Problem Solving
and Decision Making

Problem Solving and Decision Making

Hard, Soft and Creative Approaches

Second Edition

Michael J. Hicks

THOMSON

Australia · Canada · Mexico · Singapore · Spain · United Kingdom · United States

Problem Solving and Decision Making: Hard, Soft and Creative Approaches, 2nd edition

Copyright © 2004 Thomson Learning

The Thomson logo is a registered trademark used herein under licence.

For more information, contact Thomson Learning, High Holborn House; 50–51 Bedford Row, London WC1R 4LR or visit us on the World Wide Web at: http://www.thomsonlearning.co.uk

British Library Cataloguing-in-Publication Data
A catalogue record for this book is available from the British Library

ISBN 1–86152–617–2

First edition published by Chapman and Hall 1991

Reprinted 1993, 1994 and 1995

Reprinted by International Thomson Business Press 1997, 1998 and 1999

Second edition published by Thomson Learning 2004

Typeset by J&L Composition, Filey, North Yorkshire

Printed in the UK by TJ International, Padstow, Cornwall

To my mother, Phyllis Violet

Contents

List of figures and tables

Acknowledgements

I am very grateful to Professor Peter Checkland from the University of Lancaster's Department of Systems and Vincent Nolan of the Synectics Education Initiative for reading through my accounts of their methodologies, making many helpful comments and giving permission to reproduce certain diagrams and materials.

I am also grateful to Terry Gilliam from Synectics and Gerard Puccio from FourSight for providing me with information and reading through my 'write ups' of their creativity software/style inventory; and to Scott Isaksen of the CPS Group and Don Treffinger of the Centre for Creative Learning for their advice, directions to their latest work and also permission to reproduce some of it.

Mention must also be made of Arthur B Van Gundy Jnr.; the Technical Innovation Center, Thomson Learning, Prentice-Hall Blackwells, Routledge and other publishers for allowing me to reproduce material from their books as well.

A mention must also be made of my friend John Sedgwick of Managing Imaginations, Inc., St Catharines, Ontario, who first introduced me to CPS back in 1980 and who allowed me to use some of his ideas here; my ex-colleague and friend Martin Gandoff, who cajoled me into writing the first edition of this book; and my many students whose ideas are contained in the illustrative examples.

I would also like to thank the staff at Thomson Learning without whose help none of this would have been possible; in particular, Anna Faherty for commissioning this second edition, Geraldine Lyons for renegotiating deadlines and being extremely patient, Giulia Vincenzi for dealing with 'delivery' problems and getting permissions, Helen Parry for her meticulous copy-editing and Stuart Giblin for calmly coping with the production side despite some late changes.

And last, but of course not least, I must acknowledge my wife Teresa, who allowed me to take early semi-retirement recently, without which I would probably never have completed this work. Now I can finish the kitchen as well!

Introduction

This book is about problem solving, decision making and creativity in business, management, information systems, the sciences, psychology, sociology, engineering, tourism, in fact life, the universe and everything (as Douglas Adams, in *The Hitchhiker's Guide to Galaxy*, would say)!

What do we mean by 'problem solving' and what does it mean for you?

Every day of our lives, we are faced with situations that require us to decide what to say and do. They may require us to resolve circumstances which we perceive as being unsatisfactory in some way or simply to choose between several courses of action. We want to be able to deal with these problems as efficiently and effectively as possible, but do not always know how to do so. We are unclear perhaps about what options might be available to us, how we should choose between them and what their potential consequences might be.

These problems are further compounded by the fact that change and uncertainty now seem to be an inevitable part of our lives. However, decision making has always been a problem, and this in itself is not really something new. The world around us is more 'turbulent' than it used to be, susceptible to rapid and often unpredictable changes. We need to be creative to survive in these conditions.

If one surveys what has already been written about problem solving and decision making elsewhere, there does appear to be some variation over what is thought to constitute these processes, and hence also over the meaning of phrases such as 'problem-solving techniques', 'decision-support systems' and so on. Some people see problem solving and decision making as two separate but almost inextricably linked processes, while others see one process as a part of the other. (We shall be returning to this point briefly in Chapter 1.) Vincent Nolan (1989, p.14) describes the first of these views as follows:

> Decision making ... consists of making the best choice from the known options, whereas problem solving is the process of creating the options and the greater the skill [we employ] in problem solving, the easier the decision making becomes.

Whether we consider them as one process or two, this book is about problem solving *and* decision making, although for convenience I shall mostly refer to these processes collectively as 'problem solving'.

A corollary of the viewpoint taken above seems to be that any significant difficulty experienced with decision making will usually be due to the options not being 'entirely satisfactory'. The position I have adopted is to devote the greater part of this book to ensuring that we are able to generate plenty of (better than) satisfactory options (that is, we are effective problem solvers), and then supplementing this with the provision of a relatively simple way of choosing between them.

The need for systematic, yet flexible, problem-solving processes

The 'one-off' trial-and-error approaches to problem solving that we have used in the past now often appear to be less satisfactory than before. Although in the past we have used these *ad hoc* methods and on occasions been successful with them, this has not necessarily resulted in an enhancement of our problem-solving skills. What we need is more systematic, yet still flexible, problem-solving strategies. Systematic problem-solving strategies are useful in that, by understanding the process of applying them, we are better able to see their potential advantages and disadvantages when applying them elsewhere. The 'try it and see' approach seldom gives us any guidance on how to approach the next new situation that comes along.

An ability to think creatively, usually considered an asset in problem situations, is often perceived as being incompatible with the concept of systematic procedures. Creativity is frequently thought of (incorrectly) as a non-logical process that 'just happens', and which can rarely be called up at will in the middle of a methodical problem-solving process. So we also need to find a way of stimulating and maintaining our creativity whilst adopting a more systematic approach for dealing with our problems.

In the past 60 years or so many different problem-solving processes, techniques and methodologies have been devised. They have all claimed that they could help us tackle the problem situations we encounter in the real world and most of them have something to offer. They have each spawned a substantial following of devotees!

Around the middle of the twentieth century some people were realizing that the scientific method and mathematics were not sufficient both to investigate and understand the world we live in, and to deal with the problems and opportunities that world throws at us. Hence the creation of **(soft) systems thinking** and **Creative Problem Solving** (CPS).

I believe that, at the present time, there is no *one* problem-solving process or technique that is universally applicable to all the types of problem situation that we are likely to meet in this imperfect world. Some come very close to this ideal though, and are therefore more generally usable than others. In this book I am presenting a carefully selected subset of these strategies which together *will* help us tackle almost all types of problem situation.

It is for that reason that the three main approaches to problem solving described in this book are the **creative approach**, the **rational (logical) approach**, and the **soft systems approach**. These approaches should not be thought of as discrete alternatives; in fact, there is quite a lot of 'overlap' between them, and they can certainly be usefully merged at times, as we shall see. Furthermore, the importance of creative thinking in all problem solving cannot be understated. This is why the 'creative' theme runs throughout the book, even when we are apparently considering other problem-solving approaches. The success of applying a predominantly rational or soft systems approach to a problem relies greatly on the amount of creative thinking that has gone on along the way!

The portrayal of these three approaches collectively is the unique feature of this book. I believe that by studying them as a set will not only reveal their innate interreliance but may also instil a comprehensive problem-solving approach to life and thus help to rectify the unbalanced learning that is believed to have taken place on many education courses.

Although I will be giving some explanation of the rationale underlying the processes/techniques described, I will not be quoting extensively from research findings which validate them. Amongst the books listed in the Bibliography will be found the original texts where these processes/techniques were first explained, and where full justifications can be heard first hand from the originators. These books also relate many examples of the applications of these strategies to *real* problems.

My aims are:

- to present the processes/techniques which I consider to have had the greatest impact in improving our problem-solving abilities and/or are also representative of others I have had to omit;
- to provide sufficient background information about them (including illustrative case studies) to provide a practical guide for their use;
- to show how the different approaches complement each other, and thus provide a complete problem-solving system.

This is the subject matter of this book.

How the business environment has changed and what this means for today's managers

The modern business/organizational environment in particular, with its emphasis on competition, building larger markets, strategic planning, team-working, performance appraisal and so on, has created the need for a range of new problem-solving and decision-making strategies. These strategies need to be systematic enough to enable people to be trained in them and flexible enough to enable users to adapt them to the various situations where they could be applied. This need is often thought to become greater as we move up through everyday tactical (operational) decisions towards long-term policy (strategic) choices.

At an operational level, it could be said that we have many quantitative techniques available to assist in the decision-making process already. Quantitative methods, although frequently providing useful information, are equally often found to be inadequate for resolving problems. Blind reliance upon them can indeed be disastrous! They should be employed within an enlightened view of the problem situation. For example, it would be wise to ensure that we really do have an imbalance in capacity between sections of our production line causing the 'queuing' problems we have detected, rather than a machine operative who is working slowly because of his or her dissatisfaction over a recently assigned new task, before trying to use queuing theory or mathematical simulation to solve the problem. Most of the problem-solving processes/techniques described in this book (because they are intended for what we shall later call 'people' problems) are equally applicable, and just as important, at all levels of management.

Many organizations, both commercial and non-commercial, do not recruit solely on the basis of qualifications any more, but consider also the extent to which potential employees possess certain personal and interpersonal skills; skills such as:

- problem solving and decision making*
- self-confidence
- self-awareness and awareness of others*
- self-esteem
- self-reliance
- self-management
- leadership and team/group membership skills*
- maturity.

In particular, these organizations have realized the importance of having personnel with good problem-solving abilities, and who are prepared to use them. This is not just true of opportunities/careers in business and management, but of those in virtually every field.

Much has been said, both in a an academic context and elsewhere, about the desirability of developing 'enterprise' skills as well. Various attempts have been made to identify precisely what constitutes enterprise, and there would appear to be a reasonable amount of agreement about this. A recurring theme in the various definitions are all the skills listed above plus:

- displaying initiative
- generating and developing ideas*
- imagination*
- open-mindedness*
- inventiveness
- ingenuity
- adaptability
- a positive attitude*
- amenability to change
- ability to manage change.

Training in creative thinking and problem solving not only develops the skills marked with an asterisk, but is also believed by many people (those working in commerce and industry as well as academics) to develop and improve *all* these skills. This is because, if we actively assimilate these 'new' approaches to tackling problems, it is highly probable that they will change our outlook on, and attitudes to, many aspects of our personal and working lives for the better. But, like most skills, if they are not practised regularly, our ability to apply them will become less effective. This is why it is important for us to find out as much as we can about them, so as to understand them well enough to employ them frequently and in a variety of situations. In this way we can avert any tendency to neglect these skills which might occur during our 'socialization' into new 'home' or working environments.

But this book is not about processses/techniques that can *only* be used in business/management.

Who should read this book?

Anyone and everyone.

The attitude described above is being reflected in the guidance and training offered by educational bodies and institutions. The Business and Technician Education Council (BTEC) and, more recently, the Qualifications and Curriculum Authority (QCA) have been promoting the development of problem-solving and creative-thinking skills in the UK for many years now. They have 'encouraged' providers of training and undergraduate/postgraduate education to incorporate the development of problem-solving skills into *all* the various modules or units of *any* particular course. There are also several innovative MBA courses placing considerable emphasis on problem solving and creativity.

The original spur to write this book was the apparent need for a general text on problem solving for students following BTEC higher education courses. I believe that problem-solving skills cannot be developed by *just* subjecting the student to a series of progressively more complicated problems. There has to be some explicit input from the trainer on problem-solving processes and techniques and their underlying rationale. Because the bodies mentioned above believe (and I would tend to agree with them) that it is undesirable to provide problem-solving training as an entity separate from the rest of the course, this book has been compiled in such a way that certain aspects of problem solving can be extracted and used wherever appropriate. It is not my intention that the book should be used as a text for a separate module or unit in problem solving, although even that should be possible.

Since its original inception, however, the idea for this book has grown, and while writing it I have tried to keep in mind a much wider potential audience. I believe that this book will also provide an introductory text for students on both undergraduate and taught masters courses, as well as being of general interest to people in business and management, or anyone else wishing to find out more about the intriguing process by which we resolve problems and make decisions. Much of the book should also be useful to students on further education courses.

This book contains academic citations and references to permit it to be used to further the above aim of being used as a textbook. If you are reading this out of general interest, just ignore the citations/references.

There is nothing in this book that requires 'rocket science' to be understood.

In some ways it is sad that, although the problem-solving methods offered here are not new but are between 10 and 60 years old, as yet very few people are aware of them. This was another reason for writing this book; for although it is primarily (but not solely) intended for students involved in higher education, it will also be another book on the shelves of the bookshops and libraries, and this means that there will be a slightly greater probability that other people will find out about these valuable ways of improving their problem-solving skills.

How the book is organized

The idea of this book is to build on and enhance the problem-solving skills that the reader already possesses, and my starting point will be to assume that everyone reading this book has already 'endured' many years of full-time secondary education. This should have given the reader at least some 'grounding' in logical thinking, and the way we apply this to solving problems which are well defined and which often have only one desired answer. Some readers will have a good deal of work experience as well, and this may have given them a chance to develop their creative-thinking skills in addition to this.

It is because of the quite widespread belief that the educational process and the society we were brought up in have often been responsible for a reduction of our ability to think creatively, and that only the fortunate few will, through their subsequent working and personal lives, have had the opportunity to 're-awaken' their latent creativity, that we will encounter very early on a discussion on creative thinking.

After a brief discussion of what constitutes a problem or decision (Chapter 1) and how we usually go about tackling one, the stages involved and the approaches we can take (Chapter 2), I will explain why and how the attenuation of the creativity we were born with has taken place, and then show how we can reawaken or restore these creative abilities (Chapter 3). In the next six chapters we will look at the techniques we can employ at various stages of the problem-solving process: before problem solving (Chapter 4), Data Gathering (Chapter 5), Problem Identification (Chapter 6), Ideation (Chapter 7), Problem Resolution (Chapter 8) and implementation (including the management of change) (Chapter 9).

After this I will present a full account of a CPS process (**Synectics**) (Chapter 10) and a soft systems approach (**SSM**) (Chapter 11) showing how some of the techniques outlined in the previous chapters can be brought together in a complete problem-solving process. It is hoped that this will enable the reader to dip into the earlier chapters to find techniques to suit a particular problem-solving task, or apply a complete problem-solving process, depending on their needs.

Next we will attempt to tackle rather more complex problems using the Synectics (a highly developed and sophisticated form of) CPS process and the SSM (Soft Systems Methodology), noting any similarities and/or differences between the two 'philosophies', and discussing how they may be used in conjunction to good effect (Chapter 12).

Since most CPS techniques work best in a group environment, we will go on from there to look at some of the 'dynamics' of group problem solving (Chapter 13).

Finally, we shall conclude with a discussion of some topics closely linked with creativity (Chapter 14), mention some software that claims to help with our problem-solving efforts (Chapter 15) and provide a catalogue of useful information sources regarding many of the things discussed in this book (Chapter 16).

To provide a programme which gradually develops problem-solving skills is difficult, because there is no obvious intellectual progression in the ideas presented here. Vincent Nolan (1989, p.84) has described many of these techniques as 'mostly *common sense*, in that there are sound reasons for using them where appropriate, which will be readily accepted when explained simply'. The soft systems approach may need to be prefaced by an explanation of 'systems' and 'systems thinking' concepts (Appendix 2), but that is all. Success in the exploitation of the techniques described here depends more on the relative maturity of the practitioners and their experience of life.

The best that can be done, therefore, is to present increasingly more and more complex problems, from those for which there is a relatively obvious approach, to those where a combination of approaches may be the best ploy. This is what I have generally tried to do.

In Peter Checkland's book (1981) the author insisted on the idea that any problem-solving 'system' should be a flexible, modifiable and continuously evolving thing. And so, instead of a highly prescriptive 'flow chart' approach which says, 'Right. Here are the techniques. If this, this and this are so, then use method x, etc. . .', my intention is to offer what I believe to be the most useful subset of these tools which the reader can then use in any permutation he or she thinks is appropriate.

Most of the illustrations, cases, etc. given in this book are fictitious or semi-fictitious. I make no apologies for this, as they have been specifically designed to show the reader the various facets and intricacies of the methods described.

1 Problems, opportunities and decisions

This chapter explores what we mean by problem solving and decision making, puts forward the case that most of the time these are essentially the same thing, and identifies the types of problems and decisions which the processes and techniques[1] described later in this book help us to deal with.

Problems, problems, problems!

What is a problem?

Before we look at how to solve real-world problems, we should agree on what actually constitutes a problem. Listed in Frame 1.1 are some descriptions of what a problem is. There are four things implicit in most of these descriptions:

- We have *recognized* that there is a problem.
- We *do not know how* to resolve this problem.
- We *want* to resolve it.
- We (perceive that we) *are able* to implement a solution when we find it.

Frame 1.1 *What is a problem?*

Problem solving is the art of finding ways to get from where you are to where you want to be (assuming you do not already know how). The problem, therefore, is the gap between the present situation and a more desirable one.

Vincent Nolan (1989, p.4)

A problem can be defined as any situation in which a gap is perceived to exist between what is and what should be.

Arthur B. Van Gundy Jr. (1988, p.3)

> We usually refer to ourselves as having a problem if things are not as we would like them to be, and we are not quite sure what to do about it.
>
> *Colin Eden, Sue Jones and David Sims (1983, p.12)*
>
> [A problem is] any situation in which an expected level of performance is not being achieved and in which the cause of the unacceptable performance is unknown.
>
> *Charles Kepner and Benjamin Tregoe (1981, p.34)*
>
> A problem . . . is a condition characterized by a sense of mismatch, which eludes precise definition, between what is perceived to be actuality and what is perceived might become actuality.
>
> *Peter Checkland (1981, p.155)*
>
> A problem is a situation in which a decision-making individual or group has alternative courses of action available, . . . the choice made can have a significant effect, and . . . the decision-maker has some doubt as to which alternative should be selected.
>
> *Russell Ackoff (1981, p.20)*

Do I have a problem? Recognizing a problem

A problem situation must be perceived by someone; otherwise, there is not a problem. But who needs to perceive this problem situation? Someone may think that we have a problem; but if we do not perceive it as a problem for *us*, we may not feel the need to do anything about it. But does that mean we can deny the existence of this problem? We may not realize that we have a problem, but that does not stop us from having one:

Managing director to sales manager: The performance of your salespeople in our south-east region was pretty poor last month: you had better do something about it.'

As sales manager, we thought that things were fine. We did not have any problems . . . But we certainly have one now! Whether the problem is that our salespeople are not reaching their targets, or that the managing director thinks that we are not doing our job properly, we are now in a situation which is no longer how we would like it. Unless we have an immediate solution there is a real problem, and it *is* ours. So, we do not have to know about a problem in order to have one. But we do need to have perceived a problem before we can be expected to do something about it.

Can I solve this problem? Having the power to act

If we do not know how to resolve a particular problem situation, we may have two difficulties. We may have difficulty in defining precisely what the problem is and/or we may have difficulty finding a possible solution when we have decided on the best way of looking at (or defining) the problem. But, directly or indirectly, we *must* be able to do something about a problem situation once we have decided what this should be, or there is very little point in doing any problem solving in the first place. As a lone problem solver, if we do not have the authority and resources to implement our solution, then implementing it will be made more difficult because we have to rely on our skills to influence somebody else who does have that power. And motivating others to do something is seldom an easy or a simple task.

Our perceptions play a key role in many aspects of problem solving, and here they are of particular interest because they determine what we think we are able to accomplish by way of a solution. It is our perception of our *power to act* (or of our skill to influence) that is really important; this needs to be considered when starting to tackle a problem situation. Our perception will be modified by the prevailing culture in which the problem solving is to take place. In organizations with a 'flat' structure and an empowered workforce, we are likely to feel that we have more personal power than we would do in a more bureaucratic organization. This perception of our power will also vary with time, as culture changes and opportunities come and go.

There are inherent difficulties in influencing other people and persuading them to do things. Some people believe that if we do not possess the power to implement a solution *directly*, there is effectively little we can do about a particular problem. In such circumstances, we would be better off attempting to resolve a different but related problem about which we do have the power to do something. For example, I have a problem:

I wish we could abolish all forms of chemical, biological and nuclear weapons.

As an individual, there is little or nothing I can do about this problem directly. However, stating the problem as:

How can I help to increase the awareness of others to the potentially devastating effect that the use of these weapons would have on the whole of our planet?

gives me a direction I *can* move in:

- I can join/make donations to organizations already working towards this end.
- I can write letters/articles about the subject and send them to anyone who I think might publish them.
- I can start a discussion on the subject in the bar of the 'World's End' public house.

Who owns a problem? Problem ownership

Tied to these notions of whether or not we recognize a problem and are able to do something about it is the whole question of problem ownership. There are differing views as to who qualifies as a problem owner of a particular problem situation and how much power and influence is a prerequisite for this. For instance, can someone who fails to recognize that he or she has a problem be a problem owner? There is general agreement that the problem owner is any person who is 'dissatisfied' with a situation and wishes it were otherwise, which assumes recognition of the problem. However, there is less consensus over the importance of a problem owner's ability to implement a solution. Definitions of potential problem owners seem to spread along a power-to-act continuum stretching from those who have direct power to implement a solution to those who are merely the 'victims' of the situation, will be affected by any solution that is proposed and often have very little power or influence.

This difference of opinion is most prevalent in discussions concerning circumstances where several people share the same problem. These people can (and are likely to) see the same problem situation in many different ways. Which definition of this problem situation are we the owner of, and can we do anything about the problem when viewed in that way? If we redefine a problem in such a way that it comes within our own domain of power and influence, then our definition of the problem can be made to reflect not only our particular perception of the problem situation but also our individual power to effect a solution. When we embark on joint problem solving, we should each consider the limitations imposed (by our situational and contingent power) on our abilities to implement a solution, and define the problem accordingly. Then, no matter who we are or how much power and influence we have, not only do we have a valid stake in the problem, but we should also be able to accomplish something with regard to its resolution. This view of problem ownership should remind us of the possibility that other people may have a stake in any problem situation that concerns us and it is likely that there are other valid and differing views as to what this problem is.

But what of situations where we are asked to help somebody else who has a problem – where initially we have no ownership of the problem? If we are called in as an outside consultant for this purpose, we cannot and should not attempt to solve that person's problem for them. Our role is solely to help *them* resolve their own problem. We should endeavour not to get involved with the *content* of the problem situation: we are there to facilitate the problem-resolving *process*.

Problem solving, resolving or dissolving

I have been using the word 'resolve' above, where I might have used the word 'solve'. This is deliberate. I prefer the word 'resolve' because it describes better what we actually mean by 'real-world' problem solving. *Chambers Twentieth Century Dictionary* (1972) offers the following meanings of 'resolve':

> To make visible the details of; to separate into components; to analyze; to determine; to transform; to free from doubt or difficulty; to dissipate; to solve.

When involved in the process of problem solving we may do some, many or all of these things.

Other authors have found the term 'problem solving' to be inadequate and many find it necessary at least to distinguish between problem identification and problem solving. In particular, Russell Ackoff (1981) has gone further in an attempt to clarify what it is we do with problems in order to improve a problem situation, and has spoken of 'resolving', 'solving' and 'dissolving' problems. Frame 1.2 contains a brief summary of the meanings he ascribes to these terms.

> **Frame 1.2** *Resolving, solving and dissolving problems*
>
> To **resolve** a problem is to select a course of action that yields an outcome that is good enough, that satisfices . . . this approach relies heavily on past experience and current trial and error for its inputs. It is qualitatively, not quantitatively, oriented; it is rooted deeply in common sense, and it makes extensive use of subjective judgement.
>
> To **solve** a problem is to select a course of action that is believed to yield the best possible outcome, which optimizes . . . this approach is largely based on scientific methods, techniques and tools. It makes use of mathematical models and real or simulated experimentation; therefore, it relies heavily on observation and measurement and aspires to complete objectivity.
>
> To **dissolve** a problem is to change the nature, and/or environment, of the entity in which it is embedded so as to remove the problem. [This approach idealizes because its] objective is to change the system involved or its environment in such a way as to bring it close to an ultimately desired state, one in which the problem cannot or does not exist.
>
> *Russell Ackoff (1981, pp.20–1)*

Ackoff suggests that only when using scientific methods, where our intent is to optimize the situation through experimentation and quantitative analysis – for example, management science's **Operational Research** (OR) techniques, – should we refer to what we are doing as solving problems. There is some debate as to whether such optimization is ever actually possible with the sort of problems that we will be dealing with (see later).

This book is mostly about how we go about identifying which is the most useful way of looking at a problem situation and resolving what courses of action we should take in order to improve things. And according to Ackoff's classification system, most of the processes/techniques mentioned (for example, **Synectics** and **Morphological Analysis**) appear to be primarily problem-resolving processes/techniques; although the **Soft Systems Methodology** (SSM), due to its holistic approach, is the most likely to be considered a problem-dissolving process. The use of any of these processes/techniques may subsequently indicate the desirability of employing OR and other quantitative methods to optimize a chosen course of action, thus solving a problem. However, I shall use the term 'problem solving' because of its common and widespread usage.

We will be looking into what precisely is involved in problem solving (or rather, resolving and dissolving) shortly, but first I think it is useful to investigate whether there are different sorts of problem and, if so, whether we should treat them differently.

Are there different types of problem?

Consider a couple of situations that might be thought of by some people as being problematical:

We are constructing the flat triangular structure shown in Figure 1.1 according to the measurements given. Although we have sufficient information to build the structure, it would be useful if we knew the size of the other angle because this information could be used to check the accuracy of our construction when we are finished. What is the angle?

The solution to this 'problem' is 42°, which can be found by the application of simple geometry. This is a fairly straightforward problem and some people might dispute that it qualifies as a problem at all.

Let us look at another problem, described in Frame 1.3.

Frame 1.3 *Peripherique S.A: Another problem?*

Peripherique S.A., an electronics manufacturing company, produce and sell three computer peripheral products: a 5760 dpi photo quality ink-jet printer (the CP57), a high capacity 2×60 GB RAID backup drive (the CD60) and a high quality 2400×4800 dpi colour flat bed scanner (the CS24). Their production draws different demands on the resources needed to produce them, as shown in Table 1.1. The estimated contribution (to profit) from the CP57, CD60 and CS24 are £135, £95 and £105 respectively.

Table 1.1   Peripherique S.A.

Product	Machine time (min)	Labour (hr)	Raw materials (£)
CP57	10	2	90
CD60	15	3	45
CS24	25	2	50

The machine time available for moulding, cutting, folding and drilling the case and chassis components is limited to 40 hours per day, until such time as additional machinery can be purchased. Likewise, labour which is mostly used for the completion of the final units from subassemblies is restricted to

▶

Figure 1.1

Triangle problem

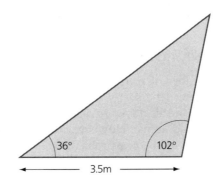

210 hours per day and there is no possibility of hiring any more staff in the foreseeable future. With regard to 'raw materials', since the greater part of this cost is the purchase of ready-built Far-Eastern subassemblies, there is no externally imposed limit on the number available. However, with an eye on its cash-flow, it is the company's present policy not to tie up more than £6000 per day on this.

Due to Peripherique's relatively small production capacity they believe they can sell as many printers and high quality scanners as they can make. The market for the RAID backup drives, however, is limited and for the moment the company feels that they are unlikely to sell more than 50 units per day. Peripherique want to ensure that they are making the best use of their available resources and have asked us to advise them on how many of each product should be produced per day in order to maximize their profit.

The solution to this 'problem' is that (on purely financial grounds) they should make 12 CP57s, 24 CD60s and 76 CS24s per day. But this is not a problem; it is a decision waiting to be made. There may have been a problem once, for example: 'How can Peripherique rationalize its operations so as to be in the best possible position for the next financial year?' But to get to the situation described above they should have identified all the possible courses of action that could have been taken, which were both feasible and desirable, and *decided* that a solution to the problem of how to get into the best possible position for the next financial year was to modify their production mix, solely on the basis of maximizing their profit. *That* is the solution, not the mathematical calculation that follows it.

It could be said that determining the most cost-effective product mix is part of the research Peripherique needs to do in order to decide whether altering the production schedule is one of the most appropriate actions to take. That still does not make it a problem. **Linear Programming** and the other mathematical/statistical techniques often grouped together under the heading of OR, and the computer software that assists their implementation, are correctly termed **decision-support systems**. They help us make decisions, not solve problems.

The problem-solving processes and techniques described later in this book should be thought of as a 'front end' to the traditional methods of management science. There are many good books already on OR, and so very little further mention of these methods will be found in this text.

Classifying problems

A number of problem classifications exist. These only help to distinguish real problems (the sort which the problem-solving processes and techniques mentioned in this book are designed to help us resolve) from situations like the two described above. However, we will briefly examine these classifications as they bring to light some problems we often have with problem solving.

Reducing problems to size! Restructuring problems

We can differentiate between **complex** and **simple** problems. This describes the structure of the problem situation, not the ease or difficulty with which we can write down a statement of what we think the problem is. The complexity of this structure reflects how far reaching a problem and its implications are, and whether it involves people — an example of complex might be a problem situation with lots of interacting 'components'.

The triangle 'problem' was simple by anyone's definition; Peripherique's 'problem' was simple to anyone familiar with the techniques of OR.

Some people suggest that complex problems should be broken down into manageable portions. Others say this is often the worst thing to do. This is because we may fail to consider the interactions between the small part we have chosen to solve and its immediate environment, and end up with an incomplete and/or imperfect 'solution'. The breaking down of a problem in order to facilitate its solution is referred to as **restructuring** the problem. We should also be aware of the danger of 'missing the problem' completely in situations where we are obliged by circumstances to do this: we may break down the problem into bits, 'solve' all these bits and fail to realize that a problem existed solely in the inter-action between these bits. This is what systems people call a **boundary problem**, and the soft systems approach described later is an attempt to overcome this dilemma. The following scenario provides a simple illustration of this.

> The marketing section of a company complains that the production section is not effective. They feel frustrated because after all their efforts seeking out new customers and obtaining more orders than ever in the past, they are being embarrassed by complaints from these customers about the failure of orders to arrive before agreed delivery dates. The production section, on the other hand, claims that they are already working to maximum capacity, and that impossible demands and deadlines are being imposed on them by unrealistic promises that the marketing section has been making to customers.

The fault may lie within a particular section; perhaps marketing *is* making unrealistic promises, perhaps production *is* understaffed in relation to the recent increase in business. But the problem may be one of bad communications between the sections:

- Marketing not fully realizing the scheduling limitations that production works to.
- Marketing inadvertently/inappropriately referring to every order as high priority.
- Marketing failing to appreciate the notice production require for a special 'one-off' run.
- Production not keeping marketing furnished with up-to-date information about finished goods in stock, work in progress and production commitments.

If this complex problem were to be broken down on a sectional basis it might never be solved. (In Chapter 11 we will use a **holistic** approach for solving a problem very similar to this.)

At one time OR was heralded as the answer to every manager's problems. It claimed to be able to deal with the problems of management in all their complexity. The OR Society defines it thus:

> OR is the application of the methods of science to complex problems arising in the direction and management of large systems of men, machines, materials and money in industry, business, government and defence. The distinctive approach is to develop a scientific model of the system, incorporating measurements of factors such as chance and risk, with which to predict and compare the outcomes of alternative decisions, strategies or controls. The purpose is to help management determine its policy and actions scientifically.

Enthusiasm for the techniques of OR, transferred from wartime operations to the practice of management in the 1950s, quickly turned to disillusionment during the 1970s.

In reality, most of the effort in adapting OR for use on management problems was concentrated on refining certain quantitative methods and developing these for use on specific and recurring situations. The belief that certain management problems turn up repeatedly encourages managers to assume that any given problem situation is likely to be one or more of the following specific 'problem' types (Wild, 1972):

- allocation problems
- inventory problems
- placement problems
- queueing problems
- sequencing and routing problems
- search problems (i.e. concerned with location)
- competitive or bidding problems.

Not only does this tendency tempt us to restructure problem situations and to do so in a restricted way, so that we may end up solving entirely the wrong problem and missing the real one completely, but it is also based on a false premise. Often it is the uniqueness of a situation that makes it problematic, and this apparent contradiction between theory and reality could explain why few managers actually use OR. An antidote to this is to recognize that the real problem often lies several stages before the point at which we decide whether we need to employ OR techniques or not. OR can be useful in certain circumstances – it allows us to model certain specific situations and (so long as we do not oversimplify reality in our model) provides us with answers to questions such as 'Which is our most cost-effective product mix?' 'How many service points do we need in order to reduce customer waiting time to a couple of minutes?' But it is of little use with a majority of real-world problems. Jay Forrester (1961) contended that this was not because managers were incapable of understanding or applying the techniques of OR, but because the techniques themselves are not capable of handling the complex decisions that managers have to make.

The problem of knowing what a problem is! Redefining the problem

We can also classify problems on how **well defined** or **ill defined** they are. Are we sure of what the problem really is? Do we feel confident we know in which direction we should look for a possible solution? The 'triangle' problem in Figure 1.1 was extremely well defined. We knew exactly what we are dealing with: a plane triangular structure some of whose dimensions were known exactly. There was only one possible problem definition, and there could only be one solution. We knew precisely what we had to find out – the third angle – and how to do this. Exactly the same comments can be made about Peripherique's problem.

When a problem is ill defined, and even when we think we know what the problem is, we should try to view the problem from many angles to ensure that we are actually attempting to solve the 'right' or most appropriate one. A simple example of this is illustrated in Frame 1.4. This process of looking around the stated problem is referred to as **redefining** the problem. The Synectics approach described later places great emphasis on this concept.

Frame 1.4 *Breakdown: Redefining the problem*

You are travelling alone in your car to a very important meeting. Fifteen minutes from your destination (30 minutes before the meeting), your car engine loses power, cuts out and you glide to a standstill on a busy clearway in the middle of a thunderstorm.

You certainly have a problem. But what is it?

1. How to get the car started again.
2. How to effect an immediate repair to the . . .
3. How to reach my destination as quickly as possible.
4. How to find alternative transport.
5. I wish I had wings.
6. I wish I could teleport to my destination.
7. I wish it would stop raining.
8. I wish I had stayed in bed today.
9. How to get the car off the clearway into a safe parking area.
10. How to communicate with the RAC/my office/my destination.
11. I wish I could think up a new excuse for my boss/wife.
12. I wish I could afford a more reliable means of transport.
13. I wish I knew how to fix cars.
14. How to get myself and/or car back home.
15. I wish I could afford the repair.
16. How to get the car to a scrap yard at no cost.
17. How to keep warm and dry.
18. I wish I were a member of the AA.

▶

19. I wish I had a Rolls Royce (they 'never' break down).
20. I wish I had a mobile telephone.

Tame and wicked problems

Yet another classification system, which again only separates real problems from the others, divides problems into **tame** and **wicked**. The features of a wicked problem are paraphrased in Frame 1.5 to illustrate the type of situation we *are* hoping to deal with.

Frame 1.5 *Wicked problems*

Wicked problems have the following features:

- they do not have a definitive problem description,
- there is no certain way of knowing when you have reached the best solution,
- their possible solutions are not true or false but somewhere between good and bad,
- there is no immediate or ultimate way of testing the merit of a solution,
- they have an infinite number of possible solutions,
- the problem situation shows no precise indications as to what are/are not permissible ways of reaching a solution,
- each problem is essentially unique,
- there are many ways of looking at (defining) the problem and each one suggests a 'different' direction in which we should perhaps look for a solution,
- every wicked problem can be thought of as a symptom of another problem,
- there is seldom any opportunity to determine a solution by 'trial and error',
- it is usually imperative that we find a 'correct' solution, preferably at the first attempt.

Rittel and Webber (1974)

Simple, well-defined and tame problems are not our major concern here. Taken one at a time, they are relatively easy to deal with. However, even simple problems can be difficult to handle if they arrive together in large numbers. If they are not to overload our problem-solving efforts, we will need to prioritize them and plan a schedule for their resolution. It is mainly the wicked variety with which we need help, and we will look at these real problems again later (in Chapter 2), to see if their nature suggests the use of one problem-solving approach, process or technique rather than another.

Opportunities!

Not all problem situations are 'unpleasant'. We may be having problems planning something nice, for example a holiday; exploiting an opportunity; or inventing a new way of doing something. The term 'problem situation' as used herein intends to cover these possibilities as well, and certain decisions, as we shall see shortly.

Decisions, decisions!

Among the definitions of a problem given in Frame 1.1, you may have noticed that Ackoff's definition was somewhat different. It seems to describe a decision, not a problem. Is decision making a different process from problem solving; is one part of the other, or are we really talking about two aspects of the same thing? If we described problem solving as something like 'finding ways of getting from a situation perceived as unsatisfactory, to one that we would rather be in', and decision making as 'making a selection between various courses of action', these processes might be thought of as separate. However, as we consider the full implications of what is involved, perhaps by expanding these 'definitions' into a number of stages, the fallacy of considering them as discrete processes becomes apparent.

In Frame 1.6 we can see two lists typical of those which people come up with when asked to identify the stages in problem solving and decision-making. It is clear that there is at least one decision-making stage – 'select the best solution' – within problem solving, and often many more. Moreover, people tend to find it difficult to make decisions because they have a problem 'generating alternative ways of meeting the objectives', 'determining the evaluation criteria/techniques' and sometimes 'identifying the objectives of the decision'.

Frame 1.6 *Problem solving v. decision making*

Problem solving	Decision making
Identify and try to understand the problem	Identify the objectives (goals) of the decision
Collect relevant information and reflect on it	Find alternative ways of meeting these objectives
Generate some ideas	Determine evaluation criteria/ techniques
Develop solutions	
Select the best solution	Select best course of action
Implement it	Implement it

Looked at in this way, one process is obviously part of the other and vice versa. But which is the superior process and does it matter? The answers to these questions depend mostly on the view people take of the decision-making process itself. It is worth digressing slightly to explore these viewpoints, in order to place the problem-solving processes/techniques about to be described in context.

Decision making: a choice between alternatives?

Decision making is often thought of as a relatively simple choice between several courses of action. This is an oversimplified view because such a definition can imply that the decision-making process is a single-stage affair, which happens in a fairly short space of time. It is true that some decisions we make, for example, whether or not to have another cup of coffee, do appear to be like this. We make a lot of rapid, simple choices and often are not conscious of doing any complex analysis or comparative evaluation of available alternatives. Some routine decisions (including business ones) may be like this, but many are not!

We could settle for the **rational** view of decision making, which has been advocated as an appropriate method for dealing with decisions other than trivial ones such as the coffee example, as our description of the decision-making process. (The list of steps in Frame 1.6 provides a rudimentary summary of the rational view, but its modern-day counterpart is better exemplified by Charles Kepner and Benjamin Tregoe's (1981) **Decision Analysis** described in Chapter 8.) While to a large extent it supports the idea that a decision is a fairly straightforward choice between alternatives, the rational model does identify a number of steps we usually need to go through, and implies that the process is a conscious one. However, it also assumes that the decision-making process can be, is and should be rational. It leaves no room for intuition. You may feel that this is not the way things are with many of the decisions you have to make. If this is the case we need to think of the decision-making process as something rather more than just a choice between alternative courses of action, but what?

The problem with decisions

The rational model, though seemingly an eminently sensible way of approaching choice situations, is difficult to apply in practice. Herbert Simon (1955) criticized the rational view on the basis that it assumed that an exhaustive set of alternatives were readily available along with a full knowledge of their consequences, and that it was also possible to measure the extent to which the consequences of each of these alternatives would achieve the desired objective. Furthermore, the rational model claims that we could then establish a consistent order of preference from these measurements, and could thus choose the alternative that came out best. He maintained that seldom were these assumptions valid in practice.

Simon demonstrated that in reality the essential 'ingredients' of the rational model were often compromised out of sheer necessity, resulting in an oversimplification of the whole process. He further claimed 'there is a complete lack of evidence that, in actual human choice situations of any complexity, these computations can be, or are in fact performed'. In his **principle of bounded rationality** (1955), he even seems to suggest that the capacity of the human brain is not up to handling the magnitude of the task of making a truly rational decision with complex real-world problems. Most of the time, he said (1955), managers were settling for a satisfactory solution that suffices for the time being (**satisficing**), rather than pursuing the optimum solution the rational model purported to yield.

Many real-world decisions are highly complex, because of:

- multiple and often conflicting objectives (see Appendix 2);
- difficulties encountered devising alternatives and deciding or reaching a consensus about what the evaluation criteria should be;
- the personality and prejudice (see **mental set**, see Chapter 3) of the decision maker(s);
- the politics of the situation (see Chapter 5); and/or
- difficulties in getting reliable and relevant information.

Even if we ignore the issue that many of the factors we might want to consider when comparing alternatives are unmeasurable, things would have to be drastically simplified to make them fit the rational model, even if finding an optimal solution under these circumstances were not virtually impossible anyway. Furthermore, as Cyert, Simon and Trow found (1956), there are many decisions we have to make which involve just a single alternative, usually made by comparing this one possible course of action with 'some kind of explicit or implicit "level of aspiration"'. We are not searching for the best alternative, but deciding whether the one we have is good enough. Ackoff (1983) also notes that what seems rational to one person is not necessarily rational to someone else. Therefore, if objective, rational decisions exist, they must depend heavily on consensus for their validity (see Decision Analysis, Chapter 8).

If the rational model of decision making is often not viable, what can we use instead? Charles Lindblom (1959) says that what managers actually do in practice is to make **successive limited comparisons** restricting themselves to one (or a few) objectives at a time, often initially disregarding the social issues. They then compare the few alternatives that come easily to mind, more on the basis of past experience than anything else.

This choice involves selecting alternatives and evaluation criteria simultaneously, because the appropriateness of the latter varies between alternatives. Since this process can result only in a partial solution, it is repeated endlessly as conditions and aspirations change and as the accuracy of predictions improve. Decision making has thus been perceived as a cyclical, 'incremental learning process'. Though still in widespread use, the 'successive limited comparisons' style of decision making cannot, as Lindblom points out, guarantee we will not overlook potentially excellent options in our limited search for alternative courses of action, nor can it ensure that we will consider all relevant criteria in our comparative evaluation of alternatives. Complex decisions are evidently more than a simple choice between alternatives: they are starting to look like problems! The decision-making process appears to be heuristic (guided trial and error, based on past experience) and stochastic rather than rational.

Simon (1960a) argues that the decision-making process consists of three phases, 'intelligence', 'design' and 'choice', which he describes as follows:

- searching the environment for conditions calling for a decision;
- inventing, developing and analysing possible courses of action;
- selecting a particular course of action from those available.

Clearly, this view indicates more than a 'choice between alternatives', implying the existence of two stages (phases) before we get to any 'choice' situation. Simon believes that executives spend far more time on the first two phases (particularly the second) than the third phase, although he concedes that this varies between individuals and the organizational levels at which they operate.

An alternative view, from Sir Geoffrey Vickers (1961), describes judgement as 'the power of reaching the "right" decisions when the apparent criteria are so complex, inadequate, doubtful or conflicting as to defeat the ordinary man'. He distinguishes three broad types of judgement (increasing in levels of complexity):

- *reality* judgements – about the state of affairs 'out there';
- *action* judgements – deciding 'what to do about it' and committing yourself to action on this basis; and
- *value* judgements – about 'what result was most to be desired'.

He maintained that 'the higher the level of judgement involved; the less possible it is to find an objective test by which to prove that the judgement is good'. Both action and reality judgements involve the mental processes of analysis and synthesis (fundamental components of problem solving), and an ability he calls ingenuity (compare with **intuition**, page 57), and latent in value judgements is a creative process (see also **EQ** and **SQ** in Chapter 14).

These last two viewpoints seem to suggest that making decisions is often the same process as problem solving, and that we should attempt to classify decisions in some way before we look any further at how we should be making them.

Types of decision – some are really problems!

The nature and types of decision that members of a typical organization may have to take can vary considerably. At one extreme, we have the vital, often complex, 'one-off' decisions that may determine the future of the organization; and at the other, the still significant but relatively simple routine (and often repetitive) 'day-to-day' running decisions. H. Igor Ansoff (1968) has classified business decisions as 'strategic', 'operating' and 'administrative' (see Frame 1.7). While distinct, these categories of decisions are interdependent and complementary.

Frame 1.7 *Types of business decision*

Strategic

These are long-term decisions that resolve the organization's relation to its environment. Questions include: what are its objectives and goals, whether to diversify and how best to develop and exploit its present

▶

position, which products or services it should be offering and where these should be marketed.

Operating (tactical)

The bulk of the decisions an organization has to make. These are short term and concerned with maximizing the efficiency of resource allocation, including such things as production scheduling, quality management, inventory control, pricing, choosing a marketing strategy, budgeting, etc.

Administrative

These decisions ensure harmonious and effective collaboration over the implementation of strategic and operational decisions, and are concerned with organizational structure (chain of command, areas of responsibility, work flows, communication channels, location of facilities and distribution networks) and the acquisition and development of resources (personnel, finance, raw materials, facilities and equipment).

Ansoff (1968)

Using this classification, strategic decisions tend to be less well structured in that objectives are less clear, often conflicting, more open ended in the number of possibilities and issues we should consider, and hence problematic and less amenable to the rational approach. Operational decisions tend to be less complex, more routine, and the techniques of OR are available to assist decision making here. However, as we have seen before, it is doubtful whether such optimizing techniques are really capable of handling even this type of problem (see also Appendix 2). Apart from illustrating the diversity of decisions, this classification does not help in deciding how we should attempt to deal with them, because some operational decisions can be exceedingly problematic, and at the other extreme, the appropriateness of certain policy decisions may be obvious to all. Administrative decisions can be both routine and complex, involving as they do the actual organizing of people.

Paul Diesing (1958) has classified a manager's decision making into two parts depending on the type of decision being made. Some decisions, termed 'economic', could be dealt with in a rational (and quantifiable) way as above, by identifying objectives and alternative courses of action and evaluating them according to how well they achieved these objectives. But managers also have to make 'social' decisions, which 'attempt to change personalities and social relations in a direction of greater fundamental harmony and stability'. Decisions of this type involve intangible and unquantifiable factors such as stress, morale and self-confidence and, although necessary, are not made on a rational basis.

Around the same time, Simon (1960a) suggested it was possible to position all decisions along a continuum running from 'highly programmed' at one end to 'highly non-programmed' at the other. 'Decisions are programmed to the extent that they are repetitive and routine, to the extent that a definite procedure has been worked out for handling them' and '. . . are non-programmed to the extent that they are novel, unstructured and consequential. There is no cut-and-dried method for handling the problem because it has not arisen before, or because its precise nature and structure are elusive or complex, or because it is so important that it deserves a custom-tailored treatment'. The implication seems to be that some decisions *may* be amenable to a rational approach. But there are other decisions which deserve a different kind of treatment altogether.

Problem solving, decision making and management

Although Simon (1960a) has suggested that the whole process of decision making can be thought of as synonymous with managing, most traditional management texts define the process of management as something like planning, organizing, motivating, coordinating and controlling. Although decision making must play a central part in planning and organizing, what about the rest? Ansoff (1968, p.15), claims 'a major part of a manager's time is occupied in a daily process of making numerous and diverse decisions'. Conventional wisdom maintains that 'managers make decisions', perhaps not all the time, but certainly a lot of it. Charles Handy (1985, pp.360–5) however, believes this to be an inaccurate stereotype and maintains that a manager 'does not just, or mainly, "take decisions"', and goes on to summarize and group Mintzberg's ten roles (Mintzberg, 1975) (see Frame 1.8) into 'leading', 'administrating' and 'fixing'. The balance of these roles varies, Handy says, with the level of the job, the size of the organization and the organizational culture (see Chapter 9), but underlying all these is that 'the manager, like the GP, is the first recipient of problems', the implication being that a manager spends a lot of time identifying problems and finding out what can be done about them. Is this not what Simon meant?

Frame 1.8 *A manager's job*

Arising directly from his or her formal authority, we have . . .

Interpersonal roles:	Figurehead
	Leader
	Liaison

which give rise to . . .

Information roles:	Monitor
	Disseminator
	Spokesperson

and these two sets of roles enable the manager to play . . .

Decisional roles:	Entrepreneur
	Disturbance handler
	Resource allocator
	Negotiator

Mintzberg (1975)

Any apparent difference here is mainly semantic. A certain activity is occupying a lot of a manager's time, and this activity is an important part of managing. It is simply that we call it by two different names, one of which, 'decision making', is ambiguous!

Concluding thoughts

I have tried to show that if we dismiss the trivial type of decision we are left with two basic types: the relatively straightforward choice-making situations – programmed or economic decisions – and the rest – the ones likely to cause difficulties and require some problem solving; many planning decisions will be of this latter type. Whether we lump together these awkward decisions with our wicked problems and call the process for dealing with them 'problem solving', or carry on calling this process by two names is immaterial, so long as we realize that the way of dealing with them is essentially the same. I shall continue, in the main, to speak of this process as problem solving, because that is what we are doing most of the time.

An attempt is made to summarize what has been said here in Figure 1.2. We spend a lot of our time making decisions where the mental processes we use are those usually referred to as problem solving (including Ackoff's problem resolving and problem dissolving). At times, we will face relatively straightforward choices (of which some may benefit from rational analysis whereas others will be intuitive selections), in particular within the problem-solving process itself. Chapter 8 presents a choice-making method, Decision Analysis, for making relatively straightforward decisions, for example, after our problem solving has ascertained what alternative courses of action are available to us and we have thrashed out how we should compare them. The rest of the book is about problem solving, or how to deal with awkward decisions and wicked problems!

If we have an important and complex decision to make, and we feel that the rational method or successive limited comparisons to be inadequate or inappropriate, then we must add some **Creative Problem Solving** (CPS) processes/techniques to the 'front end' of our choice situation to help sort out our objectives; generate a comprehensive set of alternatives and gain agreement over suitable selection criteria; or adopt a systemic (holistic) approach to the whole thing.

Decision making involves:

Figure 1.2

Problem solving and
decision making

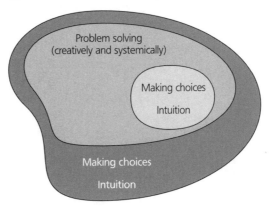

Summary

In this chapter we have established that there are certain kinds of problems (complex, ill defined, wicked) and decisions (requiring a high level of judgement, unstructured, complex, social, non-programmable, awkward), actually the majority of the ones we face, for which we require the processes and techniques described later in this book.

Endnotes

1. We shall be using the term *process* to describe a problem-solving 'method' that spans several stages of the problem-solving process (see Chapter 2), and the term *technique* for one used within a particular stage, for example Ideation.

2 Approaches to problem solving and the stages involved

This chapter introduces three approaches to problem solving, explains why we need these different approaches and when one approach (or a combination of approaches) may be more appropriate than another. It also outlines the stages usually involved in problem solving no matter which approach (or combination of approaches) is adopted.

Different approaches to problem solving

The three main approaches to problem solving (and decision making!) described in this book are:

The creative approach

This approach starts from the assumption that we have a large amount of knowledge and experience locked in our minds and there is always something in there that is 'approximately relevant' to a given problem situation, but we do not always realize this. The processes and techniques that fall under the 'creative' heading enable us to make connections between this material and the problem we are tackling (for example, between an overflowing bath tub and a method for testing gold) and often produce innovative solutions, and invariably ones that are new to us. How often have you said something like 'That's a really clever/new/elegant idea – it's so simple! If only I could think of things like that . . .' It is not just people like Archimedes who can do this, we all can!

Frequent exposure to **Creative Problem-Solving** (CPS) processes used in a group setting has been found to improve communication skills and teamwork as well. This is because of the open and supportive group climate that needs to be created in order for people to be willing to think and say the often 'strange' things required by these CPS processes and techniques. **Excursions** (see Chapter 7) are often used early in the problem-solving process as much for their climate-setting tendency as anything else.

The rational (logical) approach

When we say that we are dealing with something in a 'rational' or 'logical' way, we usually mean that we are carefully and methodically proceeding from one stage to another, letting our analysis of each stage dictate where we should go next. On many occasions this is the most appropriate way of proceeding, but we often 'forget' the importance of our choice of starting point. Before we can apply this approach we must have examined the problem situation, analysed some of its features and formulated some assumptions about it (that is, defined the problem and decided on the 'right' way of solving it). If these assumptions are wrong or inappropriate, so will be our solutions.

The soft systems approach

It is the realization that most of the real-world problem situations that we encounter, like the world we live in, are by their nature exceedingly complex and also interrelated, that make us strive for a way of tackling the situation as a whole. If a problem is detected in some aspect of our lives it is possible, if not likely, that we will need to look outside of that aspect – for example, with a work problem – perhaps even wider than the organization itself, in order to find a way of resolving the problem. We need to take a holistic view of things. It is this that systems thinking attempts to do; that is, to 'model' the situation in all its complexity.

C. West Churchman (1968), cited in Flood and Jackson (1991, p.121), whose work was an inspiration for many (soft) systems thinkers, summarizes this approach thus:

> The [soft] systems approach begins when first you see the world through the eyes of another . . . [and] goes on to discover that every [such] world view is terribly restricted. There are no experts in the systems approach. The systems approach is not a bad idea.

We can think of a group of people 'working' with a common purpose, or an organization trying to fulfil its mission, as a **human activity system**. The **soft systems** approach **SSM**[1] helps us improve problem situations by building abstract systems models purporting to have that same purpose or mission, and comparing the activities 'taking place' in these 'ideal' models with that actually occurring in the real world.

Traditional (or **hard**[2]) systems thinking tended to look at the problem situation with a view to detecting what was wrong with how things were being done, and then putting it right – which often in reality meant (and resulted in) patching up a basically defective set-up. The soft systems approach looks beyond the present implementation of the system and tries to discover its underlying essence. Asking not how something is being done, but why, questions the original design rather than the implementation.

Which approach?

The logical approach on its own is seldom enough, and will always benefit from some creative thinking. There is a danger with a purely creative approach that we can get 'hooked' on the generation of ideas and shy away from the (logical) discipline required to develop and implement these ideas. If not carefully applied both of these approaches may fail to appreciate the problem in all its complexity. And to use the (soft) systems approach effectively requires some understanding of, and experience in using, various systems concepts; and it is debatable if this approach can deal with situations involving conflict and coercion (Flood and Jackson, 1991).

It should be said here that there is some 'confusion' with this classification of approaches! First, although this is probably mostly down to semantics, Koberg and Bagnall's (1974) book *The Universal Traveller* was subtitled *A Soft Systems Guidebook to: Creativity, Problem Solving, and the Process of Design* and was about CPS techniques; whereas Flood and Jackson's (1991) book *Creative Problem Solving: Total Systems Intervention* was about hard and soft systems approaches to problem solving! More significantly, however, we now have the terms 'systematic innovation' and 'technical creativity' (coined by Genrich Altshuller, 1999) and a theory (**TRIZ**) that seeks to provide us with a better way of dealing with inventive problems and is considered by many as a creative approach, which was born out of a very analytical approach to innovation and has a rational underlying 'philosophy' (see Frame 2.1).

Frame 2.1 *Systematic innovation and technical creativity*

Lev Shulyak (1997) tells us that Genrich Altshuller investigated literally thousands (200 000+) of worldwide patents in the leading engineering fields, and then analysed the solutions which were, in his judgement, the most effective. Altshuller's research provided the first understanding of the trends/patterns in the evolution of technical 'systems'. It also laid the foundation for the development of an analytical approach to solving inventive problems, which became TRIZ. Altshuller came to believe that all technical 'systems' are governed by objective laws, such as the Law of Ideality which states that 'any technical system, throughout its lifetime, tends to become more reliable, simple, effective . . . more ideal' (Shulyak, 1997).

If we try and solve a problem (especially an inventive one) by our 'usual' trial-and-error method, the search for a solution is often sought, says Altshuller (1999), along the 'inertia vector' (near to where we have been before), which is invariably in the opposite direction to where the solution in reality lies (if only we knew it!). At best we look in all directions. What TRIZ can do for us is to reduce drastically the search sector, finding the most promising direction in which to search by imagining the parameters of an 'Ideal Machine' (compare with **Visioning**, see Chapter 4).

So, these approaches should not be thought of as discrete alternatives, never to be used in conjunction with one another. In particular, the importance of creative thinking in *all* problem solving cannot be understated.

Why we need creativity in all problem solving

We live in a rapidly changing world, where the pace of change seems to be forever increasing. Many people believe that in order to cope with these changes it is often appropriate, if not necessary, to apply some creativity in most things that we do. For example, Tony Proctor (1999, pp.7–10) maintains that when considering the area of business and management. Creativity is important because:

- of the inadequacies of logical thinking, which seldom produces the necessary insights into a problem situation,
- it provides the means for coping with/responding to the accelerating pace of change,
- it is necessary to gain/maintain a competitive edge in these days of rapidly growing competition,
- an increasing number of problem situations have few or no precedents,
- it is a vital asset for any person in a leadership role.

Many of these points could be said to 'extend' beyond the workplace into all aspects of life, not just work.

John Sedgwick (2000, p.123), analysing the sort of thinking that typically goes on in organizations, proposes a five thinking skills continuum:

- *Patterned thinking* – 'being able to take specific instructions and follow them exactly, again and again without retraining and without error'.
- *Troubleshooting* – knowing the process and when it is off track, to be able to think of a reason for this and immediately take the appropriate corrective action.
- *Problem solving* – Root Cause Analysis – not just patching things up, but being able to make an intervention into a process which is likely to have a significant long-term effect.
- *Visioning* – creating in their mind a picture of some future state, then laying down the steps which would make that state a reality.
- *Innovation* (inventing) – breaking out of the pattern and finding and communicating new, different, relevant and, one hopes, better ways of seeing a given situation.

Clearly, as we move 'down' this continuum, the thinking described becomes more unstructured, open and creative. All these thinking skills are useful, Sedgewick says, but in the interests of productivity and quality of working life (and I would say life in general) there is an increasing need for more people who can think at the problem-solving, Visioning and inventing end of the continuum.

My stance is that I believe that the success of applying a predominantly rational or a soft systems approach to a problem relies greatly on the amount of creative thinking that has gone on along the way. It is for this reason that the creative theme runs throughout the book, even when we are apparently considering other problem-solving processes and techniques.

We shall now return to our earlier discussions (in Chapter 1) about classifying problems, in an attempt to determine where the use of (predominantly) one approach might be more appropriate than another.

Choosing a problem-solving approach

Machine problems *v.* people problems

When something goes wrong with a piece of machinery, be it a car or a computer, a drilling press or a packing machine, there is always a cause or combination of causes that have produced the malfunction. Careful logical analysis of the situation *will* determine what has gone wrong and it is usually possible to verify that we have found the cause, and hence *the* solution. Problems involving machinery can certainly be **ill defined** – we may not know precisely what the (cause of the) problem is. If we did, we would not have a **machine** problem. We might have a replacement-part problem or a work-rescheduling problem but not a machine problem. But although the problem may have arisen from a combination of causes, which all need to be identified, there is only going to be one solution – to do whatever is necessary to rectify the fault (or possibly two solutions, if we include the possibility of scrapping the machine and buying a new one).

Most problems in the real world are not quite like this. Invariably there are a number of potential and possibly interrelated causes and, what is worse, a variety of possible solutions, some of which may be better than others. How do we know that we have thought of *all* the possible solutions? Such problems very often seem to involve other people. Another method of classification therefore, albeit somewhat simplistic, is to divide problems into those concerned with purely mechanistic 'systems' (machine problems), and those which involve people in some way (**people** problems).

A 'logical/rational' approach, such as the Kepner-Tregoe (KT) problem-solving strategy, **Problem Analysis** (see Chapter 6), or perhaps the (more often used!) method of what we might call 'probabilistic replacement' (where you assume that the cause is the most likely one and replace the supposed faulty part, then if that doesn't do it, you move on to the next most likely cause, etc.) seem ideally suited to machine-type problems. However, although it is claimed that KT's Problem Analysis can deal with all forms of problem, the general opinion is that there are better ways than this for dealing with people problems: adopting a *creative* approach like **Synectics** (see Chapter 10) for instance, or a soft systems approach (see **SSM**, Chapter 11).

Some people will doubtless say that all problems have people involved in them somewhere, and quote situations such as the one described in Frame 2.2.

Frame 2.2 *Zenith Engineering Ltd: a 'machine' problem?*

A new machine bought recently by Zenith Engineering Ltd is not performing up to specification. It will not shape the thickness of alloy used to the desired level of precision. On contacting the designer of the machine, Zenith Engineering Ltd were told that their problem was due to the fact that they were expecting the new machine to do something for which it was never intended, so what did they expect!

There will inevitably be a grey area between the two poles of this classification system, and we shall have to rely on common sense when choosing a problem solving method.

Obviously Zenith Engineering had a machine problem, and presumably using KT's Problem Analysis they have discovered a possible cause, which has now been verified by the designer. Whether they still have a machine problem or now have a people problem will depend on how they define their current problem situation. It is more likely to be a people problem from now on, since problem descriptions such as the following suggest themselves:

- How do we encourage the designer to work with us to modify the machine to deal with the necessary alloy thickness?
- How could we persuade our customers to accept the slight reshaping of our product that is necessary with the new machine?
- How do we redesign our product to use either the same alloy only thinner, or a 'softer' alloy of the same thickness so that the machine can cope with it?
- How do we persuade the machine's supplier to exchange it for a more powerful variant or offer us recompense for the bad advice received?

A notable exception to the rule of thumb given above is medical diagnosis, obviously a people problem, but one for which the rational approach is usually better suited.

What we have loosely defined as people problems still encompass a diversity of real-world problems. Is there no way that we could subdivide these into classes where one problem-solving strategy is better than another? The answer to this is probably 'no', but there are additional guidelines that can be offered.

Innovation

Do we require a particularly innovative solution to our problem situation? Such might be the case if our problem could be stated as:

- How can we 'invent' a new range of products/services?
- How can we improve an existing product/service to make it more appealing to our customers?

This list is by no means exhaustive. If a problem requires a novel or innovative solution, then every creative skill we can exert during the problem-solving process will help. Most people would argue that we do not only need creativity when looking for something new. If we have considerable difficulty resolving a problem, this is probably because we keep drifting back to some old solutions, none of which is particularly satisfactory – we are in a 'thinking rut'. What is needed is for us to take an apparently irrational sideways leap (**Lateral Thinking**[3]) to discover fresh ideas, because carrying on in the same direction means continually bumping into the same 'brick wall'.

If innovation is paramount in our considerations then we must adopt a creative approach such as **Brainstorming** (see Chapter 3), or the full **Osborn-Parnes** CPS process (pages 35 and 410) and Synectics (Chapter 10), or, for a 'technical' problem, TRIZ pages 36, 100, 125 and 173. Brainstorming is included here primarily because it was the first serious attempt to apply the 'psychology' of creativity to real-world problem solving, and because its underlying 'philosophy' forms the basis of all creative problem-solving approaches that have followed.

Although there are many CPS techniques, there are only two generally applicable CPS processes. One is the Osborn-Parnes CPS process which was developed from Alex Osborn's original Brainstorming process by extending it with some additional CPS techniques, Brainstorming coming from a marketing environment. The other is the Synectics CPS process which came from a research and development background. Although similar in many ways, they have differences both in their approach/rationale and in their techniques that can be traced back to these origins.

Brainstorming is still a useful technique for acquiring large numbers of conceptually simple ideas; for example, product names, ideas for adding value to an existing product, etc. Synectics, however, is a far more sophisticated process. In the area of idea generation alone Synectics is more powerful because, where Brainstorming relies on 'connection making' to happen by relatively passive random association, in Synectics it is actively encouraged, stimulated and forced to occur. You are more likely to find that novel solution/invention with Synectics or TRIZ.

Sometimes the problem situation is likely to require considerable development of an idea before it becomes a possible solution. For example: 'How can we increase our revenue from tourism without spoiling the environment?' One idea might be to 'attract only rich tourists'. This idea has possibilities, but most of us would have some concerns over it – it needs developing (we need to think about its merits, and whether there are any ways of overcoming our concerns) before we can judge whether it is a possible solution or not. Brainstorming, and to a slightly lesser extent the Osborn-Parnes CPS process, have severe limitations in this area; they are not really equipped for this type of situation at all. The Synectics CPS process is good at **Idea Development**. Another area where Synectics is strong (as is the Osborn-Parnes CPS process) is in Problem Identification, when our need is to 'open up' the problem situation, view it from many angles and give ourselves a reasonable chance of checking that we are attempting to solve the right problem.

One of the CPS techniques we will look at is **Morphological Analysis** (Chapter 7). This comes in several variants, evolved from a scientific context (astrophysics) and is also often applied in situations where innovation is sought.

The importance of an innovative solution is thus a guide to which process/technique we might use, but not a way of classifying real problems. Don't forget though that the use of creative-thinking and CPS techniques is beneficial in the resolution of *any real* problem.

Large numbers of problem owners

A creative approach that is particularly suited to problem situations with multiple ownership, about which more than one person feels dissatisfied, and where they should all have a part in resolving it, is Synectics. However, as a group problem-solving process, Synectics works best with relatively small groups of six to eight people. And since a key feature of the Synectics approach is that a problem owner plays a vital role within the group in the problem-solving process (see

Chapter 10), this has implications for its use in situations where problem owner-ship is wider than a handful of people. We may have to restructure the problem into appropriate parts (with the problems that can entail, see pages 15, 87 and 304) and have several groups working on it, or try something else. The soft systems' holistic approach, as in SSM, avoids the need to restructure the problem situation and could be a better alternative in this situation (see Chapter 11).

Solving someone else's problem

When we do have a situation in which too many people are involved for one group to be practicable, and subdividing the problem so that various groups can tackle a part of it is unmanageable or undesirable, there is a tendency for organ-izations to call in 'outside' consultants to help solve their problem. Whilst these consultants will work in close collaboration with the actual problem owners, it may ultimately be the responsibility of the consultant to 'solve the problem'. He or she will analyse the problem situation and suggest the feasible and desirable changes that might resolve it. In other words, an external consultant may be expected to and inevitably does get involved with the 'content' of the problem-solving process. Synectics insist that the leader of one of the groups involved should not do this (see Chapter 10); SSM makes allowances for this *modus operandi*.

These situations often arise because people feel that they do not have suffi-cient time or resources to solve their own problems, and for this reason they resort to outside assistance. Whether we consider this attitude right or wrong is immaterial; these situations exist and if *we* are the external consultant it is likely that a soft systems approach (such as SSM) is the most viable problem-solving one to adopt, simply because Synectics does not permit the problem owner to 'opt out' of the problem-solving process in this way. Having said this, the choice between SSM or Synectics should not be determined by whether you find your-self in the role of an external problem-solving facilitator or not. If it has not been determined by practical considerations due to the complexity of the problem or widespread problem ownership, it is likely to be determined by the extent to which the problem owners are prepared to take an active part in the problem solving (including development of the solution). Every attempt should be made to encourage as much participation by the problem owners as possible.

The reason for these repeated references to the undesirability of trying to solve another person's problem is that if people are not involved with the derivation of the solution to a problem situation in which they have a stake, they cannot realistically be expected to be committed to it, or its implementation (see Chapters 9, 10, 11). Even SSM used 'carefully' in these circumstances could be doomed to disaster.

Organizational climate

The would-be problem solver may find that, whether or not a particular problem-solving approach is appropriate, the climate in which s/he has to work may pre-clude its use. For example, in many 'hi-tech' environments, relying heavily on computer systems, or in traditionally conservative organizations such as banks and insurance companies, the employment of the creative techniques mentioned here may well be met with little understanding or sympathy. Even today, many people feel that CPS techniques are at best new-fangled, strange and American. New they are not! Unorthodox and American they are, but there is nothing intrinsically bad in this. Fortunately, this is not a hard-and-fast rule; there are organizations operating at the frontiers of science and technology and financial institutions which employ these problem-solving techniques.

A general problem-solving model

The stages in problem solving

No matter which approach to problem solving is adopted, the problem-solving process generally goes through a number of stages. Many variations on the required/desired stages have been suggested. There are several (problem-solving) models around, based on a list of steps or activities such as these. It is not necessary either to know of or to strictly adhere to any particular model in order to be an effective problem solver. In fact, most of the problem-solving processes discussed later tend to have their own steps or stages; for example, Version 3 of the the Osborn-Parnes CPS process had six (Isaksen and Treffinger, 1985) (see Frame 2.3 and Appendix 7).

Frame 2.3 *Comparison of CPS stages*

Osborn-Parnes	Synectics	Generic
Mess Finding		
Data Finding	Analysis	Data Gathering
Problem Finding	Goal Wishing (Springboards)	Problem Identification
Idea Finding	Idea Generation (Excursions)	Ideation
Solution Finding	Idea Development	Problem Resolution (Turning ideas into possible solutions)
Acceptance Finding		Implementation

Notes

The first stage of the Osborn-Parnes CPS process, 'mess finding', apparently missing from the generic stages we are going to use, is the basic 'time management' concept of proactively looking for problems and opportunities and prioritizing them, and thus is not considered here as part of the problem-solving process proper.

Although the Synectics CPS process seems to be missing an 'acceptance-finding' stage, this is not so, because it believes that the implementation process is a problem in itself and would reuse appropriate stages from its process again to deal with this.

In a similar way to the development (of the stages) of the Osborn-Parnes CPS process, ARIZ, the algorithm for inventive problem solving (used in TRIZ) has been through many versions, and 'grown' stages at its beginning and end to 'make analysis easier, and provide better results after the analytical stage is completed'. It has also had various stages segmented into more steps 'for increased solution reliability' (Altshuller, 1999, p.119) – see Frame 2.4.

Frame 2.4 *Versions and stages of ARIZ*

ARIZ 61 had three stages: analytical, operative and synthetic, broken down into five, six and four steps respectively. ARIZ 71 had six stages: choosing the problem; defining the problem more precisely; analytical; preliminary analysis of the arrived-at concept; operative; and synthetic, with six, five, eight, five, nine and three steps respectively. ARIZ 85C had nine stages: analysis of the problem; analysis of the problem's model; formulation of the ideal final result; utilization of outside substances and field resources; utilization of standard solutions and physical effects database; change or reformulation of the problem; analysis of the method that removed the physical contradiction; utilization of found solution; and analysis of steps that lead to the solution.

However, Boriz Zlotin and Alla Zusman (1991) have criticized ARIZ 85C for losing the 'problem clarification and formulation' stages possessed by ARIZ 71, and describe the development of ARIZ SMV91, which became the basis of a computerized ARIZ and a 'simplified' version, ARIZ SMVA91, for manual use.

Interestingly, though, the last stages of both ARIZ 85C and ARIZ SMVA91 review our problem-solving efforts. When employing a structured problem-solving process we should always do that, so that we can learn from what we did and, one hopes, improve the process or use it better the next time. No other process has this 'built in', although the authors of those processes would no doubt recommend such a practice – Synectics certainly do.

ARIZ 61 and ARIZ 71 can be found in Altshuller (1999), and a summary of ARIZ 85C in Lev Shulyak's 'Introduction to TRIZ' in Altshuller (1997).

In order to classify (by their usage) the problem-solving techniques presented later, we will be using the following generic (and non-proprietary) stages (although taken from CPS, and based on the Osborn-Parnes process, they are applicable wherever): **Data Gathering**, **Problem Identification**, **Ideation**, **Problem Resolution** (or dissolution/solution), **Implementation** (which can be a problem in itself!), prefaced by a 'pre-problem-solving' stage. Frame 2.3 compares these steps with the 'equivalent' ones from the Osborn-Parnes and Synectics CPS processes. The model shown in Figure 2.1 serves as a reminder of the various stages we *may* need.

The Osborn-Parnes CPS process recommends (Isaksen and Treffinger, 1985) that at each stage we first employ some **divergent thinking**, to open things up, followed by a phase of **convergent thinking**, where we try and get some degree of closure (see Chapter 3 for a fuller explanation of these terms). This is sound advice for our stages also, but the degree of closure felt necessary or desirable can vary, according to circumstances and the CPS process being employed. For example, the Synectics CPS process does not attempt to determine the significance of data obtained in the **Data Gathering** stage, and progresses from the **Problem Identification** to **Ideation** to **Problem Resolution** stages by selecting problem statements/ideas on the basis of appeal, without attempting to formally 'evaluate' any or all of them or precluding any return to those not so chosen. A brief description of each of the generic stages follows.

The 'mess' – really a pre-problem-solving stage

We start with the realization that problems (or opportunities) exist. Since this implies that things are not as we wish them, we will probably experience feelings of uneasiness, doubt, etc., but to bring order out of this chaos we must at least be prepared to get down into the middle of it. Any real-world problem situation will appear immensely complicated at first sight. We feel intimidated by its complexity, and will long for some way of simplifying it – some way of imposing order on the chaos. We feel threatened and inadequate, anxious about how we can demonstrate our competence, about how we can demonstrate that we are on top of the situation. But we must resist the temptation to 'rush in' to things.

Figure 2.1   A problem-solving model

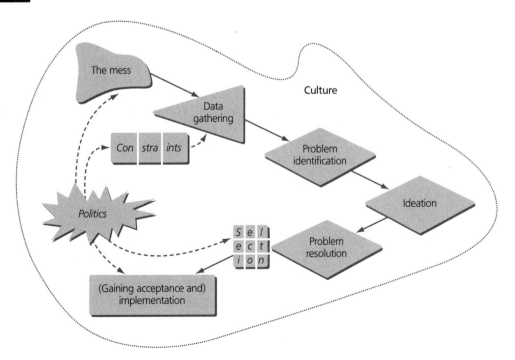

We could also be experiencing excitement if our problem situation is in reality an opportunity.

What we need to do is to identify the things we need to address and prioritize them. Techniques for helping us with this will be presented in Chapter 4.

Data Gathering

In this 'fact'-finding stage it may be necessary for us to gather:

- *objective data* – the who, what, where, when, why and how of the problem situation;
- *subjective data* – opinions, attitudes, feelings and beliefs;
- details of any *constraints* that exist (or are thought to exist) on what we can do about the situation – legal, financial, time, etc.;
- anything else (!?).

Techniques for helping us with this will be presented in Chapter 5.

Problem Identification

This crucial stage in problem solving can also be referred to as 'problem redefinition' as there may be several valid ways of viewing the problem that all need to be considered. If we do not start from the right place we will be lucky to stumble on a lasting solution. General advice is to note the problem definition as given, or first thought of, then take time to think of other ways of describing it – trying to get different 'angles' on the problem situation (as in Frame 1.4). Techniques for helping us with this will be presented in Chapter 6.

Ideation

Generating ideas is another important stage in problem solving. At this stage we should remember not to evaluate our ideas too soon, for reasons we will see later in Chapter 3. Although some selection of ideas will be necessary before we move to the next phase, no judgements or criticisms should be made whilst we are actually trying to generate them.

Many techniques for helping us with this stage will be presented in Chapter 7.

Problem Resolution

This stage is probably where we need to be the most creative. Now we gently evaluate and develop the most promising of our ideas. Very seldom are we lucky enough to get an idea (for a possible solution) that 'arrives' fully developed (new, appealing and feasible) and whose merit is obvious; usually if it's that new it needs some development. This will need to be done first. Then, if we have several possible solutions we may need to compare them by evaluating them against some appropriate criteria in order to select the best one(s) to implement.

Techniques for helping us with these things will be presented in Chapter 8.

(Solution) implementation (including possibly gaining acceptance)

Finally, and (as we have discussed before) often a problem in its own right, we need to implement our solutions.

In addition to this, we may be required to 'sell' the merits of our possible solutions, gain acceptance for them and elicit the commitment (from others) necessary to implement them. There are many factors that determine success in this, as will be seen later. It does not matter how innovative, imaginative, spectacular, accomplished and eminently sensible our solutions might be, if we lack the authority or interpersonal skills necessary to persuade others to our view. The brilliance of our solution alone is rarely sufficient to guarantee its implementation.

Furthermore, not only is most organizational problem solving a group process, but often other groups have a stake in the problem-solving group's operations. So what constitutes an acceptable solution is often not decided by the problem-solving group itself, and may also be constrained by these wider interactions (see Frame 2.5). It may involve 'political' considerations as well, and is often an involved and complex decision-making process.

Frame 2.5 *Acceptable solutions to real problems – 'pollution'*

A simple illustration of the difficulty of deciding what constitutes an acceptable solution is to consider the following solutions to the problem of 'How to combat air pollution from car exhausts', all of which are possible. Which would be appropriate in a management report from say the research and development (R&D) department to the managing director of a major car manufacturer:

(i)   ban all cars

(ii) ban internal combustion power

(iii) invest £x million in R&D into alternative energy sources

(iv) redesign *all* of the company's engines to run on, hydrogen or biofuel liquid petroleum gas (LPG)

(v)   fit catalytic converters to all new cars

(vi) conduct an advertising campaign *saying* that all his company's cars are cleaner?

Presumably the first two are unacceptable, but what of the other four? Most car manufacturing companies have gone or are moving in the direction of the fourth solution, the fifth seems eminently reasonable and is now mandatory in many countries if you wish to sell your cars there, but would a company unable to adopt immediately either of these two consider the last? A rich and far-sighted company might even contemplate adopting the third solution.

Techniques for helping us with these things will be presented in Chapter 9.

Following the model

You can return from any stage to any previous stage and repeat part (or all) of the process, if appropriate. You may wish to take several problem definitions through to a solution, to generate additional ideas if difficulties are encountered developing possible solutions from your initial ideas, or even go back to get additional data if needed. While it is useful to know what stages we might have needed to go through, it should never be thought that we must:

- go through every stage;
- do this in the order prescribed, starting at stage 1 (or 2 depending whether we have a specific problem in mind)
- never consider the possibility of 'looping back' to repeat an earlier stage or stages, if that seems to be desirable or necessary;
- assume that the stages are discrete and never overlap.

Although often we start at stage 1 or 2 and go through all the stages methodically, this is not always the case. Often our problem is identifying what is causing us concern about the situation. Once we have satisfied ourselves as to how best to describe (or define) the problem, the solution or the means of arriving at it may be fairly standard or obvious and we may only complete the first three stages of the model. If we already have a couple of ideas, and our problem is determining their feasibility, we might start with a developing/evaluating stage (stage 5). This will uncover doubts or concerns we may have about these ideas and require us perhaps to start at the 'top' again, stating each concern as something we need to resolve (stage 3, or perhaps stage 2 if we think we need to gather more data), and then generating some ideas (stage 4) about ways of overcoming the concerns that we have.

Specific problem-solving processes

Four of the five problem-solving processes we shall encounter – Osborn-Parnes (Brainstorming), Synectics, Kepner-Tregoe's rational approach,[4] TRIZ and SSM are reckoned to be 'complete' problem-solving processes. That is, they contain their own steps or stages, through which we progress, and which should be comparable with those in our model. You will be able to judge how comprehensively the four processes address the issues raised by the model as we go on.

The separate techniques described later, such as Morphological Analysis, can be usefully employed at different stages (sometimes more than one) during our problem solving.

Summary

In this chapter we have become acquainted with three approaches to problem solving, discussed and explored some problem situations where predominantly one approach may be more appropriate than another, and established that creative thinking is important no matter which approach is the main one used. We have also seen that the problem-solving process normally involves several distinct stages.

Endnotes

1. Peter Checkland's **Soft Systems Methodology** (SSM).
2. The rational or logical approach can also be seen as a 'hard' (though not often a systems) approach due to its common underlying assumptions, for example, there is a well-defined (and universally agreed) objective to be achieved.
3. Lateral Thinking is a name coined by Edward de Bono (1990) and is roughly synonymous with **divergent thinking**.
4. Four 'aspects' of this approach, Situation Analysis, Problem Analysis, Decision Analysis and Potential Problem Analysis will be described as separate techniques in the later chapters because (a) some of them have been adopted at least in part by the Osborn-Parnes process, and (b) some people consider Problem Analysis to be only suitable for a specific *type* of problem (machine ones).

3 Where has all our creativity gone?

This chapter describes the concepts of creativity and creative thinking in the sense that they are to be used here. It also offers two reasons why we may feel that we are not creative, or not as creative as we used to be. It concludes by offering some initial advice on how we can revive our creativity, including an introduction to Brainstorming.

What is creativity?

Creativity is apparent in many fields of human endeavour, though common usage of the word often erroneously limits it to the fields of art and invention. However, if we consider only these two very visible environments, our conception of creativity will tend to look only at the *products* of someone else's creative process in terms of their *value* to us as marketable or functional commodities, when attempting to assess the degree of creativity employed.

Our main interest here is the application of creativity within both our working environment and life in general; for example, in developing new products and services, and looking for opportunities for economic and personal growth – in managerial terms, surmounting barriers to desired goals and objectives. So, although the commodified view of creativity given above may not be totally inappropriate here, to encourage this narrow view of creativity would be wasteful of many of the ideas and processes/techniques discussed in the later chapters.

Carl Rogers (1954, in Parnes and Harding, 1962, p.65) maintained that 'there must be something observable, some product of creation' in order for us to talk usefully of a creative process having taken place. He further insists that the product must be a 'novel construction' and have 'the stamp of the individual' who created it evident upon it. But he also suggests that one of the inner conditions for creativity is the realization that determining the value of these products should reside with the individual who created them and not with someone else (see Frame 3.1).

> ## Frame 3.1 *Conditions for constructive creativity*
>
> Carl Rogers (1954, in Parnes and Harding, 1962, pp.67–8) suggested the following 'inner conditions' are closely associated with our creative potential:
>
> ### Openness to experience
>
> 'A lack of rigidity . . . [a] permeability of boundaries in concepts, beliefs, perceptions, and hypotheses . . . a tolerance for ambiguity where ambiguity exists . . . the ability to receive much conflicting information without forcing closure upon the situation.'
>
> ### An internal locus of evaluation
>
> A belief that the value of our creative products is established not by the praise and criticism of others but by ourselves.
>
> ### The ability to toy with elements and concepts
>
> 'The ability to play spontaneously with ideas, colours, shapes, relationships – to juggle elements into impossible juxtapositions, to shape wild hypotheses, to make the given problematic, to express the ridiculous, translate from one form to another, to transform into improbable equivalents.'

Another view of creativity is that it is (just) a 'connection-making' thought process; that is, making connections between apparently disparate ideas, observations, experiences, etc., which helps us to solve problems or realize opportunities. Sidney Parnes (1992, p.136) argues that: 'the essence of creativity – the "aha" – might be considered to be the association of thoughts, facts, ideas data, etc., into a new and relevant configuration, one that has meaning beyond the sum of the parts – that provides a synergistic effect', and goes on to say that 'the product, if one exists, may be new and relevant to a group or organization, to society as a whole, or merely to the individual concerned' thus 'extending' the definition of new/novel.

The **processes/techniques** discussed later can help us be more creative in dealing with many aspects of our lives, and will not always result in a tangible product, let alone one that someone else thinks is creative. Here, we will also consider as creative, situations where although the solution of a problem may not be novel or unusual, the process by which it has been attained is nevertheless ingenious, demonstrating both flair and imagination. Here the *process* is creative. Simply 'surviving' in our everyday lives can be a creative process; is being an entrepreneur, an inventor or a Van Gogh any more creative than bringing up four children as a single parent drawing state benefits?

Wherever and however true creativity is manifested, it is commonly believed that the same mental process has been used to produce it. According to Rogers, 'there is no fundamental difference in the creative process as it is evidenced in painting a picture, composing a symphony, devising new instruments of killing, developing a scientific theory, discovering new procedures in human relationships . . .' (Rogers, 1954, in Parnes and Harding, 1962, p.65). Much research into creativity has been directed at attempting to discover what is actually involved in these mental processes. The best known of these are the Factor Analysis studies of J.P. Guilford (1962). **Factor Analysis** is a sophisticated statistical method that attempts to uncover the underlying factors or variables that give rise to a set of observed measurements. For example, if we have a group of tests that purport to measure some aspect of creativity and we apply these to a number of people, then Factor Analysis will help us to identify what factors constitute creativity. In Frame 3.2 we can see a summary of the results of Guilford's research (1962).

Frame 3.2 *What is creativity?*

The psychologist J.P. Guilford initially hypothesized (1962) that there were at least seven distinct creative-thinking abilities:

- *sensitivity* (alertness) to problems
- *fluency* of thinking
- *flexibility* of thinking
- *originality* of thinking
- ability to *analyse* and (in particular) *synthesize* information
- ability to *redefine* things ('to transform the meaning or use or function of an object so as to give it a new role', p.157).

Guilford was able to validate all but the abilities to analyse and synthesize. He concluded that these abilities must exist but because they are not uniform processes they did not 'show up' in his tests. He did establish four types of fluency: 'word', 'ideational', 'associational' and 'expressional' – and two types of flexibility: 'spontaneous' and 'adaptive'.

Along with **cognition**, **memory** and **evaluation**, Guilford identified two types of productive thinking which 'generate new information from known and remembered information' (p.160): **divergent thinking** 'in different directions, sometimes searching, sometimes seeking variety' and **convergent thinking** which leads 'to one right answer or to a recognized best or conventional answer'. Most creative abilities Guilford found came into the category of divergent thinking, but sensitivity and redefinition are classified within evaluation and convergent thinking respectively. For creative thinking to exist we must have cognition – 'without having information there is no intellectual performance of any kind' and we must have a good memory in order to retain learned information.

Parnes (1992) also provides a 'context' for creativity, associating it with knowledge (and by implication, the traditional concept of intelligence[1]) amongst other things.

> Creativity can be considered a function of knowledge, imagination, and evaluation. Without knowledge, there obviously can be no productive creativity. ... The effectiveness of creative productivity also depends, of course, on the evaluation and development of embryonic ideas into usable ideas. Without knowledge, imagination cannot be productive. Without imaginative manipulation, abundant knowledge cannot help us live in a world of change. And without the ability to synthesize, evaluate, and develop our ideas, we achieve no effective creativity. (Parnes, 1992, p.137)

Proctor (1999, p.6) seems to support this view, but points out an interesting contradiction concerning creativity: 'immersion in one's subject matter can be an important factor in gaining creative insights ... [they] appear to be easiest to gain in fields where we have considerable prior knowledge and experience.' But (as we saw in the last chapter when we discussed the inertia vector, and as we shall see later), 'existing ideas tend to make us myopic about new possibilities'. The paradox is 'creative ideas do not come to us unless we spend much effort engaged in just the activity which makes their emergence most difficult'.

Since we are concerned with problem solving, we will take these mental processes as our main concern and not worry about whether any end product is also creative. From now on this is what I shall refer to as creativity.

Parnes (1972) refers to the three S's of creativity – 'sensitivity', 'serendipity' and 'synergy':

- *Sensitivity* can mean both an increased awareness of those little peculiarities of life – those inconsistencies, discontinuities and disparities associated with people, things and ideas – which are a fundamental part of the world we live in, and an increased awareness of the processes involved in the personal and social interactions between ourselves and others.
- *Serendipity* is usually defined as the faculty of making happy chance finds.
- *Synergy* is the name given to the phenomenon associated with systems of people, things or ideas, whereby these entities (or 'components') are more effective, more useful, more significant and/or exhibit some behaviour or property, in combination, that could not have been predicted by an examination of their individual attributes, behaviours or properties.

Sensitivity implies being more observant and more knowledgeable about 'the way things are', thus increasing the likelihood of our producing fortuitous ideas, relationships, etc. But to be truly creative we must also appreciate the relevance of these random 'finds' to the task in hand. In brief, then, the essence of creativity is the ability to make connections between seemingly irrelevant and unrelated objects, ideas, information and events.

Parnes's definition is less orientated towards the end product than some but, more important, it provides us with a starting point for our search to find out ways of facilitating the mental processes of creativity. It suggests that we should strive to be more aware of what is happening around us and be more open-minded, and that there might be a 'connection-making' skill we can develop. The practical processes and techniques (for improving creative thinking) in use appear to validate this view of creativity.

However, this definition of creativity could also be said to reinforce the idea that creative thinking is an exceptional occurrence, that most of us do not experience it or do so only to a small degree and then infrequently. Debates on the nature of creativity will doubtless continue. However, I do not believe that creativity is an exceptional process. Most of us can be, and probably are, more creative than we perceive ourselves to be; though in some of us this ability may be inhibited. However, our creative-thinking skills *can* be enhanced with practice like any other skill.

Creativity v. innovation

Having adopted here a definition of creativity that does not 'require' the outcome to be in any way absolutely new, it seems worthwhile spending a paragraph or two defining the process of innovation. This is also not unproblematic! EACI[2] (1995), attempting to provide working definitions of creativity and innovation, gathered key words associated with each term from thirty of its members, and found that there was considerable overlap between the two, as one might expect. The nearest they got to a definition of innovation was ... the process of introducing new and 'creative' products!

Michael Kirton (1994a) believes that as individuals we adopt a particular (cognitive) style when it comes to creativity and problem solving, and that each of us can be placed somewhere along his adaption-innovation continuum. The characteristics of typical adaptors and innovators can be found in Chapter 14. Kirton (1994d) maintains that adaptors prefer to improve things by small evolutionary modifications, whereas innovators prefer to 'throw away the mould' and do things in totally new, revolutionary ways.

But is incremental improvement innovation? Jon Coldwell (1996), after also discussing the difficulty in pinning down exactly what innovation is, argues that continuous (incremental) improvement is *not* the same as innovation, and uses the Cusp Catastrophe theory model to illustrate this (see Figure 3.1). In his view,

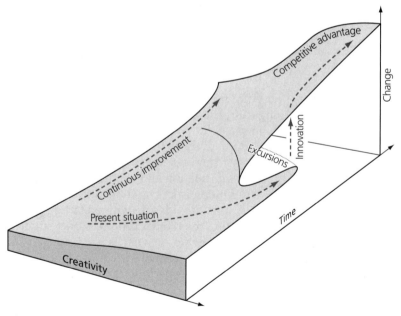

Figure 3.1

Cusp Catastrophe Model of Innovation

Adapted from Coldwell (1996)

innovation requires a sudden, discontinuous, stochastic, *breakthrough* and holds a greater potential for positive change and thus competitive advantage. The sort of ideas that come from employing **Synectics excursions** (see Frame 14.1) tend to lead to innovative solutions such as these, though ones that get less 'distance' from the problem are likely to be developed into little more than incremental improvements.

Genrich Altshuller (1999), when introducing 'technical creativity/systematic innovation', defines five levels of 'innovation': given below are Lev Shulyak's (1997, p.16) description of them:

- 'Level 1 A simple improvement of a technical system. Requires knowledge available within a trade relevant to the system [not really innovative].
- Level 2 An invention that includes the resolution of a technical contradiction. Requires knowledge from different areas within the industry relevant to the system.
- Level 3 An invention containing a resolution of a physical contradiction. Requires knowledge from other industries.
- Level 4 A new technology is developed containing a breakthrough solution that requires knowledge from different fields of science. Improves upon a technical system, but without solving an existing technological problem. Instead, it solves the problem by replacing the original technology with a new technology.
- Level 5 A new phenomenon is discovered that allows pushing the existing technology to a higher level.'

At first sight the 'lower' levels 1–3 might appear to be similar to (or little more than) incremental improvement, even though level 4 and 5 problems will certainly be seen to be something else altogether! But when Altshuller's ideas are looked at in more detail, he goes on to say (1999, p.91) that 'from the engineering perspective, creation of a new invention always manifests as the full or partial overcoming of a technical contradiction' (which is the case with level 2 problems and above); this I feel meets Coldwell's definition of an innovation.

We need both incremental improvements and breakthrough innovations. Most of the creative problem-solving processes or techniques described later tend to produce the latter, but we will not worry any further whether a particular process/technique normally delivers the former, the latter or both.

The downturn in creative thinking

As young children we produce uninhibited drawings and appropriate but technically or grammatically incorrect descriptions of the world we find ourselves in, and invent imaginative adventures in which to act out roles. Because everything is new, there are many opportunities to demonstrate our creativity as we explore the world.

As we grow into adulthood we develop levels of competence in order to deal adequately with the problems of life. For most of us, our artistic endeavours become a secondary (leisure) activity. We strive for precision in our communications so as to be better understood, and we stop making up dream worlds.

Dealing with perceived reality is paramount. Our activities might require a degree of creativity, but others are less likely to see them as interesting or creative and our chances of appearing to be creative diminish accordingly. Whether we are actually less creative than we were as children; whether we have less opportunities to display our creativity, or do display it but in different ways; or whether we just *perceive* ourselves as less creative, our creativity appears to diminish.

There are two major explanations of this hypothesized creative downturn. The first argues that we have 'lost control' of certain thinking operations that are fundamental to creativity. To regain full command of these processes we need to accept that certain childlike thinking operations do have a place in adult problem solving. In the second explanation the existence of various psychological blocks, some of which are innate while others form as we mature, hinders our ability to get ideas.

The common theme in both of these views is that at least part of the problem stems from our upbringing. Our society, our culture and our educational system equip us adequately for most aspects of our lives but at the expense of our ability to think creatively. George Prince, W.T. Weaver and Kathleen Logan-Prince (2000, pp.23–5) cite the research of George Land and Beth Jarman in the early 1990s that attests to this 'decline' in creativity, and offer the belief that it is caused by 'certain kinds of transmissions that convey criticism, rejection, disrespect or humiliation [that] have a remarkably negative effect on the early stages of learning and creating ideas'. We shall discuss these **discounts** further, below.

Also common is the idea that all the 'material' necessary for producing creative ideas *is* available at a sub- or non-conscious level in our minds: what we require is the means of making them conscious.

MindSpring theory

Prince (1976) devised his **MindSpring** theory (see also Frame 3.3) in an attempt to show the relationship between our learning and creative problem-solving skills and to suggest why they are often perceived to have diminished by the time we reach maturity. He suggested that six thinking operations are involved in learning and problem solving:

- wishing
- retrieving
- imaging
- comparing
- transforming
- storing.

The following example demonstrates how we might use these six thinking operations in a typical learning/problem-solving situation. We are sitting at a personal computer trying to use a new piece of software when the machine responds with an incomprehensible error message and/or refuses to do what we want it to. We start to do some wishing:

- I wish I had just saved all the work I have done in the last hour.
- I wish that I could back-track from this impasse.

- I wish I knew how to get out of this mess.
- I wish I knew what I have done wrong, so that I don't do it again.

In other words, we make an attempt to determine what really is our problem. We then start *retrieving* any past experiences we have of using other computers and other pieces of software that have ended in a similar situation. We *form mental images* of these situations, replaying in our minds how they occurred and what we did in an attempt to recover from them. We *compare* these past experiences with the present situation and *transform* or adapt them in line with our most recent perceptions. It is these modified mental images that will (we hope) help us to understand and thus resolve the present problem. At the end of all this we *store* away this new experience for future reference.

Frame 3.3 *George Prince's (1976) MindSpring theory*

- There are six discrete thinking operations: wishing, retrieving, imaging, comparing, transforming and storing.
- All thinking operations are purposeful and their products will fall somewhere on the spectrum: irrelevant – approximately relevant – precisely relevant.
- Learning involves the same thinking operations as problem solving.
- Certain of these thinking operations (wishing, transforming and imaging) tend to be repressed as we grow older and this decreases our learning and problem-solving efficiency. (Our culture 'inadvertently' causes us to associate these operations with wrongness.) This situation is worsened by the natural decline of our mental abilities that often happens with age.
- These repressed operations can be restored to awareness, increasing learning and problem-solving efficiency. This is not a difficult task, though the use of them tends to bring on anxiety.

When we were young virtually all our experiences were new, and we spent most of our time trying to make sense of them. To do this we had to make considerable use of *all* six of these thinking operations. But the novelty of the circumstances ensured that we used the thinking operations of wishing, imaging and transforming in particular.

As children we did a lot of wishing. We wished that we had the toy that we saw someone else playing with. We wished that we were someone else, or could be somewhere else. We wished that we knew how to deal with all these new situations. When things seemed to be unobtainable our usual way of dealing with this was to imagine what they would be like, but we had to do this on the basis of limited past experience. When wishing for the impossible and when trying to make sense of the actual, we had to rely heavily on our ability to transform mental images, as most retrieved experiences were only approximately like the new situation. It was also essential that the images we formed from retrieved memories were vivid and detailed enough so that we *could* adapt them and play with them in our attempt to understand.

What Prince noticed was that as we grow older we appear to use the operations of wishing, imaging and transformation less and less. We do not actually stop using them, we just cease to be aware of using them. Yet they may be the basis of all creative thought. According to Prince (1976, p.291):

- Wishing is an efficient form of goal setting, a technique for Problem Identification, 'the natural first step in affecting change' and a powerful motivator.
- Transforming is at the very heart of learning. We learn by refining the precision of our stereotyped memories. Without transforming there can be no change, no learning.
- Imaging not only facilitates the comparison and manipulation of ideas, but is also an essential part of our memory processes.

Prince suggests that as adults these operations have become internalized and are usually carried out at a non-conscious level. He accounts for this phenomenon by suggesting that as we grow up we associate these operations with wrongness, and we soon learn that being 'wrong' can be painful. Essential though these operations are, we find it difficult to perform them consciously and repress them to an unconscious level. We learn that we cannot have everything that we wish for. Our parents, teachers and peers tell us that is wrong to wish for certain things. We find it difficult to differentiate which things it is all right to wish for and which are not, so we curtail our wishing perhaps more than we need to.

We are able to manipulate mental images much faster than another person can talk, and so we tend to 'think ahead' of the speaker. We try to imagine what the other person is going to say. Inevitably we find out that many of these images are wrong. Unfortunately we come to believe that it is the process itself which is 'wrong'.

We have already noted that transforming is a very important part of learning. However, when we were children (having already encountered and appreciated the concepts of buses and birds) and described an aeroplane as a 'bus with wings' when seeing one for the first time, we may once again have been told that we were 'wrong' and others may have laughed at us for making such 'mistakes'. Being very resourceful at that age we soon learned to ask what the mystery object was, rather than to risk another 'incorrect' transformation.

To complete this discussion on Prince's theory, Frame 3.4 lists those things which he believed were characteristics of *routine* and *creative* thinking (Prince, 1976, p.292). Prince and Logan-Prince (2002) have now extended the MindSpring theory into a concept for everyday living called **MindFree** (see Chapter 14).

Frame 3.4 *Routine and creative thinking*

Routine thinking is characterized by:

- wishes that are reasonably attainable;

▶

- retrievals that fit the situation perfectly, and which require little transformation;
- comparisons that result in precise fits;
- logic and precision;
- a feeling we have of being comfortable and certain;
- little or no learning that takes place;
- a high degree of rightness;
- little worth storing (nothing new!).

Creative thinking is characterized by:

- wishes that may not be achievable;
- retrievals that are at best approximate, but may not fit at all;
- a necessarily high level of transformation;
- comparisons that lead to more wishes, transformations, retrievals, etc;
- being non-logical and approximate;
- a feeling we have of being confused, uncertain, anxious, excited, afraid;
- a high propensity for learning;
- a feeling of wrongness;
- things worth storing.

Prince (1976)

Conceptual blocks

We can take an alternative view of our apparent lack of creative talents if we picture our mind (as mentioned above) as containing all the necessary raw materials (memories and experiences) for creativity. This is the stuff from which we should be able to make connections with the problem situation that will eventually lead to the production of novel ideas and possible solutions, but, unfortunately, these ideas and innovative solutions are prevented from emerging from our subconscious minds by various mental blocks. In this respect our mind is a bit like a dormant but not extinct volcano: the creative fire is being held back by the natural movements of the rocky substrate and the crusty cap that has formed over many years as a result of the external pressures of the environment. Only very rarely (and with difficulty) does our 'volcano' erupt with an idea. These mental blocks affect each of us in different ways. Some of them could be the mechanism for what Prince (1970, 1998) calls our **self-censor**, which severely filters and evaluates our ideas, only letting (if we are lucky) some of them to emerge from our subconscious mind, and of those only allowing us to voice the 'carefully thought out' ones. These blocks certainly work at a conscious level, but may be working at a deeper level than this, inhibiting the thinking processes themselves.

James L. Adams (1979) compiled a list of 30 of these **conceptual blocks** that make it difficult for us to think creatively, classifying them as perceptual, emotional, cultural, environmental, intellectual or expressive blocks. Those, merged with a few others, are described below.

Perceptual blocks

It is well known that our senses can easily be misled when the mind receives 'confused' data from the sense organs. However, perceptual blocks result from the way the mind naturally tries to manage all of the data it receives from our senses. Whilst this process may be optimized for most of our everyday living (including basic survival! – see, the feint, fight or flight response below and EQ/SQ Chapter 14) it has inappropriate side effects when it comes to problem solving. Because our senses are so critical to us in perceiving the world these blocks are probably the most significant factors undermining our creativity.

1. Stereotyping It would be impossible to remember every detail of every experience and so our mind only stores in its long-term memory 'important' information. It appears to do this by looking for patterns in the data that will permit it to 'pigeon hole' new information along with similar experiences. When we recall this information we get an imprecise image of the original experience with the 'irrelevant' details removed. Consequently, we often see only what we expect to see based on the pattern of our previous experience. Perhaps the most common manifestation of this is the tendency, on meeting people for the first time, to form instant and lasting judgements about them based on obvious features such as clothes, hair or accent, and even other things such as names.

Unfortunately, our attitudes, opinions and beliefs affect our perception as well. The tendency we have because of this to notice certain things (of particular interest to us) more than others (**mental set**) only serves to reinforce these preconceived notions ('halo effect'), and can also lead to what is called a 'self-fulfilling prophecy' (where, because of our inappropriate responses based on this reinforcement, the other party is 'encouraged' to react to us in the way we 'predicted' they would): see Frame 3.5.

Frame 3.5 *Example of the self–fulfilling prophecy*

If we take an immediate dislike to someone (or a certain group of people), it is likely (due to our mental set) that everything they appear to do will confirm that our dislike is well founded. We will then tend to respond to them negatively, and they will probably not know why but assume that it is because we are not very nice persons, so will treat us in a similarly negative way that they think we deserve. In other words, in a way that we always felt that their type of person would!

If we take our stereotyped memories too literally we may overlook a significant feature of a new problem situation because we do not remember it (as being important) on some previous occasion, or incorrectly assume something exists or is significant simply because that is the way we remember things were the last time.

Genrich Altshuller (1999, p.86), when talking about systematic innovation, reminds us that 'habitual concepts [stereotypes and preconceptions] besiege the inventor, blocking any directions that lead to fundamentally new solutions'. He goes on to say about his way of dealing with them: 'A directed search does not by any means exclude intuition. On the contrary, a structured thought process creates that special mental tuning which helpfully promotes intuition.'

2. Difficulty in isolating the problem   It is often true that 'you can't see the wood for the trees'. We can experience difficulty in isolating the problem from the masses of irrelevant data surrounding it. If we allow ourselves to become enmeshed in these superficial details our solutions may be inadequate, or worse, we may fail to recognize the real problem altogether.

3. Tunnel vision   All too often, when we start to solve a problem we make assumptions about it: we impose (possibly inappropriate) boundaries or constraints on the problem situation, and hence limitations on what we can do about it. These boundaries and constraints may exist in reality – or they may not. If they do not exist, obviously, these boundaries/constraints are 'cutting off' some mental avenues we could/should explore. But even if they do, it may still be useful to 'forget' them for a while when generating ideas, for example, there could be a cost constraint which, if initially ignored, might allow an idea to emerge that, although initially 'over the budget', is actually revenue generating in the long term. (See also, ignoring contradictions, **TRIZ**, pages 101 and 132).

Edward de Bono, who is perhaps best known for his invention of the term **Lateral Thinking** and his efforts to popularize the merits of creative thinking, describes (1990) the fundamental aspects of Lateral Thinking as:

- generating alternative ways at looking at things
- challenging assumptions.

He goes on to say (1990, pp.111–12) that

> A *dominant* idea is the organizing theme in a way of looking at a situation. It is often present but undefined and one tries to define it in order to escape from it. A *crucial factor* is some element of the situation [often connected with an assumption] which must always be included no matter how one looks at the situation.

Both these things are limiting!

Although this block may seem to be the 'opposite' of the one above, it is possible to suffer from both!

4. Inability to perceive the problem situation from different viewpoints   This block has two dimensions. First, we may have difficulty in seeing a shared problem from someone else's viewpoint. Second, we may be unable to see our own problem in a number of different ways that, amongst other things, can lead us to attribute the wrong cause or to confuse cause with effect, and thus misdirect our problem-solving efforts (attempting to solve the 'wrong' problem). Whether we are working alone or with others it is important for us to get different perspectives on the problem situation to ensure we are actually trying to solve the right one. **CPS** techniques such as **excursions** (see pages 140/51) for 'getting away' from the problem, can help.

5. Saturation   Extremely familiar inputs from our senses are often disregarded by our conscious mind to avoid 'overloading' it. Think of something you see every day, your television set perhaps, and try to draw it. Did you get every detail correct? Tape record an evening at home with the family: do you remember that clock ticking on the wall and the aircraft or bus passing by outside?

We may overlook these everyday phenomena when one of them is, or could give us a clue to, the actual cause of a problem.

6. Failure to use all our senses effectively   Blindfold yourself and hold your nose. Then try to tell the difference between the taste of a raw potato and a piece of apple. Without your senses of smell and sight, your sense of taste may be inadequate. Our senses frequently work in an interconnected manner. Failing to use all of them efficiently may cause us to miss an important part of a problem.

Emotional blocks

Our emotions and desires can interfere with both our ability to form thoughts and mental images, and the freedom with which we can then transform and manipulate these. They can also inhibit us from voicing our ideas. These emotional blocks seem to be linked to motivation, that 'something' which drives us to expend effort, enthusiasm, emotion, etc., in doing certain things (Frames 3.6 and 13.5).

Frame 3.6 *The desire to be creative*

To Calvin W. Taylor (1962, p.181) motivation may be a strong component of creativity. Here are some 'motivational characteristics' that have been suggested:

- curiosity or an inquiring mind;
- an intellectual persistence;
- a need for recognition to feel achievement;
- a need for variety;
- a need for autonomy;
- a preference for complex order;
- a tolerance of ambiguity;
- a need for mastery of a problem;
- an insatiability for intellectual ordering.

7. Obsessive desire for security and order A desire for security and order is a common trait. We develop habits to make our lives easier, more predictable, more secure and free from anxiety. An extreme desire for this state can result in an intolerance of ambiguity that inhibits creativity. We must be able to tolerate chaos, to immerse ourselves in the 'mess' of the problem situation in order to resolve it.

8. Fear of making a mistake No one likes appearing naive or foolish and being laughed at as a consequence. Our self-image is important to us and can depend heavily on what we feel other people think of us. Making mistakes is a natural part of learning, but we are often afraid of making mistakes because we believe that others will think less of us. The only thing about making mistakes for which we should ever be criticized is not learning something from them.

9. Unwillingness to take a risk Although there is some debate over what precisely motivates us, a common factor seems to be a desire for self-fulfillment. Unfortunately, attaining this invariably involves taking a risk. It may be relatively harmless or could involve something as drastic as our professional credibility, financial ruin, or life itself. We are wisely taught to err on the side of safety and not to take any unnecessary risks, but are seldom told how to assess these risks. So, we tend not to take *any*. Because most people fear to take risks, it is important to be gentle and constructive when evaluating and criticizing other people's ideas.

10. Lack of motivation Since problem solving is a risky business, we need to be highly motivated to get involved. For some it is the expectancy of the exciting mental challenge of the problem (see Frame 3.7), for others the chance to pursue a personal interest. Sometimes the possibility of monetary reward can be the stimulus. But without sufficient motivation of some kind we may well fail at our problem solving by either not doing it when we should, or not doing it effectively (say by not being speculative enough).

Frame 3.7 *Kepner and Tregoe's views on problem-solving motivation*

Charles Kepner and Benjamin Tregoe (1981, p.33) believe that people at any level within an organization will not only accept problem-solving tasks, but will actually seek out problem-solving situations, so long as the following four conditions exist:

- They possess the appropriate problem solving skills needed.
- They experience success in using these skills.
- They are rewarded for successful problem solving.
- They have no reason to fear failure.

▶

The converse of this is also true: people will avoid problem-solving situations when they are unsure of how to solve their problems, when they do not experience success after trying to solve a problem, when they feel that their efforts are not appreciated, and when they sense that they have less to lose either by doing nothing or by shifting the responsibility.

11. Inability to reflect on ideas   The solution to a difficult problem can often come after a daydream or on waking up after a sleep. Certainly, being able to relax, to mull over ideas calmly, away from a crisis atmosphere, and to reflect on the various possibilities, help the problem-solving process. Conversely, pressure and anxiety due to a perceived lack of time or feelings of insecurity can only hinder our problem solving.

12. Trying to solve problems too quickly   Some people are always rushing around frantically trying to get things done quickly, trying to get things back to normal as soon as possible. This may be due to an intolerance of 'chaos', emotional insecurity or perhaps a desire to hide incompetence. The danger is that by rushing at things we start with the first or most obvious problem definition, rather than the most appropriate one. We may also allocate insufficient time to reflect on our ideas or rush our evaluation, thus risking the premature rejection of unusual ideas. The end result is we are likely to end up with an inadequate solution, and we may even 'solve' the wrong problem.

13. A preference for judgement   We have a need to explain and justify why things related to ourselves are the way we perceive them to be. This process of 'attribution' is important because it enables us to determine our level of personal achievement. Because of this we are ceaselessly evaluating situations and thus get into the habit of judging and criticizing *everything*. This is undesirable in problem solving which should be approached with an open mind. Also, our fear of making mistakes 'encourages' us to criticize rather than to offer ideas. Remember that if we judge and criticize other people's ideas they are more likely to judge and criticize ours. We also need to know why others are thinking, feeling and behaving in the way they are. The process of attribution may lead us to misjudge their *intentions* as well.

14. Lack of imagination or imaginative control   Some people find it hard to use their imagination fully. They have difficulty thinking, let alone saying, apparently illogical, impractical or irrelevant things. Mental imagery and fantasy are important in CPS. However, we must always be aware of the difference between fantasy and reality, as ultimately we must interpret our fantastic speculations in the real world of our problem situation.

Cultural blocks

Our society places limitations on what is acceptable for us to say or do. Our upbringing helps to ensure that these limitations are so ingrained that they affect our thinking as well as our actions. The organizations to which we belong also have cultures that produce similar effects. Often the bases of these cultural limitations are highly dubious. Ten years or so ago, a senior policewoman was criticized in some newspapers for going swimming (at a private party) in her underwear. Would she have been criticized had she worn a bikini swimsuit, which consists of essentially the same garments? Of the many shared beliefs and values that go to make up our culture, most that affect our creativity are based on false premises.

15. Problem solving is a serious business![3]   We have a tendency to believe that problem solving should require considerable mental effort. If we are not actually experiencing 'discomfort' we are obviously not working hard enough. Problem solving is usually something we have to do rather than choose to do. Yet being comfortable and relaxed may well be the best way to approach solving a problem. Being too serious can lead to stress which will in turn decrease productivity and effectiveness and will also make us susceptible to the next two blocks.

16. Daydreaming and reflection are a waste of time!   The importance of having the time and the inclination to mull over problem situations and to reflect on ideas and possible solutions cannot be overstated.

17. Fun and playfulness are only for children!   Laughter at a business meeting is often taken to indicate that group members are not taking things seriously enough. For adults, work and leisure are normally disjoint activities, yet CPS can and should be fun. Indeed 'childlike' mental playfulness can considerably enhance creativity. J.G. March (1976) wrote: 'Playfulness is the deliberate, temporary relaxation of rules in order to explore the possibilities of alternative rules.' Playfulness allows experimentation, which is very important in CPS. This seldom gets out of hand since experienced practitioners of CPS seem to develop a natural awareness of when their enjoyment of the situation could be becoming detrimental to a group's productivity.

18. Logic is better than intuition!   Popular myth in Western cultures holds that something which can be proved by scientific method has more merit than something felt intuitively to be correct. We have a tendency to overvalue logic, objectivity, quantitative data and practicality, and undervalue intuition and subjective quality judgements. In fact, there has been much interest and research in recent decades into what Doris Shallcross and Dorothy Sisk (1989) refer to as 'an inner way of knowing'. One thing seems certain however: no matter what causes the (bodily) sensations, feelings, ideas and thoughts, and occasionally mystical experiences (which Francis E. Vaughan (1979) links with four distinct levels of awareness: physical, emotional, mental and spiritual) to 'leap out' of our subconscious minds, they are worth valuing and paying attention to. We should even attempt to improve our intuitive thinking skills. Effective problem solvers need a good balance between logical and intuitive thinking. And remember, *'intuition is the initial spark of creativity'* (Shallcross and Sisk, 1989, p.8).

19. Tradition is better than change!   Some cultures put much time and effort into preserving traditional ways of life. To attempt change in such a culture means that the benefits of the change must be sold effectively. There is nothing wrong with keeping up traditions, provided that they are good traditions.

However, if we are going to challenge a tradition it is important to show that we are not doing so just because it is old. And an over-protectionist attitude to tradition, which gives rise to a dislike, distrust or fear of change, and inhibits creativity and progress. Without new ideas we stagnate.

20. Taboos Some things are not just unacceptable to say or do, they are unthinkable, or at least difficult to think of without feelings of guilt. However, these taboos often block off from our conscious minds areas of thought that might provide ideas for a solution to our problem. Thinking of taboo subjects offends no one.

21. Organizational taboos Typical of organizational taboos are certain ideas, policies or processes that were tried once before and which resulted in 'disaster'. Everyone takes great delight in putting right the innocent newcomer who dares propose such a discredited solution, but what if this solution (perhaps in a modified form) is now feasible and we refuse to reconsider it? Who is being foolish? Contravening organizational norms (see page 211, Chapter 9) is another common form of taboo.

22. Management and leadership style The intuitive judgements, fantasies and the often wild and unconsidered ideas that are so essential for creativity seldom occur except in an atmosphere of mutual trust within a group where normal cultural and emotional blocks have been lifted. Whether or not an organization encourages participative management generally, a problem-solving group must be democratically run. In an autocratically governed work group, we will not be encouraged to run against organizational norms and we are thus unlikely to be creative.

23. Lack of group support To produce an environment that supports creative thinking the group dynamics must be appropriate. We need the emotional support, cooperation and approval of our fellow group members. Everyone needs to be committed to the group's objectives and must be willing to 'sacrifice' their own position or opinions for the common good.

24. Reluctance to implement ideas Any unwillingness by an organization to implement new ideas will be frustrating and dampen the creative effort. Expectations again; if little or nothing ever actually gets done about the situations we are trying to improve, we will be less likely to try so hard next time around. This problem is further compounded because successful CPS groups may come up with too many ideas to implement, or with ideas at the wrong time (that is, a time when they are not wanted). The first of these we will just have to live with, and to overcome feelings of guilt about not pursuing *all* our ideas. The second requires further consideration. We will want to tell someone of our ideas but the offering of an **unsolicited idea** may be treated as an unwelcome distraction or it may cause offence because it is seen as an implied criticism. The solution to this may be to have an organizational policy similar to that suggested by Synectics Limited, whereby the originators of ideas may freely publish them on the understanding that the recipient is under no obligation to adopt, consider or even acknowledge receipt of the idea.

Environmental blocks

25. Distractions   Some organizations will take employees away from the office when problem solving has to be done. This is to combat the common mental block of physical distractions such as phone-calls and interruptions. Obviously distractions can only hinder problem solving, but one person's distraction (for example, loud music) may be an essential element of another's ideal working environment.

The next three blocks were suggested by Stevens (1988, pp.51–2).

26. Monotony   When dealing with monotonous tasks we often switch our brain onto 'auto-pilot'. In consequence, we may fail to notice a problem when it arises. We may also be more susceptible to distractions, especially other matters that require our consideration. A good way to combat this specific distraction is regularly to take a few seconds' break, to write down any thoughts concerning this other matter, and then return to the task in hand.

27. Physical and mental discomfort   Poor lighting, uncomfortable seating and inadequate heating/air conditioning can be a cause of distraction. They can also make us tired and irritable and contribute to feelings of lethargy or stress. Pressure of work, whether due to unrealistic deadlines or previous procrastination, also causes stress. Stress and anxiety are not normally conducive to problem solving.

28. Lack of communication   Getting access to the data we need to solve a problem usually involves us in talking to other people. We may also feel that they too should be involved in our problem solving and that we should get together for this purpose. Inability to achieve these things hinders problem solving as well as leading to frustration and yet more stress. An organization's structure will have implications with regard to the form and efficiency of its communication channels and the ease with which we can gather information and meet with others – 'tall', hierarchical organizations are not renowned for their 'good' communication.

Intellectual and expressive blocks

29. Incorrect choice of problem-solving language   There are variety of problem-solving languages at our disposal; for example, visualization (using mental images), verbalization and mathematics. A given problem is often easier to solve using one rather than another. And so, we should experiment with different problem-solving languages.

30. Inflexible or inadequate use of problem-solving skills and strategies   Using a particular problem-solving skill too exclusively or at the wrong time can hinder problem solving. Often, it is appropriate to use creative thinking to open a problem up when first starting to solve that particular problem. Later, logical or analytical skills may be an appropriate way of refining the solution. But using analytical skills too early in the process of Problem Resolution can be a mistake. When using a particular problem-solving process (such as those described later), be prepared to use them flexibly; for example, it may not always be appropriate to start at step one.

31. Lack of correct information   It is usually important to have all the possible relevant data and to sift through it looking for directions, implications, limitations and connections, before embarking on problem solving.

32. Incorrect or inadequate means of expression   Accurate communication with another human being is always difficult. Many factors increase this difficulty, such as the use of jargon, giving quantitative information in written rather than tabular or graphical form, describing something in words when a small sketch would illustrate the object being described more simply and quickly, using a complex photograph instead of a simple diagram emphasizing important features, etc. Always make sure you are using the most effective method of communication. Paraphrasing back to someone what they have said to you is an effective way of ensuring that you have understood their idea or possible solution.

Do not despair! We have ways of ameliorating the effects of these blocks.

Creativity revived

Now that we have seen how and why our creative talents may have become inhibited, what can we do to improve matters? The advice offered in the 'rules' listed below, which are all based on the findings of people working in this field, 'offers' a good start.

Ground rules for creative thinking

- Welcome every idea: no matter how wild it is, it has some merit. If nothing else it will fire our or someone else's imagination.
- Hold back on criticizing an idea – remember that it is difficult enough to get an idea past our self-censor, so don't be too quick to criticize somebody else's idea (see also the 'destructive force of discounts' below). *And* make sure you understand another person's idea before you evaluate it.
- Remember that we always have some knowledge or experience that can help us solve a given problem.
- Don't be afraid to indulge in some 'childlike' thinking – as in wishing, imagination, mental playfulness, etc.
- Never forget that other people perceive problem situations in ways different from you – treat this as an advantage, a way of helping you get different viewpoints that help you establish which is the most appropriate one to work with.
- Always think of a mistake or failure as an opportunity to learn, not as a thing we did 'wrong'. If we just forget about it, we could do it again!

These 'ground rules' are largely interdependent, and we should try to incorporate *all* of them within our everyday problem-solving strategies at once. More realistically though, we could use them as a sort of checklist to indicate how creative our current behaviour is, and for identifying and initiating corrective actions.

The beginning idea

We should learn to value the **beginning idea**; that is one that has not been carefully thought out. We have seen that cultural disapproval of being 'wrong', making mistakes and appearing foolish can lead us to voice only carefully thought-out ideas. Rarely do we 'publish' beginning ideas and then only in climates where we are sure not to be ridiculed or taken advantage of. Ideally, we need to promote a climate in which we can all safely 'let our hair down' and feel able to disregard the inhibitions that normally limit our creative thinking. The problem is that we cannot always guarantee that we will be called upon to problem solve in such a 'friendly' climate.

Given that ours is a less than perfect problem-solving environment, we should begin by supporting others brave enough to voice beginning ideas. The least we can do is not to reject their beginning ideas because they are naive, unusual or incomplete, and to refrain from gaining emotional capital out of their willingness to offer them. We should indicate unambiguously that we are pleased to receive their beginning ideas, and where appropriate, credit people for having inspired one of our ideas. Also, since someone has to make the first move, we should try to be less reserved about offering our own beginning ideas. In a potentially 'hostile' climate, I find that prefacing a *beginning idea* with an appropriate 'apology': 'This is just a wild idea, I don't know if we can do anything with it . . .' or 'A thought has just occurred to me, but I haven't had the chance to think it through as yet . . .' makes me feel less anxious about voicing it. Even so, someone is almost certain to say 'Yes it certainly *was* a wild idea!' or 'We can tell that you haven't thought *that one* through!', but such criticism will probably be seen by others as the deliberate put-down it was intended to be, unhelpful, and of less worth than our beginning idea.

If we do feel unable to voice beginning ideas, and only offer carefully thought-out ideas, others will not have seen how these ideas have evolved or been able to contribute to their development. All that is left for them to do is to accept or reject our idea. Also, by not offering ideas early, we do not get the benefit of other people's thoughts, ideas and opinions and our idea may be the poorer for that. We need to overcome our (natural) inhibitions and be more prepared to 'publish' imperfect ideas.

The destructive force of discounts

A discount is an interpersonal interaction, either verbal or non-verbal, that conveys criticism, rejection, disrespect, humiliation, etc. Prince *et al.* (2000, p.25) maintain that discounts can have 'a remarkably negative effect on the early stages of learning and [which is important to us here] creating new ideas'. Even though often they are not 'rationally dangerous or even threatening', our reaction to them can be strong 'because they trigger involuntary emotional and physiological reactions, especially anxiety, that lead to defensiveness and avoidance. This anxiety is associated with earlier "irrational" fears, for example, being "abandoned" when a baby'.

Prince *et al.* (2000) and Goleman (1996) both warn us about the amygdala (a key component of our limbic brain[4]) that monitors our senses for any 'message' that might indicate the existence of a threat (to our survival), and initiates an (usually) appropriate emotional response (the feint, fight or flight response (see also EQ/SQ, Chapter 14) before 'higher levels' of the brain (the cortical areas of the cerebral hemispheres) have had a chance to determine the real potential (danger) of the situation. The more intense the feeling of what Goleman (1996) calls an 'emotional emergency', of which there are two kinds – physical danger and threat to meaningfulness – the more dominant the emotional mind is over the rational.

In a group problem-solving situation, the usual reactions of a participant to a discount are withdrawal, remaining silent and not participating. Suspending judgement – the central tenet of Alex Osborn's **Brainstorming** – can reduce many opportunities for discounting; however, we may still feel anxious offering ideas, especially initial contributions, beginning ideas, etc. Prince (1970) and Prince *et al.* (2000, p.47) offer a 'safer' alternative to my 'apologies' mentioned above. They recommend we label these things *wishes*, because they found (through action research) that when wishing, rather than opinions or conclusions, was encouraged, 'the effect was an immediate reduction in scepticism and competitiveness'. The 'mechanism' behind their suggested reaction to discounting, that of listening for meaning, rather than listening defensively, 'demands modifying much of what we believe is good listening, that is, being good at being critical, judgmental, evaluative and listening for flaws' (Prince *et al.*, 2000, p.51).

Next time you do some problem solving 'Do some wishing, and, even though it makes you anxious, allow yourself to be confused and uncertain and do some mistaken thinking. It won't hurt you; you don't have to act on it' (Prince, 1980).

Brainstorming

All the CPS techniques described in the next few chapters employ the original Brainstorming 'philosophy' which, as we have just said, was intended to counter some of the negative effects of the criticism/discounts mentioned above. Let's now have a look at what exactly this is.

The Brainstorming philosophy

When a group of people get together to produce ideas, solve problems, etc., often the first thing that happens to the ideas or possible solutions put forward is that they are criticized, torn apart or dismissed from further discussion. Sometimes ideas may deserve this fate, but often they are useful, interesting or appealing ideas that have a few minor 'faults' that could be remedied if we were to try. In this situation the best that is likely to happen is that an idea from which we might have developed a solution is lost, one hopes only temporarily. Unfortunately, as we said above, this may deter the idea-giver from contributing fully to the group; the group may then lose a potentially valuable resource. At worst, the idea-giver turns against the group, or against the member responsible for the criticism. We then have what Synectics call a 'revenge cycle'. The idea-giver retreats into his or her 'shell' thinking mainly about 'crucifying' any opponents the next time they speak.

The main difference between Brainstorming and previous methods of problem solving is its insistence that absolutely no criticism whatsoever (whether spoken or implied by visual expressions, body language or grunts) is allowed during the generation of ideas. This does not mean that there is no evaluation of ideas, just that it is postponed until later, usually in a separate session.

It is not easy to create an atmosphere in which criticism is postponed, even temporarily. In our prevailing culture, people often come to meetings with differing viewpoints and desires, and a self-concept to enhance or protect. These things, coupled with the usual differentials of status and power that exist within groups, tend to lead to an atmosphere of competition, especially when group members are trying to impress others with their contributions. But neither is creating such an atmosphere impossible.

A key characteristic and benefit of a Brainstorming session is the much larger quantity of ideas produced compared with individual problem solving or the use of previous group problem-solving techniques. Not all the ideas produced will be brilliant, but there are usually many useful ones. This productivity of Brainstorming groups has been attributed to several factors. The power of association of the human mind is well known (though perhaps not really understood), and when a group of individuals are assembled and encouraged to produce ideas by association the effect is a dramatic increase in the number of ideas produced: what Alex Osborn (1957) refers to as '*social facilitation*'. When judgement is suspended, one person's idea quickly triggers ideas in the minds of others, causing a 'snowball' effect. Groups also usually come up with more ideas than the same number of individuals working alone. It has also been demonstrated that the more wild or speculative these ideas are, the more dramatic is this effect. A certain amount of constructive rivalry – the challenge to produce more, better or wilder ideas – also acts as a stimulant.

The rules of Brainstorming

The creative 'climate' within the group is developed and maintained by the group leader's 'gentle enforcement' of strict adherence to the four rules of Brainstorming; these are summarized in Frame 3.8. The leader in this context is not a typical meeting chairman but a process leader, as defined in Chapter 13.

Frame 3.8 *Rules of Brainstorming*

- No criticism is allowed – evaluation of ideas must be withheld until later.
- 'Free-wheeling' is encouraged – just let the ideas flow out, 'the wilder the idea, the better'.
- Quantity is wanted – the greater the number of ideas, the more likely is the chance of having useful, interesting or appealing ones.
- Seek combination and improvement – try to 'build' on other people's ideas.

There are a number of reasons for this insistence on the observance of these rules. Apart from the earlier comments about 'losing' ideas and 'upsetting' fellow group members, permitting criticism at the idea-generation stage affects the productivity of our imaginations and the 'flow' of ideas. We tend to use our imaginative resources to construct defences for our ideas (and our self-esteem) rather than for thinking up new ones. This reduces the quantity of ideas that we are likely to produce, let alone the quantity we will express and record (see Figure 3.2).

We should never dismiss 'wild' or unorthodox ideas as silly or irrelevant. A conscious effort to produce 'wilder', more speculative ideas is almost as important as the postponement of criticism. Not only do these ideas tend to set and maintain the 'atmosphere', reducing tension, relaxing the participants and providing the 'fun' element of problem solving, they also fire the imaginations of other group members.

All this ultimately leads to the acquisition of a larger number of innovative ideas. Although this is the main purpose of the wild ideas, a surprisingly large proportion of them do lead to a problem solution. Who would have thought that such a 'stupid' idea as repeatedly striking overhead power lines with the wing tip of a light aircraft as it flies over them would lead to a solution of the problem of a three-inch build-up of frost along 700 miles of overhead power cables, which had been causing them to break and disrupt supply! A simple modification of this idea worked; replace the aircraft with a helicopter and use the downdraught of the rotors to dislodge the frost.

Finally, experience has shown that the best ideas often come from a combination and/or development of several other ideas, and so we are encouraged to 'build' on other people's ideas whenever possible (see Frame 3.9 and Chapter 7). We will also see later (Appendix 3) that Osborn (1957) recommends that further 'builds' should be attempted, when we subsequently begin to evaluate the ideas we have generated.

Conducting a Brainstorming session

Since all CPS techniques employ the Brainstorming 'philosophy' described above, and are often used in a group setting, it may be appropriate to mention here some general advice on running Brainstorming sessions.

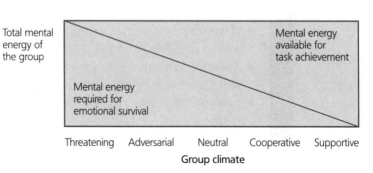

Figure 3.2

The trade-off between defensiveness and productivity

Adapted from Nolan (1989)

> **Frame 3.9** *Building on other people's ideas*
>
> Whilst seeking names for a new unisex perfume the following ideas may have been suggested:
>
> - The Master and Mistress
> - How about something French sounding?
> - Messieurs et Mesdemoiselles
> - Maestro
> - Deux Chevaux
> - Lovebirds.
>
> 'Deux Chevaux' is a simple 'build' on the idea of trying something French and the car name 'Maestro'. It has a certain 'ring' to it, though people would probably not want to think that they were wandering around smelling of 'two horses'! Having said that, there was once a successful ladies' perfume called 'Tramp'.

Size and composition of the group

Group sizes from half a dozen or so up to a couple of hundred have been tried in the past, though experience suggests that approximately a dozen people is the ideal. A compromise has to be made between enough people to get a steady flow of ideas easily and a group small enough to be manageable. In too large a group, ideas may be forgotten or lost, leading to frustration, and time may be 'available' for us to evaluate and perhaps censor our own ideas. If a group contains a couple of people who are 'good' at, and willing to come up with, wild ideas, the group size can be smaller and still be as productive.

Osborn originally suggested that these groups should consist of a leader, an associate leader, five 'regulars' (experienced Brainstormers) and five 'guests' with a 'knowledge' of or experience related (perhaps tenuously) to the problem area (for example with a marketing problem these might include a 'typical consumer'). There are no hard-and-fast rules on composition, although it is generally thought that the inclusion of experienced brainstormers is very desirable, as is a group with a wide spread of backgrounds. A group made up of only 'experts' in the problem area is very undesirable, and some would say that having more than one expert can cause problems (see also page, 231, Chapter 10). The more diverse (due to experience, expertise or ideology) the participants, the more difficult it is for the leader to ensure that those opinions are voiced in a positive way; if the leader succeeds in this, the more creative will be the ideas. Osborn believes that a positive attitude towards the task in hand and the processes used is more important than proven creativity.

Life is made easier if all the participants are of equal 'rank' within the organization. This is because group members are expected to say things that, in other circumstances, might be thought silly (or worse). However, a group of equal rank is neither always possible nor desirable. If our problem was 'How can we improve communications within the organization?' an input from people at various levels in the organization should obviously be sought. This makes it important to ensure that the correct 'climate' has been established and that everyone knows the rules and what is expected from them, so that within the group they are effectively equal.

When is the best time to hold a Brainstorming session?

Timing depends largely on the group's motivation. Osborn favours morning sessions, suggesting that starting a little while before a light 'working' lunch is also successful as it improves the informality of the occasion. This should not be confused with traditional meetings and conferences which span a coffee break, lunch break, etc. where, perhaps because of inherent faults in the traditional process (see page 312), these informal breaks are often deemed to be the most useful part of the process!

There may be problems in getting everyone wanted for a particularly group together at the right time in the right place and keeping them there. This will require considerable planning.

Where is the best place to hold a Brainstorming session?

Individual Brainstorming (**Brainwriting**) can be accomplished anywhere we can cut ourselves off sufficiently from our environment (although we may want to use our environment to fire our imagination).

For group CPS sessions, we generally need an informal and relaxed atmosphere. The venue should be cut off from external distractions and interruptions such as telephone calls, the seating should be comfortable and arranged in such a way as to inhibit 'breaking up' into a number of submeetings, and there should be flipcharts and wall space so that all ideas can be put up for everyone to see. The traditional image of a boardroom (with its long rectangular table and upright chairs) is not usually considered to be an ideal arrangement. A round table would improve matters, but the general consensus seems to favour 'easy' chairs surrounding low 'coffee' tables.

Warm-up exercises

It is difficult to brainstorm from a cold start. My favourite device for a warm-up exercise is the 'Most Useless Ideas Competition' (see Chapter 7). However, this can take up too much time if one works through the whole competition, so here is an alternative warm-up exercise, 'Pet Hates'.

The members of the group are invited to divulge those relatively trivial things that cause them to spend an inordinate amount of time being anxious, concerned or angered about them. All suggestions are written up on whiteboards, flipcharts, etc. without any comments except encouraging ones – the sillier a person thinks these ideas are, the better for our purpose. 'I don't like being told I am losing my temper, when I am!' 'My wife apparently doesn't appreciate the helpful advice I always see fit to give her, before she drives my car!' A typical list of this sort of thing is given in Frame 3.10. Incidentally, James Adams points out (1979, p.113) that, when addressed specifically at aspects of products and services that annoy us, this can be a useful means of 'searching' for new products and services or improvements to existing ones.

> ### Frame 3.10 *Pet Hates*
>
> - My next-door neighbours' dog (and its habit of fouling my lawn).
> - Bindweed and couch grass.
> - People who drop litter.
> - Drivers who deliberately use the wrong lane at roundabouts.
> - People who drive at 65 mph in the fast lane on motorways.
> - The individual who 'restyled' the front wing of my car last week and did not stop to apologize.*
> - The speed at which some solicitors and insurance companies operate.*
> - Picking up my children's clothes/toys/sweet-papers.
> - My family's inability to turn any lights off.
> - The ease and speed with which my children get their clothes dirty.
> - People who leave the tops off toothpaste or squeeze the tube in the middle.

The little things which regularly irritate one person are usually amusing to others, and the laughter which inevitably occurs 'breaks the ice'. Often people share similar 'pet hates' and saying so helps to forge sympathetic and supportive bonding between group members. This exercise may also permit the airing of something that has been preying on someone's mind prior to the session, thus clearing the air of things that would have prevented them from making a full contribution to the group's efforts. (The items marked with an asterisk in Frame 3.10 are possible examples of this.) This exercise is carried on for several minutes, by which time the group members should be beginning to relax. The leader should encourage everyone in the group to contribute but not by identifying non-contributors.

An alternative warm-up exercise is to encourage group members to describe the most stupid or embarrassing thing they have done this week/month. If it succeeds, these revelations of our 'weaknesses' or failures break down the 'walls' that people build around themselves, but it does require a group leader who inspires trust, friendliness and confidence to solicit these rather more 'soul baring' responses and to 'carry off' this type of exercise.

This concludes our initial discussions of Brainstorming. Further advice on running Brainstorming sessions and an illustrative example of what to expect can be found in Appendix 3 and Chapter 7, respectively.

Summary

In this chapter we have attempted to define creativity, and have offered two theories that explain the apparent inhibiting of our creativity as we grow up. We have also provided some initial advice on how we can revive our creativity and been introduced to the 'philosophy' and practice of Brainstorming.

dnotes

1. This author would maintain that any modern attempt to define intelligence that does not include the creative-thought processes identified by Guilford and others is worthless. Chapter 14 will explore the concepts of **Emotional** and **Spiritual Intelligence**.
2. EACI is the European Association for Creativity and Innovation.
3. It is difficult to convey irony in print; I hope that it is obvious that this statement and the following four are meant to be seen that way.
4. The lower, more 'primitive', part of the brain which developed in animals first as they (we) evolved from the primordial 'soup'.

4 Before problem solving

This chapter describes some miscellaneous techniques that can be usefully applied before we actually start 'problem solving', because they help us determine how we would like things to be, and identify and prioritize the decisions, opportunities, problems, etc. that we should perhaps be tackling next in order to get there.

Introduction

As a precursor to any problem-solving or decision-making activity it is often useful to reflect on things to make sure that we are doing the right things first. Many would say that we should do this on a regular basis, as we shall see below. We will first look at some techniques for imagining our futures, and then some others for 'managing' the opportunities and concerns we may discover whilst doing this.

Visioning (creative)

John Sedgwick (2000, p.125) describes **Visioning** as a type of thinking that 'requires people to create in their minds a picture of some future state, then to lay down the steps which would make that state a reality'. Sidney Parnes (1991, p.148) says that Visioning[1] 'focuses on goals and objectives – on opportunity-making – on respecting your wishes and desires for yourself, your organization, and the society you live in – on expanding and amplifying these and then fulfilling whatever portions you can manage through CPS'.

Synectics used to offer an exercise called 'Vision of the Future' on their **CPS** courses, positioned as a preparation for going back into your 'normal' work situation and life in general, so that you do not 'lose' (through a lack of use/continuing practice) what you have just learnt after your 're-entry' back into the pressure of these everyday realities. The steps involved are:

- Imagine your life as you would like it to be in x years' time.
- Determine what you need to do to bring this vision into reality, what actions you need to take, what opportunities you need to exploit, what problems you need to resolve, etc.
- Identify which of the above you already know how to do (and presumably get on and do them!).
- Apply CPS processes and techniques to help assist you with those you do not yet know how to do.

This is Visioning. It is a technique that can be employed at any time when we feel there is a need to reassess where we are going/want to go, and it might be a good plan to do it more regularly than this.

Constructing a vision

Leif-Runar Forsth and Bodil Nordvik (1995) describe a 12-step process for producing a shared vision for an organization which they say can be adapted for use by individuals. Looking at just those steps that we would need to produce an individual vision, the process starts by looking at a set of pre-prepared pictures.[2] The idea is to identify any pictures that are telling us something about the way we want things to be, and to select a few of these that best describe what this is. Then we should articulate this in words. An alternative to using a set of pictures like this could be to do a little daydreaming, and/or draw your own picture of how you want things to be.

This (verbally described) vision is then 'widened', by describing things in more detail giving 'a more practical description of what the vision really means', and 'deepened', by asking what the vision (or part thereof) will give us if it is achieved, and why we want this, as this should strengthen our motivation 'to do what is necessary' to get there (1995, pp.255–6).

Next we need to ensure that we have some goals that express how we will know 'what it really means to fulfil the vision, and . . . when we have done this'. Finally we identify the gaps between where we are currently and where we want to be; these (as mentioned above) will be the focus for our CPS.

Forsth and Nordvik (1995, p.256) warn that vision building is sometimes no more than just a pleasurable experience – after constructing the vision nothing changes, 'there are no signs that anything is done differently from before', and nothing seems likely to create any change or 'subsequently contribute to the fulfilment of the vision'. If this is the case, they suggest that the reason is one or both of the following:

- the vision is not a sufficiently good fulfilment of the vision builders' basic inner hopes, values and beliefs;
- there is no continuation of the process after the basic vision has been built – no plan has been made to fill the gaps!

Situation Appraisal – Kepner-Tregoe (hard)

Situation Appraisal, a technique devised by Charles Kepner and Benjamin Tregoe, is being aware of what is going on around you, knowing what needs to be done in situations likely to occur and being able to carry out effectively one or more of these tasks at a time. It is knowing when it is necessary to make a decision, have a problem-solving session, prepare contingency plans or just carry on 'looking around' to make sure we have not overlooked something that we should have seen as a concern. Kepner and Tregoe frequently refer to 'concerns', which they define as 'any situation that requires action and for which you have full or partial responsibility' (1981, p.166). It is important not just to be able to handle problem situations as they occur, but actively to go out looking for things that need to be done; not creating work for work's sake, but being proactive rather than reactive.

By adopting a proactive outlook, we tend to discover the opportunities that the reactive person seems not to have time to consider. We tend to detect problems when they are still quite easy to deal with, saving us time we can use for our Situation Appraisal. Situation Appraisal consists of continuously cycling through four separate but interrelated tasks that help us evaluate our circumstances and select when and how to apply the other Kepner-Tregoe (KT) techniques[3] appropriately:

- recognizing concerns;
- separating concerns into manageable components;
- setting priorities;
- planning the resolution of our concerns.

These tasks are not necessarily sequential. We can seldom complete a whole circuit without back-tracking, because the situations that we have to deal with are 'invariably confused, multifaceted, overlapping and fragmentary' (Kepner and Tregoe, 1981, pp.164–5).

Recognizing concerns

Kepner and Tregoe recommend (1981) a four-pronged attack to this task, not all of which needs to be accomplished at the same time.

- We can make a list of
  - (a) all the situations that are not quite as we would like them to be, that is, ones likely to be candidates for some problem solving;
  - (b) situations we see as threatening to our well-being or that of any group or organization to which we belong;
  - (c) what we see as possible opportunities.
- We can compare our progress with existing activities to that which we had previously planned. In doing this, we may well discover items that we need to add to our list.
- We should do some forecasting – start planning ahead for the consequences of what we are working on at the moment: decisions which we will have to

make, solutions that we will have to implement. We should also be on the look-out for 'surprises'.

- Finally, we look for ways of improving the things we are currently doing and our methods for doing them; that is, improving both the product and the process.

We should not expect these to be four separate tasks; they are inextricably inter-linked, because reviewing our progress on one problem inevitably indicates pre-viously unforeseen problems and opportunities. Creative thinking is vital to the effective execution of Situation Appraisal. Successful appraisal of any situation depends on sensitivity, serendipity and synergy (Parnes's three S's, see Chapter 3). It may also be that indulging in some **Goal Wishing** (see Chapter 6) is not only a good means of exploring the situation, but also helps to ensure that we do not waste time resolving the wrong problem.

Separating concerns into manageable components

When performing this task, we must remember the dangers involved in attempt-ing to restructure problem situations (see Chapter 1) to make them more man-ageable. Things are seldom as simple as they first seem, and what appear to be totally disconnected phenomena are often related in some way. We should ask the following questions (Kepner and Tregoe, 1981, pp.168–9) in order to discover if we should, and how best to, break a complicated situation into a number of smaller concerns we *are* capable of dealing with.

- Do we think one action will really resolve this concern?
- Are we talking about one thing or several things?
- Are we agreed as to the reason we are concerned about this?
- What evidence do we have that says this is a concern?
- What do we mean by. . . ?
- What is actually happening in this situation? Anything else?
- What do we sense that tells us we must take action?
- What is there about the way we handled this situation that should be improved?
- What is really troubling us about this situation?

The asking of these questions in a group session can reveal that people within the group possess different viewpoints on, or information about, the situation under discussion. Done separately to any problem solving, this should lead to few com-plications, but we should keep in mind that others (Synectics, see Chapter 10) maintain that questioning can have undesirable effects. If such questioning does uncover a number of concerns where there was only thought to be one, we add these to our list of problems to be resolved.

Setting priorities

To decide in which order we should tackle our concerns we prioritize them on the basis of their seriousness (impact), their (time) urgency and an estimate of their likely growth. This can be done by asking questions such as 'What will be the consequences if we postpone consideration of a concern?', 'Will a problem get worse if we do not deal with it for a while?'. The importance and hence the priority of a concern may be determined by any or all of these factors. Assessing the importance of an activity and assigning it an appropriate priority with as little subjectivity as possible is a difficult process. The human mind is very good at justifying why we are doing something that we should not be doing. We all prefer activities that we enjoy to those we do not and thus tend to give them a higher personal priority by inflating their importance, thus justifying doing them and perhaps doing them first, no matter how important we *know* the other activities to be.

If we discipline ourselves to assess the things we have to or want to do on the basis of their seriousness, urgency and probable growth, it makes it more difficult to attribute inappropriate priorities to them than if we assign an arbitrary degree of importance to them without considering these contributory factors. Once we have organized ourselves a little better, so as to have more time for all our tasks, we can use the doing of the preferred (but less important) activities as a reward for accomplishing some of the less desirable (but more important) activities.

We are still left with the problem of combining the seriousness, urgency and growth factors into an overall importance rating. This process has to remain fairly intuitive, in the sense that it cannot be prescribed for; each situation will need to be judged on its own merits. However, in many cases urgency will be contained in either seriousness or probable growth, seriousness often being the slightly more significant factor.

In all this we must guard against any tendency to procrastinate, whether caused by the daunting number of tasks piled up ahead of us, guilt, self-pity, or whatever. Get on with something, anything! Preferably the truly important tasks.

For an attempt at prioritization to be effective, it is essential to break a complex task down into its component activities; these activities, not the task, should be given a priority. This is because it is usually difficult to differentiate between the perceived importance of the relatively few major tasks we are involved in. However, the component activities, once identified, will at any given moment in time have very different priorities from each other. Although we have already separated our concerns into manageable proportions, it is probably worth reviewing these in order to ensure that they could not usefully be considered as a series of even 'smaller' activities before we assign priorities.

This process of considering a major task or project as a series of component activities, together with the estimation of the likely time each activity will take and the determination of possible interdependencies of activities, is the basis of **PERT**[4] and **Critical Path** or **Network Analysis**, and is a fundamental part of project management (see page 193).

Planning how to resolve our concerns

Having determined and assigned priorities to our concerns, we must decide how to tackle them and what depth of treatment is appropriate. Do we need to make a decision, have a problem-solving session, prepare contingency plans or just make sure we have not overlooked something that we should have seen as a concern? The depth of treatment will depend on the circumstances. A decision may have to be made now, or we may at present only need to think about the criteria that we will use to assess the options at a later stage. Do we need to call people together for a full problem-solving session, or do we only need to schedule an uninterrupted hour to do some lone thinking about Problem Identification? We need to plan what has to be done, think about who ought to be involved and determine how much of a particular process we need to perform.

Situation Appraisal is an ongoing activity, where we continuously check to see whether something needs to be done.

Mess finding – Osborn-Parnes (creative)

In actuality, *Mess Finding* is a stage in the Osborn-Parnes CPS process not a technique, but this process contains a number of simple techniques that could be used in conjunction with Situation Appraisal so it seemed sensible to write about them together.

When trying to open things up and identify what they used to call 'messes' (compare with Kepner and Tregoe's (1981) 'concerns'), Scott Isaksen and Donald Treffinger (1985) suggest that we focus on *outcomes* – our objectives or goals that we hope to reach, things we need or want, opportunities we would like to exploit – and *obstacles* – things, people or events which stand in the way of obtaining some desired outcome. More recently, these messes have been referred to (more positively) as just 'opportunities' – 'a broad, fuzzy, and ill-defined situation, challenge, concern or goal' (Isaksen, Dorval and Treffinger, 2000, p.64) or sometimes 'challenges'; and the stage as **Constructing Opportunities**.

WIBNI/WIBAI

One technique Isaksen and Treffinger recommend (1985, p.31) for identifying outcomes (challenges and opportunities), or obstacles (threats, crises or emergencies) is to ask the 'questions' 'Wouldn't it be nice if . . .?' (WIBNI) or 'Wouldn't it be awful if . . .?' (WIBAI), and advise that the description of our 'Mess Statements' (now called 'Opportunity Statements') should be *broad* (that is, sufficiently general so as to not to attempt to 'define the problem' or 'search for *the* solution' prematurely), *brief* (like a headline) and *beneficial* (expressed in a positive way).

They also suggest that as a prompt we think about people, places, plans, processes and products,[5] and also relate our personal strengths and weaknesses to our hopes/opportunities (outcomes) and concerns (obstacles) – the latter can be done in the form of a 2 × 2 table. This prompts us to identify, for each opportunity and concern, the strengths we intend to capitalize on or need to improve and the weaknesses (or lack of resources) that need to be overcome.

Wallet checklist

Another technique that can be employed during the divergent phase of the mess finding stage is the 'Wallet checklist'. As the name may indicate, this involves rummaging through your wallet to see what you can find. The idea is that the contents of our wallet are a 'reflection of ourselves, containing those things that are important or greatly valued to us' (Isaksen and Treffinger, 1985, p.35). Each item found should evoke several thoughts, which can then be expressed as a mess statement. For example, we may have someone's business card – a possible business opportunity? – or an appointment with our doctor – a concern about health? – a receipt – time to fill in my (income) tax return form!

Mess finding checklist

In the convergent phase of mess finding we need to attempt to prioritize all the messes we have identified. For this Isaksen and Treffinger (1985) use a mess finding checklist (see Figure 4.1) that first checks out your **ownership** of the mess (see our earlier discussions in Chapter 1) by considering your **influence**, the explicit authority and decision-making responsibility you have with regard to this mess (compare with **power to act**); your **interest** (or willingness) to tackle it; and the **imagination** needed to do so. Second, the checklist assesses the **outlook** on the basis of the mess's **critical nature** (importance); its size, which will be related to your **familiarity** with the mess (how knowledgeable you are of the situation – the less the knowledge, the bigger the mess); its **immediacy** and its **direction** (is it stable, deteriorating or even improving?).

The second part of the mess finding checklist can be completed in several ways, and some typical ways of 'grading' the outlook elements are shown in the table.

Figure 4.1

Focusing on a challenge: a mess finding checklist

Ownership
First, make sure you can say 'yes' to these important questions:

Possible challengers	Can I act on it?	Do I want to?	Do I need new ideas?

Outlook
Then, use these questions to sort your challenges and focus your thinking:

Possible challengers	How important?	How big is it?	How soon must I act?	How will it change?
	A. Earth-shattering B. Moderate C. Low	A. Big B. Regular C. Small	A. Yesterday B. Soon C. Any time	A. Get worse B. Stay the same C. Get better

Does one of the challenges rise to the top of your list? Or might you construct a key challenge from the common elements of two or more?

Compare this to the not dissimilar advice in Kepner-Tregoe's Situation Appraisal above: you may prefer this way of prioritizing your concerns.

Summary

In this chapter we have seen a number of techniques that let us discover/reveal/identify our decisions, opportunities and problems, and assess their significance/importance in regard to the sequence in which we need to tackle them. In the next five chapters we will look at techniques that will help us do just that.

Exercise

Set aside some quiet time on your own, do a bit of daydreaming about your future, and develop a personal vision. Then construct an action plan – a list of things you need to do to fill the gaps between the present situation and your desired end-point.

Endnotes

1. Referred to as *visionizing* by Parnes (1991).
2. Forsth and Nordvik (1995, p.252) recommend that the pictures selected for this 'mostly evoke pleasant feelings' and are in equal numbers as follows: ones that 'directly (or symbolically) represent the whole or part of the [possible] vision' – e.g. pictures of people playing a team game that might indicate that our future may depend on us improving our ability to work with others; ones that are (indirectly) 'connected to the possible vision in one way or another' – pictures that suggest the expression of certain things, e.g. determination, security, etc.; those that are 'highly stimulating'; and 'any further kind of picture you like to look at'.
3. An overview of the original four 'patterns of thinking' that made up the KT 'process' are described in Appendix 1, and the other three techniques elaborated in more detail in Chapters 6, 8 and 9.
4. Project Evaluation and Review Technique
5. This is essentially the **Five W's & an H** prompt/checklist – who, what, where, when, why and how – that is used elsewhere in the Osborn-Parnes CPS process.

5 Data Gathering

This chapter describes some of the techniques employed by various problem-solving approaches/processes for determining which data/information needs to be found, in what ways (if at all) it should be 'filtered' and how it can best be recorded.

Introduction

The amount and types of data and/or information collected varies between the different problem-solving approaches and processes discussed in this book. This chapter looks at some of the techniques employed for determining which data/information needs to be found, in what ways it should be 'filtered' (if at all[1]), and how it can best be recorded, for example, several processes use a questioning technique to determine the data/information needed, see later and pages 93-5, 99–100.

The techniques employed to collect this data/ information are usually one or more of the 'traditional' methods of observation, interviewing, questionnaires, document inspection, working in the situation, etc. Since these latter methods are well documented elsewhere in texts on quantitative methods, systems analysis, conducting research projects, etc., they will not be pursued further here.

A **hard** approach often gathers quite specific data and/or information, is generally looking for 'facts', and does not always do this before identifying the problem – for example, an information-systems development methodology focuses on the data/information people need to do whatever activity it is that they are engaged in, where it comes from, how it is 'changed' by that person (if at all), to whom/where is it passed on, what the frequency and volume is with which this information 'arrives' and what problems there are with the existing information system. This is done *after* we have identified the problem (decided what sort of information system we need).

With the **machine** problem of 'Lowlands Distilleries' presented in Chapter 6, we will meet a hard approach: Kepner-Tregoe's **Problem Analysis**, used to identify the problem. Here the situation regarding **Data Gathering** is different, because with this technique it is an integral part of **Problem Identification**.

Because of this, I will consider that the hard approach is well covered here by the **soft systems approach**[2] (discussed below), probably the process that tries to gather the most varied information by looking for facts plus a lot of other stuff, and the **Osborn-Parnes** process, which (although being a creative one) contains techniques similar to, but less 'directed' than, the Problem Analysis technique mentioned above.

The two **CPS** processes mentioned in this book take slightly differing approaches in the Data Gathering stage. The Osborn-Parnes CPS process encourages the (individual) problem solver to gather lots of data/information, some perhaps not currently known, that might be needed in the problem solving. With the **Synectics** CPS process, the tendency is to assume that often the problem owner (as *the* problem-content expert – the rest of the group acting as naive resources) already possesses all the necessary data/information to solve the problem (although it may be 'locked up' in his/her subconscious mind), and only requires a new way of applying it to the problem situation, say from another perspective.

Political and social dimensions – Soft Systems Methodology (soft [hard])

The soft systems approach in the form of **Soft Systems Methodology** (SSM) differs from a hard approach in that it *deliberately* explores the political and social dimensions of the problem situation. We should remember always that 'every human problem situation is the product of a history, one which will dictate perceptions, judgements and standards' (Checkland, 1987b, p.4). These factors can and often do have a considerable bearing on what are culturally feasible ways of improving the problem situation (see also Chapter 11).

In an SSM intervention, we should be aware that as soon as we 'intervene' in problem situation we will become involved in its politics. Not only will the problem situation have political aspects, our intervention itself could and should be seen as a political act. In this sense, 'politics' means the process by which interested parties reach some sort of mutual accommodation or compromise, including all the manoeuvring and intrigue that this entails. The concessions invariably made during this process will be overt or covert changes in the disposition of power. (Those with the most power tend to do the least compromising!) Attempting to unravel the politics of the situation should be one of the first things we do during the initial Data Gathering stage, but since it is unlikely to remain static, we should reassess the politics of the situation repeatedly as the investigation proceeds.

To appreciate the political dimensions of the problem situation fully, Peter Checkland (1986, pp.6–10) advises that we should identify the people within the problem situation who (could) occupy the roles of:

- client – the people who commissioned us and whom it is assumed can implement any changes which we may suggest;
- would-be problem solver – those people who will be trying to bring about some improvement to the problem situation;

- problem owner – anyone who is affected for better or worse by the current problem situation.

We should do this by listing the roles and then assigning actual persons to them, rather than the other way around, thus helping to ensure that we realize that a particular person could and usually does occupy more than one of these roles. In a soft systems context, a person occupying the role of client need not also be considered as a problem owner (which is a little different from the situation with other problem-solving processes, such as Synectics, page 232); however, perhaps he/she should be.

Checkland (1981, p.294) defines a problem owner as a person

> who has a feeling of unease about a situation, either a sense of mismatch between 'what is' and 'what might be' or a vague feeling that things could be better and who wishes something were done about it. The problem owner may not be able to define what he would regard as a 'solution', and may not be able to articulate the feeling of unease in any precise way.

It is also possible for someone involved in the problem situation not to recognize his/her own problem ownership. This should not prevent us from assigning him or her that role, because we should attempt to view the problem situation from as many standpoints as we feel appropriate.

Assuming that power is expressed through the possession of one or more usually abstract 'commodities', we should determine what these are in the organization we are dealing with. Listed below are some typical examples (Checkland, 1981):

- size of departmental budget
- chairmanship of certain committees
- indispensability
- personal charisma
- intellectual expertise
- external reputation
- being under 40 years of age
- rank
- years of service
- being someone who plays squash with the MD.

Although these criteria are highly variable, subjective and possibly contradictory, they do represent examples of how we go about attributing power to others in organizations. We need to identify also how these sources of power can be obtained, exercised, protected, preserved, passed on and relinquished or lost.

Regarding the social dimensions within any group there are key roles determining the effective operation of the group. We must ascertain what these significant roles are within our problem situation, who holds them, what behaviour is expected from them and whether they are considered to be fulfilling these roles well or badly (see Frame 5.1).

> ### Frame 5.1 *Model of a social system*
>
> If the problem situation we are considering is one that can be viewed as a *social system* it is appropriate to determine its social aspects using a model which can be thought of as a continually changing interaction of three elements – roles, norms and values; each continually defines and is defined by the other two. A role is a social position recognized by people in the problem situation which is characterized by expected behaviours or *norms*. Actual performance in a role (which changes the role-occupant just as his or her way of occupying the role will change perception of that role) will be judged according to local standards or *values*, beliefs about what is humanly 'good' or 'bad' performance (Checkland, 1986).

Hard and soft data

In an SSM investigation (and to some extent with the application of the Osborn-Parnes CPS process, see below), both 'hard' and 'soft' data are needed in order to get a complete picture of the problem situation. Hard information consists of factual data, such as:

- the divisions or departments within the organization;
- noteworthy individuals;
- the organizational structure;
- products;
- reporting channels;
- data flows;
- any quantitative data.

Soft information includes such things as:

- hunches, guesses, intuitions;
- perceptions of the people involved with(in) the problem situation;
- judgements about the helpfulness, skills, competence, efficiency, perceived status, attitudes, motivational needs of individuals;
- rumours about friendships and hostilities.

(Checkland, 1981)

Soft information is highly subjective data, things that people often have qualms about saying, let alone having recorded. (There will always be exceptions to this, especially people with political, personal or organizational axes to grind.) Normally there is a natural anxiety about offering information that might offend, the meaning of which might be perceived incorrectly, the truth of which is uncertain and/or which might be relayed to the 'wrong' person. This type of information is vital and must be determined.

All this data/information is normally 'recorded' in a **Rich Picture**, see below.

5W's & an H – Osborn-Parnes (creative)

Isaksen and Treffinger (1985, pp.43–5) say that 'some data-finding will always help you to improve your effectiveness in understanding the problems that really need to be solved'.

Amongst other things, they maintain that their Data Gathering stage (called **Data Finding**, or more recently, **Exploring Data** (Trelfinger, Isaksen and Dorval, 2000)) helps us to:

- take stock of the situation by determining what we really do know about it and what we do not;
- break away from stereotyped or habit-bound thinking, and look beyond the 'constraints' imposed by assumptions;
- uncover key pieces of the **mess** (problem situation) that might have been obscured, overlooked or so obvious that they had previously gone unnoticed;
- reveal hidden patterns and interrelationships among the data;

and the different kinds of data we should be looking for are:

- *information* – knowledge, facts, intelligence, recollections – what is known and can be perceived, calculated, verified, discovered or inferred;
- *impressions* – images or effects retained as a consequence of experience and/or beliefs, reasonable expectations, intuitive guesses, hunches, vague notions, or speculations;
- *observations* – perceptions, comments;
- *feelings* – desires, emotions, sentiments, feelings of sympathy/ empathy;
- *questions* – due to lack of information, curiosity, perplexity of the situation.

In the divergent phase of data finding, to help us identify the bits of information, impressions, observations, feelings and questions we need, Isaksen and Treffinger (1985, p.55) recommend the use of the **Five W's & an H** technique on the mess (problem situation):

- *Who* – identifies the individuals/groups who might be involved.
- *What* – identifies the things, materials, resources, objects or items that are involved.
- *Where* – considers places, locations, positions or focal points.
- *When* – probes for times, intervals, schedules, dates, beginnings, ends or deadlines.
- *Why* – inquires about reasons, goals, aims or intentions.
- *How* – helps recognize previous actions that have been attempted, things now occurring, steps that might be taken.

These words are used to formulate questions to help us explore every possible aspect of the mess. For example, some less 'obvious' questions we might ask could be (Isaksen and Treffinger, 1985, p.56):

- Who has special strengths or resources pertaining to the problem situation?

- What success have I achieved so far with regard to resolving this problem situation?
- What influence do I have over people, places, resources and times that are involved in this problem situation?
- How did this problem situation happen or develop?
- How do others see this problem situation?

It is interesting to note that similar 'questioning' words are used in the hard (Kepner-Tregoe) **Problem Analysis** technique described in Chapter 6. Whereas Osborn-Parnes uses 5W's & an H, Problem Analysis uses either what, where, when, how, or who, what, where, when.

To encourage speculation in this phase, Isaksen and Treffinger go on to say, asking supplementary questions such as 'What wild guesses can we make about . . .?' and 'What puzzles and perplexes us?' can help.

It can also be useful to attempt to identify data items that we do not have but 'need/like to know'.

Isaksen and Treffinger (1985) also suggest that we use a two-dimensional table (**data finding matrix**) where the answers to the 5W's & an H (written down the side) questions are classified by 'know *v.* need/like to know' (across the top), marking any of the data items in these two columns as **very important data**. That is, the data that 'must be considered', as opposed to 'preference data' which we 'would want/like to consider'.

Hits, hotspots and relates – Osborn-Parnes (creative)

You can never find out everything about a given mess and it is often difficult to put an end to the divergent phase of the data finding stage, say Isaksen and Treffinger (1985, p.59), but they suggest that we move on (to the convergent phase) when . . .

- our attention wanders to intriguing questions and problem statements,
- we spot several areas of concern clustered around a main one,
- we can foresee several topics important for us to pursue,
- we have an *Aha!* moment (something jumps out at us and demands our attention),
- we have compiled an extensive list of data including new or unusual perceptions/observations as well as 'obvious' pieces of information, *and* we feel we have *stretched* our thinking!

To start the convergent phase of Data Gathering, Isaksen and Treffinger (1985) suggest we look through our data and mark the particularly important items or areas which warrant closer attention, data that describe the heart or essence of the situation (starting with any already identified very important data). They call these **hits**. If some of the hits deal with the same general aspect of the situation, we should group these together – such a cluster of hits they call a **hotspot** – and determine what it is that **relates** these items together.

This technique of identifying hits, hotspots and relates is a generic one – for, instance, it is used again in the Osborn-Parnes CPS process during the convergent phase of **Idea Finding** where our interest is in selecting ideas for special attention rather than data items.

Isaksen and Treffinger (1985, p.61) suggest that we allocate priorities to our **hotspots**. The priorities they use to classify hotspots are high – immediate attention; medium – act soon; low – can be put on the 'back burner'. By this means we identify our **critical concerns**; that is, which hotspots should receive the most attention, be considered first, etc. We then write beside them the reasons we have for believing this to be so, the hotspots with a 'high' priority are, or should be, our critical concerns: that is, the problems we are now going to try to resolve.

(Problem) analysis – Synectics (creative)

Because, as we said above, **Synectics** believe that often the problem owner already has all the information, knowledge, experiences, etc. to solve the problem and just needs to 'reassemble' or connect these in new ways to solve the problem, they adopt a fairly minimal approach to Data Gathering which, as we will see on pages 93–5, is as much a technique for checking out the problem and the problem owner as it is to gather data.

Synectics seek answers to the following questions from the problem owner:

- What is the present situation?
- Why/how has the problem or opportunity arisen?
- Why should/must it be resolved?
- Why is it a problem or opportunity for *me* personally?
- What have I already tried or thought of trying, and with what result?
- What is my **power to act**? (What power do I have to implement a solution, if/when I find one, . . . any restrictions/limitations on what I can do?)
- If by simply making a wish, my **ideal solution** would happen, what would this ideal solution be?
- Where (with which aspect of the problem) do I need most help?

I find attempting to answer these questions very helpful in assisting with the first look around the problem situation with a view to Problem Identification, and would recommend their use no matter which problem-solving approach or process I was predominantly using. An example of their use is given in Chapter 10, pages 240–2.

Rich Pictures – Soft Systems Methodology (soft)

A **Rich Picture** is a cartoon-style diagram used within an SSM investigation to depict all the data/information (mentioned above) that we should have collected. It helps us see the problem situation in a **holistic** way, with all its intricacies and their interrelationships.

There is no reason why it should not be used to good effect in other problem-solving approaches and processes where the benefits described below might apply.

The advantages of using a pictorial representation as opposed to a written description are:

- A picture can show far more information in the same space.
- It shows patterns, arrangements, connections and relationships far better.
- We are less likely to overlook vital links and interactions which may have given rise to unexpected or unintentional consequences.
- It permits us to see the whole of the problem situation in all its complexity, and gives us a 'feel' of its overall shape.
- It provides a representation of the problem situation that can be readily shared with others.

Guidelines for preparing Rich Pictures

When preparing for and constructing our Rich Picture we should:

- Look for and include things in the problem situation that tend to change slowly with time and which are relatively stable – the *structure* – such as the purchasing, sales and distribution sections, products, etc. of a retail company etc. Look for things that are continuously changing, such as the various activities taking place within the structure – the *processes* – for example, the product sourcing and selecting activity which goes on, and see how these elements of structure and process interact with each other (are there any mismatches or conflicts in the way they relate?) – the *climate*.
- Try not to think and certainly do not represent the parts of the situation as systems, because that would imply that they have all the properties of a system (see Appendix 2), including things such as control mechanisms and efficient communications channels providing feedback, which they may not have. Also, once identified as such, these 'systems' may become 'untouchable' entities.
- Ensure that you have shown both hard and soft data/information (see above). If there is a lot of quantitative data it is usually easier to depict this by placing on our Rich Picture an appropriate symbol annotated by an equally suitable cryptic comment, and keep the bulk of the data on a separate sheet. The subjective (soft) data must be included, even though they may be contentious.
- Determine and include which are considered to be the important, meaningful or useful social roles within the situation and note the behaviour (in a very general sense) that is expected from the people who fill these roles; in other words, examine what are the cultural norms of the organization. Be very careful not to make your own value judgements about what kind of behaviour is good, bad or acceptable!
- Include yourself in the Rich Picture along with your 'sponsor', since each of us has a set of attitudes, opinions, values and beliefs which colour our perceptions.

A Rich Picture does not have to be a work of art as long as it makes sense to us, its creator. We use vivid symbols wherever possible to represent aspects of the problem situation. For example, a big weight resting on the head of a 'pin man' would indicate that someone in the organization is under considerable pressure. The differing perceptions of people within the problem situation can be shown using 'balloons' coming from these figures. A set of useful symbols can be found in Figure 5.1.

Summary

In this chapter we have explored different views on how much and which type of data/information needs to be found when problem solving, described some of the techniques employed by various problem-solving approaches/processes for determining this and in what ways (if at all) it should be 'filtered', and shown how it can be recorded in a pictorial (as well as a narrative) form.

Exercises

1. Every time you attempt some problem solving, try answering the Synectics (Problem) Analysis questions above (page 83). When you have done this, read through your answers and let them suggest different ways of describing your problem or parts thereof.

2. Next time you are trying to resolve a relatively complex situation, try recording everything you discover as a Rich Picture. This should give you a better overall feel of what is, or should, be going on!

Figure 5.1

Some useful symbols

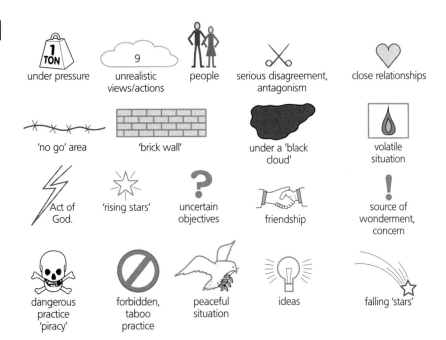

under pressure

unrealistic views/actions

people

serious disagreement, antagonism

close relationships

'no go' area

'brick wall'

under a 'black cloud'

volatile situation

Act of God.

'rising stars'

uncertain objectives

friendship

source of wonderment, concern

dangerous practice 'piracy'

forbidden, taboo practice

peaceful situation

ideas

falling 'stars'

If you are working with a small group on a shared problem get everybody to contribute to a communal picture of the problem situation as they see it. Ask the group what they see in the picture and to suggest different ways of looking at the problem or parts thereof.

Endnotes

1. The **Osborn-Parnes** CPS process, unusually, has a convergent phase to its Data Gathering stage; other problem-solving processes usually leave this stage 'open ended'.
2. Although mentioned above in the context of information systems, **SSM** is *not* an information-systems development methodology, though it is often used in combination with one to enhance the process of designing information systems.

6   Problem Identification

This chapter describes various techniques used by different problem-solving approaches/processes for identifying what the problem is or how it can best be stated.

Introduction

Some of us have the tendency to assume that the first way we think of for describing our problem is the best way; that is, the best starting point for our problem-solving efforts. As a result, we often rush off in the 'wrong' direction looking for solutions, and, if we are 'successful' in that regard, often end up solving the 'wrong' problem or at best getting a partial solution to the real problem. The **Problem Identification** stage is therefore a crucial one, one where we try and ensure (as best we can) that we are trying to solve the 'right' problem. Quite often this is over 'half the battle': with some problems – for example, medical diagnosis – once the problem has been identified, a 'stock' solution is (often) readily available to resolve it.

Generally, cutting through the tangled mess of information we have relating to the problem and seeing the problem situation through the 'camouflage' of our own and other people's opinions and attitudes is not particularly easy. This is what the **Backward/Forward Planning** and **Goal Wishing** stages of the **Synectics** CPS process and **Cognitive Mapping** seek to achieve.

The **soft systems** approach in the form of **SSM** does not attempt to identify problems in quite the same way as other approaches, preferring instead to identify changes that can be made to the problem situation or its environment that 'dissolve' the problem (see Frame 1.2 and Chapter 11); that is, that modify things so that the problem cannot or does not exist. However, there is a soft systems technique that helps to restructure the problem, **Decomposable Matrices**, and we shall start with this.

We will then look at a couple of **hard** (analytical techniques).

There are many named **CPS** techniques for identifying problems, a lot of which are very similar if not identical. Because of this, only a few representative ones (such as those mentioned above) are discussed below, along with notes giving the names of similar techniques. These many techniques are often classified as either redefinitional or analytical techniques. The latter, as the name suggests, perhaps should be called hard techniques.

nposable matrices (soft)

Van Gundy (1988, pp.53–6) attributes the ideas behind the technique of Decomposable Matrices to the work of H.A. Simon (1969), and suggests that it can give

> a clearer picture of [the] important problem elements, with some problems (those complex, ill structured problem situations typical of engineering and the social and biological sciences), that because of their 'near decomposability' *can* be broken down into a hierarchy of subsystems.

'Near decomposability' means that these subsystems 'maintain some, although not total, interdependence' with each other. For example, if a retailing organization is viewed as a system, with a sales subsystem and a distribution subsystem, there will generally be less interaction between people from the different functions than between those from the same.

Van Gundy (1988, p.54) offers the following steps for the technique:

- determine if the problem (situation) is analysable using subsystems (presumably on the basis of near decomposability),
- list the major subsystems and the components of each,
- construct a matrix of the subsystems and their components,
- using a five-point scale, weight the degree of relationship of each of the interactions between and within the subsystems,
- select the highest-weighted interactions for further analysis or generation of ideas.

Viewing a manufacturing company as an open (human activity) system, we might consider that it is comprised of the following subsystems: develop markets (marketing), sell products (sales), produce products (production), develop technology and products (research and development), and plan and control business (Wilson, 1990). Furthermore, we might consider that the 'sell products' subsystem comprises the following components: obtain orders for products, process and track orders, maintain relationships with customers (retailers), etc.; and the 'produce products' subsystem, the components: plan and control production, provide utilities and raw materials, convert raw materials into products, etc. Just filling in that part of the matrix that pertains to the information we have so far about these two subsystems, we would get something like Table 6.1.

The successful deployment of this technique relies heavily on the users' ability 'to correctly identify all [the] relevant subsystems and components and to accurately evaluate the strength or value of all their interactions' (Van Gundy, 1988, pp.55–6).

Such an approach should have identified in the Woodsons illustrative example (in Chapter 11) the major communication problem between sales and production – the matrix would presumably have given us (the need for) a strong relationship between these two subsystems when in reality there was very little satisfactory interaction.

This technique might also be usefully employed within SSM to help determine which activities in a conceptual model we might expand into subsystem models. Again referring to the Woodsons example mentioned above, both the 'sell loudspeaker . . .' and 'build loudspeaker' top-level activities probably require expanding into subsystem models, so that we can explore how these two subsystems ought to interact.

Problem Analysis – Kepner-Tregoe (hard)

Introduction

Problem Analysis is a problem-solving process which assumes that by a thorough and logical analysis of the problem situation we should be able to identify certain changes that have taken place between before the problem existed and now, and from these deduce the cause of the problem. Contrary to some people's belief and practice, it is not always sufficient to know all the things that could have caused the problem and then attempt to solve it by 'rectification' of the most likely cause (and if that doesn't work, the next most likely cause, and so on). This way of resolving problems can waste a lot of time and money, as many car repair bills confirm. This approach is connected with the tendency to assume that a given problem is so similar to a previous problem that the appropriate remedy must also be the same. The use of this 'most likely cause' approach is particularly noticeable when it is important to get a quick solution. Problem Analysis can help us avoid the pitfalls of this approach.

Table 6.1

Decomposable matrix of a manufacturing system

	Develop markets a1 a2 ...	Sell products b1 b2 b3 ...	Produce products c1 c2 c3 ...	Develop technology & products d1 d2 ...	etc. e1 ...
a1					
a2					
...					
b1 Obtain orders for products		5 3	4 1 1		
b2 Process & track orders		4	2 1 1		
b3 Maintain relationships with customers			1 1		
...					
c1 Plan & control production			5 4		
c2 Provide utilities & raw materials			5		
c3 Convert raw materials into products					
...					
d1					
d2					
...					
e1					
...					

Overview of Problem Analysis

Charles Kepner and Benjamin Tregoe believe (1981, pp.36–7) that problem situations are typified by 'a deviation between expected and actual performance' and that problem solving consists of 'a search for a specific change' that has caused this decline in performance. Despite this tight definition of a problem, they believe that many different sorts of problem can be thought of in this way and that this strategy can be used to deal with both **machine** and **people** problems.

The one type of problem that does not seem to fit this description is the 'ever since we installed that new machine it has been totally useless' situation. Kepner and Tregoe refer to this as a different but similar type, which they call a **Day 1 problem**. We use the same process as with any other problem except that we compare the actual poor performance with what we believe should have happened instead of the performance observed before the problem was noticed. There are dangers in comparing present performance with some sort of ideal performance; we should guard against setting our expectations of what should have occurred too high, or too low.

An outline of the Problem Analysis process can be seen in Frame 6.1.

Frame 6.1 *Problem Analysis*

- Definition of the problem.
- Description of the problem in four dimensions:

    identity – what it is we are trying to explain;

    location – where the problem is observed;

    timing – when the problem happens;

    magnitude – how serious and widespread the problem is.
- Use of this key information to generate possible causes.
- Testing for the most probable cause.
- Verification of the true cause.

It may not always be necessary to complete every stage of the Problem Analysis process before a solution is found, nor always essential that the full analysis is written out. Shortened and/or 'informal' Problem Analyses are often necessitated by situations which lack sufficient information for a full analysis.

Although Problem Analysis is normally thought of as an individual problem-solving process, there is nothing preventing it from being employed by a team of people. It is absolutely essential for one problem solver to have technical expertise bearing directly on the problem content, but the team should include a member with no such technical expertise and they should lead the process questioning. This helps prevent the team getting bogged down in the technicalities of the problem situation and being blinded to the consideration of an unusual occurrence. Kepner and Tregoe (1981) encourage us, in appropriate circumstances, to speculate about possible causes of the problem situation.

Frame 6.2 gives a description of a problem at Lowlands Distilleries, which we will attempt to solve using Problem Analysis. Before we start analysing this problem situation, make a note of what you think is the cause of the leak.

Frame 6.2 *Lowlands Distilleries Ltd: the problem situation*

Lowlands Distilleries are makers of rye whisky who occasionally perform commercial distillation for other companies in the food and drinks industry. One Monday morning, a couple of hours after the stills had been started up after the weekend break, a leak was reported in the main still room. This was the first problem with the stills for many months. A quantity of liquid, which after a cursory inspection was deemed to be mostly ethyl alcohol, had been found on the floor underneath the collection vat.

From the diagram of the still room (see Figure 6.1) it can be seen that there are six stills altogether. Each still has a retort which is heated from below and into which the liquid to be distilled is pumped periodically. The temperature is carefully monitored to ensure that only the appropriate vapours are allowed to pass out from these retorts up and along a network of pipes (individual to each still) and through the condensers. From here the liquid whisky is 'piped' to the collecting vat. The flow of water used in the condensers can be controlled by a valve on the exit pipe.

Figure 6.1   Lowlands Distilleries, still room

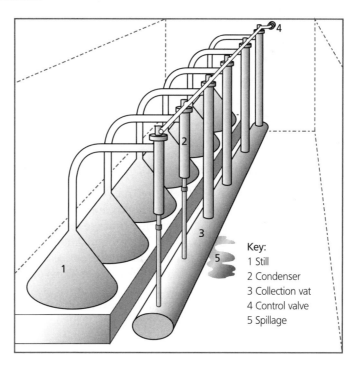

Key:
1 Still
2 Condenser
3 Collection vat
4 Control valve
5 Spillage

▶

The maintenance crew check the vats, piping, etc. every Saturday morning, after operations shut down for the weekend. They check for leaks and rectify them once found and also examine the equipment thoroughly and carry out preventative maintenance. Last weekend, Robert Jones, who had joined the maintenance crew three weeks ago, had replaced a section of the piping on No. 2 still between the condenser and the collection vat because, he had reported, it was showing early signs of corrosion.

The No. 1 and No. 2 systems are considerably older than the others, being the first stills operational. The other four have been added subsequently as demand for rye whisky has increased. The connectors joining the pipework used in these stills are of the 'compression' type. In the newer stills longer condensers have been used that precluded the need for these connectors. The maintenance crew have continued to use compression-type connectors on these old stills to make it easier to maintain and replace the ageing pipework when needed. A new batch of compression connectors had been delivered last month.

The spillage was cleaned up and the system carefully observed. After a close inspection of the pipework it was found that the leak appeared to originate from the vicinity of the replaced section of piping on No. 2 still. There was certainly liquid running down the outside of this pipe from the connector where it emerged from the condenser. This liquid was then running around the collection vat, and dripping off there on to the floor. The stills had continued to operate throughout Monday, with frequent mopping-up operations.

The maintenance crew were asked to check the new pipework on No. 2 still on Monday evening. Robert Jones drew the short straw. Jones, still finding it inconceivable that anything he had done last week could have been wrong, removed all the new piping and joints he had put in last week, and replaced them with more new items.

It is now Tuesday 11.00 a.m. The still room supervisor has just been called to the still room to inspect what appears to be a patch of liquid on the floor similar to that found yesterday.

Definition of the problem

The first step in Problem Analysis is to write up our 'deviation statement', a brief problem definition. Bearing in mind the warnings given in Chapters 1, 2, 3, 10, 11 and above about assuming that we know what the problem is, this may seem to be a retrogressive step. In Problem Analysis, however, describing the problem as a deviation (or decline) in performance from some norm or expectation is not quite the same as the problem definitions elsewhere in this book, as here we are merely attempting to describe a problem's symptoms. We will not try to hypothesize about what the problem is or its cause until we have performed a careful analysis of the problem situation. This may be the best approach to a machine-type problem.

To ensure that we do not start from a position where we know what the problem is, Kepner and Tregoe (1981) suggest we formulate the deviation statement as follows. Having written down something we ask whether we can give an explanation of the problem as currently stated; if so, we can back up one 'level' at a time until we get to a deviation statement that we cannot explain.

In the example, the problem could have been defined as 'distillation products found on the floor'. This is a problem for somebody as they have to keep cleaning it up, but a deviation statement worded this way is explainable: there are distillation products on the floor because distillation products are dripping off the side of the collection vat. Furthermore, distillation products are dripping off the side of the collection vat because there is a 'leak' in the distillation apparatus up above and the leaking fluids are running down the pipework. This leak cannot presently be explained so this is where we start. We should phrase our deviation statement carefully and precisely, because all that follows is logically dependent on it (see Frame 6.3).

Frame 6.3 *Lowlands Distilleries Ltd: deviation statement*

There is liquid running down the outside of the pipework on No. 2 still, apparently leaking from the new pipework.

Description of the problem in four dimensions

Kepner and Tregoe (1981) next recommend that we collate information about the problem in four dimensions: identity, location, timing and magnitude (see Frame 6.1). The method for determining this crucial information concerning the problem situation is probably the single most important contribution that Problem Analysis offers us with regard to the solution of machine problems. We elicit this information by determining the answers to ten questions that can be seen in Frame 6.4.

Frame 6.4 *Problem-specifying questions*

Identity

- What is the unit that is malfunctioning?
- What is the malfunction?

Location

- Where is the malfunction observed (geographically)?
- Where on the unit is the malfunction observed?

Timing

- When was the malfunction first observed?

▶

- When has it been observed since?
- When in the operating cycle of the unit is the malfunction first observed?

Magnitude

- What is the extent of the problem?
- How many units are affected?
- How much of any one unit is affected?

Kepner and Tregoe (1981)

With the Lowlands Distilleries problem we would probably answer the question 'What is the unit that is malfunctioning?' with 'Still No. 2', and 'What is the malfunction?' with 'A leakage of distillation products'. The rest of the answers for the Lowlands Distilleries example are given in the Problem Analysis chart (Table 6.2). Complete the whole analysis yourself before looking at this.

Having gathered our information, we now look for a similar situation or machine that could be exhibiting the same symptoms but is not. This comparison allows us to reduce the number of possibilities and hence the size of the search area for our cause. For example, the leak appears to be coming from the pipework of still No. 2, but not still Nos. 1, 3–6. You may notice that still Nos. 1–2 are older than the rest, and link the problem to that. We have now established that still No. 1 is functioning correctly whereas still No. 2 is not, meaning that age, though perhaps a contributory factor, is not the significant cause of our problem. We need to look elsewhere, but have at least narrowed the field of possible causes by one.

Generating possible causes

After doing the above for as many of the answers to the 'specifying questions' as we can, we look at our two sets of answers: those that say what, where, when and how the problem, or performance deviation, *is* and those that describe what, where, when and how the problem *could be* but *is not*, searching for any 'distinctive feature' that may help us unearth changes that have taken place which might have caused the malfunction. In this way, we are beginning to look for possible causes. As we note these distinctive features we should also note any changes that have occurred which come immediately to mind, and then go back through our distinctive features specifically looking for as many additional changes as we can (see Frame 6.5).

Frame 6.5 *Lowlands Distilleries Ltd: distinctive features*

The 'distinctive feature' about the fact that the leak is coming from the pipework of still No. 2 and not any of the others is that the pipework on still No. 2 has been replaced recently. This in itself is nothing particularly unusual but it suggests a change that may be the cause of the problem: this is the first time that Robert Jones, a new maintenance engineer, has done a repair in the still room and perhaps his inexperience has caused the leak.

When you have completed this analysis for all four dimensions of the problem definition, compare your results with Table 6.2. The two possible causes to the problem are repeated in Frame 6.6 below.

Frame 6.6 *Lowlands Distilleries Ltd: possible causes*

There are two possible causes of our problem:

- Robert Smith's inexperience has led to him bungling the repair job on the pipework.
- There is something peculiar about the new batch of connectors that arrived recently.

Testing for the most probable cause

Once we have determined some possible causes in the changes we have uncovered, we test whether they would give rise to all the symptoms (the answers to our problem-specifying questions) that we noted. We do this by the logical questioning of each symptom in the following manner:

If Robert Smith's inexperience is the cause of the problem then how does this explain *why* only still No.2 was affected?

Because it was the only one he worked on.

We repeat this process for any other possible causes we have, eliminating some because they cannot account for all the symptoms. Both possible causes summarized in Frame 6.6 pass this test.

Verification of the most likely cause

We now need to verify the true cause of the performance deviation that constitutes our problem. If possible, an obvious method is to swap the offending article (or person) with the identical counterpart in a working system. We could get another maintenance engineer to replace the pipework on still No. 2 for the third time, or we might investigate whether Robert Smith did use one of the new connectors, and if so, determine what difference there was between these and the older variety.

In this example, Robert Smith is absolved: the problem was later verified as due to the new connectors being made to metric specifications, whereas the older

Table 6.2 Problem Analysis for Lowlands Distilleries Ltd

Deviation Statement: There is liquid running down the outside of the pipework on No. 2 still, apparently leaking from the new pipe-work

Specifying questions		Performance deviation is	Could be but is not	Distinctions between what is and is not	Changes suggested by distinctions
Identity	WHAT is the unit with the malfunction?	Still No.2	Stills Nos 1, 3–6	No. 1 repaired by Robert Jones	New and perhaps inexperienced maintenance engineer
	WHAT is the malfunction?	A leakage of distillation products	Water, incorrect distillation products	Distillation process & condenser OK	Nothing
Location	WHERE is the malfunction observed?	On the floor by collection vat	Elsewhere	Likely source of leak is above there?	Nothing
	WHERE on the unit is the malfunction observed?	The new pipework	Other pipework, condenser, collection vat	Replaced recently	New pipe and connectors
Timing	WHEN was the malfunction first observed?	Late Monday morning	On the previous Friday and before	A maintenance check on Saturday	Nothing additional to above
	WHEN has it been observed since?	Continuously ever since	N/A	N/A	N/A
	WHEN in the operating cycle of the unit is the malfunction first observed?	Whenever the stills are operating	When stills are not operating	Pipe only contains distillation products when in operation	Nothing
Magnitude	WHAT is the EXTENT of the malfunction?	Half a litre/hour	More or less than this amount	Commensurate with with badly fitting connectors	New batch of connectors last month
	HOW MANY units are affected?	Only still No. 2	Stills Nos 1, 3–6	As No. 1 above	Nothing additional to the above
	HOW MUCH of any one unit is affected?	New pipework	Rest of pipework on Still No. 2	New connectors	As No. 8 above

ones were imperial sizes. They were similar enough to be used as equivalents, but the slight discrepancy in sizes, coupled with the old pipework, led to the leak.

Problem Analysis and people problems

Though a good strategy for dealing with machine problems, Problem Analysis has been criticized since its introduction as not really suitable for dealing with people problems. Kepner and Tregoe (1981) have addressed this point (and changed the wording of the specifying questions), but they use the term 'people problem' synonymously with 'human performance problem'. Although whether they consider that *all* people problems can be expressed in terms of performance is not clear; they still seem to believe that Problem Analysis is an appropriate way of dealing with problem situations in which people are not doing what is expected of them. They do warn us to apply Problem Analysis differently with people problems: unlike machines, people have self-esteem, and identifying their shortcomings may not have positive results!

They also admit (1981, p.186) that the cause of a person failing to perform as expected is usually rather more complex than with machines and that managing human performance problems by finding a 'reasonable adaptive action' to improve a problem situation, as opposed to solving the problems, is perhaps a more realistic expectation. This adaptive action may not always be good enough, as it can misfire and hurt innocent bystanders if the cause is not thoroughly checked out before the adaptive action is taken. For human performance problems the specifying questions have been rephrased in less mechanistic terms and reduced from ten to six questions:

Identity

- WHO is the person (or group) about whose behaviour we are concerned?
- WHAT specifically is that behaviour?

Location

- WHERE is the behaviour observed?

Timing

- WHEN did this behaviour first become apparent?
- WHEN since that time did we observe this behaviour?

Magnitude

- WHAT is the extent of the behaviour?

(Kepner and Tregoe, 1981)

However, this remains to some extent immaterial, since you will either judge them as appropriate and acceptable or not.

Kepner and Tregoe go on to suggest that often when the precise nature of a person's underperformance is specifically stated in the deviation statement, the cause is readily identified by all concerned as being a simple misunderstanding of what performance level was actually expected. Kepner and Tregoe also argue that the specifying questions give us real data, factual differences in circumstances, which are better than mere speculation in determining the causes of poor performance. The availability of this information during the testing and verification processes is what ultimately protects us from management building a case that supports a preconceived notion such as 'He's just an awkward —!' by possibly providing contradictory evidence undermining such a preconceived notion. However, this places great importance on the verification process.

It is also important, they say, when gathering information on the four dimensions of Problem Analysis that the things which people say, as well as the things they have or have not done, are recorded, no matter how unacceptable or even distasteful to the manager or the organization these comments may be. These remarks will contain clues to the speaker's behaviour.

My main concern in using Problem Analysis on people problems is in starting with too precise a problem definition. Whilst it may be appropriate to start a machine problem with a statement such as 'There is liquid running down the outside of the pipework on No. 2 still', the deviation statement 'John Smith's attitude to his manager has been getting worse and worse over the past three months' does not seem so helpful. It suggests the possibility that a value judgement has already been made and that the fault lies squarely with John Smith. It is the systematic and objective use of the specifying questions that is supposed to reveal the true cause of the problem, but this is not as reliable at rooting out the real problem, I feel, as something like Synectics' **Goal Wishing** (see later and Chapters 10 and 13). Both the **Osborn-Parnes** and **Synectics** CPS processes have elaborate ways of ensuring we are solving the right problem by forcing us to look at the situation from many viewpoints.

Whether or not human behaviour is basically rational, I question whether one person can reliably assess the rationality of another's behaviour. Attempting to deduce something logically from another person's behaviour is to me a very dubious enterprise.

Kepner and Tregoe (1981, pp.206–7) believe that their technique is an objective process and conclude that the questions of Problem Analysis, when asked with 'skill and courtesy . . . cannot help but improve matters for everyone concerned. . . . The important thing is to treat people fairly and honestly, making full use of all relevant information'. However, Vincent Nolan (1989, p.86) comments that 'It [Problem Analysis] . . . does nothing to encourage (indeed, it tends actively to discourage) creative and imaginative thinking, and completely ignores the human factors which are such an important component of most "real world" problems'. Moreover, the actual use of Problem Analysis on people problems has often been associated with the worst aspects of Scientific Management, the principles of management advocated by F.W. Taylor and others at the beginning of the last century, and which was still prevalent until relatively recently. This was mainly due to Problem Analysis' rational method and behaviourist connotations.

Comments such as 'Managing human performance problems calls for a compassionate, considerate approach' and 'Few things hurt productivity more than having people think they have been dealt with unfairly, arbitrarily, or without the intention of understanding their views and positions' seems to suggest that perhaps we may have misjudged Problem Analysis by this association. But as David McHugh reminded me (when reviewing the first edition of this book), the use of Problem Analysis on people problems (i.e. most real-world problems) is essentially Taylorist in effect, if not in intent also. Simply attaching a few human-relations-style prescriptions as caveats does not change this, nor does it make it any more acceptable than other Taylorist practices. We are both by no means alone in having reservations about using Problem Analysis on people problems.

Kepner and Tregoe (1981) give many accounts of the application of Problem Analysis to a variety of both machine and people problem situations.

Dimensional Analysis (hard/creative?)

In an interesting contrast to the above, **Dimensional Analysis**, attributed by Van Gundy (1988, pp.56–62) to J.V. Jensen (1978), seems to focus on human relations problems, and in this case the questions asked have to be modified when applied to a technical problem such as new-product development! Here a problem is said to exist whenever there has been a 'violation of values' – so you can see that it could be difficult to determine exactly what this means in relation to the problem of creating a better kettle. Van Gundy goes on to say that this technique is 'designed to clarify and explore the dimensions and limits of a problem' by examining five elements (or dimensions) of a problem.

These dimensions are elaborated into 22 questions. The following is an adaptation of Van Gundy's presentation of them:

- **Substantive (What?)**
  1. Is something being done that needs to be stopped or modified, or is something not being done that should be? (The latter being more difficult to detect!)*
  2. Does the problem stem from [someone's] attitude or observable behaviour? (Focusing on changing attitudes rather than behaviour is often the best plan, but not always easy!)*
  3. Is what we experience/observe only a symptom or the real cause?*
  4. Is the problem situation (actively) threatening to people or just an irritating obstacle?
  5. Is the real problem visible or hidden?*
- **Spatial (Where?)**
  6. Is the problem localized or far reaching?*
  7. Is the problem associated with a specific location?*
  8. Is the problem an isolated incidence or widespread?*
- **Temporal (When?)**
  9. Is the problem situation a recent or long-standing one?*
  10. Is the problem present or impending?
  11. Is the problem constant or intermittent?*
- **Quantitative (How much?)**
  12. Does the problem have a single cause or multiple causes?*

13. How many people are involved (a few or a lot)?*
14. Does the problem have general implications or are these implications specific to certain subcategories/groups?*
15. Is the problem simple or complex (having many interlocking elements)?
16. Is the problem due to an abundance of something or the lack of it?*

- **Qualitative (How serious?)**

17. Is the problem deep-rooted (philosophcally or ideologically) or superficial?
18. Is the problem a question of survival or enrichment? (The former will require immediate action!)
19. Are people's perceptions of the problem that it is of primary or secondary importance?
20. What values are being violated?*
21. What is the degree of these values being violated (very worthy or trivial)?
22. Should the value being violated be honoured or is it questionable anyway?

Some of these questions seem to be getting us to think about how or whether to deal with a problem (and as such should be used at an earlier (pre-problem-solving) stage rather than helping us identify them, but may still prove useful for this latter purpose. Those marked with an asterisk seem to have the greatest potential for Problem Identification.

Defining the problem – TRIZ (hard?/creative)

Introduction

In the early stages of the different **TRIZ** algorithms, see page 36, various stages/steps (depending on the variant of ARIZ being used) with differing advice, contribute to what might be called **Problem Identification**. In a way similar to Kepner-Tregoe's Problem Analysis (see above), the Data Gathering (rather than being a separate stage) is integrated with this Problem Identification.

Contradictions and the ideal machine

Genrich Altshuller (1999, pp.90–1) differentiates between the designer's art which, he says, 'depends, for the most part, on skills for determining what must be gained and lost through compromise', and the essence of inventive creativity, which

> is to find a way where compromise will not be needed (or, where it is disproportionately small relative to an achieved result). [That is,] from the engineering perspective, creation of a new invention always manifests as the full or partial overcoming of a technical contradiction.

A technical contradiction 'occurs when we are trying to improve one characteristic, or parameter, of a technical "system" and cause another characteristic, or parameter to deteriorate' (Shulyak, 1997). As early as we can in the Problem Identification stage we try and find this technical contradiction. Imagining the **ideal machine**, Altshuller (1999, p.103) tells us, should help with this – 'the ideal machine helps to determine the direction of search, while the technical contradiction indicates the obstacle that must be removed' – but the technical contradiction we need to deal with it is not always that obvious.

Once this is determined we might look for an '**allowable variant** . . . some deviation from the given technical condition – a compromise solution' that can be achieved by 'relaxing' one of the constraints (Altshuller, 1999, p.89). Alternatively we might try a **bypass approach**: assume the contradiction is irresolvable, and consider what higher-level problem might we try and solve wherein the cause of the contradiction no longer exists. Altshuller (1999) offers the example of the problem of getting a convoy of ships more quickly through iced-up waterways using an icebreaker. Rather than modify the icebreaker somehow (which is problematic) to permit it to cut through the ice more quickly, the bypass problem would be to achieve the desired increase in speed *without* the icebreaker (and its problems).

Then we need to decide whether to go with the compromise, try and solve the bypass problem and/or resolve our technical contradiction. If the latter, it is recommended that we draw diagrams/models of the situation before and after the attainment of the **ideal final result** (IFR), to determine which element cannot perform the required function and why, and the conditions under which it could (initially ignoring the 'how' and what must be done to the element to provide it with this characteristic). We can then describe the IFR in the form: component (or element) A of the 'system', performs action F, in a certain way H by itself, under conditions (limitations, requirements, etc.) C. For the icebreaker problem this could be: the ship (element), moves through the ice (action) at high speed (how it performs) by itself, with a normal consumption of energy – as if it were in clear water (under what conditions) (Altshuller, 1999, p.178).

Ways of overcoming technical contradictions will be given in Chapter 7 (see the **40** (Innovation) **Principles**/Contradiction Matrix.

If we are really (un)lucky a **physical contradiction** arises. This happens 'when two opposite properties are required from the same element of a technical system or from the technical system itself' (Shuylak, 1997). There is a little more about resolving these in the Chapter 7 too.

Problem documentation and preliminary analysis

A more recent and somewhat fuller account of what information we should compile about the problem, and problem situation, and what analysis we should do with it (which subsumes much of the above), is as follows:

First of all, we try and describe the problem (or innovation) situation in a simple, generic sense without recourse to using industry-specific terminology (compare with **Morphological Analysis**, page 156). Typically, such a description should be in the form:

> A technical system consisting of elements A, B and C, has [a problem P or] technical contradiction TC [if identified]. . . . It is necessary to provide required function F while incurring minimal changes to the system.

Lev Shulyak (1997) says that 'it is not important that such a result is achievable: however, it is important to state that the system should stay the same – or become simpler'.

Next we compile some information about the 'system' under investigation (see Frame 6.7), by considering the problem at different (higher/wider) systemic levels, selecting one (or more) of these that we can/want to work with and then concisely describing the chosen 'system'(s)':

- structure (its components)
- function
- environment (other related parts, systems nearby, systems interacting with it, and the general conditions around it)

plus, some information about the problem situation, as follows . . .

- the problem that should be resolved (for example, supply a need, remove a harmful function)
- the 'mechanism' causing the problem
- the undesired consequences of leaving the problem unresolved
- the history of the problem
- other 'systems' in which a similar problem exists
- other ways of resolving the problem;

along with a brief account of . . .

- the ideal (vision of a) solution
- the available resources (substance, field [energy], space, time, informational, functional)
- any allowable changes to the 'system'
- the criteria we are going to use to select our solution concept
- any (other) data about the 'system'.

(Zlotin, Zusman and Kaplan, 2000)

Frame 6.7 *The table-saw problem*

Problem description

A technical system that consists of a metal grille which protects the operator of a table-mounted circular saw from being hurt by the rotating blade. The metal grille prevents accurate sighting of the wood with the blade.

It is necessary to provide a means for cutting wood safely and accurately, while incurring minimal changes to the system.

▶

Systemic problems

- The grille – the grille must be there to stop the blade cutting the operator's flesh, but it must not impair the accuracy with which the wood can be cut.
- The blade – the blade can be exposed, but it should not cut the operator's flesh
- The saw – the blade can be removed but the wood must still be cut.

Structure (components) *of the system*

A table, an electric motor, a rotating blade, an electric motor, motor supports, and a metal grille.

Function

If we decide to work at the grille level . . .

- to keep the operator's flesh from touching the blade.

or at the blade level . . .

- to cut wood by rotating quickly with serrated edge.

Cause and effect diagrams – TRIZ (hard?/creative)

After completing our problem documentation and preliminary analysis, we can model the problem with a 'cause and effect' diagram. Figure 6.2 shows a simple model based on the case outlined in Frame 6.7. It consists of the combination of two 'chains', one showing useful functions/factors and effects of the 'system' (white boxes) and the other showing harmful factors/actions (tinted boxes).

Zlotin and Zusman (1991) describe the construction of this diagram as follows:

Starting with the 'systems' basic function the 'useful' chain can be extended either side by asking . . .

- What is the purpose of performing this function?
- What is necessary to perform this function?

And for 'harmful' chain, perhaps starting from the main harmful factor/action . . .

- What is the cause or result of this harmful factor/action?'

The separate chains are connected where the following situations occur:

- A harmful effect is caused by a useful function/factor.
- A useful function/factor is introduced to correct an existing harmful effect.

As a result, for each link from a useful or a harmful chain two additional questions should be asked. For a link from a useful chain:

- Does this useful function cause a harmful factor?
- Is this useful function introduced to correct a harmful factor?

Accordingly, for a link from a harmful chain:

- Is this harmful factor caused by a useful function?
- Is any useful function introduced to correct this harmful factor?

Answers to these questions help connect useful and harmful chains, and add new chains that were not obvious from the beginning.

Looking at each of the links in this diagram, we can now generate lots of alternative problem statements by forming ones that describe:

- the elimination of a harmful factor/action
- an alternative way to realize a useful function
- a way of doing without a useful function
- the elimination of a harmful effect without giving up a connected useful function (the **key correcting problem**)
- an alternative way to perform a useful function so the harmful factor disappears
- a way to do without the useful function together with a connected harmful factor.

Figure 6.2

The table-saw problem: cause and effect diagram

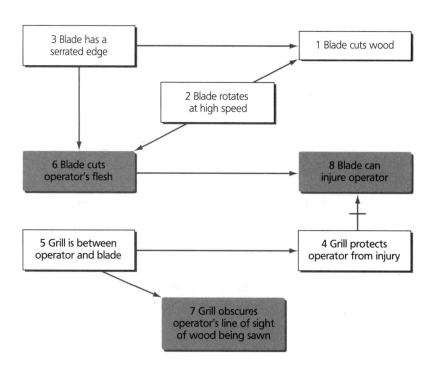

Basic directions for innovation are thus obtained (most of them will not contain a contradiction). The key correcting problem (there could be more than one) is used as a basis for formulating the so-called 'mini-problem', where 'everything remains the same or becomes simplified, while the required action or property emerges or the undesired action or property disappears' (Zlotin and Zusman, 1991). That is, where the technical contradiction is to be resolved in the most ideal way.

We would now sort these problem statements according to how drastic are the changes to the 'system' they imply (least drastic, first) and prioritize them according to the criteria we listed above and any 'specifics associated with the user' to select the ones we are going to continue with. Where we go from here depends on whether the chosen problem statement is a key correcting problem or not (see Chapter 7).

Cognitive Mapping (soft?/creative?)

As we keep saying, determining exactly what the problem is, or deciding the initial direction(s) we should go in to search for ideas and possible solutions, is often the most crucial stage in problem solving, particularly when we are helping other people solve their problems. This difficulty with Problem Identification has also inspired the development of a relatively new technique called **Cognitive Mapping**. In simple terms, this technique is an extended and more systematic version of the early stages of the Synectics process in the form of a cause and effect diagram; however, its purpose is to demonstrate an empathetic understanding of the problem situation, rather than simply obtaining a number of different ways of seeing it.

The originators of **Cognitive Mapping**, like many others in the field, believe that in trying to resolve a problematical situation our perception of it is shaped by our particular mental framework of beliefs, attitudes, hypotheses, prejudices, expectations, values and objectives. They offer their technique as a means of 'capturing' these concepts, describing it as 'a modelling technique which intends to portray ideas, beliefs, values and attitudes and their relationship one to another in a (diagrammatical) form which is amenable to study and analysis' (Eden *et al.*, 1983, p.39).

By attempting to 'map out' these concepts and showing the interrelationships between them, Colin Eden *et al.* believe the process of Problem Identification is facilitated. Cognitive Mapping seems to be particularly useful in uncovering and identifying the essence of a problem situation with multiple ownership.

Because problems are not 'objective entities', but actually belong to someone, our starting point when helping others to resolve problems should ideally be 'an empathetic understanding' of the problem as that person sees it. (This may appear to be contrary to what we will say later when discussing the Synectics CPS process, see pages 240–1, but here we are talking about problem-solving facilitators, there about the 'naive' resources.) Eden *et al.* suggest that we achieve this by listening to the 'language, descriptions, theories and beliefs that are expressed' as the problem owner describes the problem situation. In the first instance, the map we are building shows we have been listening carefully and we are making an attempt towards empathy.

To construct a cognitive map we start from a 'label' of the problem as given; for example, 'insufficient time and resources to do a good job', written in the centre of a large sheet of paper. Then, in discussion with the problem owner(s), we 'map' out various perceptions of the problem situation, showing their causal interconnections with arrows. We solicit these perceptions by asking questions such as:

- Why does . . . matter?
- What reasons come to mind as explanations for . . . ?
- Why is . . . like that?

For the question 'Why does insufficient time and resources to do a good job matter?' we might get the answer, 'Because of it everyone's morale is low'; to 'What reasons come to mind as explanations for insufficient time and resources to do a good job?' we might get, 'It's the result of having poor leadership'. For each of these perceptions we try to write down beneath them what the problem owner considers to be a 'satisfactory alternative to this circumstance'; and gradually our map builds, as in Figure 6.3. The minus sign on an arrow shows that the problem owner believes an inverse (rather than a direct) relationship exists between the

Figure 6.3 A cognitive map

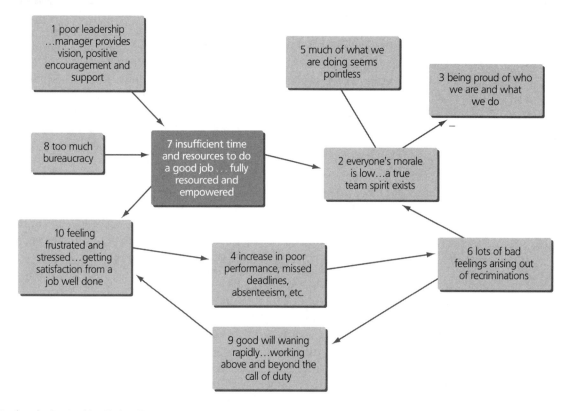

Produced using Decision Explorer™

first item in the pair of concepts. Eventually, we should be able to discern 'clusters' of perceptions within the map we have been building that indicate the main area(s) of concern.

Often, during discussion with the problem owner, we may encounter phrases with the same or a linked meaning, or that describe attributes of a particular concept rather than being causally related to it. These 'connotative links' can be shown on the map with non-arrowed lines or depicted separately in attribute diagrams. The 'discovery' of these links is important because they provide us with a better appreciation of what a person means by that particular concept. For example, 'everyone's morale is low' may be thus linked with 'much of what we are doing seems pointless'.

Once a map has been drawn it can be examined for 'loops', some of which will be self-stabilizing (negative feedback loops), while others indicate the manifestation of vicious circles (positive feedback loops, such as concepts 10, 4, 6 and 9)). Individuals caught up in the latter are usually only too well aware of being so, but seeing it shown on the map makes it clear to everyone concerned that an untenable position exists and helps us to find ways of breaking free by revealing the outcome we might expect from 'severing' any one of the links in the circle.

In a multiple problem-owner situation, Eden *et al.* (1983) advise that we first produce a separate map for each problem owner and then form an aggregated map showing the group's perception of the situation. As we study 'completed' individual maps, we may notice that the same or similar concepts appear on different maps, which may indicate that certain perceptions of the problem situation are shared. However, great care must be taken when attempting to 'merge' concepts such as these. We must ask the contributors whether they really *do* mean the same thing, even if they say the same thing. When combining maps in this way, it is best to do it in a group situation so that all the contributors can check with each other on the meaning of similar concepts, perhaps using Synectics-style paraphrasing (see pages 246 and 253). By comparing individual maps we get an idea of the diversity of viewpoints and discover potential areas of conflict, as well as determining which perceptions are shared.

There is obviously far more to Cognitive Mapping than this, for example a good rapport needs to be built between the problem-solving facilitator and the problem owner(s) in order to gain answers to our questions. Anyone interested in learning more about Cognitive Mapping should read Eden *et al.*'s book, which uses an extended case study to present very clearly the difficulties of helping other people decide on what their problem is and then resolving it.

Backward/Forward Planning – Synectics (creative)

Backward/Forward Planning is a fairly structured technique used within the Synectics CPS process to encourage the problem owner to consider alternative ways of viewing his or her problem alongside the initial 'problem (statement) as given', or task headline, by considering higher-level problems and subproblems. We will use the problem outlined in Frame 6.8 to illustrate it.

> **Frame 6.8** *Operations room access problem*
>
> Su Ling, the database administrator of WorldOutThere.co.uk, can only get 'administrator' access to the company database from one terminal which is located in the computer (operations) room. Access to this room is strictly controlled for security reasons. At present Su Ling has to seek out and ask the computer operations manager to let her into the room, and she can only stay there whilst he is there! Su Ling has asked for an electronic pass key ('swipe card'), but the operations manager is reluctant to give her one for reasons he does not seem prepared to say, apart from 'security'.

Suppose Su Ling initially states her problem as: 'How can I persuade the operations manager to give me a pass key to the computer room.'

This problem statement also illustrates a potential hazard in problem solving which Backward/Forward Planning can help alleviate. This is the fairly typical tendency with people problems for a problem owner to express his/her problem in terms of 'motivating others to think or do something'. That is, the problem statement refers to persuading/making someone else change his or her attitudes or actions in some way. This is nearly always a difficult thing to accomplish. The human species seems to be extremely good at perceiving when another human is trying to manipulate them in some way, and invariably reacts to this with an equally effective (and usually total) resistance to this effort, irrespective of whether the change is seen as good or bad.

As a problem owner I should try and rephrase the problem statement in terms of 'How can *I* change *my* own attitudes or actions in such a way that this might encourage others to . . .' on the basis that it is much easier (and is likely to be more effective in the long run) to change ourselves rather than to attempt to change other people. Backward/Forward Planning *may* help us move towards this view of the problem situation.

In an attempt to expand the problem statement to include some different perspectives on the situation we first go 'backwards' and look for higher-level problems. This is accomplished by Su Ling asking questions such as:

'If this problem could be resolved instantly by just making a wish, what (higher-level) problem would this solve, what would it allow me to do?'

'I could work on the database at times that suit me',

We rephrase/rewrite this response in a 'I wish/How to' form (for reasons given below, on page 110), such as:

I wish I could work on the database at times that suit me . . .
    and what would this allow me to do?

'I could get far more done in the same amount of time.'

'*How to* get more work done in the same amount of time?'

We can carry on asking the same question as above or – 'By not having this . . ., what is it that I am being prevented from doing?'

'Doing my job effectively and "hitting" my targets.'

I wish I could do my job effectively and 'hit' my targets

. . . and again, if possible, 'and not doing my job effectively and hitting my targets prevents me from . . . ?'

'Getting promoted to another (more challenging) job.'

I wish I could get promoted to another (more challenging) job.

Then we go 'forwards' looking for 'sub-problems'. For this we ask:

'What is stopping me resolving this problem?'

'I cannot convince him (the operations manager) of the serious impact this is having on my work.'

I wish I could convince him of the serious impact this is having on my work.

'The operations manager's "attitude" to me.'

How can I demonstrate that I am a competent and trustworthy enough person to have access to the computer room?

'My boss not intervening on my behalf and sorting things out.'

I wish my boss would intervene on my behalf and sort things out.

And to get additional benefits:

'If the original problem was now solved, . . . what would this mean to me, what additional benefits would come from this?'

'I would be able to get help on certain technical matters from the operators in the computer room (they are not allowed to "waste time" helping me when the manager is there).'

I wish I could get help on certain technical matters from the operators.

Backward/Forward Planning helps counteract the conceptual block of **tunnel vision** (see Chapter 3) should the problem owner appear to suffer from this.

Backward/Forward Planning is also a good starting point for certain personal 'decisions', for example 'I wish I could give up smoking/lose weight etc.' These are not problems but decisions waiting to be made – we choose to give up smoking/lose weight! And we call upon known solutions – nicotine patches, diets, etc. – to assist us if necessary. But there may be (and probably is) a problem that is stopping us make the decision – this is what we need to identify and address.

The Osborn-Parnes CPS process now has a very similar technique referred to by Isaksen and Treffinger (1985, pp.78, 81) as the 'Abstraction Ladder'. Here the higher-level problems are obtained by asking 'Why?' do we want to solve a particular problem, or 'What is my objective/reason for attempting this?'; sub-problems are obtained by asking 'How?' or 'What is preventing me from . . .?'. To 'stretch' our thinking a little further they also suggest subsequently asking 'Why else?' and 'How else?'. The Abstraction Ladder seems to have been derived from a combination of techniques: the 'Why Method' described by Van Gundy (1988) and attributed to Sidney Parnes (1981); and Progressive Abstractions (Geschka *et al.*, 1973)/Relevance Systems (Rickards, 1974). In the

Progressive Abstractions technique the question 'What is the essential problem?' replaces 'How?'.

Backward/Forward Planning is often done in a Synectics CPS session as a prelude to Goal Wishing, see below and Chapter 10.

Goal Wishing/springboards – Synectics (creative)

Goal Wishing (aka goal orientation, **springboard** [generation]) is the name given to the primary technique in the Synectics CPS process to assist with Problem Identification, often following on from Backward/Forward Planning. In its simplest form it involves Brainstorming (see Chapters 3 and 7) different ways of looking at/describing the problem (see the car breakdown problem in Frame 1.3).

Springboards are/can be far more than just problem definitions and may fulfil many uses, especially in a group problem-solving session. Apart from paraphrasing the problem situation and providing the means for expressing individual interpretations of it, they can also be an acceptable means of challenging restrictions (real or perceived) that seem to have been placed on possible solutions. They can even question the validity of a particular problem definition by allowing an airing of conflicting viewpoints, especially when problem ownership is shared. By using springboards to 'constructively misunderstand' aspects of the problem situation, to make wishes, to offer intuitive feelings or non-expert opinions, or simply to voice a free association of ideas, we can build up a wealth of views of the problem situation. Finally, if we have already started to make connections, we can volunteer a **beginning idea** with a springboard, without the risk that it will be heard as any more than that (see examples of this in the Northcliffe Sands illustrative example in Chapter 12).

Synectics encourage the use of the (problem redefinition) prefaces 'How to' and 'I wish'. The use of 'How to' conveys a positive direction. Rather than 'We cannot afford to do more research', which sounds negative and constraining and could put a damper on ideas that might involve more expenditure, expressing it as 'How to find ways of affording more research' is more positive and less restrictive, implying the need to actively go and look for ways of raising more money and/or cutting the costs of existing research, without precluding any ideas. The 'I wish' preface supports and encourages more speculative problem definitions.

The problem of starting with a problem statement requiring someone else to do something was introduced above in the example of operations room access. The Osborn-Parnes process uses the preface 'In what way might I . . .' (IWWMI) in addition to 'I wish' and 'How to' – use of IWWMI tends to 'throw' the emphasis back on us to do something – it is more difficult to 'start' an inappropriate/ill-advised problem (re)definition, suggesting making someone else do something, with IWWMI.

If, after generating a few (say 15+) springboards, none of them appeals to us as the problem owner, or they don't give a sufficiently new or insightful view of the problem situation, then a (Synectics) **excursion** (see Chapter 7) can be used to encourage the generation of further, more speculative springboards. (An example of this is given in Chapter 10.)

Key Word Variations – Osborn-Parnes (creative)

Key Word Variations is an interesting variation on the previous (redefinitional) techniques for generating additional problem statements, described by Isaksen and Treffinger (1985, pp.75–6). It produces 'many variations on one particular viewpoint'. However, if our need is for 'deliberate and totally different perceptions' then it is best to employ other techniques.

We identify key words within a particular statement; for example, those shown in italic in 'IWWMI *employ* my *energy* more *effectively*', and then (possibly using a thesaurus) think of several variations for these key words, for example: employ – organize, channel; energy – time, interests; effectively – efficiently, lucratively, etc. and replace one or more of these keywords with them, thus giving additional problem definitions, such as:

IWWMI organize my interests more effectively.

IWWMI channel my energy more lucratively.

IWWMI organize my time more efficiently.

Selecting by appeal – Synectics (creative)

At some point, we need to decide which of our springboards (problem redefinitions, beginning ideas, etc.) we wish to take on to the next phase of our problem solving. The advice from Synectics is short and simple – select the springboards that *appeal* to you (intuitively), do not be too concerned at this stage whether you can see an obvious way forward and/or it seems feasible to solve the problem from that starting point.

The Osborn-Parnes CPS process offers a little more advice, for the convergent phase of Problem Identification, but very much in the same vein. In the convergent phase of **problem finding**, Isaksen and Treffinger (1985) suggest we start by **highlighting: hits, hotspots and relates** (we will use an almost identical technique in Chapter 7 to select ideas). In this context, a 'hit' refers to a problem statement that 'strikes you as a breakthrough, an Aha! or a direction to be pursued' and seems to be insightful or is appealing to us. Hotspots are groups of similar or related hits.

It can be helpful sometimes to combine a couple of hits in a **restatement** prior to idea finding.

Check for Idea Finding Potential – Osborn-Parnes (creative)

Finally, Isaksen and Treffinger (1985, p.89) also offer a 'Check for Idea Finding Potential' which uses the following criteria to assess the potential productivity of our Ideation with that statement:

● it looks as if it might lead to lots of ideas,

● it is the question about which you want to find ideas,

● it locates the ownership clearly,

- it is worded in an affirmative/positive way,
- it is free from criteria,
- it is stated clearly and concisely.

(If a statement does not seem to meet these criteria then (if possible) it should be reworded so that it does.)

However, if you have been following the Synectics philosophy/principles you should not need to ask these questions, being able to assume that they would be answered in the affirmative.

Summary

In this chapter we have looked at a number of hard, soft and creative techniques used by different problem-solving approaches/processes that help us identify what the problem is or how it can best be stated. We may now have a 'stock' solution to fix the problem; if not, we need to get some ideas about how to solve the problem using the techniques in the following chapter.

Exercises

1. Taking any problems that you subjected to the first exercise at the end of Chapter 5 (Synectics Problem Analysis questions), read through your answers and generate some springboards. For example, you may have said that X is a problem for you because it's occupying too much of your time and preventing you from doing Y properly – an obvious springboard could be 'How to find more time to do Y' or 'I wish I could manage my time better'. Also, one of the things you may have tried or thought of (to solve the problem) was to delegate (dealing with X) to someone else (Z) but it took almost as much time to help/supervise that person doing it; this suggests the springboard, 'How to get some training for Z' or 'How to show Z that they can do X very competently on their own'.

2. Here are a few springboards for the 'Operations room access' problem in Frame 6.8:
   - I wish I could get administrator access from other terminals (not in the computer room).
   - I wish the operations manager would 'chill out' a bit.
   - How to copy someone else's pass key.

Generate a few more.

7 Ideation

This chapter describes various techniques used by different problem-resolving approaches/processes for generating ideas for solving a problem as identified, that later we should be able to develop into possible solutions, and selecting those to take on to the next stage.

Introduction

Most of the techniques presented below come from the creative problem-solving approach. The reason for this is that the hard (rational) approach tends to assume that sufficient and acceptable options are readily available and do not therefore have any **Ideation** techniques as such. If, as is often the case, these options are not readily available and/or universally acceptable, then creative techniques can (and should be) applied to rectify these situations.

Having said that there are no hard Ideation techniques, **Morphological Analysis** (see page 154), which is essentially a (structured) systematic search for 'opportunities' (such as new product ideas, new markets, etc.), and thus appears to be a fairly rational (logical) way of doing things, could be classified as fairly **hard**, if it were not for its reliance on **Forced Relationships** to actually get the ideas. And, I include first another systematic search discovered on a CRAC (Careers Research Advisory Council) course some twenty years ago. Also, the main Ideation technique from **TRIZ**, the contradiction matrix, being derived as it was from the analytical study of patents, could also be seen as pretty hard, though it can require a lot of creativity to employ the answers it gives within the problem situation.

The **soft systems** approach **SSM** has but one Ideation technique, which will be described second.

Classification of CPS idea-generating techniques

Many attempts have been made to classify creative problem solving (Ideation) (divergent) techniques. Van Gundy (1988) classifies both individual and group idea generation techniques by the two 'dimensions': whether ideas are produced by free association or Forced Relationships, and whether problem-related or unrelated material (or a combination) is used as a stimulus.

For group idea generation techniques he adds a third dimension: whether the technique is essentially **Brainstorming** or **Brainwriting**, but then goes on (slightly confusingly) to suggest that there are five types of Brainwriting (based on physical proximity of participants, and whether ideas are shared to provide additional stimulation), two types of Brainstorming (with or without any agreed procedure, rules, etc. – the latter I would not call Brainstorming!) and one hybrid! Certainly whether group Brainwriting (or any other technique) is interactive or not could be a significant factor in any classification system, but we will not use that here. In my opinion there are very few techniques (only those that *depend* on interaction to work effectively) that could not be used by a lone problem solver; for example, a **Synectics imaging excursion**, though most techniques are more effective in an interactive group setting.

Elspeth McFadzean (1996a) has more recently suggested classifying **CPS** techniques by positioning them along a continuum ranging from 'paradigm preserving' – that is, no new elements or new relationships (between the problem elements) are introduced (e.g. Brainstorming, Brainwriting); through 'paradigm stretching' – where either new elements or new relationships are introduced (e.g. Forced Relationships [object stimulation], **metaphors**); to 'paradigm breaking' – when both new elements *and* new relationships are introduced (e.g. **Wishful Thinking**, imaging excursion [guided fantasy]).

Whatever, Morphological Analysis (in its various forms) is a classic example of Forced Relationships, albeit a complicated one: the other extreme is a force fit using random words (**Catalogue**). **Attribute Listing** and **checklists** are examples of free association *and* the use of related stimuli. And most **excursions** are classic examples of the use of unrelated stimuli. These and other techniques are shown in Van Gundy's classification in Figure 7.1.

Figure 7.1

Classification of CPS Ideation techniques

| | | Problem | |
		Related	Unrelated
Forced relationship		Absurd solutions/ Wishful thinking Catalogue (forced relationships) Morphological analysis Analolgies/metaphors	Excursions (most)
Free association		Attribute listing Brainstorming Brainwriting pool Checklists	Creative visualization

Analysis of CPS idea generating techniques

There are many CPS Ideation techniques. Van Gundy (1988) describes 61! Because a lot of these techniques are only minor variations of others, nearly all of Van Gundy's listed techniques could be covered by:

- Attribute Listing
- Absurd Solutions/Wishful Thinking
- (Classical) Brainstorming
- Brainwriting (interactive – Trigger Method; non-interactive – Crawford Slip Method)
- Catalog (simple Forced Relationships)
- Checklists
- Excursions (line drawing, plus a 3D 'sculpture' and a picture variant; career; example; imaging, and an individual variant: creative visualization, plus a storytelling variant, the President's idea, book titles)
- Morphological Analysis;

which, in effect, is the whole of the Synectics CPS family of techniques called excursions, plus a few other techniques. We will therefore only describe this 'short list', below.

Selecting our most promising ideas

This chapter closes with a technique, **highlighting**, from the **Osborn-Parnes** CPS process for selecting our most promising ideas. With the Synectics CPS process we simply pick the ideas that we intuitively think are promising, sometimes (if appropriate) combining/(re)forming some of them (if related in some way) into a **concept**. This concept or the individual ideas are then taken on to the development stage. Highlighting, below, is a more formalized version of this formation of concepts.

Isaksen and Treffinger (1985, p.112) offer a virtually identical technique to 'Advantages, Limitations and Unique Aspects' (see Chapter 8) called 'Advantages, Limitations and Unique Connections' for situations where you have 'so many ideas that you need to sort them out and take stock of your progress, or perhaps you really are not certain which ones hold the greatest potential'. To my mind it is slightly confusing to categorize this technique as a (convergent) **Ideation** technique when it must involve some evaluation, albeit presumably not as much as would be employed when **Solution Finding** (now called **Developing Solutions**)!

Approximate thinking

Each of us has a vast, diverse and essentially unique collection of thoughts, images and experiences stored away in our memories. Probability alone suggests we must have something relevant to dealing with a new situation or resolving a particular problem, but we often fail to realize this. Research in CPS indicates that we all have some recollections that are approximately relevant to any given problem that we have to tackle.

'I have an approximate experience that's approximately relevant to anything – doesn't matter what it is! Getting myself to realize that it's not mistaken to use that, enables me to dip into a huge amount of my potential.' (Prince, 1980)

Systematic search for opportunities (hard)

It is not just the ability to make inspired connections between apparently unrelated things that can lead to new ideas and profitable ventures. There are a number of 'known' sources of opportunities, relatively mundane situations which many of us tend to overlook or fail to realize the full potential of. Many a successful entrepreneur has been able to take advantage of such opportunities. If you are looking for a business opportunity, it is worth periodically going through the following list of questions:

- What problems do other people have? Can you offer them a solution?
- Are there any changes in legislation imminent? How can you take advantage of them?
- Can you foresee any social changes, for example crazes?
- What new technologies have recently been announced? Can you think of an application for any of them?
- Is it possible to copy and/or improve something that someone else is doing/making?
- Can you do anything with local raw materials and/or people's skills?
- Can you make something different from somebody else's 'sub-assemblies'?
- Can you do something with other people's waste materials?
- Does anybody require a particular service in your area?
- Can you capitalize on any gluts or scarcities?

Conceptual Models – Soft Systems Methodology (soft)

Introduction

In Soft Systems Methodology (SSM), **Conceptual Models** (of **human activity systems**) are normally used as a foil (one could call them an 'ideal' system) against which to compare a real-world organizational problem situation, so as to get ideas as to what changes to the real-world situation should/would improve things. When used this way (see Chapter 11), I feel that they act in a similar way to the excursion material generated in Synectics (see below and Chapters 10 and 12). They can also be used to get ideas regarding a 'green field' situation, whereby a newly formed group, organization, etc. is determining what activities they should be involved in, to deliver their mission/fulfil their prime objective/purpose.

These Conceptual Models are 'built' from a concise description of the system to be modelled, called a **Root Definition**.

Relevant systems (soft)

Before formulating and deciding upon which Root Definitions to model we usually generate (by Brainstorming) some so-called **Relevant Systems**. These are brief statements of what the overall purpose of the human activity we are observing could or should be, obtained from studying the Rich Picture of the problem situation (see page 83). As well as stating the more obvious reasons for all this activity, be speculative, contentious, even wild in your suggestions, and do not be constrained by the word 'relevant' – that cannot be determined until later in the SSM process.

Let us suppose that the situation we are studying is a rugby union football match: how might we view the purpose of this phenomenon? An obvious one would be to think of a rugby match as merely a recreational system or a revenue generating system, but how about a thirst producing system, a system for preserving 'amateur status' in sport, a system for the 'safe' release of pent-up communal rivalries, a system for attracting potential male voice choir members, a system for permitting intimate contact between adult human males within a society that generally disapproves of overt displays of such behaviour, a product testing system for washing powder manufacturers, a system for utilizing misshapen footballs?

Or let's take a fashion show: is this a system for encouraging new ideas in clothes design, a revenue generating system, a system for selling 'new' designs, a system for establishing how outlandish one can be in clothes design, a system for conning rich people into buying 'the latest fashion', a system for providing models with a living, a system that provides egotistical people with a 'high profile' public outlet for their egos, a system for supplying the needs of certain voyeurs, a system for promoting the clothing industry?

The most promising Relevant Systems are then 'fleshed out' into Root Definitions.

Root Definitions (soft)

Because a systems model has to be built logically from them, these Root Definitions need to be worded with care and precision without inhibiting imagination. Smyth and Checkland (1976) believe that the following elements should be found explicitly in a well-formed Root Definition, though all except the transformation process (what the system does – its purpose) may be deliberately omitted, but only for a very good reason.

- Transformation process – 'the means by which the defined inputs to our system are transformed into its defined outputs'.
- Ownership of system – some agency that has 'prime concern' for the system and which has the ultimate 'power to cause the system to cease to exist'
- Actors – the people (expressed in terms of roles) who 'carry out or cause to be carried out the main activities of the system, especially its main transformation'.
- Customers – the people within or outside the system who will be the beneficiaries or victims of the effects of the system's activities.

- Environmental constraints – features of the system's environment (including any wider systems of which our system is a component) which have to be taken as given.
- World view (Weltanschaung) – the standpoint from which we have chosen to view the system. Because of its nature this element is not usually explicitly stated in the Root Direction.

Frame 7.1 shows how a combination of the Relevant Systems: 'a system for building and testing hi-fi loudspeakers', 'a system designed to enhance the quality/esoteric image of UK hi-fi, particularly its excellence in loudspeaker design' and/or 'a system for improving the design of loudspeaker systems' (Frame 11.6) might have been 'fleshed out' into a Root Definition.

Frame 7.1 *John Smith Institute: root definition*

A not-for-profit system that conducts research into the design and manufacture of loudspeaker enclosures, and which builds prototype loudspeaker systems that it demonstrates to hi-fi manufacturers in order to generate revenue from the sale of its designs and manufacturing expertise.

Customers:	Hi-fi manufacturers.
Actors:	Employees.
Transformation:	Conduct research into the design/ manufacture of loudspeaker enclosures, and build and demonstrate prototypes.
World view:	It is possible and worthwhile to improve loudspeaker systems.
Owner:	John Smith (and the other two members of his old R&D team).
Environment:	Hi-fi manufacturers, other research establishments, suppliers, auditors, etc.

Conceptual Models

Since Root Definitions are descriptions of human activity systems, activities are the entities which form the components of our model. The Root Definition determines which activities are incorporated into the model. We call it a Conceptual Model to stress the fact that the system modelled is an abstract thing that exists only in our minds and because an implementation of it may never exist in the real world. We represent our model diagrammatically because that is the best form in which to compare it with our **Rich Picture** representation of the real-world situation (see page 83 and Chapter 11).

Essentially an SSM Conceptual Model is a number of oval shapes representing the activities taking place within our system, linked by arrows denoting the logical dependency of one activity upon another (see later Figure 7.3). How then do we actually put this model together?

The Conceptual Modelling process is or should be a purely logical process, using our knowledge of typical business/organizational systems.

Steps in producing a Conceptual Model

There are essentially four steps in building a Conceptual Model:

1. identify the main activities that comprise the transformation process from the active verbs in the Root Definition,
2. identify the other main activities, the existence of which is logically implied by these main activities,
3. determine the logical dependency between the activities identified in steps 1 and 2,
4. 'bolt on' an appropriate monitoring and control mechanism.

Peter Checkland (1989, p.93) demonstrated this logical model-building process by building a Conceptual Model from a totally meaningless yet perfectly constructed Root Definition. I have adapted this, with influences from one of the comedian Kenneth Wiliams' characters, to make the words in it even more meaningless.

An 'absurd' Root Definition (adapted from Checkland, 1989)

A Tragg-owned nurd wangling system that within the futtling restrictions wangles nurds that satisfy the crad criteria.

Customers:	Nurds.
Actors:	Skilled nurd wanglers.
Transformation:	Wangle nurds meeting the crad criteria.
World view:	It is a good thing to wangle some nurds.
Owner:	Tragg.
Environment:	Nurds, the futtling restrictions, other nurd wanglers.

Building the model

Running through the steps given above:

What then are the main activities of this system that are indicated explicitly by the active verbs in the Root Definition?

A Tragg-owned nurd wangling system that within the futtling restrictions *wangles nurds* that *satisfy the crad criteria.*

- Ascertain which nurds satisfy the crad criteria.
- Wangle nurds satisfying the criteria.

What other activities are implied by these two main activities? That is, logically (from our previous knowledge of similar systems!), what other things must we do in order to perform these main activities?

Presumably . . .

- attract, obtain or perhaps catch some nurds,
- appreciate what these futtling restrictions are all about,
- appreciate how to apply the crad criteria, and
- know/decide how to wangle nurds or get/maintain some skilled people who can already.

... and possibly ...

- reject, (humanely) dispose of, return, release those nurds obtained which did not meet the crad criteria.

There is only some uncertainty here as how to best describe these implied activities because we have little idea of what nurd wangling is all about! In a real-world investigation there should be far less doubt as to what the implied activities are and how they should be described. Let us say the implied activities are:

- obtain some nurds,
- appreciate the futtling restrictions,
- appreciate how to apply the crad criteria,
- maintain a supply of skilled nurd wanglers.
- reject nurds not satisfying the criteria.

We now have seven main operational activities to go on to our Conceptual Model. Next, to determine their logical dependency, Checkland (1981) has suggested the use of a 'dependency matrix' such as the one shown in Figure 7.2. This is essentially a table which has a list of activities as both row and column headings. By asking the question 'Does activity A logically depend on activity B?' repeatedly we are able fill in the upper right portion of the table with a tick denoting where logical dependency exists. This leaves the bottom left of the table unused.

It is suggested we should use this part of the table to indicate logical dependency in the sense of feedback, where one activity benefits (learns or changes) on the basis of what (usually information) it receives from the other activity.

This technique will help us to systematically ensure that we have the right arrows in the right place on our diagram, but it does not help us to actually determine logical dependency, and becomes somewhat cumbersome with a large model anyway. Ian Woodburn (1985, p.102) suggests another way of determining logical dependency, using the mnemonic DIME:

D   Dependency
I   Information
M   Material
E   Energy

For there to be dependency there must be a significant amount of information, materials or energy given out by activity X which is also a significant input to activity Y. If there is then Y logically depends on X. The choice of what constitutes a significant amount is determined by the analyst and depends on the level of detail at which his or her analysis is conducted.

In Figure 7.2 the activity 'Appreciate the futtling restrictions', wherein the restrictions mentioned are assumed to be some sort of environmental constraint on the system (such as a code of conduct imposed by a professional or trade body on its member organizations), has been placed outside a circle to indicate that many, if not all, the activities inside the circle depend on it (thus avoiding lots of crossed arrows). Note, none of the circles on the model represents the system boundary; this is not shown but would be the edge of the diagram.

Now we need a monitoring and control mechanism. According to Checkland (1989), we need to monitor the performance of our system with three criteria relating to efficiency, efficacy and effectiveness. Additional measures of performance have been suggested, including elegance, ethicality and economy (actual efficency *v.* theoretical efficiency) (Wilson, 1990). They are all determined by entities within the system, but effectiveness is what we (the system) feel the owner(s) want out of their 'ownership' of the system; what we think *they* would consider as 'being effective'. If the owner is outside the system we require a different control mechanism (a 'seven-blob' one) than if s/he/it is a part of the system (a 'three/four-blob'[1] one). It has to be said though that other authors (Flood and Jackson, 1991; Stowell, 1995; Wilson, 1990) seem to adopt a different approach than this, often using less 'blobs' to represent the existence of a monitoring and control mechanism. Stowell (1995), for instance, uses the four-blob one (shown in Figure 7.3) for situations where the owner is outside the system.

If we now suppose that the owner, Tragg, is outside the system we will need a seven-blob monitoring and control mechanism. Putting all this together we get the Conceptual Model shown in Figure 7.3.

Standard 'criteria' (performance measures) for our system's control mechanism can be determined from the questions (p. 123):

Figure 7.2	Activities:						
Depend on:	A	B	C	D	E	F	G
A. Appreciate the futtling restrictions		✓	✓	✓	✓	✓	✓
B. Appreciate how to apply the crad criteria				✓			
C. Obtain some nurds				✓			
D. Ascertain which nurds satisfy the crad criteria						✓	✓
E. Maintain a supply of skilled nurd wanglers						✓	
F. Wangle nurds satisfying the criteria							
G. Reject nurds not satisfying the criteria							

Dependency matrix

Figure 7.3 A Conceptual Model

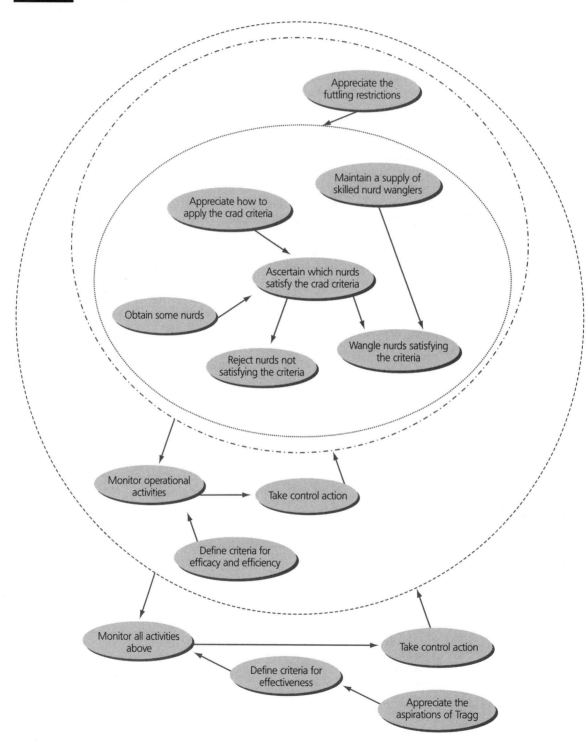

Efficacy – Do the means work? Is there some output of the appropriate quality?

Efficiency – Is there minimum use of resources?

Effectiveness – Is the right thing being done (to achieve the expectations of the owner)?

Therefore we might define them for this system as follows:

Efficacy – Nurd wangling is being successfully accomplished within the futtling restrictions.

Efficiency – Number of nurds wangled/cost of resources used.

Effectiveness – Tragg's aspirations are being met.

A proper example

Let us suppose that John Smith, formerly the R&D manager for Woodsons Ltd (see Chapter 11), having parted from his previous employment (with a 'golden goodbye'), now hopes to set up his own research institute as described in Frame 7.1.

Following the model-building steps again, we have:

1. The main activities of the system indicated explicitly by the active verbs in the Root Definition:
   - conduct research into the design and manufacture of loudspeaker enclosures,
   - build prototype loudspeaker systems,
   - demonstrate prototypes to hi-fi manufacturers,
   - generate revenue from the sale of designs and manufacturing expertise.
2. Other activities presumably implied by these four main activities:
   - obtain raw materials,
   - maintain relationships with suppliers,
   - determine research areas,
   - appreciate market demand, quality design, other research, etc.,
   - maintain relationship with hi-fi manufacturers.

With a 'top-level' (overview) model like this one (see Figure 7.4), we should depict only the major logical dependencies, not each individual flow of materials, energy, information (and influence), etc. The control mechanism we will use is the four-blob one because we are assuming that the three owners are within the system.

When we feel our Conceptual Model is complete it is possible to check out, verifying that our model contains all the components it should have by comparing it with the **Formal Systems Model** (see Appendix 2). This is supposed to contain all the elements and properties that an open system such as our human activity system should have. The Formal Systems Model suggests that we should ask of our model questions such as:

- Are the system boundaries clearly defined?
- Are there the means to measure the system's performance somewhere in the model? What is considered to be 'good' and 'bad' performance?
- Where in the model is the decision-making process located?
- What subsystems are there in the model? Are there effective interconnections between them and the rest of the system?

(Checkland, 1981)

Figure 7.4

The John Smith Institute Conceptual Model

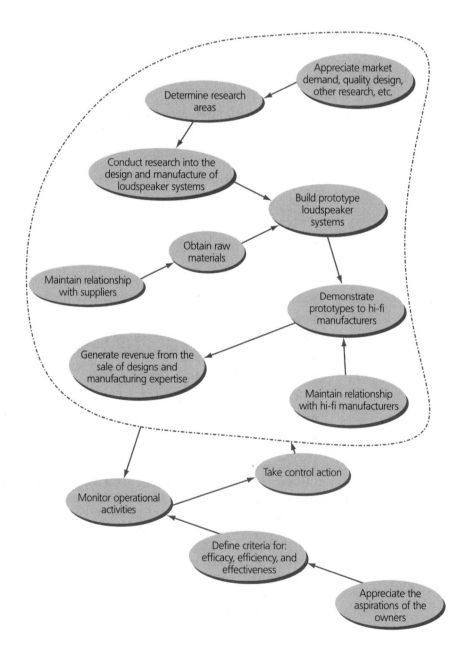

Although we cannot guarantee the validity of our model by this means we 'can at least ensure that it is not so sloppily constructed as to be useless'[2] (Checkland 1981, p.176).

If the Conceptual Model does not provide enough detail for our purposes, one or more of the (operational) activities can be 'expanded' into a subsystem (conceptual) model, as we will see later in Chapter 11.

Forty (innovation) Principles/contradiction matrix – TRIZ (hard?/creative)

Introduction to TRIZ Ideation

As **TRIZ** has evolved over the years, various innovation 'tools' have been derived from the vast knowledge base of patent information first researched and developed by Altshuller and subsequently expanded by others. Amongst these are the 40 Principles/contradiction matrix, the (Scientific) Effects, the Standard Solutions, the Separation Principles and the Lines/Patterns of Evolution (of technical Systems). This has caused a number of problems (Zlotin and Zusman, 1992). Apart from there being some overlap between some of these tools anyway (the **40 Principles** started out as a mixture of what became the later tool types), when the Standard Solutions 'replaced' the 40 Principles, it precluded the possibility of looking for solutions earlier on in the process (once the technical contradiction was known), and the Standard Solutions did not contain some useful recommendations that the 40 Principles did. Zoltin and Zusman, amongst others, have been trying to rationalize this situation with just one set of 'operators', containing all the important content from the previous tools, appropriately categorized.

Also, the **Ideation** stage of TRIZ is not as clear cut as with other problem-solving processes, because the present wisdom now seems to be that as we proceed through the problem analysis there may be opportunities to resolve a different/simpler (but perhaps less ideal) problem, without the need to address any particular technical contradiction (though we probably will eventually want to solve the mini-problem (see page 105).

It is impossible in a few pages to adequately explain/demonstrate all of the current tools, so we will restrict ourselves to one, probably the simplest to apply: the still-useful 40 Principles, and give a hint of another, but first . . .

Early on in the evolution of TRIZ (ARIZ 61) a set of ideas similar to Osborn's checklist (see pages 138–40) were offered as possibilities for resolving a technical problem. These ideas explored the possibility of:

- making changes (to the shape, material, temperature, pressure, speed, colour, relative positions of parts, working conditions of the parts with the purpose of maximizing their workload) in the object (the given machine, device and/or technological process);
- dividing an object into independent parts (so as to isolate 'weak' and 'necessary/adequate' parts, or separate it into identical parts);
- changing neighbouring (interacting) objects or altering the (outside) environment of the object (by changing its parameters, replacing it,

separating it into several mediums, utilizing its characteristics to perform useful functions)

(Altshuller, 1999, p.105)

Although these have now been subsumed into other tools, a quick look through them may still give us some ideas.

The 40 (innovation) Principles and contradiction matrix

The 40 (innovation) Principles can be found in Frame 7.2. The way we use them is as follows. Once we have identified our technical contradiction, we look along the row of the contradiction matrix (see Appendix 6) corresponding to the characteristic that must be improved until we get to the column of the contradiction matrix corresponding to the characteristic which becomes unacceptable, if a known means is used to try and resolve our problem. In the box where row and column meet will be the innovation principles we should consider.

A well-known technical problem with vehicles is that if you want them to go faster, you normally need a bigger engine; however, the weight of the bigger engine is likely to slow you down! Looking along row 9 (speed) of the contradiction matrix (Appendix 6) until we get to column 1 (weight of a mobile object), we are offered principles 2, 13, 28 and 38. Some of these do not seem immediately useful, but principle 28 (replacement of mechanical system) is suggesting that we look for a different type of engine (motive power) that has a better power-to-weight ratio which could be a possibility.

Frame 7.2 *The 40 (innovation) Principles*

1. Segmentation

a. Divide an object into independent parts.

b. Make an object sectional (for easy assembly or disassembly).

c. Increase the degree of an object's segmentation.

2. Extraction (Extracting, Retrieving, Removing)

a. Extract the 'disturbing' part or property from an object.

b. Extract only the necessary part or property from an object.

3. Local Quality

a. Transition from homogeneous to heterogeneous structure of an object or outside environment (action).

b. Different parts of an object should carry out different functions.

▶

c. Each part of an object should be placed under conditions that are most favourable for its operation.

4. Asymmetry

a. Replace symmetrical form(s) with asymmetrical form(s).

b. If an object is already asymmetrical, increase its degree of asymmetry.

5. Consolidation

a. Consolidate in space homogeneous objects, or objects destined for contiguous operations.

b. Consolidate in time homogeneous or contiguous operations.

6. Universality

a. An object can perform several different functions; therefore, other elements can be removed.

7. Nesting (Matrioshka)

a. One object is placed inside another. That object is placed inside a third one. And so on . . .

b. An object passes through a cavity in another object.

8. Counterweight

a. Compensate for the weight of an object by combining it with another object that provides a lifting force.

b. Compensate for the weight of an object with aerodynamic or hydrodynamic forces influenced by the outside environment.

9. Prior Counteraction

a. Preload countertension to an object to compensate excessive and undesirable stress.

10. Prior Action

a. Perform required changes to an object completely or partially in advance.

b. Place objects in advance so that they can go into action immediately from the most convenient location.

11. Cushion in Advance

a. Compensate for the relatively low reliability of an object with emergency measures prepared in advance.

12. Equipotentiality

a.   Change the condition of the work in such a way that it will not require lifting or lowering an object.

13. Do It in Reverse

a.   Instead of the direct action dictated by a problem, implement an opposite action (i.e., cooling instead of heating).

b.   Make the movable part of an object, or outside environment, stationary and stationary part moveable.

c.   Turn an object upside-down.

14. Spheroidality

a.   Replace linear parts with curved parts, flat surfaces with spherical surfaces, and cube shapes with ball shapes.

b.   Use rollers, balls, spirals.

c.   Replace linear motion with rotational motion; utilize centrifugal force.

15. Dynamicity

a.   Characteristics of an object or outside environment, must be altered to provide optimal performance at each stage of an operation.

b.   If an object is immobile, make it mobile. Make it interchangeable.

c.   Divide an object into elements capable of changing their position relative to each other.

16. Partial or Excessive Action

a.   If it is difficult to obtain 100 per cent of a desired effect, achieve more or less of the desired effect.

17. Transition Into a New Dimension

a.   Transition one-dimensional movement, or placement, of objects into two-dimensional; two-dimensional to three-dimensional, etc.

b.   Utilize multi-level composition of objects.

c.   Incline an object, or place it on its side.

d.   Utilize the opposite side of a given surface.

e.   Project optical lines onto neighbouring areas, or onto the reverse side, of an object.

18. Mechanical Vibration

a.   Utilize oscillation.

b.   If oscillation exists, increase its frequency to ultrasonic.

c.   Use the frequency of resonance.

d.   Replace mechanical vibrations with piezo-vibrations.

e.   Use ultrasonic vibrations in conjunction with an electromagnetic field.

19. Periodic Action

a.   Replace a continuous action with a periodic one (impulse).

b.   If the action is already periodic, change its frequency.

c.   Use pauses between impulses to provide additional action.

20. Continuity of Useful Action

a.   Carry out an action without a break. All parts of the object should constantly operate at full capacity.

b.   Remove idle and intermediate motion.

c.   Replace 'back-and-forth' motion with a rotating one.

21. Rushing Through

a.   Perform harmful and hazardous operations at a very high speed.

22. Convert Harm Into Benefit

a.   Utilize harmful factors – especially environmental – to obtain a positive effect.

b.   Remove one harmful factor by combining it with another harmful factor.

c.   Increase the degree of harmful action to such an extent that it ceases to be harmful.

23. Feedback

a.   Introduce feedback.

b.   If feedback already exists, change it.

24. Mediator

a.   Use an intermediary object to transfer or carry out an action.

b.   Temporarily connect the original object to one that is easily removed.

25. Self-service

a.   An object must service itself and carry-out supplementary and repair operations.

b.   Make use of waste material and energy.

26. Copying

a. A simplified and inexpensive copy should be used in place of a fragile original or an object that is inconvenient to operate.

b. If a visible optical copy is used, replace it with an infrared or ultraviolet copies.

c. Replace an object (or system of objects) with their optical image. The image can then be reduced or enlarged.

27. Dispose

a. Replace an expensive object with a cheap one, compromising other properties (i.e., longevity).

28. Replacement of Mechanical System

a. Replace a mechanical system with an optical, acoustical, thermal or olfactory system.

b. Use an electric, magnetic or electromagnetic field to interact with an object.

c. Replace fields that are:
    1. Stationary with mobile ones.
    2. Fixed with ones changing in time.
    3. Random with structured ones.

d. Use fields in conjunction with ferromagnetic particles.

29. Pneumatic or Hydraulic Constructions

a. Replace solid parts of an object with a gas or liquid. These parts can now use air or water for inflation, or use pneumatic or hydrostatic cushions.

30. Flexible Membranes or Thin Films

a. Replace customary constructions with flexible membranes or thin film.

b. Isolate an object from its outside environment with flexible membranes or thin films.

31. Porous Material

a. Make an object porous, or use supplementary porous elements (inserts, covers, etc.).

b. If an object is already porous, fill pores in advance with some substance.

32. Changing the Color

a. Change the color of an object or its environment.

b.   Change the degree of translucency of an object or its environment.

c.   Use colour additives to observe an object or process which is difficult to see.

d.   If such additives are already used, employ luminescent traces or trace atoms.

33. Homogeneity

a.   Objects interacting with the main object should be made out of the same material (or material with similar properties) as the main object.

34. Rejecting and Regenerating Parts

a.   After completing its function, or becoming useless, an element of an object is rejected (discarded, dissolved, evaporated, etc.) or modified during its work process.

b.   Used-up parts of an object should be restored during its work.

35. Transformation of Properties

a.   Change the physical state of the system.

b.   Change the concentration or density.

c.   Change the degree of flexibility.

d.   Change the temperature or volume.

36. Phase Transition

a.   Using the phenomena of phase change (i.e., a change in volume, the liberation or absorption of heat, etc.).

37. Thermal Expansion

a.   Use expansion or contraction of material by changing its temperature.

b.   Use various materials with different coefficients of thermal expansion.

38. Accelerated Oxidation

a.   Make transition from one level of oxidation to the next higher level:

  1.   Ambient air to oxygenated.

  2.   Oxygenated to oxygen.

  3.   Oxygen to ionized oxygen.

  4.   Ionized oxygen to ozoned oxygen.

  5.   Ozoned oxygen to ozone.

  6.   Ozone to singlet oxygen.

39. Inert Environment

a. Replace a normal environment with an inert one.

b. Introduce a neutral substance or additives into an object.

c. Carry out the process in a vacuum.

40. Composite Materials

a. Replace homogeneous materials with composite ones.

This information was reprinted from The Innovation Algorithm, *ISBN 0–9640740–4–4 with permission. All rights reserved.*

Published by Technical Innovation Center, Inc., Worcester, MA, USA.

It should be remembered that the 40 Principles and the contradiction matrix were created out of a long-term study of patents (that was completed over 12 years ago), but new patents keep appearing; that is, life moves on. These tools will need to be updated regularly in order to maintain their usefulness. Darrell Mann and Simon Dewulf (2002) make the point that with software and electronic problems (in particular), the matrix may send users off 'in directions that are significantly different to those being used by the most successful inventors of the last 15 years'. However, they also mention current research (see www.creax.com, also have a look at www.ideationtriz.com) that is already underway to update these and other TRIZ tools.

Physical contradictions

If we are (mis)fortunate enough to have a problem involving a physical contradiction, we need to employ different tools for resolving it. A fairly straightforward approach is to consider separating the contradictory requirements in space or time, or changing the physical state of a substance (Shuylak, 1997).

Attribute Listing

Attribute Listing is a technique accredited to Robert P. Crawford and usually linked with **Value Analysis** (see page 140). Described below is a cut-down version of this technique that is particularly useful when applied before searching for alternative uses for existing products. Essentially this involves **Brainstorming** (see Chapter 3 and below) the assets, features or properties that the item has. The 'full' version of the technique continues by considering systematically how each of these attributes could be improved, but for our purposes the simple listing of these attributes should (if 'alternative uses' rather than 'improving the product' is our problem) make finding alternative uses easier. Let's assume that as a prelude to resolving Dispensable Plastics' problem (see Frame 7.3 and page 135) we need to do some Attribute Listing.

> **Frame 7.3** *Dispensable Plastics Ltd: the problem situation*
>
> We have been asked to participate in a Brainstorming session for Dispensable Plastics Ltd, one of the major manufacturers of plastic cups for automatic drink-dispensing machines. This company is concerned that they have virtually only this one market for their products, apart from a small proportion of retail sales which they make through chain stores for private catering, for example, for children's parties. They would like to find a new outlet for their products, just in case anything should ever go wrong with the drink-dispenser business.

Some of the attributes of our plastic cup are given in Frame 7.4.

> **Frame 7.4** *Dispensable Plastics Ltd: attributes of a plastic cup*
>
> | | |
> |---|---|
> | Round | Cylindrical |
> | Brittle | Can be cut |
> | Cheap | Hole at one end |
> | Washable | Holds hot liquids |
> | White/coloured/patterned | Stackable |
> | Indentations on bottom | Reinforcing ring/lip at top |
> | Some have insulating properties | |

Having listed as many features of the humble plastic cup as we can, we would now move on to have our main Brainstorming session to find some alternative uses (see below).

(Traditional/classical) Brainstorming (creative)

Introduction

Brainstorming was originally conceived as a 'complete' problem-solving process (see Appendix 3) by Alex Osborn, a marketing executive, in the 1950s, and was intended to provide the means for dealing with several stages of the problem-solving 'model' presented in Chapter 3. This process has now been superseded by what is known as the Osborn-Parnes CPS process (see pages 33, 35 and Appendix 6). Here we will describe Brainstorming simply as a CPS technique for generating ideas.

Brainstorming is essentially a group problem-solving process because it relies on the interactions between the ideas and imaginations of group members for its success and productivity. This does not mean that when faced with solving a problem alone we should not utilize Brainstorming, but, because we only have our own mind from which to draw inspiration, we will probably need some assistance from additional techniques such as a checklist like the one given in

Frame 7.7, and Forced Relationships (see page 137). Even in group problem-solving situations advantages can be gained by breaking off from the normal proceedings and individually writing down some brainstormed ideas (in what are called 'trigger' sessions) and/or using these additional techniques.

Presented (again) below (in Frame 7.5) are the rules of Brainstorming; however, the reader is advised to read about the philosophy of Brainstorming in Chapter 3 (if s/he has not already) before continuing.

Frame 7.5 *Rules of Brainstorming*

- No criticism is allowed – evaluation of ideas must be withheld until later.
- 'Free-wheeling' is encouraged – the wilder the idea, the better.
- Quantity is wanted – the greater the number of ideas, the more likely is the chance of having useful, interesting or appealing ones.
- Seek combination and improvement – try to 'build' on other people's ideas.

When to use Brainstorming

'Straight' Brainstorming is probably best used on problem situations where the merit of the ideas or possible solutions once acquired is fairly self-evident and/or they do not require much further development before they become feasible; for example, finding a name for a new product.

An application of Brainstorming: new markets for an existing product

Another common use of Brainstorming is the search for new ways of using an existing product. This search is usually instigated by a perceived need to find alternative markets for the product, thus permitting diversification without too many operational changes. Some reasons why a company might want to do this are:

- Someone has asked the question: 'Are there any opportunities being missed?'
- The demand for the product is beginning to tail off, because it is coming to the end of its natural life cycle and its manufacturers may be trying to 'stall' the coming demise of their product whilst they build up other aspects of their business to compensate.
- A catastrophic change in the market has occurred.
- The longevity of the product's life has surpassed all reasonable expectations and, although the product is still selling well, this must come to an end soon and the company wishes to investigate contingency plans for what else they can do with their product.

A 'favourite' product for demonstrating this application of Brainstorming is the common red house brick. However, for the purposes of illustrating the process here I will relegate the red brick to a reader's exercise and have chosen another well-known item to investigate instead, the plastic cup. We will assume that we have already had our warm-up session (see page 66), and are ready to Brainstorm some new uses for this product.

Following on from the Attribute Listing we did for Dispensable Plastics above (see Frames 7.3 and 7.4), the problem we are going to Brainstorm is 'What other things can we use a plastic cup for apart from serving hot and cold drinks?'

Frame 7.6 gives some typical responses that we might expect from our Brainstorming session.

Frame 7.6 *Dispensable Plastics Ltd: uses of a plastic cup*

Flower pot
Strawberry protector
Disposable egg cup
Emergency toilet
Inkwell/eye wash/birdbath
Paint pot/mixing jar
Dice shaker
Waste bins (if bigger)
Decorations – bells, flowers (if cut)
Party crackers
Column: stacked, glued rim-to-rim and base-to-base
Fire lighter
Trumpet/megaphone
Decorative combs (if cut)
Party hats (with elastic)
Practice golf
Protective surround (cut in random shapes or whole)
Spacers
Pencil/Sellotape/string/wool holder
Warning device (breaks with a 'crack')
Children's toy sand-buggy wheels
Telescope/microscope/pin-hole camera (with lenses)
Lamp reflector/shade
Pastry cutters
Bottle labels (cut to slip over neck)
Temporary lens hood for camera
Paper-weight (with heavy filling)

The 'slump' and the 'wildest idea'

Eventually in all Brainstorming sessions the number of ideas emerging from the group starts to tail off. This 'slump' is particularly noticeable after the initial ideas are exhausted, if there has been little or no 'building'. Adams (1979) stresses the importance of 'pushing' ourselves through this period, since it is usually in these later stages that the best ideas appear; failure to do this means that the session 'will not live up to its potential'. One technique for rejuvenating a session, particularly if it is languishing due to a lack of speculative ideas, is a wildest idea competition (see below) whereby the group is asked to suggest the most fanciful ways they can think of for resolving the problem. As a leader of such a group, we could also use this technique if no one was trying to build on the more speculative ideas – we would use any speculative idea as the starting point for some Wishful Thinking.

Concluding thoughts on Brainstorming

Checklists (like the one described in Frame 7.7) can make an invaluable contribution to the 'straight' Brainstorming session we have just had with this sort of problem. When leading a group we could use this list prior to the session to produce a number of 'directions' in which we plan to take the members. Checklists can also be used as a regenerative device when a group finds it difficult to 'get off the ground' or are in a rut (the 'slump') because they believe they are unable to come up with any more than fairly obvious and mundane uses.

Having Brainstormed a list of ideas concerning alternative uses for plastic cups, we will probably need to run it through some sort of selection procedure. First of all though, we eliminate the 'non-starters', such as emergency toilets, then possibly hold an additional Idea Development session to generate some builds on the ideas we have. After this we will want to evaluate the most promising possibilities: techniques for doing this can be found in Chapter 8.

Brainwriting

Introduction

Group **Brainwriting**, in its many forms, is essentially the same as Brainstorming in so much as the group participants generate ideas without evaluation, but instead of voicing them and the leader writing them up on flipcharts, the ideas are written down on bits of paper or cards.

Many forms of Brainwriting have been described (Van Gundy, 1988). Some are interactive, some are not. A non-interactive variant (for example, Crawford Slip Writing) apparently (Van Gundy, 1988, p.149) allows a large number of ideas to be collected, quickly, from as large a group of people as you like, using a relatively untrained facilitator/leader, without worrying about the physical layout of the meeting room or the potential conflict that can occur with interactive sessions. If this is what you need to do, then fair enough; but in my opinion, the value obtained from interaction usually outweighs the difficulties of acquiring a trained facilitator (to handle things), setting up an appropriate physical environment, working in smaller groups, etc.

Interactive Brainwriting

The various forms of interactive Brainwriting differ only in the method of interaction. After the problem has been introduced/explained, one or more ideas are written down by each individual participant on their own bits of paper/cards.

These are then:

- passed on to the next person in the round (**Pin Cards**),
- passed on to a specific person,
- dropped into a central pool (**Brainwriting pool**), or
- pinned up on boards, to be accessed by the other participants (**Gallery Method**).

This is so that people can look at the ideas and build on them or use them to inspire other ideas, etc., which are usually written down on the same paper/cards but can be on new ones. This exchange of ideas can happen as many times as you wish.

The 'pool' method offers a certain amount of anonymity to the idea's originator and so should give the advantages of interaction with little risk of conflict or (critical) comments (about the merit of ideas) that could destroy the delicate creative climate we have so carefully tried to set up and maintain.

Forced Relationships (creative)

Aka Catalogue (simple Forced Relationships)

The concept of **Forced Relationships** is attributed to Charles S. Whiting and is described as ways in which we can induce original ideas from two normally unrelated ideas by 'forcing' ourselves to think of some connection between them. One variation on this theme is picking words (usually only nouns and verbs) at random from a dictionary to help with the development of an idea.

For instance, supposing we were looking for new ideas for a table lamp, the word from the dictionary might be 'fluke': a flounder, the barb on an anchor, an accidental success. Forcing a connection would lead us to think of such ideas as:

- A lamp with a large flat base (perhaps the whole 'work surface'), that will not fall over.
- A lamp with a 'flatter' reflector, that provides a greater area of illumination.
- A lamp with a hook, magnet or suction pad, that could be attached in any convenient position.
- A lamp that switches itself on (or off) in response to 'accidental' movement.

There is nothing particularly revolutionary about these ideas, but 'fluke' was only the *first* word I picked from the dictionary.

Next time you are having difficulties thinking up ideas, try deliberately forcing some connections, but do not even think about evaluating them at this time. Only when you have lots of ideas (useful, interesting, speculative, whatever), is it time to think about their merits – and even then it may be too soon (see Chapter 3).

Checklists (creative)

Another useful technique to stimulate new ideas is the use of **checklists**. These contain many questions designed to stimulate the imagination by acting as prompts to look at the problem situation from different aspects.

Suppose our problem is: engine oil for cars is often sold in five-litre tins. When these tins are full, it is notoriously difficult to top up the oil level in an engine without pouring oil all over it. How can we improve this 'delivery system'?

Osborn (1957) discusses at length the questions we can ask ourselves to encourage our imagination. The checklist shown in Frame 7.7, is intended to be useful for many problem situations, but should be particularly useful for our current problem. Situations where this type of checklist has been found to be particularly useful are finding applications for new synthetic materials, e.g. neoprene, cellophane, nylon, glass fibre; deciding what to do with waste products, scrap, etc.; and a specific example, finding new functions for telephones – time, weather, travel information, text/picture messaging, answering service '1571', etc.

Frame 7.7 *Ideas checklist*

PUT TO OTHER USES

New ways to use it as it is?
Other uses if modified?

ADAPT

What else could be adapted?
What else is like this?
What can I make this look like?
What other ideas does this suggest?
Does the past offer a parallel?
What idea can I incorporate?
What other process could be adapted for this task?
What could I copy?
Whose style can I emulate?
How can we make this better and cheaper?

MODIFY

New angle?
Change meaning?
Change colour, motion, sound, odour, taste, form, shape?
Other changes?
What other 'packaging'?

MAGNIFY

What can I add?

▶

Extra feature, ingredient?
Stronger? Larger? Higher? Longer? Thicker? Extra value? More time?
Greater frequency?
Duplicate?
Multi-purpose?
Multiply? More in a package?
Exaggerate? Over-state?

MINIFY

What can I subtract?
Omit? Eliminate?
Smaller? Condensed? Miniature? Lower? Shorter? Lighter? Streamline?
Split up? Separate parts?
Under-state?

SUBSTITUTE

What can I substitute?
What other ingredients, materials, process, power can I use?
Another place and time?
Another approach?
Other senses, emotions, attitudes?
Who else instead (could do this better)?
What else instead (could do this better)?

REARRANGE

Interchange components?
Another pattern, combination?
Another layout, position?
Other sequences?
Change pace, timing? Slower? Faster? Earlier? Later?
Change schedule?
Transpose cause and effect?

REVERSE

Transpose positive and negative?
How about opposites?
Turn it back-to-front, upside-down, inside-out?
Reverse roles, e.g. with client, competitor?
Turn 'the tables', 'the other cheek'?

COMBINE

What materials, processes can I combine?
What could be merged with this?
How about a blend, an alloy, an assortment, an ensemble?

◀

Combine units (into a single entity)?
Multi-purpose?
Combine appeals?
Combine ideas?

(Compiled from Osborn, 1957, Chapters 21–4.)

With our oil problem, this checklist might have suggested that we add something to it (Magnify – What can I add?), such as the plastic tube with a lip at both ends commonly inserted into the screw cap fitting and pulled out to form a primitive spout on these tins. Another question from the checklist (Substitute – What other ingredients, materials?) might suggest that we make the 'tin' out of another material – some form of plastic in which we could mould a better spout. (I suspect, however, that the move to plastic containers may have been more the result of **Value Analysis**, see Frame 7.8.) Some of you may have already noticed the 'ultimate' solution. One oil company now sells oil in a 'highly modified' plastic container that comes with a proper spout and can subsequently be used as a petrol can (Magnify – Multi-purpose?).

Frame 7.8 *Value Analysis*

Value Analysis is a technique which examines the components that go to make up a particular item, and compares the cost of producing them to the value of the function that they perform. If the cost of producing a component is disproportionately high compared with its utility, better ways are looked for to provide its function.

Do not expect your ideas to emerge fully evolved and perfected. That idea you may have had about selling oil in polythene sachets, or large cardboard 'milk' cartons where, if you are careful, you can tear them so as to be able to refold the top of the carton into a spout, may not be as silly as it first seemed. You can get wine and tomato ketchup in bags, and all manner of milk products, fruit juices and sieved tomatoes in cardboard cartons at the moment. Do not be too critical too soon!

Analogies, metaphors and excursions (creative)

Introduction

William J.J. Gordon (1961, p.54) (co-founder of Synectics), suggests that the essence of creativity is the mental act of 'making the familiar strange', a 'conscious attempt to achieve a new look at the same old world, people, ideas, feelings, and things'. He describes how we might use techniques variously referred to as analogies or metaphors to facilitate the making of these unlikely connections.

Analogies are a 'correspondence or partial similarity' between two things, for example organizations and ant colonies (they both have life forms rushing around on their behalf, they have a hierarchy of 'members', they are interesting to observe from afar, they can both 'sting' you, etc.). Gordon identified (1961, pp.36–56) four types of analogy: personal, direct, symbolic and fantasy. **Metaphors** are 'the application of a name or descriptive term or phrase to an object or action to which it is imaginatively but not literally applicable' (*The Oxford Modern English Dictionary*, 1992), for example muscles of steel, heart of stone, 'the last comment s/he made really wound me up', etc.

These analogies (and metaphors) became incorporated by Synectics into a set of idea generation techniques called **excursions**, because they provide on demand the ability to take our mind away (or get some 'distance') from the problem, to 'free it up', thus enabling it to make connections. It is a well-known phenomenon that we can often 'waste' time staring for 'hours' at a blank piece of paper, trying unsuccessfully to get ideas, then after we have given up and started doing something else, even if it is just dozing (under the strain of our idea generating efforts), ideas come to us. Probably the most cited example is that of Archimedes who, whilst bathing, realized that his overflowing bath gave him the solution to the problem he had been tasked with, that is, determining if the emperor's crown was made of gold or not.

All excursions work in the same way:

- (try to) forget the problem,
- generate some irrelevant material,
- generate ideas by relating the irrelevant material back to problem.

What differs between excursions is the method used to generate the irrelevant material, and the method used determines how much distance we get away from the problem. Note also that the greater the distance we get from the problem the more likely we will need to first produce some **Absurd Solutions**, see below.

First we will look at some techniques that use analogies and metaphors directly to generate ideas and then, second, some excursions.

Personal analogy

With a personal analogy, we imagine what it must be like to 'be' the object of our interest or concern, and use this 'experience' to help resolve a problem. Suppose we were looking for ways of improving a 'propelling' pencil. In your role as a propelling pencil, you think: 'Every time my lead breaks somebody twists my extremities with both hands (painful!) and this interrupts my writing. It's not my fault. It's that idiot holding me who was pushing too hard! I was doing OK and deserve a pat on the head and not a punishment. Anyway, why don't they give me unbreakable lead or at least protect the normal stuff somehow: it doesn't break when it's inside me.' It may be that such a personal analogy was responsible for the 'new' breed of pencils that were introduced a decade or so ago that extrude more lead when pressed on top like a retractable ballpoint pen, and which have a protruding metal tube protecting the lead.

Direct analogy

With a direct analogy, we make a fairly straightforward comparison between the object or situation under consideration and something similar but from a totally different environment.

Return to the propelling pencil and the problems we used to have refilling them, having to take them apart to transfer lead from the store at the top of the pencil. An image that came immediately to mind was of some friends of mine hand-milking their goats. Could we use a squeezing and pulling motion (fed by gravity) to draw in a new lead for our pencil whilst the old one is being used up? Biology is a useful field to examine when looking for parallel situations such as this. One of my refillable pencils actually does have such a gravity-fed 'autofeed' mechanism that funnels a 'new' lead towards the tip of the pencil, where it is grabbed by a 'ring clamp' device. I noticed this after I had my goat idea and confess to being both pleased and disappointed to find someone had already perfected 'my' idea!

This example illustrates two very important points. First, it is totally immaterial that I do not really understand how a goat's mammary glands operate; my 'approximate knowledge' of the way a goat's teats are manipulated was sufficient to start me thinking about a possible solution to my problem.

Second, direct analogies work best when living entities are used as an analogy for an inanimate object, as in the example above. They also work well the other way round. Take for example the problem of dealing with redundant employees with whom there is nothing 'wrong' except that their services are no longer required. We might think of them as empty wine bottles. Rather than just throw these people on the scrap heap of life, we could ponder the merits of bottle banks. Because of current altruistic feelings about ecology and the conservation of resources, people are prepared to sort bottles by colour (clear, green, brown, etc.) and transport them to a bottle bank, thus reducing collection costs to glass manufacturers and making recycling more of an economic proposition. Could we identify transferable skills that our redundant employees might possess and classify them accordingly? Are they really redundant (it may be that they can be retrained more cheaply than training a new person from scratch)? If they are redundant, do they qualify for subsidized retraining schemes, which will increase the likelihood of their finding alternative employment?

Symbolic analogy

For this type of analogy we need to be able to sum up the essence of our problem situation in some symbolic and highly evocative way.

In the early days of Synectics, **Book Titles** were often used for this purpose. Prince (1970, pp.95–6) suggests that first we should try to write down the indispensable characteristics of the object, action or idea that we are investigating, providing us with a list of words. Then we ask what is paradoxical or contrary about one or more of these words in connection with this object, action or idea. We then try to form from these thoughts, word pairs (the so-called Book Titles) that are 'aesthetically pleasing, surprising, even poetic'. Examples of the sort of thing Prince means are:

- a familiar surprise
- a disciplined freedom
- a dependable intermittency
- an ephemeral solidity.

If we return to the redundancy problem discussed above, the essential characteristic of these employees is that they are:

> redundant – excessive, inessential, obsolescent, old-fashioned, superfluous, surplus, unnecessary, unwanted, useless

Now think of words connected with these employees that are contradictory to any of these. Although these employees are redundant, they still possess certain skills and experience; they are not without some 'potential' or utility

> skill – ability, accomplishment, aptitude, competence, experience, expertise, facility, ingenuity, practicality.
> potential – capability, capacity, possibility, promise, utility, value, future, hidden, latent, unrealized.

After this we combine these words into pairs (the Book Titles), for example:

- a redundant potential
- a surplus value
- an old-fashioned future
- a superfluous utility
- a latent obsolescence
- a promising uselessness.

Having generated a few Book Titles, one or more of these word pairs would be used as the 'quality' required in what is called an **example excursion** (see below and Chapter 10).

The Book Title concept was eventually dropped (wrongly I believe) in favour of a type of symbolic analogy which is not easy to describe or to generate. William Gordon (1961, pp.45–8) cites one example of its use, namely, that of using the 'Indian rope trick' as an analogy for a car wheel jack, but would we have thought of doing that? The criterion for selecting this type of symbolic analogy is that it should 'use objective and impersonal images'.

We are bombarded continuously with visual (and often intentionally symbolic) images in the form of films, television and advertisements. These images can be extremely productive when it comes to generating ideas. Extract a character or situation from a film you have seen as a symbolic analogy, and use this to suggest ideas about the problem. One word of warning, however: do not take a character or situation that too closely parallels the object of your current problem solving.

To demonstrate how we might use this idea, let us consider the problem situation described in Frame 7.9. I found it impossible not to compare Harry Pearson with the two main characters in *M.A.S.H.* The film and TV series focus on two doctors working in a US Mobile Army Surgical Hospital during the Korean War. They are portrayed as having a total disregard for the authority and morality of their (often incompetent) senior officers. They also deliberately flaunt their disrespect for unjustifiable regulations, and are able (or perhaps 'allowed') to get away with not wearing regulation uniforms, having a still in their quarters and a blatant indifference to rank. They get away with this because they are good surgeons, desperately needed by the war effort. I asked, 'Why are the two main characters in *M.A.S.H.* acting the way they are?' and then tried to transpose the answers I obtained into the VideoSonic problem situation. The results of this are given in Frame 7.10; the 'transposed' answers are shown in parentheses.

Frame 7.9 *VideoSonic Electronic Systems: the problem situation*

The management of VideoSonic are concerned about the attitude and behaviour of one of their service engineers, Harry Pearson. Harry is a highly experienced service engineer and has been with the company many years without a blemish on his work record. Six months ago, he was 'reassigned' from his usual work because his expertise was desperately needed to sort out the many problems that were occurring with a new product range of televisions.

In recent months, despite many warnings, Harry has been repeatedly breaking company 'rules' by 'extending' guarantees, supplying replacement parts at cost, replacing faulty equipment with new and often different models of television when he 'should' have repaired the fault, and by advising customers to purchase TVs produced by VideoSonic's competitors. Harry has always maintained a good rapport with those of VideoSonics's customers with whom he has dealt, and recently there has been a barrage of complimentary letters to the company about the promptness, courtesy and professionalism with which he has done his job. There has even been a letter from a satisfied customer mentioning him by name published in a national magazine.

Why is Harry recklessly going against company policy? What can be done about him?

If familiar with *M.A.S.H.*, your likely perception of its central theme will be similar to one or more of the viewpoints listed in Frame 7.10, but probably not all of them. I have tried to put my feelings to one side and to consider what *could* be an objective explanation of such behaviour. I am attempting to use this highly visual recollection to provide a number of initial ideas about what the problem could be and what should serve as the basis of discussions with Harry about the true causes of his present attitude and behaviour. Rather than having no idea as to what Harry is about, we now at least have some possibilities, and by asking pertinent questions we can determine whether we are on the right track, and if so, discuss with Harry what would constitute a mutually acceptable solution.

Frame 7.10 *VideoSonic Electronic Systems: symbolic analogy – transposition from the characters in* M.A.S.H. *to Harry Parsons*

Why are they the way they are? Because of

- an overriding altruistic interest in the welfare of . . . their patients (his customers) . . . who have been . . . conscripted (conned) . . . into a pointless, and not of their own choosing, war (buying a worthless product);

- a reaction to . . . the horror of their environment (the totally alien philosophy of the new management), . . . and the incredible wastage of . . . human life, something they value highly (his time, expertise and resources, not to mention the destruction of the quality image that the company's products used to have);

- a rebellious attitude against being . . . forced to do something they dislike, don't believe in, cannot see the point of (reassigned to service a new, cheaper, lower quality/prestige product range);

- a psychological need to . . . let off steam by behaving irresponsibly whenever the pressure is off (to avert the many 'unpleasantnesses' that *he* is now receiving from dissatisfied customers), . . . in order to preserve . . . their sanity (his self-esteem);

- a hope that such actions might lead to . . . a dishonourable discharge and being sent home (him being returned to the job that he was happy doing).

Career excursion

The first of many excursions we will look at is the **career excursion**, which is placed here rather than, like the other ones, in its own subsection because George Prince (co-founder of Synectics) did not accept this as a 'true' excursion, and because it follows on quite nicely from what we have just been saying.

There are at least two ways of performing a career excursion, building on either personal or symbolic analogies. First of all, when faced with a problem situation or problematic object, we could imagine ourselves in roles (careers) totally different from our own, and then ask questions such as:

If I were a sports personality, astronaut, school teacher, judge, monk, fireman, trucker, exotic dancer, pirate, etc. . . .

What would I think of this situation?

What would I (want to) do with this object?

How would I want things to be different?

Clipboards were once used mainly by 'time and motion' experts, inspectors and the like, but are now available cheaply in a number of different colours and styles, and are often given away free with other things, for example, promotional offers, training courses, etc. Let us suppose that we have been asked for ideas to 'add value' to this commodity. How can we add that 'extra something' to the basic design in order to encourage people to buy another before their existing one wears out? We will assume that our starting point is a rigid moulded plastic clipboard.

Our sports personality might say

> Well, what I need is a clipboard with a stop-watch built in, I know you can get pens, rulers and, as far as I know, possibly clipboards with simple digital watches in them, but that's not much good to me. A full-function stop-watch is another matter altogether. At the moment I have to fix my stopwatch to my clipboard with elastic bands. I often take groups of kids orienteering at the weekends, and we have a similar problem, only this time we could do with a built-in compass.

Our school teacher complains:

> We lend our pupils clipboards when we take them out on educational visits, so they can record their answers to questions we ask them. The trouble is, too many of them get 'lost'. We can't afford to keep replacing them. I've thought that indelibly marking them with the school's name and address might alleviate this. I've also thought of advertising the local fish and chip shop, record shop or something on the clipboard, to try to gain sponsorship from local retailers.

Both examples illustrate how putting yourself in another role can produce useful ideas, but does depend to some extent on knowing a little about the role adopted.

The 'normal' way of applying a career excursion is to ask what do we think of when someone mentions, say, an astronaut. It does not matter whether we actually know anything about what it is like to be an astronaut, something should come to mind; for example, funny looking suit, floating in space, a back pack with jets in it, the blackness of space, etc. When we have got a list of thoughts like these, we look through them, pick one that attracts our attention and just let our minds wander from there until we can think of an idea that will help us with our problem, repeating this as often as we need to. Going back to our clipboard problem, how about one with a belt strap on it for 'hands-free' carrying (this came from 'floating in space') or so we do not lose it, or one with a light on it for use at night (from 'blackness of space').

A variation on this type of career excursion is to use well-known characters (real or fictional); for example, Florence Nightingale, Winston Churchill, James T. Kirk or Jane Eyre. The only proviso is that your roles or characters should be ones that are seen by you (or others if working in a group) as 'larger than life'.

Fantasy analogy

This type of analogy takes a number of different forms. A less fantastic form involves mentally disobeying or ignoring scientific, organizational or cultural laws or rules to see the benefits of not being restricted by them. If this helps us to find some quality or thing in this fantasy world that we like or we think would resolve our problem, then we try to find ways of achieving this within the laws we have temporarily dismissed. In a similar way we can mentally realize our wishes pertaining to the problem – do some **Wishful Thinking** (see below) or 'wish fulfilment'. We then analyse what it is about these wishes that appeals to us, and try to incorporate this into a more practical solution. These forms are useful to the lone problem solver.

There are other forms of fantasy analogy such as the use of mental imagery (see below and Chapter 10), or the telling of fantastic stories, which work best with a group because they rely on the interaction of people's imaginations to add to the storyline and/or send it in unexpected directions.

Metaphors

Metaphors can be very evocative, 'visual' ways of describing things and can be used for idea generation; they are also important from the point of view of understanding/empathizing with others (see Chapter 14).

To use metaphors to get ideas could be done in a variety of ways, but typically we would take the essence of the problem statement (as a word or two), find some metaphors involving that word, list the thoughts or describe the images that the metaphor brings to mind, and then use these to get ideas for resolving the problem. It is not always easy to find/remember suitable metaphors, but computer software like IdeaFisher (see pages 350–1) should help.

If we suppose that our problem was to do with something hardening (paint, glue, etc.) we could look for metaphors involving the word 'hard'; for example, hard as nails, hard and fast, hard-core, hard-nosed, a hard nut to crack, hard-on, hard-pressed, etc. and see what thoughts and images these conjure up. The metaphor 'a hard nut to crack' may suggest squeezing or otherwise applying pressure to facilitate/speed up the hardening process, whereas 'hard-core' might suggest 'exciting' the molecules in the substance with microwaves.

Example excursion – Synectics (creative)

The *example excursion* takes us only a moderate distance away from the problem because it takes a little bit of the problem with it. It works by taking the 'essence' of the chosen **Springboard** (see pages 110, 289) or problem statement and requiring us to look for examples of this in 'other worlds' (analogies). A list of 'worlds' that are often used is given in Frame 7.11. This is probably why less adventurous problem solvers find the example excursion more acceptable (less 'illogical') than some of the more 'way out', 'off the wall' excursions such as the imaging excursion (see below and Chapter 10). For example, the essence of the problem 'How to prevent vandalism of public telephones' might be to make them more indestructible somehow. The 'irrelevant' material generated in an example excursion is one or more lists (depending on how many 'worlds' we use) of examples, in this case of 'indestructibility'. Some of these examples (the ones that appeal to us) are then chosen and related back to the problem.

Frame 7.11 *'Worlds' for example excursions*

Organic		Inorganic
biology	archaeology	physics
anthropology	medicine	palaeontology
sport	science fiction	crafts
fashion	computing	chemistry
music and dance	models	mathematics
warfare	agriculture	electronics
history	space travel	astronomy &
mythology	acoustics	astrophysics
		engineering

This (edited) list of typical 'Worlds' has been reproduced here by kind permission of Synectics Ltd.

Going back to our redundancy problem, briefly explained again, we would try to think of examples of, say, 'superfluous utility' from the worlds of, say, warfare, biology and transportation. Amongst other examples, this might yield 'nuclear weapons', 'pairs of organs in the human species' and 'spare sets of wheels on lorries' respectively. Then we try to make connections between these ideas and our original problem, that of redundant employees. Here are just a few beginning ideas that these comparisons suggested to me:

- Nuclear weapons: the super-powers have far more nuclear weapons than they realistically need to win a war, let alone to act as a deterrent. However, it could be argued that this surfeit has been useful in preventing a war, because of the fear of nuclear Armageddon. It would now seem that the sheer number of these weapons, and the expense of maintaining them, has obliged these nations to bargain for arms reductions, and that this process could lead to the development of an atmosphere of cooperation, trust, perhaps even friendship, between these nations. From the first part of this idea, I wondered whether a company might keep on in some way certain employees that they don't need rather than lose them to a competitor. Can you relate the rest of it to the problems found in an overstaffed company?

- Pairs of organs in the human species: in nature we can find many examples of 'built-in' redundancy; many of our organs, for example, our lungs and kidneys, are duplicated though we do not actually need two of them. Here nature is providing a 'back-up' provision in case one of them should go wrong. The 'spare organs' idea made me wonder whether companies may feel that it was cost-effective to keep a 'spare crew' available on call in case of illness or other emergencies. Or, if this is not viable for an individual company, then that industry as a whole might consider organizing and financing a system of 'back-up' employees. A less ambitious alternative might be to set up a register of employee skills and experience (like the existing system for supply teachers) that could be made available to others who might have a need for these people.

- Spare sets of wheels on lorries: these days, with increasingly heavier loads being carried by road, we often see spare sets of wheels on the larger lorries which are used when the vehicle is heavily laden, but are jacked up off the road when the lorry is unladen. This idea suggested the notion that it may be cost-effective to keep some redundant employees on a retainer basis, in case we may need them again. Some income and a partial connection with the company may be seen by them as better than nothing.

Another example excursion is described in Chapter 12.

Imaging excursion (Synectics) (creative)

The imaging excursion is possibly the most unorthodox form of excursion and can be a potential disaster with a conservative-minded group, though it often works dramatically well when you least expect it. Because of its 'extraordinary' nature the imaging excursion is the form most likely to produce innovative ideas. It is one of the few Ideation techniques that can really only be used with a group; however, **creative visualization** below is an attempt to apply its principles to a lone problem solver. Essentially, imaging excursion involves the building of a 'communal' mental image, which will be the irrelevant material for our idea generation.

We need an evocative word to stimulate a mental image. In practice sessions I use a 'stock' word, one that has multiple meanings (and hence will evoke different images for different people); for example, 'junk' (a Chinese sailing boat, 'fast' food, rubbish – as in shops, scrap yards, children's bedrooms, etc.) or 'stake/steak' (but do not tell people how it is spelt!) (sizzling barbecues, vampires, casinos, etc.). In a problem-solving session, where a brief warm-up session is probably desirable/needed, a simple 'round robin' word association is often sufficient, and more fruitful because it often evokes more, differing, images. It also serves the secondary purpose of helping us to start 'getting away' from the problem. If we are using this excursion to generate ideas, rather than generate additional springboards (see page 247), it is usual to start with a word taken from the springboard the group is working on.

We only need carry on the word association for a couple of 'rounds', until things start to get a little silly and laughter breaks out – this usually means that the group members have pictured/recalled an amusing image.

The group is told they are about to describe a mental picture/story inspired by the last item in the word association and that the more colourful, outlandish, weird or exotic the story the better. They are given a minute to think about this image and then someone is asked to make a start. One person will lead off, and then every other group member adds to this story, one at a time. They can do this in order round the group or are invited to jump in whenever they like.

Everybody should try to add about a minute to the story, and then someone else takes over. Change-over points can be left to the storyteller, or be deliberately chosen by the leader at the most 'inconvenient' times.

It is usually best to keep the story in the same location if possible as this makes for richer mental imagery. If the storyline stagnates in descriptions of the minute details of one particular image we, as the group leader, could ask for description of what is going on in an adjacent location or deliberately ask someone to make something surprising happen. Conversely, if images are insufficiently developed because storytellers move on too quickly to other images we can 'pin' people to one scenario by asking for more detail.

As mentioned in Chapter 3, as people talk listeners naturally form mental images of what they think people are saying, and this happens during a mental imagery exercise. As the first person sets the scene for our story, we imagine our version of it and cannot help but go ahead of the storyline as we can think quicker than they can describe their mental image. When the storyteller changes, our image is often shattered because it is likely that the new storyteller's image is different from ours and so the story goes off in the wrong direction for us. This can be unnerving, as once a mental image has been shattered like this, we are left with 'nothing' until we build another one.

We may be anxious about doing this mental imaging in public and about our ability to contribute to the story. Psychologists tell us that this 'violent' changing of direction, and our having to build another mental image after the 'destruction' of the first, is precisely what makes the story rich in speculation and evocative images. This is not very reassuring if your mind has gone apparently blank, but don't panic. After the initial shock you will find enough of the old image left (because it was so vivid) to drag the story back your way if you want to and in a few seconds you will start to build a new and possibly better image, perhaps incorporating the best parts of your last one. If all this fails, pretend, and just carry on the story.

When every group member has had at least one chance to contribute to the story we stop the imaging and ask the group to spend a few minutes replaying the (whole) story in their minds (like a video), and whilst doing so to try to think up some really absurd or impractical solutions to the problem.

An example of an imaging excursion can be found in Chapter 10.

Creative visualization (creative)

Van Gundy (1988, p.98) says that there are a variety of approaches to using mental images to generate ideas, and offers the following as a typical approach to **creative visualization**, a technique which seems to be an individual but structured imaging excursion.

First, relax, then warm up by practising imaging (create/recall a mental image, any image and examine it in detail, and repeat this four or five times – write down ideas that come to you but do not consciously look for them). Then, using a partner or recorded script, 'visualize yourself doing a variety of activities in different settings' – examine everything encountered in detail – use more than one sense! 'At some point . . . you should discuss the problem with someone you visualize'. Finally, after 10/15 minutes visualizing, stop, and write down immediately any ideas you have for resolving your problem.

Line Drawing excursion – Synectics (creative)

In a **Line Drawing excursion** a problem-solving group are asked (as usual) to try and forget the problem, and to add a line one at a time to a communal drawing. The lines can be of any shape or colour. The only rule is that somewhere it must be connected to part of the existing drawing – this is to prevent multiple separate drawings being produced. For this we need a flipchart and some coloured pens. When the drawing is 'complete' the group are asked to say what they see in the drawing.

I often use this as a warm-up exercise at the beginning of a course or problem session as people are arriving. The completed drawing is then put on one side until we have the need to use it to generate some ideas to resolve a problem.

Picture excursion aka 'Visual Synectics' (creative)

Van Gundy (1988, pp.200–1) attributes the technique **picture excursion** to Geschka, Schaude and Schlicksupp (of the Battelle Institute, Frankfurt) Originally intended to suggest analogies in Synectics sessions, it can be used to generate ideas for solutions directly.

Essentially, when we need some (more) springboards or ideas, we look at a series of pictures (say ten) and, for each one, describe (and record) what we see. Then, after doing this with all the pictures, as above, we attempt to relate the descriptions to the problem situation.

Van Gundy (1988, pp.201–2, 209) suggests that pictures should not be likely to provoke negative emotions, be too abstract and/or difficult to understand . . . or very similar to the problem . . . the best pictures are probably those that either show or imply motion, without emphasizing human figures, and be of scenes with easily identified objects, such as street scenes, a boat on a river, etc. Citing a personal communication with Geschka, he also relays the suggested use of an initial set of pictures as a warm-up. These pictures are also unrelated to the problem, but should be abstract without as much detail (though typically, more appealing aesthetically) as the main pictures, and should be of general nature scenes, such as leaves on a tree or a beautiful sunset.

Before becoming aware of the work of Geschka *et al.* (1973), I considered 'creating' a Picture excursion, and had concluded that the best pictures were likely to belong to this second category! That is, 'abstract' nature scenes; for example, cloud formations, land/seascapes, etc. All I can suggest is that you select some pictures that you find appealing and evocative and try them out.

Sculptures (creative)

Sculptures is effectively a Line Drawing excursion type exercise in three dimensions. The problem-solving group are given an assortment of materials; for example, string, (drinking) straws, pipe-cleaners, blocks of wood, coloured paper/card, sticky tape, paperclips, modelling clay, glue, and asked to jointly build an abstract structure (adding pieces in turn) which could 'in some way represent some aspect of the problem', or alternatively could be totally unrelated to it (Van Gundy, 1988, pp.163–4).

Once completed the group are asked to list what they 'see' in the sculpture and to connect these descriptions with the problem situation to get some ideas regarding its resolution.

Storywriting (creative)

Storywriting involves composing a brief (say 1000-word) fictional story which, according to Van Gundy (1988, pp.122–5), should be about but not too directly related to the problem. I believe that there is no reason why the story should not be totally unconnected with the problem, and see storytelling as an alternative to an imaging excursion (essentially a group technique) for the lone problem solver. The story can be written as a means of 'getting away' from the problem.

That is not to say that we could not have group storywriting, members of the group adding to the story in turn. Though more story 'telling' than 'writing', there is a passage in Louisa M. Alcott's novel *Little Women* (1987, pp.206–12) that shows how this could be done, except that the characters in the novel are doing it for fun rather than to solve a problem.

Prince *et al.* (2000, p.49) also describe a form of storytelling used as a warm-up exercise:

> one person tells a few instances of a story out loud to the group and then abruptly puts a twist into the developing plot. She passes it to someone else who must paraphrase what she said from the point of the plot twist and then add a few lines. That person, then puts in a twist of his own in the story and then passes it to someone else.

This can cause anxiety in the same way as the imaging excursion (see above), when your mind 'blanks' because of the 'twist'; however, 'perseverance' with it improves our creativity.

Van Gundy (1988) goes on to suggest that you should 'allow your imagination to wander and write whatever seems appropriate. Don't be afraid to be a little playful and whimsical in your approach'. Having said that, evocative passages like the Alcott one, or those you have come across in other works of fiction, poetry, etc., could be used instead of writing your own, though it's not so much fun.

After you have written (or selected) your story, carefully read it and list the major principles, actions, characters, events, themes, expressions, objects, etc. that seem interesting. Then write down ideas for problem solutions suggested by these. The more unrelated (to the problem) and bizarre your story is, the more you will probably need to go first for **Absurd Solutions**, and then to turn those into more practical ones (see below).

Frames 7.12 and 7.13 contain the beginnings of two stories I made up for this purpose. I have tried to make them as silly as my imagination would allow, but have not put many twists in them. The first one needs extending considerably (so try), the second is almost long enough to be used as is, or you could combine them. See if you can use one of them (or both) to help resolve one of your problems.

Frame 7.12 *Storywriting example 1*

Picture a quiet rural setting, rolling hills, green fields, the autumn tints invading the trees, and a typically cloudless late-summer sky. It is mid-afternoon as we approach a rise. As we come over the brow of the hill, we notice a group of four people, two young couples picnicking in the valley laid out before us. They are sitting by a clear fast-running stream, in the shade of a weeping willow. A few hundred yards behind them is a picturesque group of farm buildings.

Suddenly the stillness of the afternoon is broken by a roaring sound apparently coming from one of these buildings. The doors of a barn slide open and a cloud of black smoke belches out. The picnic party turns around in unison to ascertain the source of the noise. As the black smoke begins to dissipate, they are alarmed to see a large green-and-yellow dragon bearing down upon them at great speed.

As the dragon is about to devour one of the couples, the female partner of the other couple, using a trick she had learnt from Crocodile Dundee, manages to persuade the dragon to desist, explaining that his potential dinner were much in love and wanting to get married. The dragon promptly puts on a 'dog collar', conducts a marriage service, eats all the remains of their picnic, burps loudly and thunders off into the sunset. Our newlyweds (shaken and more than a little bemused) and their friends catch a passing albatross and go back to the city. (258 words)

Frame 7.13 *Storywriting example 2*

Picture a young couple who have just returned to their city flat after having spent the evening celebrating their first wedding anniversary at a local restaurant. He had had prawn cocktail, T-bone steak and Black Forest gateau; she had tried something more adventurous. The first thing they do on entering the flat is to pour themselves a nightcap and then together, arm in arm, they walk out onto their balcony, high above the city traffic, to admire the silent beauty of the stars.

She is the first one to notice and points excitedly to a shooting star falling out of the Pleiades. They stand there transfixed as the shooting star traverses nearly a third of the night sky. Instead of burning up in the Earth's atmosphere, this speeding light comes to an abrupt halt, just hanging there a few degrees above the horizon, its clear white light changing first to a pulsing blood red and then to a searing steel blue. So fascinated are they by the light show that the couple does not notice initially that the light is moving rapidly towards them. The space ship eventually comes to rest over the Parliament building. A thin yellow beam of light streaks earthwards from the ship.

The thin yellow beam is a kind of short-distance probe. The aliens are using it to scan the minds of the people in the Parliament building. Unfortunately, they

▶

◀

had set its intensity too high and it 'burns out' all the minds into which it comes into contact. As it turns out, Parliament was in session the next day as normal but nobody notices that its members are mindless individuals!

Now the aliens, realizing the incredibly stupid mistake they have made, decide that they should look for a suitable number of other inhabitants of the planet, and make copies of their minds for later reinsertion into the heads of those they had relieved of their wits inadvertently.

Our happy and mesmerized couple on the balcony are the first people that the aliens encounter. All they feel is a warm yellow glow and then they awake inside this incredibly dirty, evil-smelling, steam-laden room. It seems that one of our members of Parliament had been dreaming about taking a Turkish bath when his mind was removed – the aliens assumed that the image found in this mind constituted a typical human habitat, and had replicated it in minute detail so as to make our adventurous couple feel at ease.

They are just beginning to take in their surroundings when once again they are totally dumbfounded by the sudden materialization of red double-decker bus in the middle of everything. A ticket collector wearing Bermuda shorts and carrying a deckchair gets off the bus and asks them where they want to go.

As the steam in the space ship's reception area cum temporary Turkish baths clears, the green-and-yellow dragon from the first story can be seen swinging from the chandelier!!! (492 words)

Have a quick look at the description of the problem situation at Wessex Telecom plc, described in Frame 8.1 (page 171) in the next chapter. Essentially this problem is about managing the IT support of two regional offices geographically separated from the head office in London. Here are just a few ideas I got from the second of my stories:

- Do something that makes them feel less like mindless individuals: trust them, give them more responsibilities, etc.
- Spend a week in the Manchester (or Exeter) office sitting in a deckchair watching them work.
- Give a free pair of Bermuda shorts to everyone who reports a request for support.

Although not particularly absurd, you may feel that some of my solutions are less than practical, useful, etc. . . . but for 'Bermuda shorts' read 'incentives'; 'sitting in a deckchair' read 'install monitoring equipment e.g. CCTV', etc.

Morphological Analysis (creative/hard?)

Introduction

Morphological Analysis (MA) is an extremely pretentious name for what can be a simple and effective way of making a systematic search for new (usually product-type) ideas. There are several morphology techniques described in the problem-solving literature, but they are all founded on the same basic theme; namely, the use of some form of n-dimensional grid to permit a systematic and logical search for ideas. First of all we will look at an example of MA in its original form (Zwicky, 1969).

When looking for an idea for a new product, we choose two or three independent attributes that the product must have, and represent these on the axes of a two- or three-dimensional grid or matrix, subdividing each of these into several independent ways in which the attribute can be accomplished. The result is a diagram consisting of cells or boxes, similar to those shown schematically in Figure 7.5. Each of the cells represents one of the many possible combinations of the subdivisions of each attribute.

There is no reason why we should be limited to three attributes, except that more than three aspects are virtually impossible to represent diagrammatically in this particular way and are almost as difficult to manage by any other means. This last point is also why the number of subdivisions is normally restricted to a small number, say, six.

Inventing a totally new way of doing something

Superficially, the process of MA seems similar to the full **Attribute Listing** technique mentioned above. Both start off by trying to list the main features or attributes of the item we are trying to invent. When using Attribute Listing to design, say, an 'improved hammer', we would note that it has a metal lump, with a flat face on one end, a rounded one on the other and a hole in the middle for

Figure 7.5

Grids showing the schematic way of representing the essential attributes of a possible new product

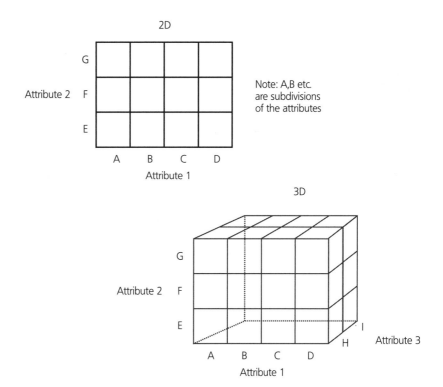

inserting a round wooden shaft, and that it is heavy; and then we would think of ways of modifying each attribute. For example, we might think of replacing the rounded face of the hammer head with a nail-removing claw or a cold chisel blade, or having a hollow metal shaft with a nail storage compartment in it.

If we are using MA to help us design a totally new way of 'inserting nails into wood', we need to think in far more general terms about the attributes we desire. We would not derive them from observing an example of the latest state-of-the-art hammer. Instead of the attributes suggested in the previous paragraph, our attributes would probably be something like some sort of driving force (to push the nail into the wood), a method of holding and/or positioning the device, a means of gripping nails. Our starting position, 'a new way of inserting nails in to wood', is necessarily more generic as well.

Once we have chosen the main attributes, we need to generate various ways in which these attributes can be provided. For instance, the driving force of the nail inserter could be compressed air, explosive force, mechanical leverage, elastic potential energy (for example, compressed springs and stretched strings), electromagnetic repulsion or angular momentum of a heavy weight (simply swinging it around your head as you do with an ordinary hammer). The holding and/or positioning device could be a free-standing structure, something that adheres to the surface (for example, suction pads), a (horizontal) surface-skimming mechanism (for example, rollers, air cushion), a handgrip appendage (for example, D-shaped handgrips on the side, or a pistol grip, or even a long round shaft). And the means of holding the nails could be fingers, a built-in 'spring' clamp mechanism or a groove/gun barrel attachment.

We now need to represent all this information on a three-dimensional grid (see Figure 7.6). Then we explore the cells, systematically looking for presently existing ways of inserting nails into wood and new ways of doing this which are worth pursuing.

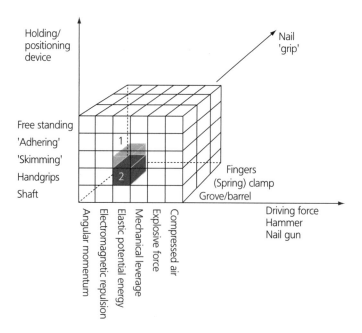

Figure 7.6 shows two existing products:

- the hammer (angular momentum, a long round shaft, fingers);
- the nail (staple) gun (elastic potential, a handgrip, groove/barrel).

As we look through the cells, we are bound to find some that we feel we cannot do much with, for instance, explosive force, a long round shaft and fingers! But do not give up on them too quickly. We should give every cell, or combination of attribute subdivisions, careful consideration, just in case there is a possibility there. If it is unusual, and we can make it work, we could be on to a winner. There should be many cells that offer new ideas for getting nails into wood, though some will be more practically and/or commercially feasible than others.

I wonder if anyone has thought of:

- a nail crossbow (elastic potential energy, a pistol handgrip, groove/barrel);
- a lever-operated nail-inserting tool (mechanical leverage, a D-shaped handgrip, groove/barrel) (similar to a device for getting wine corks into wine bottles);
- a nail-inserting tool based on the principle of the linear motor (electromagnetic repulsion, a pistol handgrip, groove/barrel);
- a 'shooting stick' nail gun (elastic potential energy, a long round shaft, groove/barrel): you push a nail into a spring-loaded shaft until a clamp with a quick release mechanism grabs the nail head; useful for getting into recessed places;
- a cross between a roller skate and a stapler (mechanical leverage, surface-skimming, spring clamp) which would be foot operated and would hold the nails in a magazine clip (as in a rifle) on the skate, and take the back/knee ache out of nailing floorboards;
- a miniature pile driver (explosive force, free standing, spring-release clamp): a small internal combustion engine drives a cam that raises and releases a weight that drives large nails into really hard wood.

MA is a powerful technique for generating ideas as long as we work at trying to do something with the combinations of features it suggests. With the nail-inserting problem there are theoretically 90 combinations in total. If we manage to get ideas from most of them, our productivity is comparable to what might be expected from a Brainstorming group session.

More on choosing attribute subdivisions

I encountered a number of problems with selecting the 'right' attribute subdivisions for this example, so below I have outlined my thought processes, as I feel this could be instructive.

In my initial attempt at resolving this problem, my holding and/or positioning device attribute (which in the first instance was just a holding device) had D-shaped handgrips and pistol handgrips as *two* different subdivisions (along with a long round shaft). I soon realized that it was going to be extremely difficult to think up ideas for a particular power source and nail holder in *both* of these (layers) that would represent substantially different tools! They would be basically the same apart from having different grips. Then I thought, perhaps either a holding device is not a very important attribute or the choice of subdivisions for that attribute have not been sufficiently thought through.

Realizing these subdivisions were not independent, I tried to be more inventive with them. Revising the 'holding device' attribute's subdivisions, I began thinking about the 'positioning' aspect of it because I saw simultaneously several possible ways of improving the present technology:

- some form of nail gun (on rollers) tracking along a metre ruler (possibly with an L-shaped cross-section for butting up to the edge of a piece of wood) that would facilitate the insertion of a number of nails at equal spacings;
- a (height-adjustable) free-standing nail gun that would make the nailing of vertical wood panels a little easier.

Then I started thinking of whether the concept of positioning should include the use of some sort of artificial sighting device for situations where the bulk of the tool prevented us from seeing the nail's point in order to line it up. We could even stretch this idea of a sighting device further and include a nail gun with a built-in metal detector – no more nails through pipes and cables! The idea of a gun made me wonder if you could fire a nail as you would a bullet and whether, using the principle of a rifled barrel, it could be used with screws as well.

Forcing myself back to my grid I eventually got to the 'pile driver' idea and realized I could do similar things with an electric motor. Should I have included electrical power? I managed to convince myself that this would probably be turned into some form of momentum, so I left my attributes as they are now.

Even so, the first idea above came from the same cell as the nail gun. This indicated to me that I may still have not thought carefully enough about my subdivisions. There would seem to be two 'energy source' categories here rather than one: perhaps I should have compressed springs and stretched strings/wires as two different ways of producing the driving force.

With MA, there are often many possibilities, so we need to think carefully about our choice of attributes and their subdivisions before we compile a grid and start searching through it for ideas!

So a good method for improving your ability to select attributes could be to take a problem, select some attributes, *fail* (unintentionally) to get much out of the subsequent analysis, and then force yourself to do it again, this time remembering to:

- express the problem and/or the attributes in (more) generic terms;
- use your imagination when choosing attributes – do not let yourself be constrained by images of existing products and services;
- ensure that your chosen attributes/subdivisions are independent – trying a few experimental grids should reveal if they are not.

Systematic search for unexploited opportunties

Instead of letting the axes of a grid represent two or three attributes of a product, they can represent two or three aspects of an organization's operations (an idea developed by John Carson, which he discussed on a training course at Manchester Business School in 1980). For example, a manufacturing company might analyse its operations against the three variables:

- manufacturing processes available;
- raw materials used;
- markets for its products.

This way of using an MA grid is illustrated by the manufacturing company WC Louis described in Frame 7.14.

Frame 7.14 *W.C. Louis Ltd: the problem situation*

WC Louis manufactures and sells bathroom furniture, using wood composites, clay, plastics, glass and some metals as raw materials. They have processing facilities for cutting, drilling and shaping metal, wood and glass; for applying decorative finishes (paint, colouring, engraving, electroplating, etc.) in or on most of the raw materials they use, and for the moulding of ceramic and plastic shapes including the production of glass-reinforced polyester (GRP, fibreglass)

At present they have only one market, 'bathrooms', although this could be split down into builders' merchants and retail DIY outlets. They are particularly interested in expanding their product range and diversifying into new market segments, but do not wish to invest a lot more of their funds in new manufacturing processes or stocks of new raw materials.

We have been asked to assist them in the task of thinking up some new ideas for products and markets.

With what we already know about WC Louis, the raw materials they currently have to hand and the manufacturing processes they are equipped for, the first thing to do is to help them think of possible market segments that appeal to them and which they might be able to move into, say, household products and leisure. Next, we should think about the processing capabilities WC Louis possesses. Often, just listing the different processes involved in the manufacture of the products (drilling, cutting, shaping, painting, colouring, engraving, electroplating, making ceramics, GRP moulding, etc.) and representing all of them as subdivisions along a process axis is not too helpful. This often produces no-go areas on our grid because some of these processes are specific to certain raw materials. For instance, one would not apply GRP moulding technology to metals, electroplate clay, or put a plastic item into a kiln. It is also necessary here to rationalize the production processes to prevent a lot of 'repeat' cells containing the same ideas. For instance, products made from certain materials for certain markets will require drilling, cutting and shaping, and would thus occur in three cells. It is usually best to think of the processing capabilities of the organization in terms of generic areas of expertise. In the WC Louis example, one area is applying decorative finishes. Another is moulding/curing. Drilling, cutting and shaping can be put together. Implied expertise can also be included; because of the products that they manufacture, WC Louis must know a fair amount about waterproofing and insulation.

We can now build a three-dimensional grid, with raw materials, manufacturing processes and markets as the axes and fill in on this grid the extent of the company's current operations, as shown in Figure 7.7. The grid has been drawn differently this time, as three separate planes as opposed to a three-dimensional box: an easier arrangement to work with.

There are a lot of open spaces on this grid which might contain opportunities for expansion and diversification. The main use of this variation of MA is to show companies how they can easily (with minimum cost and disruption) and safely diversify. Initially, we examine the 'home' layer, the market that WC Louis knows best – bathrooms. Then we move up to other layers, the markets identified earlier as possibly suitable for expansion into. Frame 7.15 contains some possibilities for new products.

Figure 7.7

Morphological Analysis for WC Louis Ltd

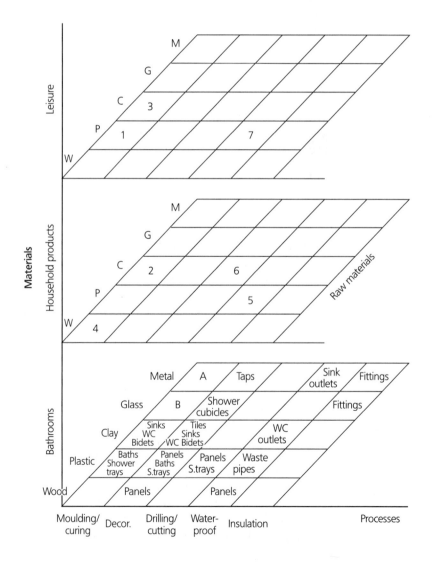

Frame 7.15 *WC Louis Ltd: Possibilities*

Bathrooms

A WC Louis might apply their moulding/curing expertise to the production of aluminium replicas of Victorian cast iron baths.

B Their expertise in moulding and shaping glass products might allow production of smaller bathroom products, for example soap dishes, toothbrush holders, splash backs and many household products as well.

Other markets

1 With their supply of plastics materials and their existing GRP production facilities could allow a venture into the leisure industry, making surf boards, dinghies and canoes.

2 They have the appropriate raw materials and processing facilities to make large ceramic items; perhaps they could move into smaller household items such as cups, plates or even 'old fashioned' jugs and wash basins, potties, etc., which are now very popular.

3 Ceramics in the leisure industry – clay pigeons?

4 Applying moulding techniques to wood laminates could open up possibilities in furniture production.

5 These are not really household products in the usual sense, but WC Louis have the necessary expertise to manufacture gutters and drainpipes, etc. (this idea could be found in a number of cells, for example, moulding-plastic or decorative-plastic); I put it only in the cell where I first thought of the idea, because I wanted to leave the other cells blank to force me to think up additional ideas for them.

6 A variation on the theme of idea no. 2: drilling/cutting clay might allow production of parsley pots and the like.

7 Another possibility might be waterproof 'plastic' clothing, bags or enclosures generally, for use in connection with water sports.

These possibilities would have to be evaluated very carefully. WC Louis would need to perform a careful analysis of the present use of their production capacity, do some costing and attempt to assess the likely share of the new markets they could realistically attain. In other words, they need to do a full feasibility study on the most promising ideas. After they have collected some of these data they may determine the most likely candidate for a new venture using a simple **grid method** (see Chapter 8, or the more sophisticated Kepner-Tregoe Decision Analysis (see Chapter 8).

When considering moving into a new market, two questions should be asked: how familiar are we with the market; and can we exercise some control over it? For example, WC Louis is probably better off considering household products than leisure because the behaviour of the former is far more akin to their present market, the market for leisure products being highly seasonal and subject to rapid changes in fashion. They probably already have connections with distributors and retail outlets operating in the household products market. Only after investigating known territory that is currently not exploited, should areas further afield be looked at, first considering new materials, then new processes and avoiding materials and processes that are not understood. A process similar to this can assist with the development of corporate strategy.

Morphological forced connections

We are now back to the search for new products. Although based on exactly the same principles, this variation (Allen, 1962; Koberg and Bagnall, 1974) on the use of morphology (the study of shape, form, pattern) does not have a cell on the grid for every combination of attribute subdivisions. Instead of each axis representing an attribute, all the attributes are represented on *only one* axis. The two-dimensional grid has the attributes written across the top columns and the ways these attributes can be accomplished written in the cells beneath. A combination is represented by a line linking a cell from each column. A grid set up to generate new ideas for a garden-refuse carrier is shown in Frame 7.16.

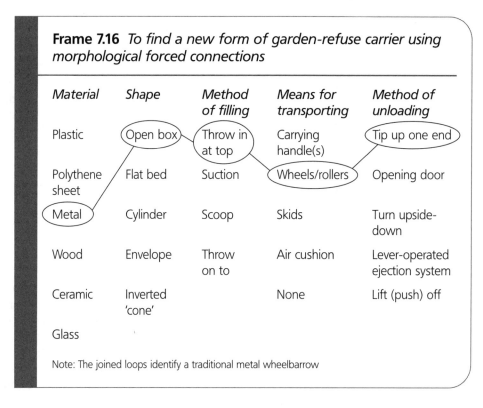

Frame 7.16 *To find a new form of garden-refuse carrier using morphological forced connections*

Material	Shape	Method of filling	Means for transporting	Method of unloading
Plastic	Open box	Throw in at top	Carrying handle(s)	Tip up one end
Polythene sheet	Flat bed	Suction	Wheels/rollers	Opening door
Metal	Cylinder	Scoop	Skids	Turn upside-down
Wood	Envelope	Throw on to	Air cushion	Lever-operated ejection system
Ceramic	Inverted 'cone'		None	Lift (push) off
Glass				

Note: The joined loops identify a traditional metal wheelbarrow

Note that we did not say 'new ideas for a wheelbarrow', because, as we said before, it is important to specify the object of the search in generic terms. Using MA on a problem such as designing a new bed would lead to finding just a few 'cosmetic' attributes, like shape and construction material. These attributes would probably only enable you to identify some new styles of bed, although if we were really lucky we might come up with a minor improvement such as a three-legged bed. The reason for this general lack of success is that the fundamental bases of the objects concerned are not being questioned.

However, suppose we were to define our problem as 'design a new item of furniture for sleeping/relaxing on'. This starting point would suggest far more significant attributes such as:

- 'method of bodily support' (air, water, foam, springs, fabric, the structure itself)
- 'type of surrounding structure' (rigid frame, folding frame, non-rigid free-standing, none, so that the 'method of bodily support' can be rolled up, etc.).

With these attributes and the cosmetic ones (shape and construction material) we should be able to come up with some really innovative ways of fulfilling the functions desired.

So, thinking in the same way about the fundamental attributes of a garden-refuse carrier, we come up with: how we fill and unload it, and the mechanism by which we transport the device from one place to another. If you immediately think of a wheelbarrow the way these things are done is taken for granted: if we start from a narrow description of what we are looking for in a new product we could well miss important attributes. A list of attributes for a garden-refuse carrier and some suggested subdivisions for them were shown in Frame 7.16. As you will easily see, I should perhaps have spent more time thinking about even the 'cosmetic' attributes (like 'material'): there is not much difference between a metal, wood or plastic wheelbarrow!

It is more difficult to progress through all the possible combinations, but try. Once again, do not dismiss the apparently impossible combinations too quickly. They can sometimes be very fruitful.

In this sort of grid it is often useful to build in the option of 'none' where this seems appropriate. We should be careful, however, not to use this 'none' option as a means of avoiding selecting from a certain column just because what the combinations might give are difficult to do anything with. There is also a temptation to incorporate an 'other' category or subdivision in certain columns, just in case we think up some wonderful idea using a category we do not have halfway through our analysis. A better ploy, under these circumstances, is simply to add this new category to the list and then deliberately try to make some more connections with it.

In Frame 7.17 some existing garden-refuse carriers are listed, with a couple of new ideas.

Frame 7.17 *Garden-refuse carrier: existing products and new ideas*

Existing products

- Metal/Open box/Throw in at top/Wheels/Tip up or rollers one end is a wheelbarrow.

▶

◀

- Plastic/Inverted ('chopped off') cone/Throw in at top/Carrying handle/Turn upside-down is a bucket.
- Polythene sheet/Flat bed/Throw on to/None/Tip up one end is a grass mat (a small groundsheet that you throw grass cuttings on to and which you then drag along the ground by two of its adjacent corners).
- Wood/Flat bed/Throw on to/Wheels or rollers/Lift (push) off is a wooden trolley (with skids instead of wheels, we have a sledge being put to good use in the summer).
- Polythene sheet/Envelope/Throw in at top/None/Turn upside-down is a dustbin bag.
- Plastic/Open box/Suction/Carrying handles/Opening door? is a garden vacuum cleaner.

New ideas

- Wood/Cylinder/Throw in at top/None/Turn upside-down – I envisage something like a wooden barrel one of whose ends is removable. You stand the barrel upright on its 'fixed' end, throw stuff in it, and replace and fasten the removable end. Moving it is achieved by pushing it over on its side and rolling it to its destination, whereupon we undo the removable end and tip the whole thing upside-down.
- Plastic/Open box/Suction/Air cushion/Lever-operated ejection system? – a converted hover mower that, by operating a lever, can redirect its air-flow three ways – reversing its thrust to suck small bits of garden debris into some receptacle – like a vacuum cleaner – acting in 'hovercraft' mode so that it can be pushed easily to its destination or, for unloading, blowing the air and contents out of some other orifice to land in the right place.

This variation of MA is intended for situations where we wish to consider more than three attributes. If we had had only two or three attributes for our garden-refuse carrier, we could have drawn up our grid in exactly the same way as before.

Concluding thoughts on MA

MA has been used here as an idea generating technique, it can also be used, in the **Problem Identification** stage, to (re)structure the problem.

MA can also be used in a group setting, with the group participants helping to determine the attributes and their subdivisions, as well as making something out of the combinations the MA grid produces. Simon Majaro (1988) describes the details of how this can be done.

As has been implied already, probably the most difficult part of any form of MA is the finding and selection of the attributes (or the dimensions of the problem if we are employing it for Problem Analysis) that are to be represented by the axes of the grid, and the subdivisions (or components) that we need to break these down into.

An idea (attributed to M.S. Allen by Van Gundy, 1988) reckoned to help with this is to collect all the information possible relating to the problem without any consideration at all of its importance. Each bit of information is then written on a separate card and these are gathered together at random into groups of, say, 12. We study all the cards carefully, and then go and do something else for about 30 minutes. On returning to the cards we regroup them in such a way that all the cards in a particular group are related in some way. Give a title to each group (a provisional attribute name) and write the titles on a different set of cards, each of which is placed with its appropriate group. Repeat this process, but this time working with the groups as units – in other words, group the groups by rethinking the group titles. Try to end up with between four and seven final groups. With the attributes thus decided upon turn to the original cards associated with each of them, and rationalize these down to about seven subdivisions per group. All this can take a little time, but it can be a useful exercise if we have no clear idea what our attributes and their subdivisions should be.

Most useless ideas 'competition' (creative)

As a means of freeing the mind, this exercise should be equally effective carried out individually or in a group. The idea is to find the most useless, ridiculous, totally impractical application for a common, everyday item.

I often find that a useful article for these exercises is a clear acetate overhead projector transparency. A typical set of responses is shown in Frame 7.18 (they have only been slightly censored!).

Frame 7.18 *Most useless ideas for an acetate sheet*

Nuclear fallout shelter	Paperweight
Spare wheel	Contraceptive
Spectacles	Nose warmer/ear muffs
Parachute	Cooking utensil
Headware	Incinerator
Missile launcher	Fire extinguisher
Aqualung	Piggy bank
Furniture: chair, table, stool	Toilet
Footwear	Handkerchief/toilet paper
Channel Tunnel excavator	Pea shooter
Transportation: boat, car, plane	Car park
Clothing: trousers, dress	Glass cutter
Ovenproof dish	Windows
Food	Crash helmet
Knife, razor blade, etc.	Golf clubs
Jet engine	Key
Tower block foundations/support	

Some even more creative ideas often appear by taking each of the ideas in turn and trying to find five good points about the suggestion. For example, 'If we did make our nuclear fallout shelter out of a sheet of acetate, what would be the advantages of this 'building' material?'

- You could see the bombs coming.
- You could see when it's safe to come out again.
- It is waterproof; the fallout would be washed off by the rain.
- It would be portable; fold it up, put it in your back pocket and carry it around with you just in case.
- It's cheaper than conventional methods, and about as effective as the advice offered in the government pamphlet 'Protect and Survive'.

There is a 'moral' to this exercise which is worth stating: 'No matter how stupid an idea may seem to be it has *some* value'. Do not underestimate the value of those wild ideas. They are the source material which we need to spark off our imagination.

If you are desperately trying for new ideas to help resolve a particular problem, but without success, then try this technique on something directly related to the problem. Imagine the wildest, most impractical or stupid ways in which you could solve the problem. Then list the good points of your useless ideas: it is possible that you will make realistic connections with the problem. At the very least you will begin to clarify some of the qualities you need in your solutions.

Wishful Thinking/Absurd Solutions – Synectics (creative)

Wishful Thinking is described by Van Gundy (1988) as, assuming that *anything* is possible, make statements about what could/needs to be done to solve the problem if we were living in this fantasy world. Then, by examining each of our 'fantastic' solutions, try and think of a way of making them more realistic. This is very similar to a technique often used in conjunction with excursions (see above) in the **Synectics CPS** process as follows.

Imagine 'The wall' (in Figure 7.8) is the problem that you are banging your head against. You might take an **excursion** to get (a lot of) distance from it; for this you would want to take a long 'run up' so that you can leap over the wall with ease. If you are not careful you will land on the same side of the wall as you started! You need a gentle gliding descent.

Figure 7.8

The wall

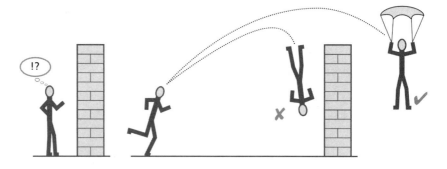

Because some excursions take you a long way away from the problem it may take you several stages to 'connect' your irrelevant material to the problem – so first we try for an Absurd Solution. An Absurd Solution to your problem might be 'to kill my boss' (far from being absurd this may well be possible, but . . .). We then take the essence of the idea (getting the boss 'out of the way') and make the idea a little more feasible, e.g. 'find some adverts for conferences I know my boss would be interested in going to'. Further examples of the use of Absurd Solutions can be found in Frame 10.15.

Highlighting (Osborn-Parnes) (creative)

Van Gundy (1988, p.232) describes **highlighting** as a 'relatively efficient idea evaluation and selection technique' which he attributes to R.L. Firestien.

First we take our list of ideas and identify the **hits**. In this context we mean 'ideas that are obviously interesting and attractive to you', 'the ideas that just seem to jump out at you as being appealing, promising, or worthy of more detailed consideration'.

We then look for groups of hits that are somehow related to each other, the **hotspots**, and try and combine them (in a similar way to Synectics' concept (see above), recording what the connection or relationship is.

Summary

In this chapter we have looked at a number of hard, soft and creative techniques used by different problem-solving approaches/processes that help us generate ideas which we hope will eventually lead to possible solutions, and, if appropriate, select the most promising ones. In the next chapter we look at techniques to develop these ideas.

Exercises

1. **The Birmingham Brick Company**

   The management of the Birmingham Brick Company has for some while been unhappy about the dependency of their business on the frequent fluctuations in the construction industry, and wish they could find other 'avenues' for their expertise, that can slowly be built up as an attempt to 'smooth' their long-term profitability.

   The company's main product is the common red house brick, although it does come in a variety of shades of red, brown and grey. They have already diversified into 'specialist' types of brick – for example, the fire bricks industry – but this only accounts for a few per cent of its business.

   When a recession hits the construction industry, the workforce has to be pared down to its absolute minimum level; but even then, large quantities of bricks quickly accumulate in the storage yards. So far the company has managed to avoid stopping production altogether.

Either individually or as a group, using **Brainwriting/Brainstorming** along with **Attribute Listing** and **Checklists**, address the problem 'What else can we use a house brick for apart from building houses?'

2. **The President's Idea**

The **President's Idea** is an exercise frequently encountered on Synectics courses, and is based on the following context: the company's president has been talking to your line manager about the work you are doing and with his limited knowledge of this has offered you a somewhat 'off the wall' idea. Your manager wants you to do something with this unsolicited idea and report back to her, so that she can tell the president about what you have done with it next time she sees him!

The exercise involves asking a small group of people to write a problem headline on a sheet of paper: these are then collected. After an imaging excursion the problems are given back, but to anybody except the original problem owner. The recipient is asked to use the excursion material to generate a really totally absurd, impractical solution and to write it on the paper. This 'solution' is then given back (with the original problem headline) to the problem owner, who is asked to produce a more sensible solution from this, by developing the idea that comes from the absurd solution.

This exercise illustrates, and provides the opportunity to practice, many things: the **Imaging Excursion**; the ability to help with resolving a problem despite knowing nothing more about the problem situation other than the problem headline, i.e. with the minimum of information; the use of **Absurd Solutions**; **Forced Relationships**; **Itemized Response**, etc. Try it with a group of friends.

Endnotes

1. If the organization concerned was more of a 'co-operative', we could have got away with a 'three blob' control mechanism; being all owners of the system we would not need to appreciate the aspirations of our own ownership.
2. This process is little used now, being replaced by checking that the model is defensible – each phrase in the root definition can be linked to an activity or connection in the model (Checkland and Scholes, 1990b).

8 Problem Resolution

This chapter describes various techniques used by different problem-solving approaches/processes for progressing our most promising ideas into possible solutions.

Introduction

The next stage in our generic problem-solving process, **Problem Resolution**, is where the most promising ideas from the previous stage are 'progressed', so as to become **possible solutions**. Sometimes this is just a question of deciding which of our most promising ideas to go with. If these ideas are already sufficiently developed (that is, we can action them straight away), a sufficient set of criteria for comparing them are readily available and we (all the problem owners/stakeholders) are happy with ideas and agree on the appropriateness of the criteria, then a **hard** (rational) decision-making technique like Kepner-Tregoe's **Decision Analysis** (see below) might well be employed to determine the 'best' idea to implement as our solution. If any of these prerequisites does not exist (which is usually the case), then more work must be done at this stage and perhaps later to obtain our possible solution.

Although referred to as a stage wherein ideas are developed, the **Solution-Finding** (aka **Developing Solutions**) stage of the **Osborn-Parnes** CPS process is mainly concerned with the *evaluation* of ideas. This evaluation is often/normally also done on the basis of criteria. However, Isaksen and Treffinger (1985) do offer a brief note to the effect that if you have many **hits** from the previous stage you should try and incorporate aspects of several (perhaps all) of these in your solution, and not go for one 'best idea'; and Van Gundy (1988) advises trying to combine your best ideas (hits) if you can see some relationship between them (see **highlighting**, page 167). But this is usually done as part of the convergent phase of the previously described **Ideation (Idea Finding)** stage. As said elsewhere, I consider the lack of explicit **idea development** techniques the weakest point in the Osborn-Parnes process.

The **Synectics** CPS process' *Idea Development* stage (below), on the other hand, attempts (usually successfully) to take an appealing (but less than perfect) idea and build in feasibility.

Since the **soft systems** approach in the form of **SSM** concludes with some systemically desirable changes, which are offered to the problem owners/solvers, who then decide whether they are culturally feasible and whether they wish to implement them, deciding on the 'how' of these changes is left to them. So there will not be any ideas to be developed as such within this approach. However, the problem owners/solvers may need to adopt some CPS techniques to generate and develop ways of making these changes.

Because I believe most promising ideas will need some development before they can be considered possible solutions, and it is only possible solutions that may need to be compared against each other in some rational way, we will start this chapter with Synectics' Idea Development (a creative technique) and conclude with Kepner-Tregoe's decision analysis (a hard technique). In between, we will look briefly at how technical creativity/systematic innovation in the form of **TRIZ** deals with Idea Development.

Idea Development – Synectics (creative)

As noted in Chapter 3, our tendency to classify ideas as good or bad with no degree of merit in between is a mistaken practice both philosophically and practically. In the Synectics CPS process, there are no binary judgements like this until we get to a possible solution; and even then, we can only judge a solution's merits *after* it has been implemented. Nolan (1989, p.60) comments,

> ideas . . . are only words and pictures they do not change anything in the real world. So we do not need to make an instant judgement on them; we can explore them in a more gentle, open-minded way. They are neither good nor bad just more or less interesting and appealing . . . .
>   This belief is a fundamental aspect of the way we handle judgements, and 'goes to the very heart of Synectics'.

For example, how do we classify an idea that we (as problem owner) like a lot, which has promising potential for developing a possible solution, but about which we have a number of concerns. An 80 per cent good idea or a 20 per cent bad idea? This surely suggests that a binary judgement is unworkable. Even if we classify ideas on a continuum from good to bad, we would probably attempt to determine an idea's 'position' by trying to pick holes in it. If it survives this, it must be 'pretty good'. Sadly, many other pretty good ideas would be rejected by this same process. Very few ideas come out perfectly formed: they should not be rejected just because of this. Dismissing ideas because they are not perfectly formed is typical of situations where hole-picking is allowed at the outset of evaluation. Nolan (2000, p.21) tells us that 'most new ideas need a period of incubation and development, to allow them to grow into feasible solutions'.

Synectics have developed a simple technique, the **Itemized Response**, that allows a possible solution to be developed from any idea, using a gentle, constructive evaluation that encourages the ironing out of minor concerns rather than dismissal of the idea. It starts from the assumption that *all* ideas have value, and thus before any flaws and imperfections in the idea are pointed out, some of the things we like about it (say three) are identified first – the practical, helpful or attractive aspects of the idea – and listed, giving reasons wherever possible. This reinforces the value of the idea and justifies the additional time that will be spent overcoming our concerns about it.

Then we identify the most serious concern we have with the idea, expressing this as a 'How to/I wish' in order to give a direction for the further development of the idea in order to overcome this concern.

Now we generate some ideas for overcoming this concern. If the suggestions only partially overcome the concern, the itemized response process is repeated with this latest suggestion. As the idea develops in this way it becomes more difficult to get three 'new' good points each time, but the time spent trying is usually worthwhile.

Having, we hope, resolved the major concern, we now tackle any other concerns.

It may appear that we are running the risk of spending an inordinate amount of time going round in circles, resolving concern after concern, trying to make something of an idea of little or no potential. In practice Itemized Response is not a long-winded process. First, the problem owner selects the idea to take through Itemized Response on the basis of its interest and appeal; the group would not be allowed to spend time on ideas of little value to the problem owner. Second, as the major concern is being tackled, the minor ones often dissipate or are resolved at the same time.

Apart from developing ideas, Itemized Response can be used in conflict situations where various stakeholders have different perceptions of the problem situation and the ways it can be best resolved, or in (multi-problem owner) situations where we are not starting our problem situation from a 'blank sheet' because of the existence of a preconceived solution. To illustrate this technique we will use Wessex Telecom plc's problem described in Frame 8.1: apart from illustrating the 'mechanics' of Itemized Response it gives an indication of how the (preconceived) head office 'solution' could have been presented to the other stakeholders, as an *idea* so as to resolve any consequential problems.

Frame 8.1 *Wessex Telecom plc: the problem situation*

Wessex Telecom plc is a national telecommunications provider. Apart from their main head office (HQ) in London, they have two other regional offices, in Manchester and Exeter. Until recently the company's IT (information technology) support was provided by three autonomous groups of dedicated personnel, one at each site. As a result of a recent reorganization, IT support is now managed centrally from HQ. Every request for support received at Manchester or Exeter, along with a description of the 'solution' provided, has to be reported to London; also, anything that the regional teams cannot handle should be notified to HQ as well.

The main reason given for this change was that they wanted to encourage a sharing of knowledge which could benefit all regions, and that some specialist expertise recruited recently only at HQ could be made available to the regions. However, underlying this perhaps is a desire at HQ for more control over the regional groups, maybe eventually requiring all the IT support staff to operate out of HQ.

▶

> IT support has always been under great demand at Wessex Telecom plc, and what has resulted from this change is that the backlog of jobs in the regions has now actually increased, due to more time spent on the additional administration. And HQ is frustrated because of (as they see it) missing/incomplete reporting, the regional offices still trying to offer support they are not equipped to do because (they say) of delays getting the HQ experts to do anything for them, etc.

Wessex Telecom plc HQ's 'solution' to whatever problem they perceived they had was:

> Get the regional IT support groups to report any support requested and given and support they could not provide, as soon as these things occur.

If, say, the team leader of the Manchester (or Exeter) office had been invited to do an itemized response on this 'solution' when it was first mooted, she may have responded:

- (Three or more things she likes about the idea . . .)
    + if they do share the information we give them we could learn some new things;
    + we might actually be able to provide a better service;
    + they would realize how under-resourced we are;
    + taking an interest in us like this may make us feel less of a 'poor relation'.
- (And her main concern was . . .)
    − the extra time it is going to take to report everything.

This needs to be expressed as a problem definition indicating a direction for us to go in: 'How to "release" the extra time it is going to take to report everything.' We now need to generate some ideas to overcome this concern:

- automate the reporting process
- ask for some more clerical support
- work more overtime, etc.

If we suppose the team leader picks the first idea, we need to subject this to the itemized response process (remembering that it is a modification of the original solution).

- She says, if we could do this . . .
    + reporting wouldn't interfere with our normal workload
    + HQ will be happy
    + it would get them off our backs.
- . . . We could (given the money/equipment) automate some things, and semi-automate others, using standard, tick box forms for request logging and forwarding, but . . .

- there are quite a few situations where only a human would be able to detect the problem, and write up about the support provided.

We do not have a solution for our team leader yet: we need to get some ideas to overcome this additional concern now. Alternatively, we could return to 'ask for some more clerical support' and ask her if there is any future pursuing that idea. If she says yes, we would probably start with an itemized response on that.

It may be that, after 'spiralling' through this process several times, we feel that we are not getting anywhere. We then need to go back to the original concern and try to generate some more ideas to overcome it or, had the 'solution' we started from here been one of *our* promising ideas, then back to the other ideas we had before selecting this one for development. Failing that we go back to a different **springboard**.

This technique sounds as if it could be long-winded, but it is not usually. Even so, a lot of novices do not 'spiral' through it enough times, leaving themselves with an unusable 'solution' with which they still have concerns. More examples of the application of itemized response can be found in Chapters 10 and 12.

Development of (solution) concepts – TRIZ (hard?/creative)

Because of the number of different ways we can tackle the Ideation stage depending on the nature of the problem we have chosen to resolve, it is not always easy to distinguish with TRIZ where **Ideation** becomes **Problem Resolution** (Idea Development); however, the following technique seems to fit the latter description.

TRIZ provides two general approaches for achieving close-to-ideal solutions:

- use of resources
- use of physical, chemical, geometrical and other effects.

A **resource** in TRIZ is any material (including waste, system elements, substance flows, etc.) available in the system or its environment, an energy field, time (for example, idle time, pauses, etc.), space (for example, vacant space, space inside an object, etc.), additional functionality, information. Identifying them and wondering what you might do with them can improve your 'solution' (see below).

Effects are well-known scientific and other effects that have been 'logged' over the years, and which can be found in TRIZ knowledge bases. Likewise, considering how these might be incorporated within the system could provide ideas for improving your solution

Development of (solution) concepts

Boris Zlotin, Alla Zusman and Len Kaplan (2000) suggest that if we have two ideas that resolve the same problem but in different ways, we should try and combine them into a **concept**.

We do this by first comparing these ideas, to determine each one's advantages. Then, considering the idea that has better functional features as the **source** of resources, and the other idea is the **recipient** of resources, determine the elements (what it is) that provides the better functionality of the source idea, and apply these elements to the recipient.

Then consider if some of the elements of the recipient can also perform functions of the newly applied elements and simplify the system. The best possible result is to arrive at a new system consisting of elements of the recipient and having the features of the source.

Altshuller discovered eight lines/patterns of evolution of technical systems:

- lifecycle (every system goes through one!)
- dynamization (a transition from being rigid to more and more flexibility)
- multiplication (a single system becomes two, three, more systems combined together)
- transition from macro- to micro-level
- synchronization
- scaling up or down
- uneven development of parts
- replacement of humans.

By considering where in (some of or all) these lines of evolution our concept is, we may get further ideas for improving it.

Selecting (evaluation) criteria – Osborn-Parnes (creative)

If it *is* appropriate to (just) evaluate our **most promising possibilities** in order to determine our best solutions, a simple grid method (see below) may be sufficient, where we assess each of our most promising possibilities (or ideas) against various appropriate criteria.

Some care must be taken when it comes to choosing suitable criteria, as there is a possibility of 'overlap'. If we return to Dispensable Plastics' 'new uses' problem (Frame 7.3), the ones which spring easily to mind in connection with commercial viability (our main interest) do overlap. For example, the amount we can spend on research and development, and in additional production costs 'modifying' the existing product, depend on what price we believe we might then be able to sell the product for, the quantity we believe we can sell and all of this affects the profitability of the project. Some other possible selection criteria are given in Frame 8.2.

Frame 8.2 *Dispensable Plastics Ltd: some selection criteria for new uses*

- Profitability
- Likely demand
- Marketability: how easily can we sell it?
- Lifetime of product.

Criteria checklist

The main techniques used in the Osborn-Parnes CPS process to generate suitable criteria are either 'straight' **Brainstorming** (see page 133), or the use of a generic criteria **checklist** containing various questions. Originally these questions related to cost, time, feasibility, acceptability and usefulness. Isaksen and Treffinger (1985) said that criteria should be relevant, clear, concise and consistent. Their latest thoughts on typical categories of criteria can be found in Frame 8.3.

Frame 8.3 *Criteria checklist*

Cost – will the options be cost-effective to implement? Will they require expensive resources? Will it be necessary to obtain many costly resources? Will it exceed our budget or funds available?

Acceptance – will this possibility be acceptable to others? Will it be acceptable to those who need to support it? Will it be acceptable to the public? Will it be acceptable to me in the long run?

Resources – will the materials needed be readily available? Will any special support materials or equipment be needed and available to carry out the option?

Time – will the option fit into our schedule? Will it fit our time requirements? Will it make excessive demands on anyone's time? Will the critical resources and people be available when needed?

Space – will we have the space or room we need to act on this possibility? Will any special facilities be required and available? Will there be room to do what's needed?

©2000, Center for Creative Learning, Inc., and Creative Problem Solving Group, Buffalo. Reproduced with permission from Treffinger, D.J., Isaksen, S.G., and Dorval, K.B. (2000) Creative Problem Solving: An Introduction. *Third edition, p.53. Waco, TX: Prufrock Press.*

If, once you have generated your criteria, you feel there is a need to weight them, you can do this with a technique called **Paired Comparison Analysis** (see below).

Treffinger and Isaksen (1985) also suggest that it may also be appropriate to sort the criteria into MUSTS and WANTS in essentially the same way as is done in Kepner-Tregoe's Decision Analysis described below.

Paired Comparison Analysis – Osborn-Parnes (creative)

The **Paired Comparisons Analysis** technique can be used to 'evaluate' our most promising possibilities (ideas) or to rank our evaluation criteria. We will use it for the latter.

To perform a **Paired Comparison Analysis**, we need to write our criteria across and down the 'diagonal' of the triangular-shaped grid shown in Frame 8.4. As an example, we are going to use Life's Alternatives, a monthly magazine available through subscription only. Life's Alternatives needs to increase its revenue, and is considering various options. We will return to its case later in this chapter. Going across the square boxes in each row of the grid we make a one-on-one comparison of the criteria as follows. In the top left box we will write either A or B depending on whether we think criterion A is more important than criterion B or vice versa. So in our example we have decided that idea B 'increased circulation' is more important than criterion A 'even more revenue'. Then we assign a 'weighting' to that relationship depending on whether we see criterion B as being slightly, moderately or much more important than criterion A. In this case we think that criterion B is much more important than criterion A. Hence 'B3' is written in the top left box. Then we continue this process all the way across the top line of squares comparing criterion A with C, D and E in turn.

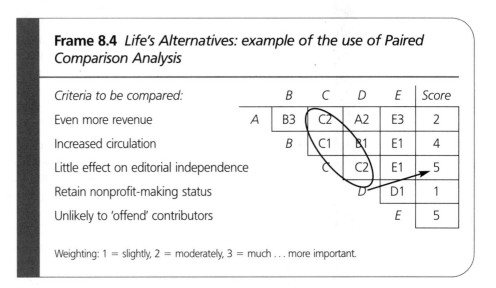

Frame 8.4 *Life's Alternatives: example of the use of Paired Comparison Analysis*

Criteria to be compared:		B	C	D	E	Score
Even more revenue	A	B3	C2	A2	E3	2
Increased circulation	B		C1	B1	E1	4
Little effect on editorial independence	C			C2	E1	5
Retain nonprofit-making status	D				D1	1
Unlikely to 'offend' contributors	E					5

Weighting: 1 = slightly, 2 = moderately, 3 = much . . . more important.

After completing the top row of boxes, we do the same thing in the second row (comparing criterion B with criterion C, D, etc.), the third row, and so on. Finally, we total up all the 'weights' for each criterion, so for criterion C 'little effect on editorial independence' we have three boxes with 'C' in with 'weights' C2, C1, C2 – this gives a total score of 5, which we write in the right-hand side column 'score'. These scores give the weight that should be given to our criteria when evaluating our ideas (most promising possibilities, see pages 183).

If we use this idea to select ideas (in the previous stage) then we would keep the ideas with the best total scores. Isaksen and Treffinger (1985, p.164) recommend the use of this technique when 'there are several promising ideas which should be compared, ranked or prioritised'.

Reverse Brainstorming

A simple (if somewhat crude) technique that can be used to sift/evaluate ideas (if this is felt necessary) is **Reverse Brainstorming**. There is, however, some uncertainty as to what constitutes Reverse Brainstorming. My use of the term means taking each idea (say for a product name) and thinking of everything that is wrong, missing or bad about the idea. In other words, we unleash the critical faculties that we have been holding back on for so long now whilst generating the ideas, and become as destructive and negative as we can. The ideas (for product names) that end up with the least wrong with them (in terms of quantity and seriousness) should be our best ones. There is, however, nothing inherent in the reverse Brainstorming process which distinguishes the more serious faults from the minor ones.

Before embarking on a reverse Brainstorming session we should have some idea of what sort of faults we might be looking for. (**Attribute Listing** could help with the selection of these 'damning criteria'.)

Advantages, limitations and unique aspects – Osborn-Parnes (creative)

Isaksen and Treffinger (1985, p.164) recommend the use of the **advantages, limitations and unique aspects** (ALU) technique if 'there is one dominant idea, or a small number which might *all* be considered'. But say, elsewhere, that if we have a lot of ideas and want to take stock of where we are with our ideas or are unsure how to tell which ones hold the greatest potential, we should use ALU. Whatever, ALU is a slightly more sophisticated way of selecting which of our ideas is to proceed to 'more extensive analysis, evaluation and development' in the Osborn-Parnes Solution Finding stage.

The technique involves listing each idea's **advantages** (its strongest points, what makes it attractive/appealing to us, what do we see as its potential), **limitations** (any flaws, weaknesses and/or trouble spots it has; what might limit its attractiveness and/or effectiveness) and **unique aspects** (has new or unusual connections with other things, hidden potentials) (Isaksen and Treffinger, 1985, p.112). Once these advantages, limitations and unique aspects have been listed the ideas can be better compared using any criteria that you have available.

The Grid (Evaluation) Method – Osborn-Parnes (creative)

With a problem like Dispensable Plastics' 'new uses' problem (see Frames 7.3 and 7.6), when we have reduced our list to the most promising ideas, we will probably want to conduct a rather more sophisticated evaluation process than that offered by reverse Brainstorming. Or, as Isaksen and Treffinger (1985, p.164) say, if we have 'numerous ideas that need additional screening or selection' we should use a **solution finding matrix** aka the **Grid Method**.

Table 8.1 shows such a grid on which we have written these ideas in such a way that we can score them against each of the criteria we have decided should be used to determine, in this case, commercial viability. Simply scoring each idea on a five-point scale will be sufficient for most purposes; the system used in Table 8.1 is 4 = very good, 3 = good, 2 = average, 1 = poor and 0 = very poor. If we feel that one or more of these criteria are more important than the others, then the scores on those criteria can be weighted as appropriate. For example, if 'likely demand' is deemed twice as important as the other criteria we would multiply the score our ideas obtained on this criterion by two. From the total score we decide which of these ideas should be considered for implementation. We can also record our decision regarding whether we are going to 'use' the idea now or 'hold',[1] 'modify' (or combine it with others) or 'reject' it.

Kepner-Tregoe's Decision Analysis, described below, is a yet more sophisticated technique for making these sorts of choices.

Decision Analysis – Kepner-Tregoe (hard)

Introduction

Kepner and Tregoe maintain (1981, p.85) that good decisions depend on the quality of:

- our definition of the specific factors (criteria/objectives) that need to be satisfied by the chosen course of action;
- our evaluation of the available alternatives;
- our understanding of the consequences of these alternatives.

Their method of decision making is an extension of the common-sense approach that has been around for some while, and which is also the basis of the simpler Grid Method used on page 177.

Many people believe that decision making is not a problematic process, and that decisions are simply a choice between several alternative courses of action, one of which may be to do nothing. In taking this stance we have to assume that we already have a *sufficient* number of alternatives of an *appropriate* quality. It is difficult to define these terms precisely, other than to say that if they are not met then the decision may be difficult to make. The first problem with decision making is the acquisition of these alternatives in the first place. The only real guidance that can be given about this is that the problem-solving session that generates them must be carried out to the best of our abilities.

Having decided what the decision is that we must make, we must select the criteria which will be the basis for our choice, the factors which we feel we must consider in assessing the relative merits of the alternatives. These will consist of the objectives we believe to be important to our overall aim (the purpose of the decision) and which need to be satisfied by the chosen course of action. This selection of criteria can also be a problem in its own right.

| | | | Criteria | | |
Idea	Profit	Demand	Marketability...	Total	Decision
Flower pot	2	3	3	8	Use now
Paint palette	1	1	1	3	Modify
Bottle labels	1	0	1	2	Reject
Egg cup	2	1	2	5	Hold
... ...					
... ...					

Table 8.1

Dispensable Plastics: Grid (Evaluation) Method

The Decision Analysis process involves six steps (see Frame 8.5), and the two 'problem-solving' stages, namely the selection of the criteria and the generation of alternatives, are thought to be part of this whole process. Whether the problem solving is done chronologically within the sequence shown or beforehand is immaterial; what is important is that we recognize the existence of these problem-solving stages and do not attempt to mix the evaluation stage with the determination of the alternatives and criteria. Failure to do this usually results in thinking and meetings that 'go round in circles'.

Frame 8.5 *The Decision Analysis process*

- Decision statement
- Establish objectives
- Classify objectives into MUSTS and WANTS
- Generate alternatives
- Evaluate alternatives
- Compare and choose

. . . balancing alternatives with potential risks.

Note: MUSTS and WANTS are discussed later in this chapter.

It can be argued that decision making in meetings or groups will generally be inferior to individual decision making. Conversely it is argued in Chapters 12 and 13 that if a group can argue its way to a consensus opinion, the resulting decision is often better than either a decision based on an average of individual opinions (such as can be obtained by voting) or that from any one individual.

Harold J. Leavitt (1978) believes that the factors which can make a group decision better are:

- the group can bring more information to the decision-making process,
- the group is able to analyse the information critically and with more objectivity, and
- a strong commitment to the group and its success develops amongst its members.

If an individual can obtain all the information needed, is capable of processing it, and the quality of a decision is important, Leavitt says that individual decision making may be the best means of proceeding. However, if commitment to the decision is the overriding issue, a group decision is essential.

Before we look in detail at Decision Analysis, it is worth pointing out that the term is used not only in this context, but also to describe a branch of mathematics that deals with uncertainty. It has also been used to describe a genre of computer software packages that assist in the process about to be described.

The Decision Statement

The first step is to state the decision we intend to make: the type or kind of action we intend to take and the results we are hoping for. The wording of the 'Decision Statement' must be considered carefully as the rest of the process derives from it. In particular, we should include guidance on the level at which the decision is to be made, otherwise we may not compare like with like and our Decision Analysis will be impaired. An example of the level at which the decision is to be made can be illustrated by supposing we wanted to make a decision on 'How to improve our company image'. Some alternatives that spring to mind are:

- Redesign the company logo.
- Change the company name.
- Improve the presentation of correspondence, catalogues, lists, etc.
- Conduct a nationwide lifestyle TV advertising campaign.
- Move the company's office to a better district.
- Acquire some prestigious brands.
- Sell off all our diversified subsidiaries so that we can concentrate/specialize in one area.

This is deliberately a disparate and incomparable list of alternatives. The budget required to implement any one of these alternatives except the last one varies from a few thousand pounds up to perhaps tens or hundreds of millions of pounds. We need to impose some limitation on the range of alternatives that should receive our consideration. This is what must be included in our decision statement. We could impose these limits later on when declaring which features our alternatives must have, but by then we would have wasted time arguing over which criteria we should use for assessment, because of the difficulty of selecting criteria that can operate effectively across such a diverse range of options. The last alternative might actually be a cost saver in the long run, releasing funds for other expensive options such as a TV advertising campaign.

The details of the process of Decision Analysis will be shown by using an illustrative example concerning the fictitious magazine mentioned earlier in this chapter, *Life's Alternatives*. The decision situation we have is described in Frame 8.6.

Selection and classification of objectives

The next couple of steps involve the selection of the objectives or criteria we are going to use to compare and evaluate our alternatives, and the classification of them into MUSTS and WANTS. MUST objectives are mandatory, that is, the alternatives *must* meet this requirement. We use our MUSTS to make the initial screening of our alternatives – those not satisfying the MUST criteria are rejected. In order to perform in this way a MUST criterion must be measurable; even a very important item may have to be used as a WANT criterion if it is not measurable. For example, a very important characteristic when recruiting a new employee might be 'being a good team member', but measuring this is difficult (and subjective) and so it cannot be used to select alternatives for further consideration. We would need to use something like 'minimum qualifications' or 'years of experience', although these too are not always a good guide.

Frame 8.6 *Life's Alternatives: the problem situation*

Life's Alternatives is a monthly magazine of interest to such people as organic farmers and fruit and vegetable growers, smallholders and private individuals who feel that there are better and healthier ways of producing food and living our lives than the predominant methods and lifestyle current today.

Life's Alternatives, currently only available by subscription, at the moment has some 50,000 subscribers. The cost of subscription, now £20 per annum, has had to increase several times recently to keep up with printing costs. The publishers of *Life's Alternatives*, GIP – a nonprofit-making organization, will shortly be faced once more with the need to generate additional income if the publication is to continue to exist. However, they fear that raising the subscription again, despite the upsurge in interest in 'Green' issues, will not necessarily yield the needed increase in revenue if the number of renewed subscriptions falls as a result.

The magazine currently survives because it receives good and informative articles, from well-known people in the field, at little or no cost. Most of the contributors write for the magazine either because of their belief in, and commitment to, its aims, or because they believe that they will personally benefit from their contributions to the magazine in other walks of life.

The publishers are pleased by the reputation the magazine has acquired for the quality of its articles and its independence of viewpoint. *Life's Alternatives* does not carry any advertising.

GIP believe that the alternatives open to them are:

- Increase the subscription by 10 per cent.
- Cease to be subscription-only and 'go public' – this will entail accepting as much advertising copy as they can get.
- Seek sponsorship from government or private agencies.
- Accept limited (and selected) advertising to 'top up' the existing subscription revenue.

All but the first of these alternatives are seen as potentially compromising of editorial independence. Another fear is that a more commercial orientation might at best encourage the present contributors to seek payment for their articles and, at worst, the possibility of editorial interference from sponsors or advertisers may cause some of them to decide they no longer want to be associated with the magazine.

Decision statement

Select a method for generating an additional £100,000 revenue p.a.

WANT objectives are the features that we would *like* each alternative to possess, and which we can use to distinguish between the relative merits of the alternatives. It is quite reasonable for a criterion to be both a MUST and a WANT. For example, in our recruitment example above, we could insist that a potential employee has, say, five years' experience in the business, and use the number of years over and above that as a means of differentiating between applicants.

If the criteria are being chosen by a group of people, we should be watchful that the final choice of criteria does not favour one particular viewpoint.

The final task at this stage is to determine the relative importance of the WANTS criteria and allocate them a weight accordingly. For example, 'editorial independence' may be seen by the publishers of *Life's Alternatives* to be of paramount importance, deserving a maximum weighting of 5, whereas bringing in additional revenue over the necessary £100,000 would be nice, but of less importance, perhaps deserving a weighting of 2. Kepner and Tregoe (1981), although saying that the precise values we use for weighting and scoring are immaterial, always use 1–10 for both weights and scores. I often find this too 'wide' a range and it exaggerates the differences in merit between the alternatives. I generally use 1–5. Let us suppose that the objectives (MUSTS and WANTS criteria) for the *Life's Alternatives* decision and the weightings they have been given are as shown in Frame 8.7.

Frame 8.7 Life's Alternatives: *weighting of objectives*

MUST

Produce an additional £100,000 revenue p.a.

WANTS	*Weight*
Little effect on editorial independence	5
Unlikely to 'offend' contributors	5
Increased circulation	4
Even more revenue	2
Retain nonprofit-making status	1

We should never look upon WANTS criteria as of secondary importance, as they are used for a different purpose, namely, to differentiate and decide between the alternatives selected by the MUSTS criteria. In summary, it is the MUSTS that decide who plays the game, but the WANTS that decide who wins. Appendix 5 gives decision alternatives which might be appropriate for part of the Northcliffe Sands case outlined in Chapter 12.

Generating and evaluating alternatives

If we find that one of our 'promising' alternatives is unable to give us all the MUSTS that we want, we should reject it. If we are reluctant to do this it suggests we need to review our MUSTS criteria (and perhaps the WANTS as well) to see whether we have chosen the best criteria, given the purpose of the decision. It is often useful if this does happen, because it causes us to think again about our assessment criteria. You have to feel right about a criterion if you are going to use it to reject a favoured alternative, and this element of doubt invariably sharpens our choice of MUSTS and WANTS. This does not mean that we can or should amend the criteria so that they give the decision we think we want, just that the surprise of seeing a favoured alternative facing rejection concentrates the mind on our choice of criteria.

The first alternative in our *Life's Alternatives* decision (Frame 8.6) – increase subscriptions by 10 per cent – might fail to meet the MUST criteria if a drop in subscriptions subsequently occurs; however I have 'kept it in' for the moment since we will deal with that eventuality when we come to discuss the consequences of the various alternatives.

After we have checked that our alternatives meet the MUSTS requirement we assess how each of them satisfies the WANTS criteria, awarding a score of 0–5. The scores are given as follows: alternative X satisfies the objective – totally 5, very well 4, by more than half way 3, some 2, only a little 1, not at all 0.

For each alternative we multiply the score it obtains on a certain criterion by the weight we have given to this criterion, and then we sum these products to obtain a total (see Frame 8.8). The alternative with the highest total score will be our tentative decision. It is useful to record comments by the scores so that the rationality of the score is obvious and can be appreciated by others. This is particularly so if the decision has to be justified to a third party, not involved in the decision making, at a later date.

Frame 8.8 Life's Alternatives: *evaluating the alternatives*

Decision Statement

Select a method for generating an additional £100,000 revenue p.a.

MUSTS

Produce an additional £100,000 revenue p.a.	Yes, if no fall off in subs.

WANTS

Alternative: 'Increase subscriptions by 10 per cent'

Criteria	Weight	Comment	Score	Weighted score
Little effect on editorial independence	5	No effect	5	$5 \times 5 = 25$
Unlikely to 'offend' contributors	5	No change	5	$5 \times 5 = 25$
Increased circulation	4	The opposite possibly	0	$4 \times 0 = 0$

▶

Criteria	Weight	Comment	Score	Weighted score
Even more revenue	2	None	0	$2 \times 0 = 0$
Retain nonprofit-making status	1	Yes	5	$1 \times 5 = 5$
			Total	55

Evaluating the other alternatives in the same way produces the following scores:

Alternative: 'Go public'

Criteria	Comment	Score	Weighted score
L. . .	Considerable – readers 'dictate'	1	5
U. . .	Half the contributors will leave	1	5
I. . .	Could be considerable increase in circulation	5	20
E. . .	Could be considerably more revenue	5	10
R. . .	Not viable	0	0
			40

Alternative: 'Sponsorship'

Criteria	Comment	Score	Weighted score
L. . .	Possibly a little	4	20
U. . .	Fairly acceptable to most contributors	4	20
I. . .	Not much, if any	1	4
E. . .	A possibility	1	2
R. . .	Would need to probably	5	5
			51

Alternative: 'Top up' advertising

Criteria	Comment	Score	Weighted score
L. . .	Inevitably some	3	15
U. . .	It would depend on who the advertisers were	2	10
I. . .	Not much	2	8
E. . .	Some extra revenue	2	4
R. . .	Doubtful if this is possible	2	2
			39

We should be wary of scores which are all high or all low. The former indicates the possibility of unrealistic expectations for our alternatives or that we have chosen undemanding and perhaps inappropriate objectives. The latter may suggest that we have included unimportant details amongst our criteria.

We should also be cautious about an alternative that stands out above all the rest as this could indicate that the criteria have been (unconsciously?) rigged to favour this alternative.

Comparing and choosing our alternative

When we have reached this tentative decision, we should vent our most destructive, negative and pessimistic thoughts and feelings about each of the alternatives in turn, starting with the best. We need to determine the adverse consequences of the choices and rate them according to both the probability of them occurring and the seriousness of the consequences if they do. Kepner and Tregoe recommend (1981, p.100) asking at least the following four questions in our attempt to discover the potentially unpleasant consequences of the alternatives:

- What are its requirements for success?
- What factors could harm its acceptance or implementation?
- What kind of changes (both inside and outside of the organization) could harm its long-term success?
- What kinds of things tend to cause problems in implementing this type of decision?

It is possible that the highest ranking alternative on the previous analysis could be rejected at this stage in favour of another, because it has a high risk of incurring serious adverse consequences, whereas another option does not (see Frame 8.9).

Frame 8.9 Life's Alternatives: *the final decision*

In our *Life's Alternatives* example, 'going public' might have been seen as having a high risk of seriously compromising both editorial independence and financial security, had it scored higher. As it is, 'increase subscriptions by 10 per cent' may be thought of as having at least a medium risk of causing a 'fall off' in subscriptions (and hence failing to increase revenue), and may thus be rejected in favour of 'sponsorship'. This latter alternative may only give a low risk of frightening away contributors, which is not considered quite so adverse as the possibility of having to close down the magazine due to additional funds from subscriptions not being forthcoming.

Are all decisions the same?

Kepner and Tregoe (1981) identify several types of decision in their accounts of the use of Decision Analysis. I believe these to be variations on only two themes. First is the type where there are several alternatives to compare and where the process described above is eminently suitable. When such a decision is complicated by the amount of detail known about the alternatives and the number of criteria involved, it is usually beneficial and easier to compare the alternatives with an 'ideal' alternative rather than with each other.

The second type is where only one alternative is under discussion, such as making a decision whether to do something or not, to change something or leave it alone, or whether one alternative is good enough. If suitable criteria can be found to permit an objective comparison between doing something or not then we can proceed in the normal fashion, with just these alternatives. The danger exists that the criteria may be stacked against one of these options; indeed the usual approach adopted is that of simply criticizing the 'do' option. The other way of proceeding here, particularly when no viable alternative is available for comparison and it is agreed that change is necessary, is again to compare our one alternative with an ideal course of action. With this procedure we must beware of not making our ideal too difficult or too easy to attain.

Finally, Kepner and Tregoe (1981) include a 'How to find the best way of doing . . .' type of decision, in which there are no alternatives currently available for consideration, not even an ideal one. In this situation they advise using creativity to generate a number of alternatives, in something very like a CPS session, culminating in a Grid Method assessment of the generated alternatives (see above).

Some final words on decisions

When the Decision Analysis is complete we should have the best decision that we could make based on the criteria chosen; what we might call the most rational decision. Sometimes the outcome may be a surprise to us; on rare occasions we may not like it. If we feel strongly that the decision given is wrong we need to reassess the situation totally. We need to think again about the purpose of our decision making and the best criteria for assessing the various courses of action we could take.

Decision Analysis can contain a learning element as far as decision makers are concerned. Whilst we should not manipulate the criteria to give the decision we desire, quite often the criteria may need some fine tuning. If done with integrity, some adjustment of the criteria may be considered to be a normal part of clarifying objectives. If we are still unhappy with a decision, it is likely that our list of alternative courses of action is lacking in quantity and/or quality. All this assumes that we are rational beings; I for one have made irrational decisions that I have never once regretted!

Summary

This chapter has described various techniques used by different problem-solving approaches/processes to develop our most promising ideas into possible solutions, and then (if necessary) to help choose between the possible solutions obtained.

Exercise

Next time you need to make what appears to be a straightforward decision, try using the Grid Method on a full Decision Analysis.

The next steps

This chapter explores the various implementation and acceptance issues concerned with realizing any problem solutions we have obtained, including the management of the change resulting from these solutions.

Introduction

The content of this chapter differs a little from the previous five chapters in so much as, although some 'techniques' are described, most of what follows is general theory and advice.

If we have followed the suggestion given earlier (pages 33–34, 61) that when seeking a consensus solution we should involve all the problem owners in the problem-solving process, we should not have any acceptance problems: having had their input into the problem-solving process the problem owners should be happy with and committed to the solution obtained. This chapter therefore starts with 'pure' implementation issues.

Because in some real-world situations it may be deemed by some that it is not practically (or culturally) feasible, or perhaps even desirable, for all problem owners to be involved in the problem-solving process, this chapter then considers how we could/should 'sell' a solution to those affected by it: how we gain their acceptance.

Finally, because our solutions will inevitably cause some change in other people's lives, the chapter concludes with the problems of being (seen as) a change agent and managing change.

Potential Problem Analysis – Kepner-Tregoe (hard)

Change is what life is all about. Success and survival depend on being able to anticipate change, and to avoid being swallowed up by its negative effects.

(Kepner and Tregoe, 1981, p.141)

Introduction

Potential Problem Analysis (PPA) is the fourth pattern of thinking employed by the 'effective manager' identified by Kepner and Tregoe (1981). It can be described as trying to determine what might conceivably go wrong with the implementation of a problem solution or decision, and preparing contingency plans against these possible occurrences. This deliberate planning for successful implementation is something that many of us often neglect.

Kepner and Tregoe (1981, pp.139–41) describe PPA as a systematic process for uncovering and dealing with potential problems that are reasonably likely to occur and therefore are worthy of attention. They believe that this process remains fundamentally 'an individual activity, whose results are guided primarily by individual motivation and concern' (1981, p.139), but once again, as with **Problem Analysis** and **Decision Analysis**, we will benefit collectively from using a common methodology. The basic questions we must ask are:

What could go wrong? What can we do about it now?

There are four stages in the PPA process, as shown in Frame 9.1, but they are not necessarily sequential. Preventative action is designed to remove completely or partially the likely cause of a potential problem. Contingent action is intended to reduce the impact of such a potential problem, particularly if it cannot be prevented. When deciding what actions can be taken, we must weigh up the cost (not just in financial terms) of performing them, against the cost of the potential disaster they are helping us to avoid.

Frame 9.1 *Potential Problem Analysis?*

- Identify the vulnerable areas.
- Identify the specific potential problems within these areas, whose negative potential is sufficient that it merits taking action now.
- Identify the likely causes of these potential problems and any preventative action that can be taken.
- Identify any contingent actions that can be taken either if preventative action is not possible or if it fails.

What these **vulnerable areas** are likely to be, and how we recognize them, will of course vary from one situation to another. Kepner and Tregoe suggest two approaches to determining the vulnerable areas. One is to rely on our experience of similar situations and our common sense, which is fine as long as it is not a totally new situation. We could try individually to **Brainstorm** (see pages 133–6) all the things that could go wrong and then identify those having the most potentially serious consequences; this is really combining two steps. The second way involves carefully going through the implementation of our solution chronologically (in our minds), listing all the things that must be done from start to finish. As we do this, potential problems should become obvious. Some common potential problems listed by Kepner and Tregoe (1981, p.145) are:

- anything that has not been done before;
- overlapping responsibilities – 'I thought Joe was handling that one';
- tight deadlines;
- any activities that have to be carried out, or coordinated from, a long distance away;

to which I would add:

- anything involving machines (particularly computers);
- interdependent activities; and
- acts of nature, God, etc.

Having identified the vulnerable areas, we need to look within these for specific potential problems.

To provide an example to illustrate PPA, let us suppose we have decided that we will hold an exhibition of products and services connected with the application of information and communications technology (ICT) in business. So how would we use PPA to ensure that we minimize the risk of anything going wrong with the holding of our exhibition?

The best way of determining possible vulnerable areas would be to gather together the people concerned with the organization of the exhibition (plus, if possible, potential exhibitors and visitors) and (as we said above) Brainstorm all the things that could go wrong. We were told first to look for the main vulnerable areas, and then look for specific problems within these areas. The Brainstorming group leader should consider possible vulnerable areas, to ensure that the group addresses all of these areas. However, group members can go in directly at the specific potential problem level, it being difficult to keep a Brainstorming group at only one 'level' anyway. After the Brainstorming session the problems can then be grouped into main vulnerable areas if so wished. For instance, problems referring to power cuts, lack of plugs, fuses, power points, etc. can be considered together under 'facilities'. Frame 9.2 gives some possible responses that we might get in such a session. They have been grouped under some possible categories of vulnerable areas, after they were generated.

Frame 9.2 *The great ICT exhibition: potential problems?*

What can go wrong?

People related:

- no visitors turn up;
- too many people turn up;
- difficulty finding the venue;

▶

- traffic jam outside the venue;
- minor accidents;
- illness of visitors/exhibitors;
- food poisoning;
- other emergencies;
- fire.

Administration:

- tickets printed wrongly;
- wrong date advertised/printed on ticket;
- planned media coverage fails to appear;
- another popular event held on the same day;
- lose money.

Facilities:

- milk for refreshments goes off;
- bar/caterers do not turn up;
- public address system fails;
- no spare plugs/fuses;
- inadequate power/lighting;
- major power cut;
- inadequate food/refreshments;
- not enough parking space;
- toilet blockage.

Activities:

- exhibitors do not turn up;
- exhibitors cannot get access to the venue to set up their stands;
- guest of honour/speakers do not turn up;
- not enough exhibition space.

Anti-social behaviour:

- everyone gets drunk;
- theft of exhibits before exhibition opens;
- theft of exhibits during exhibition;
- vandalism;
- political demonstration;
- civil riot;
- bomb scare;
- World War III.

Natural disasters

- weather-related problems;
- earthquake, storm, flood;
- Act of God.

Once we have established *what* might go wrong, we need to consider the *where*, *when* and the *extent* of these specific potential problems. This should indicate their likely causes and help us decide what can be done about them. For example, traffic problems are only likely to occur at the start and end of the exhibition and in the near vicinity. The forecasted attendance suggests that we may get a tail-back in either direction perhaps a couple of miles long (worse for those turning right into the exhibition site), which will take some half an hour to an hour to clear. The cause is obvious – volume of traffic – but things could be considerably worsened if our jam coincides with the normal rush hour traffic.

A major power cut could happen at any time. It could be an internal fault due to overloading circuits with all this extra equipment, or it could be due to external influences. In this latter case, it is likely to be coincidental with a thunderstorm, hurricane or heavy snow fall. So perhaps we should consult a local weather forecast. Another potential problem is people not turning up; the cause might be wrong dates or an ambiguous venue printed on the tickets or in the advertisements, or possibly a rival event.

Likelihood and seriousness of potential problems

As well as specifying their details, looking for causes and starting to think what can be done about them, we need to consider both the seriousness of the potential problems and their likelihood. The traffic jam is very likely, but not necessarily serious; a prolonged power cut at *certain* times of the year is unlikely, but could be devastating at an exhibition of ICT.

We might ignore fairly trivial potential problems, unless they were extremely likely, in which case we might want to guard against them being the 'last straw', particularly if they are easy to prevent. The traffic jam does not quite fit into this category, because people can find them very annoying even if they expect them. The simple expedients of starting the exhibition at say 9.30 or 10.00 a.m. after the rush hour and informing the police so that they can assign extra men to traffic duty are **preventative actions** worth considering. It may also be viable to open up another entrance to the site. The only preventative action against the unlikely occurrence of a power cut would be to hire a heavy duty mobile generator. We need to weigh up the cost in time and money of taking preventative action against the likelihood and seriousness of the potential problem.

The potential problem of people not turning up could be equally disastrous, but it is easy for us to double-check the dates and venue on the tickets and advertisements before they are released. We should also try to ensure there is no other event being held on the same day, which is likely to detract from possible attendance at ours.

Regarding the seriousness of repercussions, we should not just consider the *direct* significance of a problem, because it is usually possible to obtain insurance against weather, theft, financial losses, etc. People who attend events of this kind tend to remember the minor things. They may be prepared to accept that their favourite beer is not available at the bar, but inadequate toilet facilities is another matter. Such things contribute to the quality of service experienced by our customers.

Can we realistically do anything about a potential problem?

If we are unable to prevent a potential problem we need to develop **contingency plans** to alleviate its possible effects. We cannot prevent our key note speaker from being delayed or ill on the day of our exhibition, so we should have a reserve speaker lined up just in case. For the potential power cut problem, if it is impractical to have a second full source of mains power, we should at least ensure that the emergency lighting works and perhaps borrow two or three smaller 'portable' generators to provide enough extra light to examine key exhibits, to power essential computers, slide or overhead projectors and the public address system, so that our main lectures and presentations could carry on as planned.

There will be some potential problems we can realistically do little or nothing about, for example, the disruption of the event due to a bomb scare (except that presumably we have evacuation arrangements planned in case of a fire) or the possibility of food poisoning (apart from ensuring that we are using competent caterers) and that we have an ambulance crew standing by anyway to take care of any minor health/accident problems. It is very difficult to know where to 'draw the line'.

One final piece of advice is to be alert for the little everyday things, which we often take for granted, but which might have serious consequences. For example, suppose a regular fire alarm test was planned for the day of our exhibition, and we had overlooked this 'common' occurrence. Our visitors would hear it as a genuine fire alarm, and unless we could get to the public address system quickly and announce that this was only a practice, our carefully planned exhibition could degenerate very quickly into a situation of total disruption and panic.

The 'mechanics' of PPA

I have now described all the stages of PPA and if you are left with the feeling that these were not as clear cut as with Decision Analysis and Problem Analysis, it is because they are not. It is therefore a good idea to commit your PPA to paper as it develops. Starting with a brief **action plan statement** of what you are planning to implement, we need a document that also indicates to anyone concerned how far we have progressed in the investigation and in forestalling any potential problems. I envisage a large sheet with classified specific potential problems listed down the side, and headings across the top as follows: Likelihood, Seriousness, Can we realistically do anything?, Preventative actions, Person responsible for carrying them out?, By what date?, Other people that need to be informed, Contingent actions, Effectiveness, 'Trigger' mechanism, and Other comments. If this were implemented on a computer we would be able to sort potential problems by likelihood, seriousness or person responsible.

In this document we should also have an account of the procedures for triggering our various contingency plans – who is responsible for initiating it, and under what conditions should plan A, B or C be brought into play, etc. These plans should be widely publicized among the organizing team.

Concluding comments on PPA

To be effective at PPA, as with anything else, we must be motivated to do it. You have to want the thing you are planning to be a success, and even then, you may not always win. A half-hearted attempt gives no more than a false sense of security. I conclude by offering two well-known sayings, just in case I have not convinced you of the need for good PPA. Remember:

> Whatever can go wrong, will go wrong, but not only that, it will do so in the worst possible way at the most inconvenient time.

> The more complex a 'system' is, the more likely it is to go wrong.

Kepner and Tregoe (1981, p.161) say that 'PPA is not a negative search for trouble. It is a positive search for ways to avoid or lessen trouble that is likely to come in the future'. They maintain, not without justification, that PPA is a most rewarding experience.

Project management (hard)

If we assume that at the end of our Potential Problem Analysis, we have developed an *action plan*, then in most cases we will find it beneficial to perform some project planning/management activities to ensure that the implementation of our decision, solution or change programme runs according to plan, and that it meets its objectives on time and within budget. The very least we might do is to perform a **Critical Path** (or **Network**) **Analysis** to determine which interdependent activities are the (time-)critical ones, and produce a project schedule to monitor our progress. There are many good books on project management, so we will not pursue these things any further here.

There are also several software packages available which produce charts that show how activities should be or are progressing with time, (network) diagrams that show interdependency, and tables that help us determine whether activities are time-critical or can be delayed without affecting the total project time. These packages can also help with the costing, resource allocation and monitoring of a project's implementation.

'Synthesis'[1] – TRIZ (soft, creative)

The 'original' **synthetic** stage of ARIZ 61 was (in ARIZ 85C) expanded to three stages in which first we analyse the way in which the **physical contradiction** was removed, thus checking out the quality of the solution to our problem; for example, has the physical contradiction been removed in the most ideal way? Then we investigate the 'utilization of the found solution', which involves considering the super (or wider) 'system' to which our 'system' belongs and interacts, with a view to deciding what changes may need to be made to that super system and investigating whether our new 'system' may be used differently, and/or used to solve other technical problems. (In ARIZ 61, it was also suggested that we change the shape of our new invention – for, as Altshuller says 1999, p.106, 'a machine with a new function should have a new shape' – and tweaking the means that gives the functionality, prior to this!) And finally, we review how we *actually* solved the problem, the steps/stages 'covered' and the techniques used, compared with those suggested by the **TRIZ** algorithm, with a view to finding ways of improving the latter; that is, the systematic invention process.

Planning for Acceptance – Osborn-Parnes (creative/hard?)

Acceptance finding (now called **Building Acceptance**) is a stage in the **Osborn-Parnes** CPS process that fulfils the dual role of 'selling' the solution to other stakeholders, an activity that would probably not be needed if they had been previously involved in the problem solving (see pages 33–4, 61), and of trying to ensure a successful implementation of the solution using a technique called **Planning for Success** in a similar (but 'cut down') way to Kepner-Tregoe's PPA, from which it draws much of its inspiration. Since PPA has already been described, we will only go to the Osborn-Parnes process for the 'acceptance-gaining' techniques.

Isaksen and Treffinger (1985) suggest that a sensible first step is to complete a **Planning for Acceptance table**. This technique intends to capture (by Brainstorming) all possible sources of assistance and resistance, classified by the **5Ws & an H** (who, what, where, when why and how – see Frame 9.3). This technique could be a useful precursor of Lewin's **Force-field Analysis** (see below, Figure 9.5).

Frame 9.3 *5W's & an H applied to acceptance finding*

WHO – People (individuals, groups, organizations, etc.) who might . . . help with the implementation of your solution . . . oppose or inhibit the implementation of your solution, or limit the effectiveness of your solution.

WHAT – Things, objects or activities that might . . . be helpful to use when implementing your solution . . . impede your progress.

WHERE – Locations, places or events which might . . . be preferred/are especially useful for your situation . . . not be helpful in implementing your solution.

WHEN – Times or aspects of timing (dates, deadlines, schedules, etc.) which might be beneficial or especially appropriate . . . Particular times to avoid, or aspects of timing which might cause concerns when implementing your decision.

▶

WHY – Reasons you can provide that justify implementing your
solution, especially reasons you think will promote support for your
solution . . . Reasons for implementing your solution that might not
meet wide agreement or that some might find unacceptable.

HOW – Steps or specific actions which need to be accomplished in
order to carry out your solution effectively . . . Actions or activities
that might operate against your solutions or promote failure.

Adapted from Isaksen and Treffinger (1985, p.136)

When a solution consists of several parts, Isaksen and Treffinger (1985) suggest that you should consider the sources of assistance and resistance pertaining to each component, and develop specific courses of action for each part.

If you have used criteria to evaluate your solutions in the convergent phase of the **Problem Resolution** (Solution Finding) stage, this evaluation can be reviewed, and the criteria on which your solution was strongest and those on which it was weakest, can be listed – this should give us some other clues as to what we can do/need to do to gain acceptance for it. They call this technique **Using Criteria to Build Success**.

Having identified these sources, we need to estimate those of most importance, and any overlap – it is possible that the same source can provide both assistance and resistance, and these can be 'keys to building an effective plan of action', they certainly require careful attention – it may be possible to tip the balance in your favour. How you intend to deal with these forces can be added to your table.

Whilst on the subject of plans of action, Isaksen and Treffinger (1985) recommend that they should comprise:

- at least one immediate (within 24 hours) action to get you started,
- short-term actions to take soon,
- some long-term actions, including some ideas about how you will determine if your plan is working.

These should be **Checked for Ownership**, much as we did with **messes** initially, see page 75.

Imaging for Success – Osborn-Parnes (creative)

Isaksen and Treffinger (1985), when turning their attention to the convergent phase of the Acceptance finding stage, say that effective implementation or **action planning** 'can be stimulated by the use of imagery'. Their **Imaging for Success** technique (adapted from Lesio, 1984) has five steps:

- Goal discovery – imagine the goals you want to attain.
- Encounter discovery – form images of the people involved in gaining acceptance as they appear to you in everyday life, their looks, where and when you usually meet them, their habits, etc.

- Approach and reaction discovery – imagine meeting these people, how they and you would look and act, what you are saying and doing, what their reaction is, changing your approach, and what it would be like to be 'in their shoes'.
- Refinement discovery – consider the impact and effects of your approaches and the way these people reacted and responded. Modify, refine or improve your approach accordingly.
- Planning and rehearsal discovery – for your most promising revised actions remember the important details (time, place, mood, materials, preferences, etc.) and rehearse in your mind the whole scenario.

Implementation checklist – Osborn-Parnes

Based on the work of Rogers (1983) on **diffusion of innovations**, who identified certain specific attributes of innovations such as *relative advantage, compatibility, complexity, trialability* and *observability,* and examined how these affect acceptability, Isaksen, Dorval and Treffinger (2000) have developed an **implementation checklist** for use in the convergent phase of this stage in our problem solving. The questions are self-explanatory. The implementation checklist is intended for 'examining the effectiveness of your [implementation] plan and to identify places where it might be strong or need improvement or modification'.

Relative advantage

How well does my plan show how much better off people will be when they adopt the plan?

- Why is this plan better than what was done before?
- What advantages or benefits might there be to accepting the plan?
- Who will gain from the implementation of the plan?
- How will I (or others) be rewarded by adopting the plan?
- How might I emphasize the plan's benefits to all?

Compatibility

How well does my plan demonstrate that it is compatible with current values, past experiences and needs?

- Is the plan consistent with current practice?
- Does the plan meet the needs of a particular group?
- Does the plan offer better ways to reach our common goals?
- Who will naturally support and agree with the plan ?
- Can the plan be favourably named, packaged or presented?

Complexity

How well does my plan provide for easy communication, comprehension and use?

- Is the plan easy for others to understand?
- Can the plan be explained clearly to many different people?
- Can the plan be easily communicated?
- How might the plan be made more simple, or easier to understand?
- Is the plan easy to use or follow?

Trialability

How well does my plan allow for trialability?

- Can the plan be tried out or tested?
- How might uncertainty be reduced?
- Can we begin with a few parts of the plan?
- How might others be encouraged to try out part of the plan?
- Can the plan be modified by you or others?

Observability

How well does my plan provide results that are easily observed and visible to others?

- Is the plan easy for others to find or obtain?
- Can the plan be made more visible to others?
- How might I make the plan easier for others to see?
- Will others be able to see the effects of the plan?
- Are there good reasons for not making the entire plan visible?

Others

The following are some general questions that will help your planning and implementation efforts.

- What other resources will I need? How might I get them?
- What obstacles exist? How might we prevent or overcome them?
- What new challenges might be created and dealt with?
- How might I encourage commitment to the plan?
- What feedback about the plan is needed?

Reproduced with permission from Isaksen, Dorval and Treffinger
(2000, pp.162–7, DuBuque, IA: Kendall/Hunt)

Describing the change

Interestingly, in a similar vein, Rosabeth Moss Kanter (1983) has written about how the way that change is 'defined' affects its acceptability (see Frame 9.4). This advice is generally applicable to all change but particularly those related to an Information Systems project.

Frame 9.4 *Defining the change?*

Rosabeth Moss Kanter advises change agents to define (if possible!) their projects in ways that make them sound:

Triable – ensure that the change appears capable of being subjected to a pilot before going the whole way.

Reversible – convince people that what you are proposing can be changed back to the status quo if it falls to pieces – irreversible changes are seen as risky.

Divisible – where the change has a number of separate dimensions, present these as potentially independent aspects of a broader change programme – so when single issues cause problems the whole package doesn't have to fold.

Concrete – make the changes and their outcomes tangible and avoid expressing what will happen in abstract and general terms that do not convey an accurate feel for the proposals.

Familiar – make proposals in terms that other people in the organization can recognize, because if what you propose is so far over the horizon people can't recognize it, they'll feel out of their 'comfort zones' and start resisting.

Congruent – proposals for change should where possible be seen to 'fit' with the rest of the organization and be consistent with existing policy and practice.

Sexy – select projects that have 'publicity value', in terms of external or media relations, or in terms of internal politics.

Moss Kanter (1983)

Initiating and implementing change – advice for change agents

Introduction

Rapid change is commonplace. Complexity, disorganization and frustration are all natural aspects of our daily lives and normal features of organizational life. We would probably be surprised by their absence.

(Buchanan and Huczynski, 1985, p.410)

The basic premise underlying all that we have discussed so far has been that we need to develop and utilize a flexible yet systematic approach to problem solving and decision making. One that can help us cope with and plan for the rapidly changing environment so that we and our business and other organizations can survive and maintain their competitiveness. However, once we have a solution, or a decision on what course of action to take, it is inevitable, unless we decide to do nothing, that the implementation of our solution or decision will involve us centrally as an **agent of change**.

Further, in order to cope with the changes taking place around us, it is not merely sufficient that *we* are effective problem solvers; we ideally need everyone else, particularly those in our organization, to be so as well. The use of any systematic problem-solving and decision-making process will be much more difficult for an individual to apply alone, because that individual will require a supportive climate in which to operate effectively. This may involve anything from extra time and support facilities, through improved and flexible access to information and people, up to and including quite drastic attitudinal change. In other words, we may want (or need) to change those around us, and perhaps the whole organization, so that the use of these methods becomes the norm.

So, not only do we need to be personally able to cope with change, by alleviating undesirable effects and exploiting opportunities, we also need to be able to initiate and manage change. Whether our intention is simply to spread the use of effective problem-solving processes or just to implement their results, we will come up against the prevailing (organizational) culture, and its major manifestation, resistance; but first . . .

Types and sizes of change

Change comes in various 'sizes' and with consequently differing impacts. Getting used to a new seasonal ale at my local pub is not likely to cause me much grief, whereas a proposed downsizing of the organization I work for will probably concern me greatly. Having to employ a different computer software package is a relatively minor change. The restructuring of an organization from the traditional vertical functional structure to a much flatter, project-oriented horizontal structure with the change in business processes, work practices, reporting channels, empowerment and culture this often entails, is a very major change.

Possibly the most critical issue facing organizations today, which might well involve a cultural change, is in the case of large organizations which seek to regain a flexibility of response to environmental changes which has been lost, possibly due to cumbersome bureaucratic structures. For a smaller organization the issue is often maintaining the flexibility that it currently has, whilst continuing to grow. Central to this will be a culture that encourages and enables everyone to participate in problem solving and decision making. Such a culture would need to encourage the behaviours marked with a ^ in Frame 9.6, and should have a positive attitude to the use of the systematic problem-solving strategies illustrated in this book.

Trying to instil a culture of joint problem solving/decision making, teamwork, etc. such as this in some organizations, for example a large bureaucratic one, with many levels of hierarchy, discrete areas of functional specialism, a maze-like communication system and tightly defined areas of responsibility and spans of control, and/or one where attitudes such as 'Your job is to look after the stock cupboard, you're not paid to think, let alone use your initiative!' are endemic, would involve a great deal of structural and procedural change, and correspondingly major attitudinal changes. Some people seem to like the security and order bureaucracy affords.

When is (organizational) change necessary?

L.E. Greiner (1972) maintained that organizations ('naturally') go through five phases of (evolutionary) growth (as they get bigger and more 'mature'), and at each phase adopt common practices (not all of which are shown below), before reaching a crisis that leads to revolutionary change.

- Growth through creativity – where the structure is informal and top management style is individualistic and entrepreneurial, which leads to a crisis of leadership.
- Growth through direction – where the structure is centralized and functional, and top management style is directive, which leads to a crisis of autonomy.
- Growth through delegation – where the structure is decentralized and geographical, and top management style is delegative, which leads to a crisis of control.
- Growth through coordination – where the structure is line staff and product groups, and the top management style is 'watchdog', leading to crisis of red tape.
- Growth through collaboration – where the structure is a matrix of teams, top management style is participative, and the management focus is problem solving and innovation, leading to a crisis of . . . we are not quite sure what yet!

Whereas, Buchanan and Huczynski (1985) suggested the following three main reasons for change:

- the need to introduce internal changes to cope with developments occurring outside the organization;
- the desire to modify the attitudes, motives, behaviour, knowledge, skills and relationships of the organization's members in the interests of performance;
- the desire to anticipate future developments and to find in advance ways of coping with them.

There would appear to be little to argue over here, unless we raise the question of whether we have any right to try to change other people's beliefs and values, even if it is 'for their own good'.

However, when discussing *major* cultural changes, Terence Deal and Allen Kennedy (1982) identified five situations in which top management should consider the reshaping of the organization's culture to be something 'close to its most important mission'. These are:

- When the environment is undergoing fundamental change, and the company has always been highly value-driven (has a strong culture).
- When the industry is highly competitive and the environment changes quickly.
- When the company is mediocre, or worse.
- When the company is truly at the threshold of becoming a large corporation.
- When companies are growing very rapidly.

And, interestingly, they go on to say that, in most other situations, large-scale cultural change should simply not be undertaken.

Combining the size of change with the willingness (on the part of the recipients) to change, D.C. Dunphy and D.A. Stance (1988), by offering us four types of change and the situations in which they should be employed, seem to be implying that the need for major (transformational) change may be less 'rare'.

Given that the organization is in fit with the environment and time is available, **participative evolution**, they say, is required if the key interest groups favour the proposed change, and **forced evolution** necessary when the key interest groups oppose. And when the organization is out of fit and there is little time, **charismatic change** is appropriate if the key interest groups support radical change and **dictatorial transformation** advocated when change critical for survival is opposed by the key interest groups. (See Table 9.1.)

The implication from the above would seem to be that major cultural change should only be contemplated or attempted at certain stages in the development of an organization: when there is a potentially devastating change taking place in its environment, or as a last resort when things are about to fall apart internally. At other times we should perhaps be content with smaller changes and, if required, more modest modifications to culture.

Just because there is an external need for change – for example, changes in an organization's markets, in technology, in legislation or in society generally – we should not assume that this will guarantee or facilitate corresponding internal change. Similarly, the perceived desirability for internal changes due to factors such as organizational growth, acquisitions and mergers, internationalization or a desire to change the organization's mission, no matter how obvious their merits, may not be enough on their own to ensure that changes will be successfully carried through. Change is more likely, however, when there is both an internal and an external need present.

Resistance to change

'Resistance to change is a natural phenomenon. It does not come from sheer cussedness, it needs to be recognized, understood and managed' (Plant, 1987,

Table 9.1		Simple change (reproduction or expansion of existing state)	Transformational change (change incurred to existing state)
Four types of change depending on size of and willingness to change	Collaborate	Participative evolution	Charismatic transformation
	Coerce	Forced evolution	Dictatorial transformation

Source: Dunphy and Stance (1988)

p.29). Why *do* people consistently resist change? Roger Plant provides us with a useful list of the most frequent causes of resistance (see Frame 9.5). Some of these (marked with an *) we have encountered before (in Chapter 3), but as possible reasons for why our creative thinking skills may have become inhibited. So, if we are resisting something, it may be difficult to think about it creatively!

Frame 9.5 *Causes of resistance to change*

Fear of the unknown*

Lack of information*

Misinformation

Historical factors*

Threat to core skills and competence

Threat to status

Threat to power base

No perceived benefits*

Low trust organizational climates*

Poor relationships (for example, the autocratic boss)*

Fear of failure*

Fear of looking stupid*

Reluctance to experiment (and take risks)*

Bound too closely by tradition and custom*

Reluctance to let go (to relax, speculate, reflect, etc.)*

Strong peer group norms (or the perceived need to conform)*

Adapted from Plant (1987, p.18) (my additions in parentheses)

We will almost always have some vested interest in the way things are and we will usually resist anything we perceive as having a negative impact on our lives. We may simply identify too strongly with the part we have played in shaping current affairs, or we may perceive the effects of change as going beyond the confines of the organization or as posing a threat to an important part of our lives. As Buchanan and Huczynski neatly summarize (1985, pp.419–20):

> Organizational changes may mean the loss of power, prestige, respect, approval, status and security. Change may also be personally inconvenient for a variety of reasons. It may disturb relationships and arrangements that have taken much time and effort to establish. It may force an unwanted geographical move. It may alter social opportunities.

People attempting to implement changes often do not appreciate that *they* may have already had the chance to think through the consequences of the proposed changes, whereas the rest of us probably have not. It is a natural reaction to try to halt or slow things down until we have had a chance to do this. Even if these changes do not involve a dramatic reshaping of our lives, we still need time to satisfy ourselves of this. More serious is the possibility that the changes are being seen as having 'unpleasant' side effects, because of an incorrect interpretation of their consequences or that the resistance is due to the way changes are being suggested or implemented.

In Chapter 11, when discussing the **Soft Systems Methodology (SSM)**, we will identify four types of possible change that may be recommended by such an intervention: changes in *structure*, *procedure*, *policy* and *attitude*; and as Checkland (1981) rightly says, the last one is extremely difficult to accomplish. We can also differentiate two main forms of resistance to any of these changes The first, **cognitive** resistance, is connected with the possession or lack of knowledge; the second is due to **behavioural** (or emotional) reactions. The latter is the more difficult to deal with. However, it should not be assumed that only attitudinal changes can cause emotional reactions.

We may resist a change because we do not know or have not been told what is really going on (lack of information), or how this might affect us (fear of the unknown); because we have been fed wrong and 'disagreeable' information about the change being proposed or implemented (misinformation); or because of fear that we do not possess the appropriate knowledge, information, skills, managerial capacity, etc. to cope in the new situation. Modern business organizations attempt to minimize these uncertainties through good communications, counselling and training. However, such attempts to deal with cognitive resistance may simply push it 'underground', because we may feel there is nothing we can legitimately complain about, due to the cultural unacceptability of saying that we feel threatened or inadequate. There could still be a host of subjective, interpersonal and political factors fuelling the resistance, which will continue covertly by methods limited only by the ingenuity and integrity of those involved. We should not assume that a source of resistance which could claim to have a rational cause is necessarily amenable to rational solution!

The emotional reactions that give rise to behavioural resistance are often precipitated by the perceptions individuals or groups have of a situation, and the assumptions they make on the basis of these. These perceptions and assumptions could be incorrect or unfounded, and so could theoretically be allayed by providing the right information. However, if by then we no longer trust the initiators of the change, this will result in behavioural resistance that is difficult to assuage.

The level of a person's resistance to change is inversely proportional to the amount of involvement in and information known about that change. Thus the importance of keeping people informed right from the start cannot be overemphasized. 'Before fighting resistance, one should ask why these seemingly reasonable people are doing seemingly unreasonable things' (Sathe, 1985, p.281).

Whatever the personal sources of the resistance, the likelihood is that they will be reinforced by our next area of concern, organizational culture.

What is culture?

The study of the effects of culture, and particularly of organizational culture, is still relatively new and much work is still going on in this field. Culture is accepted as a very important aspect of organizational behaviour, and interest in cultural effects, both within an organization or group, or external to them, is a natural progression from viewing organizations as open systems. Full treatment of the topic of organizational culture requires a book in itself, thus what follows is necessarily a brief overview.

Due to its relative newness as an area worthy of research there are a variety of definitions of culture around, although the following are fairly typical:

> culture is the total pattern of human behaviour . . . embodied in thought, speech, action, and artefacts . . . (*Webster's Dictionary*).

> organizational culture is the unique configuration of norms, values, beliefs, ways of behaving and so on that characterize the manner in which groups and individuals combine to get things done. (Eldridge and Crombie, 1974, p.89)

It has been suggested that an organization's culture is a product of the environment it operates in, the technology it uses, its structure and internal functioning, its members' **psychological contract** with it manifested in their attitude to work, or even some combination of all these. Graves (1986) comments that these ways of looking at culture tend to see it as an objective phenomenon, whereas he sees it as totally subjective: the reason why a particular culture is commonly perceived by people is not because it is an objective reality, but because the *way* those people perceive it (their mental set) is the same. Graves cites as evidence for this view the fact that outsiders invariably view someone else's culture differently from those inside it. If culture is a common perception of the environment which gives rise to common behaviours (a sort of collective personality), the aspects of an organization that we as individuals are attracted to will be those that fit our personalities and through which we can fulfil our self-concepts and satisfy our needs. By the same token, organizations will likewise select us on the expectation that we will enhance their cultures.

If, as suggested, our psychological contracts are somehow interwoven with culture and if we perceive that some proposed change is likely to alter this organizational culture, it would not be unreasonable of us to be anxious or fearful that this will lead to an imminent worsening of our psychological contract. Such anxieties are highly likely to result in resistance to the change.

The basis of any culture is the set of often unstated assumptions commonly shared by the members of an organization or group, which determine the way they communicate with and behave towards others, and how such actions are justified. These assumptions include *beliefs* about the world they live in, how it functions, their place in it, etc., and *values* concerning ideals which are considered to be preferable, desirable or good and hence worth striving for. These values can be end-states, e.g. equality, self-fulfilment, freedom; or ways of conducting oneself, e.g. courage, honesty and friendship.

Beliefs and values derive both from personal experience and from the opinions of others whom one trusts and identifies with. Many of these beliefs and values become internalized; that is, they become so well assimilated that we think of them as our own to the extent that they govern what we say and do without our being aware of it. Beliefs and values often take time to become internalized, but once they do, they can become almost immutable and affect not only behaviour but attitudes as well: Vijay Sathe (1985) says that people are typically stubborn or intolerant when their values are challenged. Values occupy too central a position in one's belief system and are too important an aspect of one's personality to permit them to be readily changed. Attempts that others make directly to confront and change a person's values are rarely effective and are likely to provoke emotional reactions or hostility.

Our beliefs and values do not necessarily have any rational basis, and it is even possible for us to be unaware of an unresolved inconsistency between them, because we have repressed it rather than faced up to the 'pain' of recognizing it.

Culture can be both an asset and a liability. As Sathe (1985, p.25) remarks, it

> eases and economizes communications, facilitates organizational decision making and control, and may generate higher levels of cooperation and commitment in the organization. The result is efficiency, in that these activities are accomplished with a lower expenditure of resources, such as time and money, than would otherwise be possible.

Once formed, it can be very difficult for members of an organization to change its culture, and if the culture is no longer compatible with the needs of the organization and its members, it can become a millstone around the corporate neck. This may happen when an organization has to make a fairly major alteration to its objectives and/or operations in order to cope with some sea-change in its turbulent environment.

Culture is manifested by certain standards of expected behaviour (norms), including the way we communicate with others and present ourselves to them. These norms reflect the underlying beliefs and values that are held to be important. For example, a belief in equality might be demonstrated by the exclusive use of first names as the usual mode of personal address, or a respect for the individual might be expressed by always being punctual for meetings. Norms are what the members of an organization actually say and do, as opposed to what people might have you believe that they say and do.

Research into culture and its effects (using Factor Analysis) suggests that we may usefully group norms together under general headings (sometimes confusingly called 'climate variables') such as those listed in Frame 9.6. This essentially comprises the ten norm groups that have been identified (by Allen and Pilnick, in Plant, 1987, pp.141–2) as having the most impact on the effective performance of an organization. This list is slightly modified (to make it more complete) from other sources, particularly the Human Relations Institute's Normative Systems Indicator. There is a positive and negative aspect to each of these (the negative aspect often being simply the lack of the behaviour specified) and these norms are interrelated; for example, open and honest communication is unlikely in an organization that encourages a highly competitive attitude amongst and between its members.

Frame 9.6 *Organizational climate[1] variables*

Organizational and personal pride*
Performance: excellence* *v.* adequacy

▶

Clarity of goals, tasks and rewards ^

Leadership ^ *v.* supervision*

Collaboration and teamwork* *v.* individualism

Open communication (honesty) ^ * *v.* guardedness/secretiveness

Relationships*: warm, supportive and trusting ^ *v.* competitive

Training and development ^ *

Individual/group responsibility and autonomy ^

Participation and involvement ^ *v.* autocracy

Conflicts/differences of opinion (permitted) ^

Innovation and change ^ * *v.* conservatism and stability

Risk taking/challenges/learning from mistakes and failures ^

Customer/consumer relations* (quality, helpfulness, etc.)

Profitability and cost effectiveness*

*Allen and Pilnick's norms
^ Factors achieving heightened motivation

The list in Frame 9.6 is not a particularly definitive set of norm groups, and there is a degree of overlap between some of the individual items, especially around the 'teamwork/relationships' area. However, it does demonstrate further how norms reflect the underlying beliefs and values of a culture: the belief that one should value the contributions of individuals could well be indicated by behaviours that positively support things like 'training and development', 'participation and involvement'. In some items (e.g. 'responsibility and autonomy', 'conflicts/differences of opinion') an underlying element of structure – informal *v.* formal: rules, regulations and hierarchies – can be detected. Also, some ten of the norms are virtually the same as the factors that contribute towards achieving heightened motivation amongst followers mentioned in Chapter 13.

Organizational norms are important to us for a variety of reasons. For example, by observing these patterns of behaviour we can attempt to discern what an organization's culture is and ascertain how difficult it maybe to make any changes. The extent to which we conform to norms is perceived as a measure of our fit with an organization, and thus on how effective we can be within that organization, whether as an agent of change or anything else.

The content of an organization's culture depends on the values and beliefs its founders held and those which subsequent leaders and others brought with them when they joined, and the relative importance that these people place upon these assumptions. These will have been modified incrementally in the light of the experience of solving the organization's day-to-day problems, adapting to changes in its external environment and maintaining internal coherency.

The strength of culture, and the intensity of the related behaviour, depends on a culture's 'thickness', how 'far-reaching' and all-encompassing the shared beliefs and values are (how many aspects of our lives they cover), the clarity and consistency of the ordering of these assumptions, and the extent to which they are commonly shared by members of the organization. The number of people in the organization and its geographical dispersion are also relevant factors. The stronger the culture the more resistant to change it is, and the amount of resistance actually encountered will be a function of both its strength and the extent of the change planned.

Deciphering organizational culture

Before we try to initiate change we ought to attempt to decipher the prevailing culture, so that we can anticipate likely reactions and prepare some ways for dealing with the organizational norms we are likely to come up against. Sathe (1985) offers the following advice on where we should start looking for clues.

Both implicit and explicit forms of communication must be attended to, when examining the manifestations of culture. The former include rituals, customs, ceremonies, stories, metaphors, special language, folklore, heroes, logos, decor, dress, and other symbolic forms of expression and communication. Examples of the latter are announcements, pronouncements, memos, and other explicit forms of expression and communication.

Sathe reminds us to reflect also on what is missing, i.e. what is not seen, said or done. This will help us uncover organizational taboos. He suggests that we need to discover as much as we can about the following by both direct observation and questioning:

- the background of the organization's founders and those that followed them;
- the organization's response to crises or other critical events;
- the people who are considered to be 'deviants', and how they are dealt with;
- the most important (unspoken) assumptions about work, human nature and human relationships shared by the organization's members;
- the organization's motto;
- the people within the organization who are respected and/or considered to be highly successful, its heroes;
- that which constitutes a serious punishment in the organization, and hence the mistakes that are not forgiven;
- the company folklore, rituals, symbols and ceremonies;
- the main rules that everyone has to follow.

If we can determine these then we should be able to uncover the organization's ideology, the dominant set of interrelated ideas that explains how the important assumptions that we share fit together and make sense. It is the ideology that gives a meaning to the content of the organization's culture.

A typology of organizational culture

One way of looking at organizational culture is that proposed by Harrison (1972). He identified four types of organizational culture named according to their predominant 'orientation'. These are: power, role, task and person. Frame 9.7 gives a brief summary of their characteristics. No particular culture is more 'right' than any other, though some seem to suit certain types of organization better than others.

Frame 9.7 Organizational Culture

'God'	Power Zeus	Role Apollo	Task Athena	Person Dionysus
Location of power and influence	Centre (and power rings).	Top (rules and procedures).	At the 'knots' (control of resources).	Individual people.
Power base	Resource (some person at centre).	Position (sometimes expert) (never person).	Expert (position and person have some effect).	Expert (if needed).
Typical examples of where found	Small entrepreneurial companies, investment banks, commercial banks.	Civil service, oil industry, brokerage houses, insurance companies.	Management consultancies, high technology firms, accounts group of advertising agencies.	Barristers' chambers, architects partnerships R&D departments.
Conditions in which it thrives	Entrepreneurial situations.	Steady state, predictable or controllable markets. Long product life.	Competitive market. Short product life. Anything requiring sensitivity, creativity or integration.	
Efficiency depends on	Selection of key individuals.	Rational allocation of work and responsibility.	The right people at the right level.	Autonomous teamwork?
Strengths	Can move quickly in response to threat or danger.	Economies of scale. Depth of expertise. Functional specialisms.	Extremely adaptable, speed of reaction, ideal for creativity or integration.	
Weaknesses	Dependent on person at centre. Limited in size.	Slow to see change. Slow to change.	Difficult to control, inherently unstable, limited in size.	Control virtually impossible.
Characteristic type of activity	Policy, crisis (breakdown).	Steady state.	Innovation.	
Typical features of psychological contract	Suits those who are: power orientated, 'politically' minded, risk takers. Low security.	Good security. Chance to acquire expertise. Predictable and satisfying environment. No autonomy.	Team spirit, considerable work autonomy, judgement by results, respect based on contribution.	Organization (if any) subordinate to the individual, work autonomy.
Other comments	Effectiveness relies on trust, empathy and a bit of telepathy!		Preferred by many as place to work in.	The organization eventually takes over.

Source: adapted from Harrison (1972) and Handy (1978).

Organizations go through various stages of development, and at any given stage one particular culture might be more applicable than another. For instance, Plant (1987, p.118–19) offers a three-stage development sequence, autocratic, bureaucratic and democratic, which he relates to role, power and task cultures respectively. He stresses the importance of going through all the stages no matter how desirable the democratic stage appears to be:

> It is no use having a highly competent, forward looking, participative management team in place without a firm infrastructure of policies and procedures to bring about co-ordination and progress. People need to be clear about their responsibilities, what is expected of them and the parameters within which they can work. These are all *bureaucratic* processes.

A family business may start out as a power culture, an entrepreneurial organization driven by a single central figure. As it grows larger or the central figure ceases to be the main driving force, the organization may evolve into a role culture based on functional specialisms. New companies at the forefront of the application of technological research, however, have a tendency to (too quickly?) adopt a task culture, orientated towards individual jobs or projects, and a matrix structure, providing the flexibility and speed of response demanded by that environment. In times of dire resource limitation, the internal conflict likely to develop within such a culture may force it to change or revert to a role or power culture. Within larger organizations certain departments, for example, marketing, may have a different culture (say, a task culture) from the majority of the rest of the organization (possibly a role culture). The most appropriate culture seems to be related to the principal activity type of the organization or department. These types have been categorized by Handy (1985) as steady state, innovation, crisis and policy.

It would be extremely difficult to initiate joint problem solving and teamwork in a power culture, which actively encourages competition between its members. Likewise, the people who are drawn towards organizations with role cultures tend to be those less tolerant of change, preferring a predictable environment; and this could well be the reason why this type of culture is generally antipathetic to change. Thus, we need to take into consideration both the nature of the culture and its implications in terms of psychological contracts, when planning to effect a change.

All except the role culture are believed to be limited by size. Problems can occur when organizations become so large as to place a strain on these other cultures. One solution to this dilemma, tried by Apple Computer, a company with a strong culture, is to allow and encourage parts of the organization to split off from the 'mother' company to form separate and virtually autonomous entities, but which still retain close links. A network of smaller companies is achieved; this permits the development of new ideas and business directions, whilst at the same time preserving the 'youth' and small size of the companies that constitute the network.

More on culture

John Sculley (1988, pp.429–34), the ex-CEO of Apple Computer, warns of the down-side of culture: 'culture limits us by its emphasis on tradition, on yesterday's heroes, on myths and rituals whose sole value is that they derive from an earlier time'. He believes that this makes us look forever backwards, and suggests that a better way of preserving the best aspects of culture and of passing them on is to think of them as a 'genetic code'. This could be seen as imprinting notions of identity and values as culture does, but in so doing it suggests a sense of forward-looking, a sense that everything done today is an investment in the future, not an expression of the past.

Sculley recommends that we forget all the myths, rituals, symbols, stories and traditions, all the trappings of culture. Organizational **metaphors**, such as 'software artist' and 'hardware wizard', should replace myths because metaphors focus on 'relationships of ideas, images, symbols, and create tension collision of ideas, fusion . . . get you dreaming in two worlds'. This is creativity! Any 'heroes' should personify a process, for example 'gate-keeping' or teamworking, and not any particular set of achievements. The values (which are after all the essence of culture) are held on to but even these are not seen as immutable, and to this we should add visions that embody directions and not goals, and an identity that makes the organization recognizable without tightly defining what it is (or has) to be. The individual is free to develop in his/her own way rather than always having to conform rigidly to the 'tribal' customs more usually associated with culture. And although the basic 'hereditary characteristics' are transmitted down through the generations, they manifest themselves in different ways. This would seem to be a possible way of getting many of the benefits of a strong culture, without encumbering ourselves with a straitjacket that will hinder future changes.

Now that we know a little more of what culture is, how do we go about dealing with it and changing it?

Managing change

Following on from our comments about culture, we can predict that the ease or difficulty with which we can achieve any change is dependent on whether it can be accomplished within the existing organizational culture, by modifying it, or only through a more drastic cultural change which must be led at least partially from outside. A 'major change' is likely to involve considerable change in the culture. What can realistically be achieved depends on our standing or status within the organization, which ultimately reduces to how much power we have, or have access to, of whatever form. If a major change is being considered – as would probably be the case when trying to instil a flexible and systematic approach to problem solving/decision making throughout an organization, then many organizational development specialists would insist that changes of this type must come from 'the top'. For example, Deming (1986) is adamant that the attitudinal changes needed to bring about his management philosophy of Total Quality Management *have* to be embraced from the top down. And Reddin (1977) has likened the attempt to implement a 'bottom-up' change to mutiny.

We shall continue our discussion of change from the two dimensions of 'amount of cultural change required' and 'amount of power we have at our disposal' shown in Figure 9.1. On the way we will look at how to deal with resistance, remembering that real-life situations do not fall into neat partitions like this. We must first, however, examine the determinant factors or 'lifelines' that ought to be present if we are to be successful in promoting change.

Status, credibility and acceptance

Effecting change, particularly if it involves major modifications to the culture, means we will need to have considerable **status** in the organization. Sathe (1985) believes that status is a function of our **credibility** and **acceptance** and that high status is achieved with a high level of either credibility or acceptance and at least a moderate level of the other.

Credibility gives others assurance that we have 'the ability and intention to deliver valued results', and we gain credibility by the act of delivering them; however, credibility does not come from delivering results that the individual personally values or those one thinks the organization should value, or even those that others say are valued. It comes from results that are *actually* valued. This depends on the (content of the) organization's culture.

Acceptance implies that we are perceived as part of the community. The cultural caricatures shown in Figure 9.2 suggest that the further from being a **good soldier** we are, the less acceptance we have and the more difficult will be our task of changing things. In fact, all of the 'types' can have (some) acceptability based on what they contribute to the organization and the extent to which they

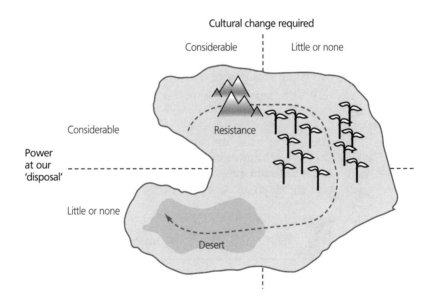

Figure 9.1

A 'change map'

Figure 9.2

Cultural caricatures

Adapted from Sathe, (1985)

transgress cultural norms. The **adapter** may work hard for extrinsic rewards, the **maverick** may supply creative energy and ideas and the **rebel** may provide useful critique of organizational policies and processes as well as being a negative role model for the good soldiers. But if you fancy yourself as a maverick and a change agent you will need a lot more credibility than your average good soldier.

Sathe maintains that high credibility requires a high level of either **power** or **trust** accompanied by at least a moderate level of the other and sees trust as being based on our perception of another's 'character' and 'competence':

Character:

- Integrity – how others perceive one's basic honesty.
- Motives – how others perceive one's intentions.
- Consistency – the sense others have of how reliable and predictable one's behaviour is.
- Openness – the sense that one is levelling with the other in discussing problems.
- Discretion – the assurance that one will not violate confidences or carelessly divulge sensitive information.

Competence:

- Specific competence – one's competence in the specialized knowledge and skill required to do the job.
- Interpersonal competence.
- Business sense.

Power and trust are not qualities that we as individuals have or can acquire, they are attributes of the relationships we have with others. There are thought to be different types of power, as shown in Frame 9.8, some of which (reward and coercion) are not considered compatible with a trusting relationship.

Frame 9.8 *Types of power*

According to Sathe, power is one person's capacity to affect the behaviour and thinking of another. Influence is the process of using power. The basis of this capacity was classified by French and Raven (1959) into reward, coercive, legitimate, referent and expert power. Plant (1987) replaces referent power (having that which makes others want to identify with us) with connection power, which we possess due to our access to and contacts with other people and groups. Handy (1985) draws particular attention to resource power, but Sathe (1985) in the list below draws all of this together very concisely. He groups legitimate power (being perceived as having some right to give orders) with reward and coercive power (being perceived as having the ability to reward and punish), and together refers to them as positional power; and he groups referent and expert power as personal power.

▶

Positional power

The power we have due to our position within the organization that permits us:

- to structure another person's tasks or formal organizational relationships;
- to reward (financially, or with promotions, recognition, etc.) and punish the other people;
- to allocate or control resources valued by another person (including his or her access to others and to information);
- to direct and organize the other people.

Personal power

The power we have due to our:

- ability to create a perception of common goals;
- charismatic appeal in the eyes of the other person;
- creating a sense of obligation in the other person;
- building a reputation as an expert in the eyes of the other person;
- fostering the other person's conscious or subconscious identification with us;
- affecting another's perception of dependence on us for resources and help;
- ability to persuade the other person;
- possession of personal information and resources valued by the other person;
- ability to reduce the uncertainty felt by the other person.

Guidelines for managing change

Plant (1987) offers the following set of key activities for the successful implementation of (any) change:

- Communicate like never before.
- Turn perceptions of 'threat' into opportunity.
- Ensure early involvement.
- Work at gaining commitment.
- Provide help to face up to change.
- Avoid over-organizing.

Deal and Kennedy (1982) admit that engineering a cultural change is still a 'black art' but offer the following tips:

- Recognize that peer group consensus will be the major influence on acceptance or willingness to change.
- Convey and emphasize two-way trust in all matters (and especially communications) related to change.
- Think of change as skill-building and concentrate on training as part of the change process.
- Allow enough time for the change to take hold.
- Encourage people to adapt the basic idea for the change to fit the real world around them.

Between them, these two lists cover most relevant factors. As we have argued before (see page 187), (early) involvement (in the change process) and participation (in the problem solving and decision making that goes with it) is or should be paramount. Likewise, the importance of good (trusted) two-way communications and training cannot be overemphasized. Providing other (practical, emotional, financial, etc.) support along with the relatively new idea, captured in the last item in both lists: conveying that what we want is for everyone to 'arrive safely' at the change destination, the route taken being less important than actually getting there, are also significant factors in a successful change.

It should not be necessary to say this, but ... we are all different, and the amount of participation wanted, the style and content of communications expected, the training and support needed, etc. by people will also be different. These things (especially communications) should be appropriately designed and targeted.

In addition to all this, Moss Kanter (1983) suggests that change management increasingly requires managers to adopt transformational skills, such as visioning, empowerment and delegation, in order that the energy and creativity of people can be effectively harnessed to the success of change.

The coping cycle

We need to consider the above in conjunction with the effects of our **coping cycle**. Carnall (1995, pp.143–4) comments that our performance during a period of change will be affected in three ways:

1. by the learning curve effect: new systems, processes, structures, etc. will have to be learned,
2. by the progress effect: it is likely that the new systems will not be implemented perfectly immediately, problems will need to resolved, modifications made, etc.,
3. by the self-esteem effect: self-esteem initially declines when change is undertaken and needs to be rebuilt,

... and all this obviously takes time.

He goes on to describe several stages within the coping cycle and the typical behaviour we should expect to see in ourselves, and from others, and the way our self-esteem changes.

Stage 1 – Denial

- People will deny the need for change and question the validity of the new ideas.
- People will find (often 'devious') value in the current situation.
- The sense of being subject to an 'external' threat can lead to increased group cohesiveness.
- Because of this, self-esteem will increase.

Since there is often a delay in the fall-off of performance, attempts to minimize the immediate impact of the change can help at this stage.

Stage 2 – Defence

- People become aware of the realities of the change and that they must come to terms with them.
- This leads to feelings of depression and frustration.
- People become defensive about their job/territory.
- Self-esteem drops.

Stage 3 – Discarding

- There is a general letting go of the past and a looking forward to the future . . . support and the opportunity to experiment with the new systems without pressure helps with this.
- The individual begins to identify with the changes involved.
- People will tend to talk openly and constructively about their experiences, and become involved in experimentation and risk taking.
- Given time, individuals will begin to recreate their own sense of identity and self-esteem.

Stage 4 – Adaptation

- Gradually the individual learns or adapts to the new way of doing things.
- Technical or operational problems are identified and modifications made.
- Anger may be encountered as attempts at improvement fail. This is not about resistance to change but a consequence of trying to make things work. Doing this for themselves often develops in people the skills, understanding and attachments needed for effective running in the future. (This is not a reason for opting out of providing training and support!)

Stage 5 – Internalization

- People involved have created a new system, process and organization. New relationships between people and processes have been tried, modified and accepted, and been incorporated into an understanding of the new work situation.

We need to get people through this cycle as quickly as possible. Carnall says (1995, pp.144–7) that to increase performance after a change requires the re-establishment of self-esteem (see Figure 9.3). He goes on to identify (1995, pp.148–54) many issues that we as 'victims' of a change need to face, for example, Can I benefit from the changes? What is the worst that can happen to me? Do I know what I want? Do I have the skills and abilities to cope with the changes? How am I expected to behave? Who can I talk to about things? How can I help myself? There is a lot of help that could and should be given on these matters by the people managing the changes; there are also things we will have to sort out for ourselves.

Overcoming resistance

No matter how mutually beneficial some changes may be, or how altruistic the motives of the change agent(s), there will be resistance. We need practical methods of analysing resistance so that effective countermeasures can be devised and applied. First, we could attempt to classify people according to the amount of resistance we think they are likely to offer. This should reveal the extent of our problem and clarify where we most need to direct our attention. Figure 9.4 offers a possible classification scheme. There is a danger in rigidly pigeon-holing people, so apply any such classification loosely. A person may hold different positions depending on which aspects of the change are being addressed. And a person hostile to one particular change may not necessarily be against change *per se,* and could actually be a change agent with regard to developments elsewhere.

Another useful tool is the often-cited **Force-field Analysis** devised by Kurt Lewin (see Figure 9.5). The idea here is that, at any particular time, a situation is held in equilibrium by forces in favour of (driving forces) and against (resistance) change. These forces could be due to ideas, people or things – we have mentioned the organizations ideology above, one source of 'ideas'; an example

Figure 9.3

The coping cycle

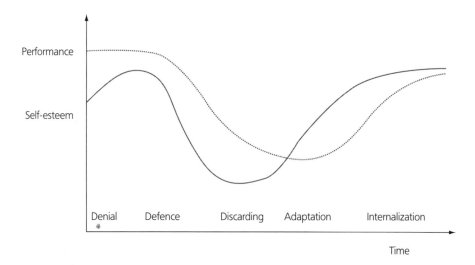

Reproduced with permission from *Managing Change in Organizations* by Colin Carnall (1995), published by Pearson Education Ltd.

of a 'thing' might be the need to keep a legacy IT system. The length of the arrows represents the magnitude of these forces, and they can be annotated with what we perceive the cause of the force to be, and (if appropriate) from which group of people it is coming. When we try to implement change we are attempting to move this equilibrium point, and in order to do this, we have to increase or add driving forces and/or reduce or remove resisting forces. Increasing driving forces may simply increase the intensity of resistance. A better policy is to try to reduce resistance.

Figure 9.4

Reaction to change

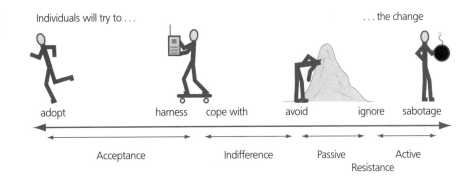

After Oldcorn (1982)

Figure 9.5

Kurt Lewin's Force field Analysis

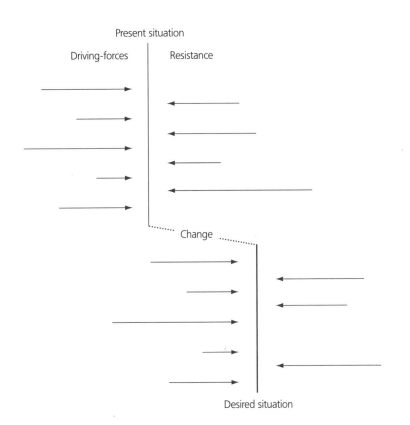

But how do we actually do this? Sathe (1985) claimed that resistance to change is overcome when people feel a sufficient incentive to change (they are motivated), when they know what new behaviour is expected from them (the new model is clear) and when the change process is appropriate to the needs of the situation (the method used is suited to prevailing conditions). For anyone who perceives a problem situation or an opportunity and is about to look for some way of resolving or exploiting it, the key words must be *motivation*, *involvement* and *commitment*. To gain commitment from others to an idea, a project or a change, we must ensure that those likely to be affected by it are involved in its development right from its conception, and have the opportunity to take part in the planning, problem solving and decision making that must go on. The only thing we can do when presented with a well-formed idea or a carefully planned set of changes is to accept it or reject it. We need to feel part of any idea or solution, to feel that our contributions were not only wanted, but have been recognized and duly incorporated into it: participation is the only effective way to ensure maximum commitment.

Allowing participation should be common courtesy – a demonstration of our respect for others, as well as an obvious means of gaining their support and commitment. Its effectiveness unfortunately means that participation is abused by unscrupulous change agents as a tactical ploy to neutralize leaders of resistance. After the real planning and decision making has taken place they are involved in the implementation of the change process by playing on their morality ('You know, the best way you can ensure that what we are saying is the truth, and that your people won't be any the worse off after this, is to help us get these changes through') or by appealing to baser motives, for example by offering to promote them 'after all this is over'.

Other methods of overcoming resistance include the deliberate use of misinformation, for example – 'forgetting' to mention the disadvantages of the change. Another aspect of the 'divide and conquer' ploy above is the disclosure of selected information intended to appeal to specific key parties. And there is always explicit and implicit coercion. These methods tend only to work in the short term, can easily misfire and are alien to the 'spirit' of this book.

The other way to overcome resistance is to try to find out its true cause and attempt to understand why people are resisting. If we can discover the cause and there is something we can do about it, then we do it. If not, we should explain why we cannot, and offer some form of compensation.

Changing the culture

Organizational culture is maintained by inculcating beliefs and values into newcomers when they join, and through the organization's recruitment process, by appointing only those who possess the right (same) values, attitudes, goals, etc. and/or would, or want to, fit in. Put simply, to effect a major cultural change, one has to do one or both of two things:

● Encourage people to accept the new beliefs and values by persuading them that the new way is better, or at least mutually beneficial.

● Appoint/promote people with the appropriate new values and beliefs, whilst removing or rendering powerless those who are hanging on to the old ones and offering resistance.

When it comes down to the practicalities of changing the culture's content, there are basically only five ways we can go. We can reorder (the importance of), modify or remove existing beliefs and values, add new ones, or attempt any combination of these things. The only guideline as to how we should do this is to accomplish the desired change with the minimum amount of disruption to the existing culture. The five options are presented roughly in order of increasing disruptive potential, except that it will probably be easier to add a new belief or value than to remove an old one.

Permanent change can only be guaranteed if people genuinely believe and value their new way of doing things. For this we need change in both culture and behaviour, but it does not follow that a change in one means a change in the other. We could change the culture in so much that individuals may change one or more of their beliefs and values, but find that due to, for example, ingrained habit or insufficient intrinsic motivation, they are unable to modify the corresponding behaviour. Similarly, people may pretend to adopt a new behaviour because they perceive they have to (usually only when being observed) although they have not accepted the new beliefs and values. Compliance can only ever be a short-term measure; for cultural change to stick people must identify with the new order, and ultimately internalize the new beliefs and values.

A corollary of the above is that we may be able to achieve desired changes in behaviour without a correspondingly major cultural change. Alternatively, there may be scope within the existing culture to utilize creatively existing beliefs and values to effect attitude change. We can do this by making minor changes to the content of a culture, perhaps by a change in emphasis accomplished by a reordering of the cultural assumptions.

If the changes we want to make are compatible with the prevailing culture, we can make the culture work for us. First, we should develop our ability to decipher culture as outlined earlier, to ascertain which things are actually valued. Second, we should ensure the views we express are in keeping with the most important and widely held cultural values; there are benefits in being seen to be a cultural standard-bearer. The degree of acceptance this bestows upon us should ensure that even unorthodox ideas will be seen in the best possible light. We should be careful not to criticize any of these higher values as we need to demonstrate actively that our idea or change fits in with, supports and even enhances the existing culture.

Other changes

In lowering our sights to more modest changes, we should be aware that a relatively minor change may have far-reaching results. For example, a company may attempt to replace a 'tea trolley service' to individual offices with a central provision where people can 'get together'. Those providing the service may resent the change because the social aspect of going around and meeting people was a satisfying part of their job; the recipients may see the imposition of a central provision as a loss of a status symbol, an inconvenience, or a waste of time. Just these few issues alone could be quite emotive and destructive.

But what do we do if we wish to bring about some change, even a fairly minor one, but our low hierarchical rank leaves us with little positional power?

Fritz Steele (1975) has described a number of 'consultant's roles' which can be adopted by an outside consultant to encourage others to do things differently (see Frame 9.9). Roles similar to those of the *advocate, barbarian* and *student* are very relevant to a person trying to make changes from within an organization. I shall discuss these shortly under the headings of being an **evangelist**, a **maverick** or a **guerilla**, respectively. Remember, if you believe that an idea or change is more important than your own well-being within the organization you could be so much of a rebel that you end up becoming a ritual pig and may not be around to see the results or get the credit when the organization eventually adopts the ideas you were suggesting!

Frame 9.9 *Consultants' roles*

Teacher – imparting knowledge by seminars, experiential learning sessions, etc.

Student – modelling a learning behaviour that we would like to encourage in the client.

Detective – trying to discover hard and soft data so as to develop an accurate picture of the system, its problems and strengths.

Barbarian – violating comfortable but limiting norms, taboos, etc. that are preventing the system from being as effective as it might be. (A counter-measure against **tunnel vision**.)

Clock – stimulating the client into getting some thinking, experimenting, etc. done by acting as a regular 'time signal'.

Monitor – providing an independent view of how the client is performing in connection with some mutually agreed task relevant to his/her problem.

Talisman – providing a sense of security and legitimacy by our mere presence, thus allowing the client to feel comfortable enough to experiment in areas he or she might not, if we were not actually there.

Advocate – advocating certain decent, non-exploitive, personally satisfying and productive principles or values pertaining to the relationship between an individual and the organization.

Ritual Pig – inadvertently serving as an 'outside' threat that, through having to be dealt with, enables a sufficient sense of solidarity and potency to develop within the client organization so that it is able to begin some difficult self-change. (A role that is usually realized retrospectively!)

Steele (1975)

Whatever we can achieve relies heavily on our personal power (see Frame 9.48) and whatever credibility we can derive from this. If we are short on positional power, then even if we possess some expert power (and it is this expertise we are promoting) it may not be valued any more than that of our peers, and any success we have will be determined by our ability to influence others and our ability to use what power we have effectively. According to Lippitt (1982), this is founded in trust, both our trust in others and their trust in us. His notion of what brings about trust is different from but complementary to that noted earlier:

- Integrity – sound and honest in character and moral principles.
- Justice – possessing a sense of right and equity.
- Ability – capable of performing well in the task or relationship involved.
- Intention – determined to achieve some desirable action or result.
- Reliability – dependable in carrying out a commitment.

Beyond this, Harrison has identified four ways of influencing others (Frame 9.10): 'assertive persuasion', 'reward and punishment', 'common vision', and 'participation and trust'. Each of us apparently feels more at ease using some of these styles than others. The last should be most effective in the long run, as it encourages involvement, which is the only sure way of gaining commitment. But Plant (1987) believes that the broader the spread of styles you can use, the more likely you are to be able to influence effectively in different situations. However, many consider the assertive persuasion style, like reward and punishment, to be totally incompatible with the qualities required to create a situation of participation and trust.

Frame 9.10 *Ways of exerting influence*

Assertive persuasion

The persistent, energetic and ingenious use of logic, facts and opinions to support the ideas and suggestions.

Reward and punishment

The overt and covert use of pressures and incentives to accomplish a clearly defined objective. (Psychologists believe that to be effective this style should involve considerably more praise and rewards than criticism and punishment.)

Common vision

The use of a shared vision of what could be a common future for everyone involved that appeals to their hopes, values and aspirations, thus releasing the 'energy' of their commitment made available by their feelings of belonging.

Participation and trust

The use of an atmosphere of mutual trust, positive support, encouragement, cooperation and openness (in fact, all of the conditions that we believe to be prerequisites of creativity), so as to gain people's total commitment through their feelings of being involved in and having contributed to the outcome.

The evangelist

We ought to be able to use the phenomenon of the self-fulfilling prophecy positively (see Chapter 3) in effecting change by adopting the evangelist approach. Raising expectations and fostering a mindset in others in favour of whatever is being advocated will draw people's attention to its good points and make them more likely to accept it. This can be particularly effective if we can demonstrate its benefits and how this innovation fits in with and enhances the existing organizational culture. This is especially true if we can incorporate appropriate cultural language and symbols, designed to evoke strong positive emotional reactions, in its packaging. We need credibility to make this approach work because the new idea or change we are extolling will be perceived in the same light as we are. Another downside to this approach is the danger that if we promote an idea too much we will put people off it. Others may not share our enthusiasm, because they are not familiar with it, have not been part of its creation or see it as an implied criticism. Nolan (1981, p.12) comments that

> it's no use trying to 'sell' your ideas. By all means present them clearly and attractively, explaining the benefits and rationale behind them (once you have established you have a willing audience for them). But no amount of eloquence, persuasion, logic or pressure will make him accept an idea that isn't on target for what he perceives his needs to be.

The maverick

Another ploy is to take on the role of maverick, a person who, despite holding the beliefs and values of a culture, does not conform to organizational norms just because they are there, but only if they are perceived as having some inherent sense. Some organizations believe it 'healthy' to have people like this around and are prepared to tolerate their non-conformist behaviour. Mavericks are prepared to stick their necks out on behalf of new concepts, constructively draw attention to deficiencies or injustices and generally fight against complacency. To survive in this role the maverick needs to be well nigh perfect in every other aspect of his/her dealings with the organization as s/he is essentially attacking the prevailing culture on the basis of his/her credibility and acceptance in that culture and/or the support s/he has from others of high status. Both of these could alter over time; the maverick needs to check periodically that his/her position is still secure.

If we as maverick persist with this role long enough, we may get the chance to try out one of our ideas on the basis of 'OK, you do something better', or just to shut us up. Alternatively, if such an opportunity does not become available, we could deliberately challenge other people to let us try. Such a challenge is often ignored on the basis that 'If it's that good a way of doing things, why hasn't he done something about it himself?' Being a maverick is by no means a guaranteed way of initiating change.

The guerilla

We could ignore Reddin's (1977) warning that initiating change from the bottom up is tantamount to mutiny and try a guerilla action, by infiltrating the organization with bits of the new idea or method we are advocating, starting first on our home ground where we possess the power to do something. Depending on the power and authority we command this may restrict us to changing only our own behaviour or method of working in the first instance. The hope is that wider acceptance of the innovation will be assisted by its own merits rather than our blandishments. Even if we are not suspected or accused of mutiny, trying to convince by example in this way can be a frustrating or even totally demotivating task. Building up the critical mass to ensure the eventual success of a change like this can take a very long time. However, this policy of discreetly applying new methods ourselves and demonstrating their effectiveness by example may be one of the few viable alternatives open to us.

Acquiring a champion

If we feel there is little we can do personally to bring about change, or we feel that we could accomplish more if we had support from others, it is suggested that we should find a **champion** for our cause. Ideally this should be one of the organization's current 'heroes'. A champion is someone in a position of power (see Frame 9.8) and authority, who controls the allocation of resources our cause might need. Having a champion increases our credibility, and helps overcome minor difficulties and obstacles. Also, those not fully committed to our proposals are less likely to resist and risk upsetting the champion. Failing this, we may add to our credibility, by seeking the support of good soldiers (see Figure 9.2).

Having a champion can be effective, but is fraught with danger as a champion's reasons for supporting us may be politically expedient rather than altruistic; our champion may withdraw his/her favour when his/her hidden agenda is satisfied and we have served his/her purpose. If the only reason we have been able to proceed with our idea is because of other people's obeisance to the champion, then, when this support is removed, we will be attacked by those people. Choice of champion is also crucial; if our champion does not have the necessary support and respect then getting support may effectively destroy our chances. Remember: to attempt to change other people in a direction they do not want to go themselves is counter-productive. Even if they comply on the surface, out of fear or subservience or even in deference to superior wisdom, their underlying resentment switches off commitment and motivation.

As a final word on this subject, a 'health warning'. The art of suppressing new ideas is well developed; many of your colleagues and managers may be well versed in it. Frames 9.11 and 9.12 list typical 'reactions' to new ideas and serve as a warning of what can be in store for a potential change agent about to embark on this stage.

Frame 9.11 *Ways to deal with new ideas*

- Ignore it. Dead silence intimidates all but the most enthusiastic.
- See it coming and change the subject.
- Scorn it: get your thrust in before the idea is fully explained or it may prove practicable after all.

▶

- Laugh it off: 'Ho, ho, ho! That's a good one, Joe. You must have sat up all night thinking that up.' If he has, this makes it even funnier.
- Praise it to death. By the time you have expounded its merits for five minutes everyone else will hate it. The proposer will be wondering what is wrong with it himself.
- Mention that it has never been tried. If it is new this will be true.
- 'Oh, we've tried that before.' Particularly effective if the originator is a newcomer. It makes her realize what an outsider she is.
- Find a competitive idea. This is a dangerous one unless you are experienced. You might still get left with an idea.
- Produce 20 good reasons why it won't work. The one good reason why it will is then lost.
- Modify it out of existence. This is elegant. You seem to be helping the idea along, just changing it a little here and there. By the time the originator wakes up, it is dead.
- Try to chip bits off it. If you fiddle with an idea long enough it may come to pieces.
- Make a personal attack on the originator. By the time he has recovered, he will have forgotten he had an idea.
- Score a technical knock-out; for instance, refer to some obscure rule.
- Let a committee sit on the idea.
- Encourage the author to look for a better idea. Usually a discouraging quest. If she finds one, start her looking for a better job.
- Accept it, but do nothing about it . . . it prevents the originator taking it to somebody else.

Nolan (1981)

Frame 9.12 *Killed any good ideas, lately?*

That's not our problem, the hole is at the other end of the ship!

- You can't save half a person.
- It isn't in the budget.
- We haven't got the staff to do it.
- The savings wouldn't come to this division.
- The intangible risks would be too great.
- We're not ready for that yet, but in the fullness of time . . . (let's not rush into things).

- This is the long-term solution . . . we're interested in the here and now.
- This is the short-term solution . . . we're in this for the long pull.
- This is a radical departure from company practice.
- Business legal/practices would never agree to it.
- There's already a procedure in place to deal with this.
- We've tried that before.
- If it's that good why hasn't somebody tried it before?

What we can actually achieve depends on how successfully the ploys above can be implemented. If we find ourselves totally stranded with little or no support, our only hope is a lucky break that allows us to demonstrate that our way of doing things will benefit everyone. If we find the culture so alien that only a major change can make it right for us, then our efforts are probably best spent finding another organization that has a culture we can survive in.

International culture

Before leaving the topic of culture we should perhaps say something about international cultures. The political, economic and sociological environments of the places in which we live and of the organizations in which we work have seen many changes in the last decade.

Since 1992 and the advent of 'single European market', wherein any citizen of any EEC country can work in any other EEC country. Enabled by the free trading relationships between these countries there has been an increase in the number of international mergers and takeovers that have taken place. The EU is about to get bigger by ten or more countries.

Whatever you may think of it, globalization is here, encouraged and enabled by improvements in international communications and transport. Many multinational organizations already face the problem of operating within differing national/ethnic cultures. Many others, hoping that the Internet will enable them to increase their potential market size, have not yet realized the implications of this.

National cultures vary more than organizational ones, which means that if we are to benefit from the potential opportunities presented by these changes, we need to be proficient in deciphering and operating within other cultures. Hofstede (1980) collected data about national culture from 67 countries throughout the world. From an analysis of 40 of these, he identified four 'dimensions' along which cultural difference could be expressed (Table 9.2). These are:

- Power distance – a measure of the extent of human inequality, e.g. the distribution of prestige, wealth and power. In organizations it relates to the difference in the extent to which a leader can influence the behaviour of followers/subordinates and vice versa.

- Uncertainty avoidance – a measure of tolerance for uncertainty and the consequent need to take action. It is ascertained from an individual's preference for rules, employment stability and level of stress.

- Individualism (*v.* collectivism) – a measure of individuals' emotional dependence on others and the organizations to which they belong, and the way others respond to this. It is reflected in the way we live together, for example in nuclear families, extended families or tribes.
- Masculinity *v.* femininity – a measure of societal preference for things thought to be important predominantly by males (tasks and things, performance and growth, achievement, etc.) or females (interpersonal relationships, quality of life, a sense of service, etc.).

Although Hofstede's work was conducted solely within IBM, and so the effects of IBM's culture cannot be eliminated from his results, there are apparently substantial differences revealed between countries, even those in the same part of the world, such as Europe or the Far East. We ignore such cultural differences at our peril!

Encouraging and managing creativity

Let us suppose that we have a culture that values our flexible, systematic approaches to problem solving (particularly the CPS strategies). Is there anything we should do as a team leader in order to encourage creativity? Nolan (1981, pp.89–90) says that 'when faced with a clear and overwhelming threat to survival, people respond with ingenuity, resourcefulness and energy that previously they did not know they had'. It is ironic that at times of crisis we can be far

Table 9.2	Country	PD	UA	I	M
Cultural dimension scores of the EU member states (excluding Luxembourg), some Far Eastern countries and the USA (higher scores indicate a greater tendency towards a particular cultural dimension)	USA	40	46	_91_	62
	Austria	_11_	70	55	_79_
	Great Britain	35	35	89	66
	Belgium	65	94	75	54
	Denmark	_18_	23	74	16
	Finland	33	59	63	26
	France	68	86	71	43
	W. Germany	35	65	67	66
	Greece	60	_112_	35	57
	Ireland	28	35	70	68
	Italy	50	75	76	70
	Netherlands	38	53	80	14
	Portugal	63	104	27	31
	Spain	57	86	51	42
	Sweden	31	29	71	_5_
	Hong Kong	68	29	25	57
	Japan	54	92	46	95
	Singapore	74	8	20	48
	Taiwan	58	69	17	45

Key: PD = Power distance; UA = Uncertainty avoidance; I = Individualism; M = Masculinity.
Source: Hofstede (1980), p.315.
Note: The scores underlined, along with Phillippines PD = 94, Venezuela I = 12, are the highest/lowest of the 40 countries whose returns were analysed.

more creative and amenable to change than when conditions are stable: yet we might benefit more from innovation and creativity when things are running smoothly. One answer might be to set people demanding and apparently impossible tasks and objectives. This seems to work so long as there is no fear connected with failing to achieve these 'impossible' missions. Nolan advises that managers who want more innovation must give a lead by doing new things themselves. By showing they are willing to make changes in what they do and how they do it, they demonstrate that they themselves are open to learning. They are prepared to take the risks of coming unstuck, making a fool of themselves, getting it wrong. These are the risks of new action, and the price of new knowledge and understanding, which only comes from experience.

And having accomplished this, how then do we 'manage' all these creative-thinking people? John Sculley (1988, pp.253–61), who when at Apple Computer led some of the most creative people in any organization, offered the following suggestions on managing creativity:

- The task is to get people to work at the highest level of creativity, not just productivity.
- The safer you can make a situation, the higher you can raise the challenge. (Tim Gallwey's theory of 'the Inner Game of Tennis')
- Don't give people goals; give them directions. We want to lead people to ideas they haven't dreamed of yet.
- Encourage contrarian thinking. There should be a level of tension between discipline and dissent . . . a little bit of anarchy in the organization.
- Build a textured environment to extend not just people's aspirations but their sensibilities. You can't buy creativity. You have to inspire it. Creative people require the tools and environment which foster their success. Above all, they require an atmosphere conducive to fun and to thinking in non-standard ways. The work environment needs to be informal and relaxed, it needs to remove the symbols of management.
- Build emotion into the system. Defensiveness is the bane of all passion-filled creative work. We keep defences down .
- Encourage accountability over responsibility. We don't give creative people traditional responsibilities . . . instead they are made accountable for the results of their work.

All these comments are still valid.

Summary

This chapter has discussed the various acceptance and implementation issues concerned with realizing any problem solutions we have obtained, including the management of the change resulting from these solutions, and the promotion/adoption of CPS itself in/by others.

Endnotes

1   This is a term I have made up to cover a number of 'closing' stages of TRIZ.

Synectics

This chapter demonstrates how some of the CPS techniques encountered in earlier chapters come together to form a complete 'basic' Synectics CPS process. Before this, the practicalities of running a Synectics session will be discussed.

Ultimate solutions to problems are rational; the process of finding them is not.

(William J.J. Gordon, 1961, p.11)

Introduction

Although **Synectics** (see Frame 10.1) can be used very effectively as an individual problem-solving technique, its full potential and benefits are realized with group participation. This is why, to illustrate how the various Synectics techniques introduced earlier can be employed together in a 'full' **CPS** process, I will be describing how an (imaginary) group problem-solving session at a (fictitious) organization called Sigma Chi Ltd would be conducted. If you are working on your own you may 'skip' to page 234 and read on from there, remembering that you are acting as both problem owner and resource.

Frame 10.1 *What is Synectics?*

Synectics is the name given to a body of knowledge, a collection of behavioural skills and a set of problem-solving techniques. It is also the name of the international group of companies that have developed this from 40 years of study and work with innovative groups, but it is far more than this as well. The greater a person's exposure to Synectics, the more it pervades the way that person thinks to the extent that it virtually becomes a way of life.

▶

In the words of John Alexander (1979, p.9), an ex-director of Synectics Ltd, the skills and procedures that comprise Synectics are designed to achieve:

- creative high quality courses of action;
- high levels of commitment and energy to agreed courses of action;
- effective cooperation between individuals and departments;
- fast progress towards objectives through innovation and conflict resolution;
- high levels of satisfaction.

Synectics achieve these benefits by enabling people to:

- develop both innovative and interpersonal skills;
- improve communication and ensure a high level of shared understanding;
- create a working climate which permits individuals to use their abilities more completely;
- reduce friction between themselves and other individuals and groups;
- increase learning abilities.

One way of viewing the Synectics body of knowledge is as though it were an iceberg that consists of techniques, skills and strategies held together by a philosophy that recognizes the uniqueness and personal autonomy of individuals. Like any iceberg, the deeper you go the bigger it seems to become.

The Synectics process was originally designed to encourage the sort of innovation and creativity that we might find in an R&D department of an organization. But it is equally applicable to any real-world problem that we are likely to encounter (especially **people** problems, as we will see shortly), due to an underlying philosophy which values our individual differences (see Frame 10.2).

Frame 10.2 *Some applications of Synectics*

Synectics has been used to good effect frequently in the area of R&D, on such disparate items as the 'Hovis' biscuit and circular saw blades that do not cut flesh. It has also produced novel solutions to such vexing problems as persuading bears not to 'vandalize' electricity sub-stations and how an oil company can extract core samples from thousands of feet down in the earth without them losing any of their chemical qualities through changes in pressure and water dilution.

◀

> The effects of Synectics can also be found elsewhere. A major brewing company has attributed to Synectics improvements made by making their meetings shorter, more effective and more focused, whilst at the same time producing more creative options. And it has enabled members of an international pharmaceutical company to change their organizational climate not only towards openness to and acceptance of new ideas, but also to fostering teamwork by encouraging mutual appreciation and commitment.

Running a Synectics group CPS session

When to use Synectics, and its limitations

Synectics is an ideal strategy to adopt if innovation is sought, or a particularly novel solution is desired, but this should not be seen as a limiting factor. It may well be that on occasion a totally new product or way of doing something is required, but the reference to novelty includes a 'newness' to the problem owner as well.

Often our real problem with resolving a particular situation is that we have been involved with the matter for so long and in such depth that we are bogged down in a rut. The more we battle to get out, the more we get stuck in the same mess, and the more the conceptual blocks of Chapter 3 will tend to make us blind to ways of escape. We desperately need a new perspective on the problem; to stand back and reflect and get right away from our problem and our previous failures to resolve it. The Synectics process, and in particular its mental **excursions**, are extremely powerful tools for digging yourself out of such situations.

The only real limitation on the application of Synectics is due to practical considerations concerning group size (see below). If the problem situation has more than a handful of problem owners, we will be unable to resolve it with them as one group (however desirable this is). The solution is to restructure the problem situation into several parts and have several groups of people working on them, or to organize several groups working on the same problem in parallel. The dangers inherent in restructuring a problem have already been mentioned in Chapter 1 and there are difficulties in the latter alternative of combining the results of parallel Synectics sessions (see Chapter 12).

A suitable (physical) environment

The actual venue should be free from the 'distractions' of the participants' working and personal lives, either by geographical separation or other means (e.g. interruptions only permitted in emergency situations, restrictions on the use/availability of telephones, etc.).

As with all CPS, we need a room with comfortable chairs, low tables, several flipcharts, plus sufficient wall space for flipchart sheets to be pinned up around the room for all to see. Although the leader would normally stand in front of the seated group in order to write on the flipcharts and to convey his/her leadership role, it is an informal setting and people should feel free to move around. In fact it will help the leader, and add to the atmosphere of friendly cooperation, if a member of the group assists with the placing of 'full' flipchart sheets on the wall.

Size of a Synectics group

The typical Synectics group is somewhat smaller than that recommended for **Brainstorming**. A group of six to eight people (excluding the leader) seems to be ideal.

Composition of a Synectics group

William J.J. Gordon (1961) laid down quite specific criteria for group membership and composition, suggesting that group members should be frequent users of **analogies** and **metaphors** (see Chapter 7), have an attitude of assistance, well-coordinated bodily movements and the capacity to generalize. They should possess personality traits such as emotional maturity, 'constructive childishness' and 'risk-taking' and be non-status orientated. They need to show commitment to the group and its purpose and be between 25 and 40 years of age! Though possession of many of these 'attributes' may well help proceedings, Gordon's views on group composition are now out of date in the sense that, by using the appropriate process 'tools', Synectics believe that all these qualities (except perhaps age – which has been shown to be irrelevant) can be 'uncovered' in everybody.

Current practice on group selection is similar to that of a Brainstorming group. Group members should have as wide a spread of knowledge and experience as possible.

The group should not have too many 'experts'. The problem owner will invariably be the problem content expert. If there are others with this content expertise from the same organization we may have a shared problem, and this type of situation needs to be tackled in a slightly different way, as we shall see later (in Chapter 12). It can be useful to have a second 'technical expert' with similar technical expertise to the problem owner, but who works in a totally different field. In one group session I was involved in, the problem owner worked for a confectionery manufacturer and was concerned about the difficulty in getting a consistent thickness of chocolate coatings on his company's products. Another group member worked for a gas utility company. His expertise in the behaviour of flowing 'liquids', coupled with our non-expert's new but wildly naive ideas concerning chocolate coatings, resulted in some feasible ideas that the problem owner was pleased to try out.

As with Brainstorming, it is easier on the leader if the group members have equal status or rank, but this is often not desirable for the problem's resolution, and anyway the process and the role of **process leader** (see also Chapter 13) is designed to cope with differences in status.

It is also very useful to have a group that contains a couple of people who are good at coming up with wild ideas, and are willing to do so; these people will encourage other members to do the same by setting the cultural norms of the group by example. Synectics Inc. used to have one of their consultants acting as a resource within the group for this very purpose. For the same reason, having some group members already trained in the Synectics process, who know what to do and what to expect, is also advantageous.

The tasks of group members

Everybody in a Synectics group plays an important part in **Problem Resolution**, but the two key roles are those of the client or problem owner, and the group leader, who is actually more of a problem-solving facilitator.

Problem owner (client)

Ideally the problem owner should be familiar with the Synectics process, or at least be warned of what to expect, so that s/he is not alarmed when proceedings appear to run off in a seemingly irrelevant direction. It is only necessary to out-line the likely stages of the process, indicating where group members should refrain from criticism, where some unusual measures might be needed to get away from the problem in order to generate some ideas to help us resolve it, and when the client is required to evaluate ideas and offer guidance or direction for future efforts. However, problem owners should not see this as their sole func-tion; they should also participate as ordinary group members. A trained problem owner is not a necessity, but if s/he knows little about Synectics it is vital that the leader keeps her/him 'informed' about what we are doing and why we are doing it, as well as telling the group how they should proceed.

Group leader/facilitator

Chapter 3 and 13 showed why using a traditional leader, or chairperson, is not the most appropriate way of running a problem-solving session. We will now deal with the practical details of leading a Synectics group.

The role described here is that of a process leader (see page 311), who guides *only* the problem-solving process. With Synectics, the group leader or facilitator should not get involved with problem 'content' in any way. S/he should lead the process, not contribute ideas, suggestions or possible solutions, let alone decide the best way of resolving the problem. However, s/he needs to assess how well the group is meeting the problem owner's wishes, and there is a temptation to do this by monitoring the content (what is being said about the problem). Although not easy to resist, the group leader should not become involved in the content even to this extent. S/he should determine the success of the process by observing, and asking for, the client's reactions to what is going on. If the suppressed desire to be involved in the content affects the leadership of the process, the group leader should, with the agreement of the client and the group, stand down temporarily and become a group resource, letting another take over the process leadership.

Because the guidance of the problem-solving process has been delegated to the group leader, s/he needs to maintain the trust of the problem owner and must be seen as working for the problem owner, not as a competitor for authority over problem content. The group leader also needs to take care of the psychological needs of other group members. We ask the group to say and do some strange things, and therefore must provide the sort of climate (see Chapter 3) which encourages and supports creativity, and ensures that every member is psycho-logically comfortable with the process.

It is the group leader's responsibility to protect members' self-images, so that everyone can win from the situation. Cooperation, mutual trust, emotional support and good communications are the key factors s/he must generate. George Prince (1970, pp.7–8) points out that

> relieved of the burden of self-protection, a member can wholeheartedly devote himself to speculating, imagining, and supporting and considering farfetched notions – in short, producing the rich variations out of which fresh alternatives and exciting decisions are made.

Many ideas sessions (not truly **Brainstorming**) appear to fail because they have been initiated and led by an authority figure who fails to appreciate the importance of such factors and why s/he may not be the most suitable person to lead the session. If a Synectics group leader is seen as serving the needs of the group, s/he will gain their commitment, enthusiasm and best ideas. If s/he is seen as serving her or his own needs, then group members will look after their own needs also and tend not to offer these things.

The group leader is also responsible for ensuring that group members obey the rules (for example, suspending judgement); encouraging speculation; logging all of the ideas; checking with the problem owner that the group is on the right track; and managing the time. A Synectics group leader, therefore, needs to be trained.

Group resources

The rest of the group act as resources offering ideas when requested by the group leader. It is likely that they will think of ideas faster than they can voice them or than the leader can record them on the flipcharts. So participants should be encouraged to jot ideas down on notepads until required. When speculation is desired, everyone should be warned to watch out for the operation of their **self-censor** (see Chapter 3), the culturally ingrained mental block that only permits us to recall relevant ideas and voice well-thought-out ones. All ideas are wanted, including beginning ideas, half-formed ideas and wild ideas.

The second most important task a group member performs, after having ideas, is to support everyone else. This can be done by genuinely complimenting them for ideas that are especially commendable for their appropriateness, novelty, practicality, insightfulness, etc., and crediting others when we build on one of their ideas.

Synectics offers useful guidelines to group participants on **open-minded communication**, which help towards encouraging cooperation and teamwork. These include:

- Make statements rather than ask questions.
- Understand what has been said (by paraphrasing it back to its author) before you evaluate it.
- Find some value in all ideas (and acknowledge it).
- Give your ideas and opinions only when requested.
- Assume a positive intent in what other people say.
- Speak up for yourself and let other people do the same.

Outline of the basic Synectics process

By describing the Synectics CPS process in the way that it is usually presented on training courses, my intention is to provide a sufficient view of what Synectics has to offer, thus enabling us to start using some of its techniques and principles. It is from the experience of using this simplified version of the process that understanding and skills will develop. This account is only a part of the story, though; Synectics is more flexible and comprises more ideas, techniques and variations than can be shown here.

Synectics uses the Brainstorming principles outlined earlier (see Chapter 3), but in a highly modified and more sophisticated way. The basic problem-solving process contains a number of steps or stages such as those shown in Frame 10.3, but it should be stressed that these are only provided for guidance. Like other problem-solving processes described in this book, we do not need to start from stage 1, nor complete all the stages in sequence; and of course iteration is permitted at any stage.

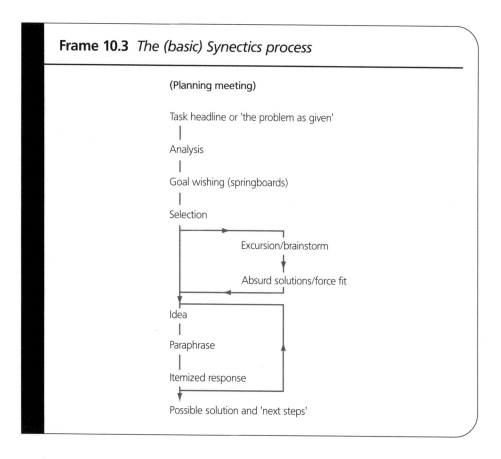

Frame 10.3 *The (basic) Synectics process*

(Planning meeting)

Task headline or 'the problem as given'
|
Analysis
|
Goal wishing (springboards)
|
Selection

Excursion/brainstorm

Absurd solutions/force fit

Idea
|
Paraphrase
|
Itemized response

Possible solution and 'next steps'

If we were to go through the whole process as illustrated then we would encounter three Brainstorming-like stages where speculation is welcomed and evaluation is suspended. First, in the '**Goal Wishing**' stage, where the problem is opened up to try to ensure that we are solving the right problem. Second, in

gathering ideas from which we hope to obtain possible soluti,
where the diagram branches into what has been called an excursion).
during the Idea Development stage (where the diagram loops back ɩ
starting with **'itemized response'**, to find ways of overcoming concerns wɩ
have with our ideas, before they can become possible solutions.

The problem-solving session

Now for our problem-solving session at Sigma Chi Ltd. A summary of the problem situation is presented in Frame 10.4. The description of the problem-solving
session will be given from the group leader/facilitator's viewpoint, and will
include some additional aspects of running a group session.

Frame 10.4 *Sigma Chi Ltd: the problem situation*

Sigma Chi Ltd (SC) is an organization working primarily in consultancy and training. Since its inception in 1982 as a government agency, SC has operated totally
within the public sector. It has been somewhat sheltered from the economic
fluctuations and traumas going on in the 'real world', with the consequence that
organizational change is rare and difficult to achieve. SC, like other government
agencies before it, has just been 'given' corporate status — it can now do more
or less anything it likes with the funds it receives from central government and
the revenue it generates itself.

For months prior to incorporation and since, the new director has been trying to implement a number of changes in the organization that he believes
will better equip it for the future. For instance, the organizational structure has
been reorganized into easily identifiable cost centres, new senior management
posts in functions previously unheard of, such as finance, marketing and personnel, have been created and the director now has a company car. At the
'shop floor' level, however, little seems to have changed! Even though the transition to a private company was guaranteed to have no initial effect on the
job security or conditions and pay of the staff employed before incorporation,
sadly, the director is frustrated by the considerable resistance to many of his
ideas.

His problem was initially summarized as:

'Sigma Chi needs to change dramatically to meet the demands of the future,
why can't people see that?'

A crucial aspect of the Synectics process is that when used in a group problem-
solving setting, it is essential that the problem owners (or clients) are members
of the group, for it is they who will be using their selection of the **springboards**
and ideas generated at various stages to give the group a direction in which to
explore next.

lanning meeting

se problem owners play such an important role in the Synectics process (see
ages 245 and 253) it is essential they are fully committed to the resolution of
oblem. Planning meetings are thus essential before a problem-solving ses-
akes place. The group leader should check out both the suitability of the
em and the motivation of the problem owner (see also Frame 10.5).

ncent Nolan (1989), formerly chairman of Synectics Ltd, suggests we, as the
p leader/facilitator (F), should get answers to the following questions (no
matter how obvious they are), before embarking on any problem solving. These
should establish whether we have the necessary preconditions for problem
solving to take place.

1. We need to know how many problem owners we (should) have:
   - Who owns the problem? Who is sufficiently dissatisfied with the
     present situation to consider it a problem that needs to be solved? Who
     is motivated to solve it?
   - Is that person willing to do something new about it or is s/he just
     seeking sympathy?
   - Is that person expecting someone else to take any consequent action? If
     so, does the other person see it as a problem that needs solving?

2. We need to know whether s/he (and we) can do anything about the
   problem situation:
   - What is the problem owner's **power to act**? What can s/he do to
     implement a possible solution? What sort of actions is s/he prepared
     to take? Does the problem owner command resources? If so, what
     are they? Under what constraints does the problem owner operate?

3. We do not want to waste our time re-inventing known solutions, or
   playing mind games.
   - Does the problem owner already have a solution? If so, is s/he trying to
     'check it out' (a candidate for **Potential Problem Analysis** perhaps, see
     Chapter 9) or are they satisfied with it and indulging in a misguided
     commitment-gaining exercise?
   - Does the problem owner want to find a solution or just prove that one
     does not exist?

Frame 10.5 *Checking out the problem owner*

A problem owner must have the authority and resources to implement a
solution when one is found. The exact nature of this power to act can be
determined by careful questioning during the planning meeting. More
difficult to determine but equally important is a willingness to solve the
problem. The group leader should look out for usage, by the problem
owner, of words like 'could', 'should' and 'ought', where perhaps s/he
might have used 'can', 'will' and 'are'.

▶

> It is possible that problem owners perceive limitations to what constitutes a feasible way of resolving the problem. Discovering what these are now need not necessarily restrict our thinking, and should allow us to explore beyond these limitations later without losing the confidence of the problem owner or causing him/her any frustration. Knowing we *are* aware of these constraints will reassure the problem owner about our competence when we do subsequently stray over the edge of the perceived problem domain, particularly if we announce this as our intention – 'just to see what might be possible' or 'to check that we haven't missed any possibilities'.

We should also encourage the problem owner to make an initial exploration beyond the problem as originally stated, to see if there may not be more appropriate ways of looking at the problem. This is especially true if the original problem statement is of a general nature, for example: 'How to prepare my company for the expansion of the EU', compared with more specific statements such as: 'How to maintain the current growth in our UK market share beyond 2004'. The technique called **Backward/Forward Planning** (see also page 107) should help with this and give the group leader a better insight into where the problem owner wants to be at the end of the problem-solving session.

Backward/Forward Planning

Suppose the problem-owner offers the following problem statement:

How to make my colleagues appreciate the need for change?

This, as we saw earlier (see Chapter 6), is not a promising start because the problem statement refers to persuading/making someone else change his or her attitudes or actions in some way. However, Backward/Forward Planning should provide some alternative views of the problem situation.

Going 'backwards' looking for 'higher-level' problems, let's suppose our conversation with the problem owner (PO) continues as follows:

F: 'If this problem could be resolved instantly by just making a wish, what (higher- level) problem would this solve, what would it allow you to do?'

PO: 'Achieve a total commitment to a common purpose.'

Checking for permission with the problem owner we rephrase this response in a 'I wish/How to' form, and write up . . .

1. I wish I could gain the total commitment of my staff to the organization's mission.

. . . and then . . .

F: 'By not having this total commitment, what is it that you are being prevented from doing?'

PO: 'Preparing for the challenges of the future'

2. How to prepare for the challenges of the future.

F: 'And not being as prepared as you might be prevents you from doing . . . ?'

PO: 'Ensuring we don't miss any opportunities.'

3. How to ensure that we do not miss any opportunities.

. . . or perhaps . . .

4. How to demonstrate that there are opportunities being missed due to our lack of cohesion.

Going 'forwards' looking for 'subproblems' we ask:

F: 'What's stopping you solve this problem?'

PO: 'I can't convince my colleagues that I have their best interests at heart.'

5. I wish I could convince my colleagues that I have their best interests at heart.

PO: 'I haven't got the resources to offer an early retirement package (that no one could refuse) to those who will never change, who are just hanging on for retirement, or are too high in the hierarchy to ignore, sack, etc.'

6. How to obtain the resources to offer an early retirement package (that no one could refuse) to those who will never change, who are just hanging on for retirement, or are too high in the hierarchy to ignore, sack, etc.

And to uncover any additional benefits:

F: 'If the original problem had now been solved and your colleagues appreciated the need for change, what would this mean to you, what additional benefits would come from this?'

Some other benefits might be:

PO: 'We could use our time more effectively, reach agreement on and implement the necessary changes, implement the changes more quickly and perhaps redirect our attention to examining the advantages of our new freedom.'

7. How to use everyone's time more effectively.
8. How to reach agreement on and implement the necessary changes.
9. How to implement changes more quickly.
10. How to redirect our attention to examining the advantages of our new freedom.

We now have ten additional possible problem statements. The problem owner now has to decide whether to start with the original one or pursue one of these alternatives. This choice is not critical as yet, since we will shortly generate more ways of looking at the problem before the problem owner finally chooses which one to use.

Another point for discussion with the problem owner during the planning meeting is the level of 'quality' desired from the solutions we hope to help them obtain. This is a measure of the compromise that often has to be made between the feasibility of a possible solution and its desired novelty or 'newness'. We would be unusually lucky if we achieved a really innovative solution that is also eminently feasible. Synectics assess the 'quality' of a possible solution on three bases, **newness**, **appeal** and **feasibility**. This indication of the problem owner's expectations can be used at the end of proceedings to gauge the success of group efforts.

The leader of a Synectics-style problem-solving session with a group familiar with one another should ascertain in advance whether there are likely to be any professional or personal conflicts between members of the group. Being forewarned of this possibility means steps can be taken at least to ameliorate any manifestations of conflict.

Finally, the planning meeting is a good opportunity for the group leader to give the problem owner an outline or review of the Synectics process so that the problem owner knows what is expected of him/her. We would explain that we will call upon him/her periodically to check that things are progressing to his/her liking, and to ask for 'direction' on where the group should most usefully turn its attention next. We should stress that the problem owner should feel free to (and that it is desirable that s/he does) contribute his/her own ideas as if s/he were an 'ordinary' group member (see later). This is one way in which the problem owner can provide direction at times other than when specifically asked to do so. We should also explain that at certain stages we will want him/her and the group to suspend any form of judgement and evaluation, and assure him/her that there is a reason for some of the strange things that we might ask the group to do. At the same time as this we should be trying to build a sufficiently good rapport with the problem owner for him/her to trust us to conduct the session in his/her best interests.

The task headline

To look at the (basic) Synectics process in more detail we will now take the Sigma Chi Ltd case study (Frame 10.4) through the steps shown in Frame 10.3. The group gathered together for this session might consist of the director (client/problem owner), two members of the senior management, say the directors of human resources and marketing, two 'grass roots' staff members, a representative from local industry and a couple of 'customers' (course participants). After greetings and explaining the administrative details, the first task for the facilitator will be to ask the client/problem owner for a **task headline** (Frame 10.6). This, a single sentence describing the problem, and sometimes referred to as 'the problem as given' – an expression that reinforces that we will not take for granted that this is either (i) the best description of the problem, or (ii) the problem definition we intend to start from – is written on a flipchart.

Frame 10.6 *Sigma Chi Ltd: task headline*

'How to convince my colleagues of the need for change?'

Note the rewording of the problem statement from that given in the planning meeting and that despite this and all that was said at the time, it sounds as if there may still be an implication in the problem owner's task headline that *other people* need to do something. As leader we should be wary of the re-emergence of this attitude as the session proceeds.

Analysis ('Data Gathering')

As facilitator, we now announce to the group that the problem owner will next be asked for some background information about the problem. We ask the group to listen to what is about to be said, not so as to understand the problem (this is not important or even desirable at this stage), but to let what is being said by the problem owner trigger off thoughts, ideas and reactions in their minds, especially those that suggest alternative and perhaps unusual ways of viewing the problem. We would say: 'Just make a note of any thoughts or ideas that come into your mind. What we would like the most is "fresh" views and ideas, no matter how wild.' Synectics call this **listening for ideas**.

We guide the problem owner's exposition of the problem by asking for a brief account of the events that led to the recognition of the problem situation described in the task headline, ensuring that all the information sought by the analysis questions (see page 83) is covered, prompting as necessary. (The questions are repeated below beside the problem owner's responses). If there is a danger of the problem owner talking at too great a length, we should explain why the group does not need to know too many of the details.

We write up the problem owner's ideal solution on the flipchart, underneath the task headline (see also Frame 10.7).

Frame 10.7 *Notes on editing and questions*

The leader should be careful not to deliberately or accidentally censor, edit or miss this or any other ideas offered. The leader should also take care with his/her non-verbal responses (e.g. body language). If an idea needs to be shortened, the contributor should do this; if the leader has to do it, the modification should always be agreed with the idea's contributor.

The problem owner should not be allowed to describe every intricate detail of the problem situation – particularly in response to questions. If a clarifying question is asked by a group member, the leader should immediately try to gently prise out from that person the idea that is likely to be hiding behind the question (see Chapter 13, page 323). For example, someone may ask 'How many people work for you?', when what they are thinking is, 'I'd like to know how many people work for you because it would be good if we could pack them all into a pub and have a totally open interchange of ideas and opinions over a few drinks'. Because of this, and because questions can be used to 'disguise' derogatory remarks, Synectics try to minimize questioning during the problem-solving session. Questions often have an important place in problem solving, but not here and now (see Chapter 6, Kepner-Tregoe's **Problem Analysis** used on **machine** problems).

Questions are often asked, not just to check out ideas before they are voiced, but because we feel we need to understand the problem before we can help solve it. A complete understanding of the problem is not

▶

likely to help produce novel and innovative solutions. Questions slow down proceedings and stop the flow of ideas. And if group members understand the problem situation in as much detail as the problem owner they may find themselves too close to the problem and in the same mental rut as the problem owner.

In this way, the problem owner is made to reiterate for the group's benefit some of the things discussed during the planning meeting. Let us suppose that the way he relates his problem is as shown in Frame 10.8.

Frame 10.8 *Sigma Chi Ltd: problem owner relates his problem*

When I applied for this post the interviewing panel were obviously looking for someone to lead the organization through privatization and into the future. I presumably got this job two years ago on the basis that my ideas concerning the way forward were deemed to be the most appropriate (b).

The first thing I did when I got here was to go round and see everyone, and asked them how they saw things (c). I asked them for their ideas! When I didn't get any I started offering mine. Since then it's been an uphill struggle (d) to implement the changes that I think are necessary. I meet resistance at every turn. I have always believed that I have an open mind, that I can be swayed by a rational argument, but when I did change my mind I was accused of being indecisive (e), two-faced, etc. Now I am just doing what I think is best. [How has the problem arisen?]

This is a real problem for me and the organization, because we are wasting a lot of time bickering when we should be out there looking for the opportunities that I know exist (f), and bringing in more business (g) to put us on a stable footing. People can't seem to understand that corporate status gives us the freedom to do all the things that we have always wanted to do! (h) [Why/how is it a problem for you?]

I have tried talking to everybody informally (a), I have set up mandatory briefing meetings to keep people informed and to collect their feedback (i) and initiated a suggestions box scheme, I have given heads of division more autonomy, but none of these things are working as well as I hoped. [What ideas have you tried . . . and thought of?]

In theory I can, as managing director of the new organization, do virtually anything (j), subject only to board approval and balancing the books next April. I can even fire people (k), something that never used to be possible except in very rare circumstances! [What power do you have to implement a solution?]

Things are changing but very, very slowly (l); the only recent thought I have had is to keep on slogging away (m) trying to get my ideas implemented. The government is partially to blame for all this because they haven't (deliberately I think) made things clear enough, and people are always afraid of the unknown (n). I did consider rewarding those who were prepared to address the changes needed (o) by salary differentials, but it seems that I do not have as much freedom in this area as I hoped, the union's attitudes and national agreements from before still seem to be the order of the day. [What ideas have you tried . . . and thought of?]

I wish I could change the cultural norms of the organization with a click of my fingers! [What is your ideal solution?]

Note: The letter references such as (b), above, are provided to show where the springboards given later have come from.

Goal Wishing (Problem Identification)

The next stage of the process has been given various names. **Goal orientation** is descriptive because what we are trying to do is view the problem situation in a number of ways, so that we look for a solution in the most appropriate direction. **Goal Wishing** stresses that speculation (including wishing) is permitted and desired. **Springboards** reinforces the idea that we are looking for launching places from which to take off into the problem. Whatever we call it, we are seeking different angles on, or **redefinitions** of, the problem.

It is useful to take the problem owner through the Backward/Forward Planning as a means of starting this stage, writing up his/her answers to the questions we asked then as additional problem definitions.

As facilitator, we now ask the group members to report their different ways of looking at the problem. We should stress that they should suspend judgement – not criticize or evaluate any of the suggestions made no matter how strange or irrelevant they seem. In particular they should not evaluate their own thoughts, but just say anything that comes into their minds. 'Way out' ideas often trigger off ideas in other group members. There will be time to evaluate these ideas later. The problem owner should be reminded that s/he can offer springboards to indicate the directions in which s/he would like the group to go. Finally, the group should be encouraged to offer springboards as short phrases, or *headlines*, expressed as the 'How to'/'I wish' statements we have seen earlier (see page 110, and Frame 10.9), followed up with a brief description of where the idea came from. This background information helps other group members see how the connections were made.

Frame 10.9 *Notes on headlines and background*

Headlining ideas has several advantages. Summarizing in this clear and succinct way conveys the essence of your idea so that others can start thinking about it and making associations. This also gives the group leader a chance to capture it on a flipchart while you continue with an explanation of what led you to it.

> Following the headline with the background to the idea is also very important, because it helps with communications by giving further insight into your thinking, and because it often contains 'colourful' material which sparks off other people's ideas.

Initially, springboards will come from the notes jotted down as the problem owner described the problem, but once captured and cleared from the participants' minds, they will have new thoughts, triggered off by others' comments. Some will be modifications or 'builds' on someone else's ideas. All should be written on the flipcharts, and the leader should ensure the problem owner also contributes some ideas! Don't forget that springboards can be more than problem redefinitions (see Chapter 6).

Almost inevitably, there will be *ad hoc* comments between group members: some are disguised criticisms, others are to check if no evaluation was really meant. We should try to capture these comments as yet more problem redefinitions. For example:

Susan says: 'I wish I could brainwash my staff.'

John replies: 'Why don't you go the whole hog and give them lobotomies?'

We intervene with something like:

John, some of us may have heard that idea as a criticism.

whilst writing up:

I wish we could give all my staff a lobotomy.

Group members will occasionally forget to give the background to their idea, and we should gently remind them.

This is the first time that our 'group of resources' will have made a contribution and, unless they are seasoned Synectics practitioners, they will still be unsure or anxious about what they are supposed to be saying and doing. As facilitator we should positively acknowledge first contributions of headlines, background, speculative ideas, or a build on someone else's idea, etc.

In Frame 10.10 I have listed example springboards for the Sigma Chi Ltd case, along with illustrations of what is meant by background to the first few ideas. I have cross-referenced these (a, b, c . . .) with the problem owner's narrative in Frame 10.8 to give an idea of where my springboards have come from. Depending on the problem and the mood and experience of the group, up to 50 springboards are perfectly possible in about half an hour.

Frame 10.10 *Sigma Chi Ltd: some springboards*

Continues list of springboards given on pages 237–8

11. I wish we could have a totally open interchange of ideas and opinions (a).

12. How to illustrate that 'traditional' roles/values/attitudes are no longer appropriate?

13. How to convince people that my ideas are the best (b)?

    Well if I could, there wouldn't be a problem would there – unless my ideas were wrong!

14. How to solicit ideas more effectively (c)?

    I was thinking of someone wandering around the streets of a town asking complete strangers questions, as religious freaks and market researchers do. Some people don't like being accosted in this way, they cross the street if they see someone like this coming, they go all shy and rush off making excuses, give misleading answers – there must be some way of doing it without people suspecting your motives.

15. How to turn resistance into support (d)?

    I had this image of school maths problems with 'bodies' being pushed or pulled up inclined planes; this led me to thinking of Newton's Laws and the one that says something like 'For every force there is an equal and opposite reaction'.

16. I wish my ideas were 'Teflon' coated.

    It's a 'build' on the last idea, thinking of things without friction, I remembered hearing somewhere that the coatings on non-stick frying-pans were used to reduce friction somehow. Can't we do something to these ideas?

17. I wish I could attribute my ideas to someone else.

18. How to gain commitment.

19. How can I engender team spirit and company loyalty?

20. How to be open-minded and decisive (e)?

21. How to demonstrate that there are opportunities to be had (f)?

22. I wish I could portray the benefits of change (h)!

23. I wish I could encourage a positive attitude to change!

24. I wish I could brainwash my staff.

25. How to minimize the disadvantages of change?

26. How to increase revenue (g)?

27. How to cut costs?

28. How to release more time for research and consultancy?

29. I wish I could institute a perfect communications system (i)!

30. I wish I were Superman, I could make all the changes I feel are necessary instantly, and no one would question their merit (j)!

31. I wish I could fire people with enthusiasm (for change) (k).

32. I wish I could sack everybody, and then select a new lot of staff.

33. How to bring about rapid and immediate change (l)?

34. How to overcome complacency?

35. I wish I could shake some of my colleagues into 'life' (m)!
36. How to counteract the fear of change (n)?
37. How can I discover, encourage and reward the creativity and innovation already taking place within the organization (o)?

Selection

We now have a number of ways at looking at the problem amongst the spring-boards written up around the session room. The problem owner needs a chance to reflect on these and select two or three that best describe the problem situation. The rest of the group can usefully take a short break at this time. As facilitator, our advice to the problem owner would be to choose problem definitions that *appeal* to her or him and which s/he would like to develop into possible solutions, regardless of their feasibility (see also Frame 10.11).

Frame 10.11 *The value of intuition!*

The problem owner should actually be warned against selecting *only* those springboards that appear obviously practical, and be advised to choose those that are intriguing, novel and interesting. A practical springboard will almost certainly lead to a solution, but one which may possibly be ordinary, uninspired or boring. A less practical but more intriguing one, though requiring more effort to develop, may well lead to a really novel solution. If a springboard appeals to us in this way, we will usually be prepared to put in the effort to see it through to a possible solution.

It is permissible for the problem owner to combine several springboards into one, and this new one should be written up with the rest.

Whatever is done next with the selected springboards, we should first ask the problem owner to say what led him or her to choose them. For instance, 'What benefits would come out of this if we could solve the problem in these ways?' The group would also be asked to start thinking of ideas that might lead to possible solutions as they are listening to this.

After the problem owner has made his or her selection of springboards, we have one of two possible ways forward. If the springboard selected implies a specific way of tackling part of the problem, the problem owner is asked to say how s/he will pursue this and what additional help s/he may need to make it happen. Supposing the director of Sigma Chi Ltd had chosen to work with:

I wish we could have a totally open interchange of ideas and opinions.

or perhaps

> I wish I could attribute my ideas to someone else.

Both of these contain a reference to a specific course of action. The problem owner might say that the first suggests to him the idea of holding an open forum for ideas, complaints, whatever. Although the staff of Sigma Chi Ltd number some 300 people, there are facilities where they can all meet together at the same time. This already happens once a year, though it is usually a one-sided communication. Our problem owner might say that s/he needs additional help over the logistics of running such a 'conference'. His/her only concern with this course of action is 'How to organize a large discussion so as to ensure that everybody has a chance and feels able to say what they like?' Although the second selected springboard is perhaps a bit 'tongue-in-cheek', if the situation is so bad that knowing something is the director's idea is sufficient to put the 'kiss of death' on it, s/he may wish to pursue it! In this case the help the problem owner might need is in finding the most convincing way of circulating 'evidence' suggesting alternative authorship of these ideas.

As facilitator, we would ask the group for ideas on how these minor concerns could be dealt with. As each of these ideas is presented, it would be evaluated by the problem owner (see later), but only after s/he has **paraphrased** them; that is, the leader would ask him/her to explain what s/he understands the idea to be, to confirm that everyone is talking about the same thing, and then will check back this interpretation with the idea's contributor. It can feel uncomfortable at first apparently echoing what someone has just said, but it pays off in the end (see Chapter 3). After the idea's contributor realizes you are not hard of hearing or lacking intellect, s/he will appreciate the trouble taken to understand what s/he is saying. We will return to this process and the springboards selected above on page 253.

If no specific action is indicated by the springboard, the next step is to generate ideas as to how the circumstances it describes might be brought about; possibly by using an excursion. Suppose the director of Sigma Chi Ltd had chosen the following springboard:

> How to turn resistance into support.

and made the following comment about it:

> I am really taken by this idea of converting resistance into support. I don't know how you do it, but if we could it would be marvellous. There is so much energy being directed against any changes, that if we could turn this about there'd be no stopping us!

No specific solution is indicated here, so we need the group to generate ways in which this 'objective' might be achieved. This could be done in the way the springboards were generated, by asking the group to suggest different means for achieving this without any judgement being imposed on them. In other words, Brainstorm a number of ways of 'converting resistance into support'. Note that the group would perhaps be asked only for beginning ideas that do not need to be fully-formed solutions at this time. Again encouragement would be given to ideas that build upon others and everything should be written up on flipcharts (note that 'actionable' ideas, no matter how crazy, are recorded *without* a 'How to/ I wish' preface).

If this does not produce the quality of ideas hoped for (the desired combination of newness, appeal and feasibility), or if we feel before we start this stage that newness is going to be a key factor in the success of a possible solution, we could use one of the many types of Synectics excursion, as well as or instead of this Brainstorming session, to generate ideas (see also Frame 10.12). My reaction to this springboard is that if I sat down and tried to brainstorm this one, I would get a few very ordinary ideas. I therefore intend to take an excursion in the hope of doing better.

Frame 10.12 *When to use excursions? Any time!*

This stage of the Synectics process, and under these circumstances, is by no means the only place where excursions can be used effectively. They can be used to generate (more) speculative springboards. They can also be a beneficial exercise whether they produce novel ideas or not. John Alexander of Synectics believes that the positive effects an excursion has on a group's cohesiveness, open-mindedness and readiness to speculate, can often be as important as its value as an idea-generating mechanism and tries to introduce them as early on in the process as he can.

Excursion (Ideation)

In Chapter 7 we came across various types of excursion used in the Synectics process in order to generate ideas. The one we will use here is an **imaging** or **fantasy excursion**. The choice of excursion depends on the degree of novelty required in the solution, the element of risk the leader is prepared to take and the material we are working on. Another type, the **example excursion**, is frequently used (and we will use it later in Chapter 12). The imaging excursion is most likely to produce innovative ideas.

The problem owner and the group need fair warning of what we are about to do before branching into any excursion. I would introduce an imaging excursion in this way:

> I think what we need to do now is to try to find some really novel ideas or solutions for this problem, so I suggest we cover up all the material we already have on the flipcharts and try to forget our problem for the moment, get some distance from it, in fact get right away from it into something totally different. You all know of people like Archimedes, Einstein, Pasteur, etc. to whom a marvellous idea has suddenly occurred apparently from nowhere, this is what we hope might happen here. We are going to take a flight of fantasy into a 'crazy' story, so as to get as far away from the original problem as possible. Then, when we have done that and collected a mass of colourful and seemingly irrelevant material en route, we will slowly come back to our problem and use this fantastic material to help us find a practical solution.

I would then explain the 'rules' and 'procedure' of an imaging excursion (see Chapter 7, page 149). And as was suggested there, we lead into the imaging excursion with a simple 'round robin' word association, taking the word 'resistance' from the selected springboard (see Frame 10.13).

Frame 10.13 *Sigma Chi Ltd: word association introduction*

Resistance	Pipe dream
Freedom fighter	Illusion
War	Magic carpet
Peace	Slippers

We will assume that (for some reason) the word 'slippers' causes considerable amusement amongst our group, and so we stop the word association at that point. As facilitator we now ask the group to descibe their mental images (in turn) relating to 'slippers', trying (if they can) to make something strange 'happen', before passing the 'baton' on. If these images were related to things like Sunday afternoons, dog walking, being on a beach, watching old sci-fi films, car washing, dreaming about holidays, etc., our mental imagery for Sigma Chi Ltd might have started off as I have shown in Frame 10.14. We will, I hope, be able to derive some novel solutions from this later.

Frame 10.14 *Sigma Chi Ltd: imaging excursion*

Let's suppose that the images in people's minds at that time were briefly:

I see a peaceful sunny Sunday afternoon in suburbia, just after lunch, and everybody is flat out in armchairs with their feet up suffering from post-dinner sleepiness. Grandad snores loudly and wakes himself up with such a start that one of his slippers flies off and hits the dog near him . . .

All of a sudden the front door of 42 Acacia Avenue bangs open and a dog comes hurtling out carrying a slipper in its mouth, and runs off down the street with a hobbling middle-aged man in a dressing-gown in hot pursuit. On reaching the pub on the corner the irate dog owner gives up the chase and . . .

Meanwhile the dog has scampered off to a nearby recreational ground because it is in desperate need of the sandpit. On reaching it, the dog sees that there are lots of circles in the sand, something is burrowing around it just under the surface. Suddenly, a small blue-and-yellow snake emerges from one of the circular furrows and wriggles sideways to the edge of the sandpit. Then he lifts up his head and hisses at nothing in a frustrated fashion 'Won't somebody get me out of here? I want to go home! Can't anyone hear me?' Then the snake seems to detect a noise, and looks up . . .

The noise the snake thought it had heard is a passing spaceship from Sirius. It is on a reconnaissance mission looking for civilization in other stellar systems. The aliens see the snake and beam it aboard their craft. After five hours of inter-

▶

rogation the aliens conclude that this Earthly life-form, although quite athletic, is not very intelligent, so they eat it . . .

Back at 42 Acacia Avenue a green Volkswagon is warming itself in the sun. The VW, who is called Spicey, senses the feelings of horror as the snake becomes the first Terran creature to examine, at close proximity, the insides of an alien being. Outraged by this wanton destruction, Spicey quickly opens his engine cover. A thin brilliantly green beam of engine oil speeds skywards . . .

The alien spaceship disintegrates instantly into an oil slick that gracefully drifts down through the lower reaches of the atmosphere like black snow, and totally covers a small fishing village in Alaska.

We should try and keep the images in one 'location' if possible, this is so as to create a rich, 'colourful' communal mental 'picture'; our session has begun to 'wander' a bit, but . . . as long as the result is evocative and linked somehow it should be all right.

As facilitator, we should also try to ensure that everyone (including the problem owner) contributes to our 'picture', but without putting anyone 'on the spot'. As we said before (Chapter 7) this excursion can be a bit unnerving! If someone is looking upwards, they are supposed to be imaging, and this could be a way for us to see who is 'ready' to offer something; but if everyone is steadfastly looking down, then we may have a problem! If anyone is having difficulty imaging, it is perfectly all right to let them 'fake' it by telling a story (rather than describing an image).

When every group member has had at least one chance to contribute, we stop the imaging and ask them to 'replay' in their minds what they have just heard, and think up some really absurd or impractical solutions to the problem. The problem statement or springboard the group was working on is uncovered and these **Absurd Solutions** are written up. Again, it is perfectly legitimate to modify, combine or build on other people's ideas as they appear. Some Absurd Solutions for the 'Sigma Chi' problem are given in Frame 10.15.

As with the springboards earlier, it is helpful if these Absurd Solutions are offered as a headline followed by some background thinking. Sometimes background is unnecessary or obvious, but with really weird Absurd Solutions we should elicit the background as it may spark someone else's imagination.

Frame 10.15 *Sigma Chi Ltd: some Absurd Solutions*

- Feed those people who are likely to resist the changes a big roast dinner . . . (the idea is that with luck they might doze off and sleep right through the actual implementation of the changes).
- Confiscate the staff's slippers . . . (in this way we can impair their ability to chase after and stop the changes).
- I wish I could pickle the resistance in alcohol . . . (I could then put it into an airtight bottle and store it away in a cupboard. I could leave it there out of

the way for some time. Then later I can take it out and eat it. It would taste better perhaps).

- Get a 'choker' chain big enough for humans . . . (I was thinking about how you train recalcitrant dogs. It's a shame there isn't a similar thing for people).

- Cause a distraction that takes people's minds away from the changes we want to make.

- Get all the staff to dance around a maypole . . . (because as they run around in circles trying to avoid the changes, the ribbons they are holding will pull them closer and closer together into a tightly bound group).

- Cover your ears so that the shouts of complaint can be mistaken for the cheers of enthusiasm.

- I wish the people that are resisting the changes could be beamed up and devoured by the occupants of a passing spacecraft.

- I wish I could wash the staff's opposition away . . . (this came from the idea of washing the VW, I thought of washing clothes and how you can remove stains (old ideas) or change colours with bleach and add stiffness (support) with some starch).

- Cover the less 'desirable' changes in curry powder so as to disguise their 'distaste'.

- I wish I were a mind reader and could look into my staff's minds.

- Fit a rocket drive to my ideas . . . (so that no one can catch up with them (and thus be able to stop them); no one will even see my ideas if I move faster than the speed of light!).

- I wish I could fire my staff through a Black Hole . . . (because it is suggested by science-fiction writers that if you survive this experience you could end up in a parallel universe where certain things are different, perhaps everything is back to front. A universe where change is seen as good, and opposition as support!).

- Bring in the Ghostbusters to dispel the evil phantoms associated with change.

- Cover your ideas with oil . . . (they would then be so slippery that other people couldn't grasp hold of them. They would just slip through their fingers).

- I wish I could freeze the resistance to my ideas . . . (it would then be so brittle that I could crush it into dust and blow it away, or I could sculpt these pillars of ice into my vision of the future).

Having moved so far from the problem with the imaging excursion it usually becomes desirable to return to the real world and our problem in several stages, the first being the attempt to dream up totally Absurd Solutions. Though, if a group member immediately comes up with a sensible and novel solution, we are obviously not going to reject it. Also, some of the Absurd Solutions are not strictly ways of 'turning resistance into support' but ways of 'diminishing' resistance; but if the problem owner seems content there is no need to draw this to the group's attention.

We, as facilitator, now need to check again with the problem owner to see if any of the Absurd Solutions intrigue, fascinate or appeal to him/her. There should be no problem with picking 'too practical' a solution as there should not be any! After the problem owner makes his/her selection we ask the group to examine the (chosen) Absurd Solutions and to try to find a way to change them into something more practical and closer to reality, whilst retaining as much of the original idea as possible. It is not necessary to change them into something practical in one step; it is better to take some time modifying them, because there is a tendency to lose the novel feature contained in the absurd solution by 'jumping' back to reality too quickly (see Frame 10.16).

Frame 10.16 *Sigma Chi Ltd: developing Absurd Solutions*

An example of trying to add a semblance of practicality to an Absurd Solution, without destroying its essence, can be demonstrated with the following Absurd Solution:

I wish I could freeze the resistance to my ideas.

We might revise this as follows:

I wish I could overcome the resistance by freezing time – by apparently slowing things down.

One of the reasons people fear change is because they believe that it will happen so quickly that they will be unprepared for it.

We then modify it again, and again if necessary, until it forms into a possible solution:

'Slow things down' by emphasizing those things which are not going to change in the near future, such as salaries, conditions of service, the bulk of our work, thus reassuring people about some aspects of the future. From this position of relative security, we can then perhaps address the things that do need to change soon.

In Frame 10.17 some possible solutions for Sigma Chi Ltd are suggested. Some of the ideas (for example 'oil') might appear a little underhand. A manager might try this: if he gets away with it and people start thinking of change as only having benefits, then half the battle is won and the whole process may snowball from there. Personally, I feel that this action cannot be recommended on the grounds that if the deception is detected, it is likely to make matters worse. However, as facilitator/process leader, I have no right to volunteer such value judgements.

Frame 10.17 *Sigma Chi Ltd: ideas for some possible solutions*

'Roast dinner'

Fill the staff up with 'good things': find out what their pet ideas are and encourage them to pursue these ideas, preferably to the benefit of the organization. Offer them all the support and resources you can, in an attempt to channel their enthusiasm in a positive direction, rather than have it being directed against you and the changes you feel you need to make.

'Maypole'

Find a way to 'bind' my staff together against a 'common enemy', perhaps by making a heart-felt plea for their support, stressing the point that everyone has a talent that could be used for the good of all.

'Beam me up, Scotty!'

Transport them off to an 'alien' environment, from which they cannot easily escape, such as one of the many country mansion residential management training centres, where you can thrash out the issues without being disturbed or distracted by other things.
. . . and/or . . .
'Enhance' and publicize the qualities of the opponents so that they are head-hunted by other organizations, or at least I do my best to support them in finding new positions elsewhere (which you have encouraged them to seek).

'Curry powder'

Use the newly acquired freedom that comes with incorporation to give all your staff a pay rise and/or better conditions of service, thus demonstrating some tangible benefits from incorporation; this might encourage support for other changes.

'Mind reader'

Invite all staff either to come to you individually and have a 'no holds barred' discussion with you or, if they prefer, to write to you anonymously, telling you what they think of the current situation and your ideas, and why they think that way; the things that they are afraid of or concerned about and the ideas that they have about what they would like to do or see happen.

'Black hole'

Find and show your staff another organization that is perceived by them to have been in a worse 'hole' than them, but who have been through more 'devastating' changes and come out the other side much better off, thus showing that the apparent disadvantages of the changes you are proposing can be turned into advantages.

▶

'Ghostbusters'

Invite some people, whose views your staff would respect, and who have been through similar changes, to come and dispel some of the myths about change that are currently being put around.

'Oil'

Describe the less desirable aspects of the changes you wish to make so that their exact nature is somewhat elusive and difficult to grasp, as is understanding their full implications.

We are now at the stage in the flowchart shown in Frame 10.3 where the two alternative branches have just come together again. We should now have a flow of ideas coming from our group's effort in overcoming the concerns associated with the springboards that indicated a specific way of addressing the problem (see page 246), or a 'pile' of ideas from our 'straight' Brainstorming idea-generating session (see page 246), or from our imaging excursion. These now need evaluating and developing further.

An excursion could of course have been usefully applied to both branches of the flowchart, but it is more likely to be needed when the springboard we are working on does not suggest a specific way of reaching a solution.

Itemized response (Idea Development)

Remembering what was said in Chapter 3 about discounts, we need to be aware of the effect of criticism on the person who suggested the ideas we are now going to ask the problem owner to (gently) evaluate. The effort that goes into getting ideas make people quite protective of them. Having withheld judgement earlier, we should not spoil things now, risking the delicate creative climate the group has developed by hasty and perhaps crude evaluation.

As facilitator, we ask the problem owner to select what for him/her are the **most promising ideas** and, one at a time, paraphrase them and identify at least three practical, helpful or attractive aspects of that idea, giving reasons wherever possible. It may be helpful to let the group contribute to this also, since they may see additional benefits not immediately apparent to the problem owner. Drawing attention to what are the positive aspects of an idea gives a sense of satisfaction to the idea's contributor and makes it easier for him/her subsequently to accept the identification of any shortcomings the idea might have.

Then we ask for the problem owner's major concern with the idea, expressing this as a 'How to'/'I wish' in order to give the group a direction for the further development of the idea to overcome this concern. We then gather ideas from the group and write them on the flipcharts while asking the problem owner to again paraphrase the suggestions to ensure understanding. If the group comes up with a suggestion that only partially overcomes the concern, the **itemized response** process is repeated with this latest suggestion.

It is to be hoped that, having resolved the major concern, the group now tackles any other concerns the problem owner may have regarding the original idea, always taking them one at a time. This is often the most difficult thing for an inexperienced group to do, due to what seems to be a natural desire to dump all the concerns on the table at once, particularly with multiple problem ownership. As facilitator, we need to be strict about this to avoid often circular arguments about which is the most serious concern, which invariably results in the idea being thrown out as an easy means of ending the argument. When working with more than one problem owner the facilitator's ultimate aim is to achieve consensus (see Chapter 12); opting out like this is not the way to achieve it.

An illustration of part of the itemized response process for the Sigma Chi problem in given in Frame 10.18.

Frame 10.18 *Sigma Chi Ltd: itemized response*

Idea ('Curry powder') from our imaging excursion

> *I use the newly acquired freedom that incorporation gives me to unilaterally give all my staff a pay rise and/or better conditions of service, thus, by demonstrating some tangible benefits from incorporation, I could perhaps solicit more support for other changes.*

What the director likes about the idea:

- It would be a popular move.
- It would show that there are some good aspects to the changes we are going through.
- I think it could improve morale and hence people's motivation.

His major concern:

> *I feel that this idea may have less impact if I am seen to be rewarding those who are not currently pulling their weight.*

Ideas for overcoming the major concern:

- Make this award only to those deemed to be competent.
- Any doubtful cases have the benefits on a 'probationary' basis.

Response from the director might be:

> *What you're suggesting is that I only offer this 'new deal' to those that I know are doing a reasonable job, but if there are some doubtfuls, we could offer it to them on some conditional basis. [paraphrasing the idea]*
>
> *That's great, that might well work, it also partially overcomes another concern that I had which was the cost, but if we could do this on the promise of an equivalent increase in 'production', I won't be worsening conditions and so I should be OK with the unions. I am concerned about one other matter, that is, there are supposed to be some national salary negotiations coming up shortly, I'm scared of 'giving away too much'.*

▶

◄
Idea to overcome second concern:

- Offer these benefits for six months at a time, renewable subject to a satisfactory review or a change in the national conditions.

This process continues, gradually homing in on a possible solution, a course of action, which the problem owner can implement without further help from the group.

Possible solution

On nearing a possible solution, we need to check again with the problem owner that the process is fulfilling his/her expectations. If the problem owner reports no need for further help from the group with the possible solution, we write up the possible solution and normally compare it with the newness, appeal and feasibility 'rating' discussed during the planning meeting, asking:

- Is it feasible?
- Is it appealing?
- Does it have newness/novelty?

This should reveal the problem owner's enthusiasm, satisfaction and commitment to the solution. If the problem owner responds favourably, as the facilitator, we can start him/her towards implementation of the solution by asking whether s/he is beginning to form a plan of action. As a check to try and ensure that the problem-solving process *has* reached **closure**, we ask the problem owner to outline his/her next (say three) steps. It is rewarding for group members to hear what the problem owner sees as the next steps in the solution's progress and, although this is not a complete action plan, it does ensure that the problem owner goes away with a solution and some idea what to do with it: s/he knows how to progress it! The meeting is usually adjourned after these next steps are written up.

Concluding thoughts on the Sigma Chi case

We leave Sigma Chi Ltd with a couple of fairly concrete ideas for possible solutions that require very little additional development, plus the idea that we have just taken through the itemized response process.

If it is felt that we have left the director of Sigma Chi in a slightly unsatisfactory way, because, for instance, you may be thinking something like 'Well if it had been me, I wouldn't have started from there', this is understandable. For, as we will see in Chapter 13, in order to gain other people's commitment to an idea or change, they really need to feel part of it, to have been in there from the start. Our director is trying to gain commitment 'after the event', but that is his problem, and we had to start helping him from where he was.

Concluding thoughts on the basic Synectics process

Now that we have been through all the stages of the Synectics process, a timely warning: because the 'opening up' stages are great fun, there is sometimes a desire to open up the problem further and further so that eventually we have hundreds of fairly specific ideas, none of which is developed enough for the problem owner to use. Letting the group do this is sometimes rationalized on the basis of 'trying to cover all the possibilities', and protecting the creative atmosphere and well-being of the group. The leader should guard against this and 'close the problem down', going into the evaluation/development phase when the time is right.

Ultimately the group is trying to help someone solve a problem, and, despite feeling that we may 'be missing something' by going into evaluation/development earlier, we can often end up in the same place. For example, earlier we had the following, quite specific, springboard, 'I wish we could have a totally open interchange of ideas and opinions'. If our problem owner had said: 'That is precisely what we need, but how do I go about it? I need help on the practical details', it is not inconceivable that spiralling through the idea–paraphrase–itemized response sequence several times could have given us an idea very similar to the one which came from our 'Mind reader' solution (Frame 10.17). If this was exactly the sort of thing the problem owner was looking for, we would not have had quite so much fun but would have resolved the client's problem quicker.

It is usual for the problem owner to be presented with all the sheets of paper from the flipcharts, carefully sequenced, or better still a typed but unedited version of the same, so that s/he can look back over the session to see where ideas have come from. More important, these sheets will contain many different aspects of the problem and probably several other half-formed solutions, which the problem owner may want to pursue at another time.

Leading a Synectics-style session is not easy, but it is invariably exhilarating!

Other uses for elements of the Synectics process

I have mentioned above that Goal Wishing is an effective way of sharing perceptions of a given situation, a 'safe' way of airing differences of opinion, and also that an *excursion* can be used in isolation to generate a mass of unusual and innovative ideas. I should add to this that itemized response, apart from being a method of developing and evaluating an idea, is valuable in taking stock of situations, presenting proposals, and in conflict resolution and appraisal situations.

Meetings, meetings meetings!

The Synectics philosophy has implications for how ordinary 'agenda'-type meetings, as opposed to problem-solving sessions, can be improved. This involves having separate agenda items for each participant in the meeting published on flipcharts around the room, which can be added to or amended as the meeting proceeds. Each item on the agenda should have a personal priority attributed to it (in case of time pressures), the estimated length of time that person believes is required to deal with it adequately and what type of item it is. For instance, the owner of the agenda item may wish to give information, collect information or ask the group to assist in some problem solving (though this may be best deferred to a separate meeting).

The facilitator/process leader (who again has no dealings with, or interest in, the likely content of the meeting) should go around the meeting participants dealing with one item per person at a time, and recording the actual time spent on a particular item. Even if several members of the meeting wish to bring up the same issue, these are dealt with as individual items as they will be seen from different viewpoints, and the time, minutes, etc. recorded for each one. If we did have several people with the 'same' problem we would doubtless call a separate problem-solving session to tackle it (much as we do with Northcliffe Sands in Chapter 12). The meeting starts on time and runs for no longer than the previously agreed duration, unless the meeting unanimously agrees on an extension.

I intend to leave Synectics for now but, just as we came across Synectics and their ideas long before this chapter started, we will encounter Synectics concepts again later.

Summary

In this chapter we have seen how some of the techniques we have met earlier come together in the complete basic Synectics CPS process, which should enable you to start using it, and been given some practicalities of running a group Synectics session.

11 Soft Systems Methodology

This chapter illustrates how the various Soft Systems Methodology (SSM) models and techniques encountered in earlier chapters come together to form the 'full' SSM. It concludes with a brief account of how SSM can be 'interfaced' with hard information systems development methodologies.

Introduction and history

To show how the various **soft systems**, models and techniques introduced earlier can be employed together to form the 'full' **Soft Systems Methodology** (SSM), I will be describing, from the analyst's viewpoint, how an (imaginary) soft systems investigation would be conducted at a fictitious organization called Woodsons Ltd to try and improve things. Before this is done, we will look at a little background information about SSM (see Frame 11.1).

Frame 11.1 *SSM: background information*

SSM was devised by Professor Peter Checkland and has been developed by him and others at the University of Lancaster's Department of Systems since 1969. SSM was conceived as a strategy for dealing with the 'soft', ill-defined, complex problems of the real world, by considering these problem situations as **human activity systems**. In other words, SSM was specifically intended to be a way of dealing with what we have called elsewhere **people** problems.

SSM evolved out of an attempt to overcome the apparent deficiencies of the traditional methods of systems analysis which, although primarily intended as a means of tackling 'hard' engineering (**machine**) type problems, were then being increasingly used (without too much success) on problem situations involving people (and sadly, still are).

◄

Briefly, the shortcomings of these methods which SSM has sought to replace are that they have tended to assume that the problem could be simply stated, and have then concentrated on what was being done and have attempted to improve this (often, some people would say, by just patching it up), without considering why it was being done or indeed whether it should have been done at all.

The product of SSM is a list of possible changes which should improve the problem situation, and which are systemically desirable and (it is hoped) culturally feasible. Traditional methods of systems analysis seldom considered the latter.

SSM was developed as a problem-solving process for those faced with resolving highly complex and interrelated problem situations, where it is best to attempt to view the situation as a whole as opposed to restructuring it (see Chapter 1). Success with SSM depends more on our prior knowledge (of systems concepts and systems thinking) and our experience than is the case with any of the other problem-solving processes/techniques described in this book. These factors suggest that SSM is more likely to be used by an external consultant or team of consultants than by someone within a group or organization. However, Peter Checkland has demonstrated that SSM is equally as useful to a manager going about normal day-to-day work as it is for a special highlighted study (Checkland and Scholes, 1990a).

Because SSM may be used by us as external consultants, it is important to remember two points pertinent to such a situation. First, we should be aware that when we make an intervention into a real-world problem situation, our presence will have an effect. Second, as 'outsiders' we should 'give' our problem-solving expertise to the participants in the problem situation, by explaining the methodology as it is being employed, encouraging them to use it and ensuring that they are in a position to continue to do so after we have left. Ideally, the problem owners should play an active part in the process while we are there!

An overview of SSM

The first stage in an SSM investigation involves the careful observation of the problem situation with all its intricate details, and the recording of all that is perceived. This involves collecting qualitative data – such as attitudes and opinions concerning the problem situation, including reactions to our intervention in matters (as external consultants) – as well as quantitative data, and recording this in the form of a 'picture'. In this way we try to capture as much as possible of the richness of the real situation. Following this, the essence of these observations is encapsulated in brief descriptions of human activity systems that we hope may later provide relevant insights into the problem situation. Then models of these systems that are consistent with the different viewpoints expressed within the descriptions are drawn. Finally, several comparisons are made of the models with the observations of the real-world situation, which are used in a discussion with the problem owners to suggest **systemically desirable** and **culturally feasible** changes that it is hoped will lead to improvements in the problem situation. Note that, unlike many other problem-solving processes, SSM does not explicitly attempt to identify problems, but through its iterative 'learning' process it is intended to make changes to the problem situation such that whatever the problems were they no longer exist (see Frame 1.2). An overview of SSM is given in Figure 11.1.

SSM was intended to be a flexible and evolving problem-solving strategy. What follows are guidelines that can be adapted or modified for a particular problem situation. A schematic outline of the process is given in Figure 11.2, but it is not always necessary to start at stage 1. Work on several stages can be carried out concurrently, and it is likely that we will need to return to earlier stages and repeat various steps again. Note the clear distinction in the figure between the 'real-world' activities and the abstract 'systems thinking'.

A soft systems intervention

The Woodsons Ltd case (see Frame 11.2) used here to illustrate this process is obviously artificial as it includes only a finite set of observations. In real life this would not be the case, and the analyst can at any time take steps to attempt to fill any gaps detected in the information so far obtained.

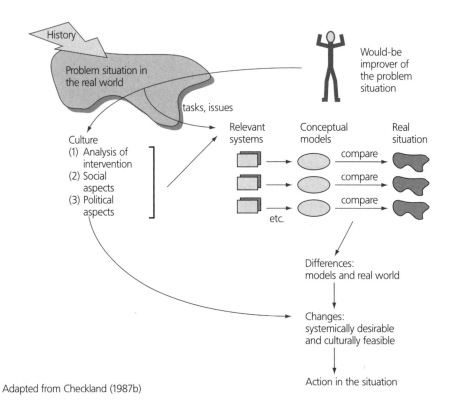

Figure 11.1

An outline of Soft Systems Methodology

Adapted from Checkland (1987b)

Frame 11.2 *Woodsons Ltd: the problem situation*

Woodsons Ltd is a small company producing and marketing loudspeaker enclosures for the hi-fi market. Originally, it was a family business which operated out of a small factory in the West Midlands. Although Woodsons design and build the enclosures themselves, they buy in speaker chassis units from LSI Ltd.

LSI is another family business. It was located on the same industrial estate, and in many ways the two companies had an ideal working arrangement. However, as the years have gone past, LSI has diversified into a variety of 'transducer' products and has become very successful supplying large electronic equipment manufacturers. LSI still supply the relatively small requirements of Woodsons, but do this more as a favour than as a viable trading proposition. Because of this and because LSI relocated to the Thames Valley, Woodsons now have to wait for 'a lorry to be coming their way' when they need to replenish their stocks of speaker units.

Woodsons was purchased in 1983 by a young entrepreneur, Rob Boston, when the company's fortunes were very low and it was on the verge of bankruptcy. Fierce competition from the Far East had almost eliminated the demand for UK mass produced hi-fi equipment. Although he still owns the company and is a member of its board, Boston has long since moved on to other things. The company is now managed by Peter Ford.

Figure 11.2

The stages of SSM

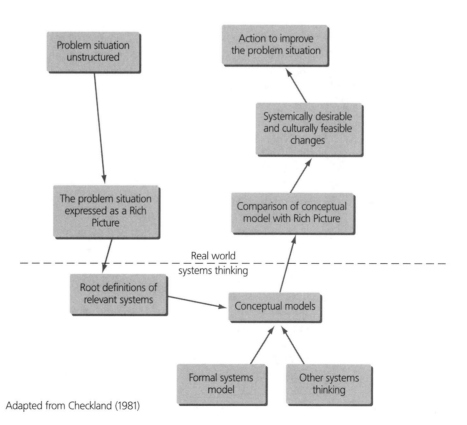

Adapted from Checkland (1981)

Boston was responsible for the drastic cuts and reorganization that took place in the mid-1980s. One of the things which ensured that Woodson survived and are still trading today is their dynamic sales team (hand-picked by Boston). Woodsons' main customers have always been small independent hi-fi retailers, though recently they have been selling any surplus 'old' stock to a hi-fi chain store. Woodsons' sales and marketing team have managed to increase orders every year, averaging a 4 per cent annual growth.

The sales and marketing section consists of the sales manager, five salespersons and a marketing assistant. Each member of the sales team is responsible for looking after the requirements of their own group of customers; they report to the sales manager monthly. They are also responsible for keeping their own customer records and two of them have home computers that they use to assist with this process.

Each salesperson passes the orders that s/he makes to the marketing assistant, one of whose responsibilities is to pass these orders on to the production section. There have now been no less than seven different marketing assistants in the last year – most have left after approximately a month. Janet has been with the company for almost seven months now, and has survived by ensuring that any abuse she receives when handing the sales team's orders to the production section is suitably deflected towards those she believes are responsible for invoking the abuse.

The other crucial factor in Woodsons' survival was John Smith. He was hired in 1984 as manager of the 'revamped' R&D team, and it was he who came up with an innovative design for a high quality compact loudspeaker system; a new product that saved Woodsons. Smith is now considered to be a bit of a maverick by his colleagues in other sections, due to his habit of forever chasing new concepts and ideas (some of which have gone down in the history of the company as 'Smith's follies'), instead of applying his team's expertise to developing and improving Woodsons' existing products. The R&D team consists of Smith, another designer and a highly skilled cabinet maker with a good working knowledge of acoustics.

Although morale has always been high amongst the sales team (this probably being due to the charisma and leadership of the sales manager, Sue Waterman), considerable frustration has been manifest in the last year at various meetings within the company. Nick Wright, one of the senior salesmen, summed it up by saying 'We are really getting fed up with the fact that after all our efforts to cultivate new customers and orders, this effort and our reputation are being ripped apart by frequent complaints from our customers about failures to deliver goods on time and receiving only part-orders'.

The production manager, Tim Shaw, and his staff of 17 consider themselves to be efficient and overworked, and morale certainly cannot be said to be good in this section. In 1983 the whole section was pared down to the bare minimum as part of a cost-saving scheme; although there has been an increasing use of technology in the manufacturing process, the number of production personnel has not changed dramatically since then. Production planning is not helped by having a succession of 'high priority' orders arriving almost continuously from certain members of the sales team who, in the opinion of Tim Shaw, 'are making irresponsible promises of delivery to their customers without first checking with me about the current production schedule, and are consequently placing impossible demands on my section'. Ironically, in recent years Woodsons have been making loudspeakers for a Far Eastern manufacturer, for sale with their equipment in the UK. These (quite sizeable) orders are invariably classified as 'high priority'.

Another aspect of the company's operation that is giving concern is the low quality of the packaging and distribution. This is done by an outside contractor, Crow Packaging. Crow Packaging are also responsible for putting together the orders prior to distribution by road carriers.

Apart from the new manufacturing systems, Woodson has a small network of five IBM microcomputers that were purchased in 1994, as part of Ford's scheme to modernize the management of Woodsons. Two of these machines reside in the general office and are used mainly for the company accounts and payroll. The managing director himself has one in his office (or, more correctly, in his secretary's office); this machine, like the other machines located outside the general office, is used mostly for word processing, much of which is normal everyday correspondence.

There is a rumour that Rob Boston is contemplating selling off Woodsons if things do not improve in the next six months. Woodsons is the least profitable of all the companies in his group. We have been hired by Peter Ford to perform an analysis of Woodsons' operations and to suggest improvements that might be made.

The problem situation unstructured

The description of the first stage of the process as the **problem situation unstructured** reinforces the idea that we should be entering the situation with a completely open mind. It is probably not obvious, though we may be told otherwise, what the problem actually is. We should not permit ourselves to jump to conclusions about it being a certain **well-defined** problem. This would tend to indicate that we know what the solution should be; it is not our place to decide what is an acceptable solution.

If the problem situation is so difficult to sort out that we have had to be brought in, then it is likely to be several interrelated problems. The people involved in the problem situation will have different views of it and there may be many valid opinions on what the problem is. It may even be that it is these differing perceptions of the problem situation which is preventing them from finding a way to resolve it. It is clear from Frame 11.2, which described the situation within Woodsons, that it is an organization with severe problems.

We shall assume that we have just begun our first encounter with the 'mess' that constitutes the problem situation, and that we have spoken to the client, who has told us what the problem is as he sees it. We have noted this for future reference and then immediately 'forgotten' it until after we have gathered all our data. We have also sorted out all the administrative details that are necessary to ensure the smooth running of the who, what, when, why and how of our information gathering, and we have made a start on collecting our data.

One of the first things we should have done is to start forming some impressions about the political and social aspects of the problem situation. We need to determine which people occupy the roles of **client**, **would-be problem solver** and **problem owner**, and also the whereabouts of the most 'sensitive areas': this has to be ascertained before the bulk of the data is obtained because it can affect our success with this (see also Chapter 5, pages 78–9).

When trying to identify would-be problem solvers we, as the external consultant, should remember that we are (and should be seen as) problem-solving facilitators rather than problem solvers. The only people likely to be able to resolve the problem will be those that have the power to implement any of our suggestions that are accepted.

Knowing the bases of power can indicate how situations have come about, forewarn us of difficulties we may encounter collecting the information we need and help us anticipate where resistance to or support for any changes we may later suggest is likely to occur.

Political issues are by nature never explicit and can be very elusive, which often predisposes people to ignore them. Checkland (1986) strongly urges us to try to determine them, recommending that a good approach is to assume good faith on the part of our fellow human beings as this often yields surprising dividends of goodwill. Having gained this goodwill we need to be careful not to say or do anything that might jeopardize it!

Let us suppose we have determined which people occupy the roles of client, would-be problem solver and problem owner, and also the whereabouts of the most sensitive areas (see Frame 11.3).

Frame 11.3 *Woodsons Ltd: essential information and early impressions*

Client – we have been employed by Peter Ford, the managing director, so he is the client.

Problem solvers – Peter Ford is obviously in the best position to implement any changes we might suggest, but he will need the support, commitment and goodwill of his three managers.

Problem owners – all the employees of Woodsons from the MD downwards have a stake in all this. And, of course, so does Rob Boston, though I'm not sure whether we can get his viewpoint in any more detail than that provided by the rumours. We might also consider LSI, Crow Packaging, and even Woodsons' customers as problem owners. This would certainly give us a good mix of viewpoints.

Political aspects

It is a little difficult to say much about the political aspects of Woodsons' problem from such a brief account. A couple of potential power 'commodities' might well be being hand-picked by Rob Boston (Sue Waterman and the five salesperons) back in the crisis years and the innovative and technical expertise of John Smith (it has brought him through several mistakes without too much damage).

Social aspects

Over the years it would appear that to be seen as dynamic and successful (by all but Tim Shaw and his staff) one needs to produce growth of 4 per cent p.a. Perhaps it is time that this norm is re-evaluated. Being hand-picked by Rob Boston and meeting their self-imposed targets seems to imbue in the sales team the feeling that they have (or at least should have) the authority to lead the organization. However, there is some dispute (from Tim Shaw) as to whether they should hold this position. Also, the behaviour of the person occupying the role of 'ideas man' (John Smith) is evidently not that which is expected by the rest of the organization.

We also need to collect other hard and soft data, of the types described in Chapter 5. See Frame 11.4 for some examples from the Woodsons case.

Frame 11.4 *Woodsons Ltd: some examples of hard and soft data and 'climate'*

Hard data

- Divisions/departments – sales (and marketing), production, R&D . . .
- Noteworthy individuals – Sue Waterman, John Smith, Peter Ford . . .
- Products – apart from being loudspeakers we don't know much about this.
- Data flows – most communications between sales and production go through the marketing assistant (currently Janet) . . .
- Quantitative data – 6 people work for sales, 18 for production . . .

Soft data

- Perceptions/judgements – R&D manager (John Smith) is seen as a maverick, production manager (Tim Shaw) thinks sales are being irresponsible, sales are 'frustrated' with production . . .
- Rumours – the owner (Rob Boston) is thinking of selling up . . .

Climate

An example of 'climate' in the Woodsons situation is that, whilst many other things may have changed in recent years – such as the growth in sales – the size of the production section has not, hence there is a mismatch between *process* (sales) and *structure* (the staffing of the production section).

The soft data is vital to our investigations and must be determined, though doing so is not easy (see page 80). Success with this will depend very much on the personality of the person collecting the information and his/her reputation for fairness and confidentiality and for being non-judgemental.

Rich Pictures, the primary tasks and the issues of concern

Once all the necessary data have been gathered, we (as the analysts) 'record' it in a cartoon-style diagram called a **Rich Picture** (see also Chapter 5). We must assemble this picture without imposing any particular preconceptions on it. This is difficult because we may have already seen some possible promising directions we could suggest to Woodsons that they might go in to improve things and we are keen to get started on the next steps.

When we are sharing our thoughts or explaining our possible systemically desirable and (we hope) culturally feasible changes later, we may wish to refer back to something 'seen' in the Rich Picture. There is therefore a case for not making it too idiosyncratic. However, the fact that it may be seen by others should not be the main criterion in deciding how to construct it.

We could construct two Rich Pictures, one complete and one omitting the (sensitive and possibly contentious) subjective comments, the latter being intended for public consumption; but this presents us with an ethical dilemma.

There is nothing to be gained by disclosing contentious information that is of no importance to the solving of the problem. However, if a contentious piece of information is significant, but has been given in confidence, we must get clearance from the originator before disclosing it. We should never attempt to disguise or give anonymity to a piece of data in order to 'publicize' it. The originator is almost certain to hear a garbled version of what was actually said, and even though that person may remain undetected as its author, our reputation for confidentiality will be compromised. Rich Pictures often need tidying up before public presentation and so could be judiciously 'simplified', though we should make it clear they are a summary of our findings and that if further details are required they will be given, if available.

Figure 11.3 shows the Rich Picture that I drew for the Woodsons example. This must not be considered an example of the 'correct' way to draw it, let alone a 'correct' answer; it has also been slightly 'tidied up', so as to give a glimpse of my thinking whilst compiling it! But it should give an indication of appropriate content and level of detail.

How do we know when we have finished? In practice, the picture will never be completely finished, as representing all the information you have gathered into a Rich Picture is not a finite activity. We will need to add to our picture as our investigations continue and we come across additional information. This makes it difficult to determine when it is complete enough to allow us to move on to the next phase. The best advice is try it and see. Later, when formulating our **Root Definitions** or comparing our Rich Picture with our **Conceptual Models** (see below), inadequacies resulting from a lack of information will become apparent. We will then need to find out this information and add it to the Rich Picture. Ultimately, experience will be our guide with this matter.

When we feel it is time to move on, we should take some time to reflect upon the picture. The transition to this next stage will be easier if we take a break between the data collection and recording process that we have just finished, and reviewing our picture to try to discover what it all means.

As we review our Rich Picture we should be looking for new and insightful ways of looking at the problem situation. We would like to find a new angle, perspective or a totally different way of viewing the problem situation. This task is often helped by first trying to determine:

- the tasks that the organization was originally created to perform,
- the activities they must engage in now in order to 'survive' the problem situation.

These are the organization's **primary tasks**, and also the things which are or should be the organization's main **issues of concern**.

The two types of primary tasks can be seen as the organization's original prime objective(s) or 'mission', or what now could or should be its mission. During our investigations it is likely that we will have discovered various (groups of) people's views on this.

Frame 11.5 identifies the primary tasks and issues of concern for Woodsons Ltd; your interpretation of the situation might be different.

Figure 11.3 Rich Picture for Woodsons

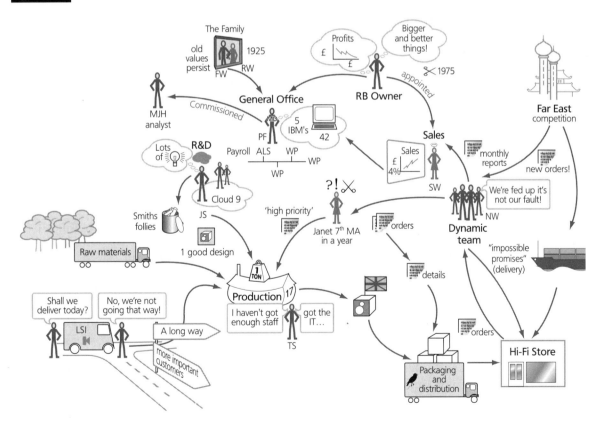

Frame 11.5 *Woodsons Ltd: primary tasks and issues of concern*

Primary tasks

Created to perform	*Must do to survive*
Design, produce and market loudspeakers	Provide an acceptable return on investment for the owner
Improve the design of loudspeaker systems	Become a 'high-end' quality loudspeaker manufacturer
Provide employment?	Become a high volume/low cost loudspeaker producer by out-sourcing manufacturing
Make a profit	

Issues of concern

'Mis-guided' R&D effort

Maintaining an adequate supply of speaker units

Poor communications between sales and production

Insufficient production staff

Low morale (particularly in the production team)

Unreliable packaging and distribution

Poor customer relations

Under-used computing facilities?

Possible sale of the company

Note: Those items marked with a ? may seem at first sight not to be quite so important and/or relevant as the other items, but have been included so that they will not be overlooked, just in case we should change our minds later.

Root Definitions of Relevant Systems

We are now approaching the crucial stage of SSM, deciding on which human activity systems to model. As we have seen earlier (pages 116–18) a Root Definition is the name given to a concise verbal description of a system we intend to model and which, when compared with the real-world problem situation, will, we hope, inspire ideas for changes that may resolve the problem. It is a major step to move from our Rich Picture to here, so how do we summarize the essence of what's going on in the problem situation from all the detail in the picture?

We have already taken some tentative steps in this direction by listing the organization's primary tasks and its issues of concern. Now we need to think of some systems which are likely to be relevant ways of viewing the problem situation, and write down brief (often 'one-line') descriptions of their purpose. How do we know that they are going to be relevant? Don't worry about this. We can only be certain that a particular system was not relevant at the end of our efforts, if the changes we suggest derived from comparing it with the real world are rejected. It is usual and a wise precaution to proceed through the next steps developing at least one possibly **Relevant System** into a Root Definition and conceptual model.

The problem situation as seen through our Rich Picture should give some clues as to which system(s) we should employ to make some sense out of all the 'furious' human activity it depicts. There is presumably a purpose for *all* this activity, and if this is worthwhile there should be a human activity system that will assist with our appreciation of the problem situation. A useful strategy for generating our Relevant Systems is to do some **Brainstorming**, as we would particularly like some unusual ones.

When searching for Relevant Systems, we should not attempt to evaluate their potential usefulness, as this will reduce the likelihood of us coming up with new and insightful ways of seeing the problem situation. Frame 11.6 lists some Relevant Systems for the Woodsons case study.

Frame 11.6 *Woodsons Ltd: Relevant Systems*

1. A commercial system for manufacturing and selling hi-fi loudspeakers.
2. A system for designing and testing hi-fi loudspeakers.
3. A system for encouraging/helping the survival of the UK hi-fi business.
4. A system for supplying independent hi-fi retailers with good quality loudspeaker systems.
5. A system for providing business for external manufacturers, packers, distributors and retailers.
6. A system for promoting the European 'sound' of loudspeakers.
7. A system designed to enhance the quality/esoteric image of UK hi-fi, particularly its excellence in loudspeaker design.
8. A system for improving the design of loudspeaker systems.
9. A system for providing employment for acoustic designers and cabinet makers.
10. A system designed to challenge/arrest/regain the inroads being made by Far Eastern hi-fi manufacturers in the UK.
11. A system for providing humans with the ability to make more noise.
12. A system for providing an effective investment for the owner.
13. A system for testing the potential of gifted staff by subjecting them to a situation which causes confusion and frustration.
14. A system for utilizing the products of sustainable forests.
15. A system for encouraging noise pollution.

When trying to generate names for new products (page 134 and Appendix 3) we said that the merit of a good one will usually be obvious. The same is true of Relevant Systems: we tend to recognize a really insightful system as soon as we have thought of it, because it provides us with an unexpected perspective on the problem situation. Remember, these systems are not intended to solve a given problem, nor are they ones that anybody is likely to implement.

We now select the most promising of our Relevant Systems. We may feel it appropriate to combine some of them in one Root Definition. The word 'mission' (although a term that some dislike) does seem to summarize nicely what we are trying to do here. We are gathering together a number of Relevant Systems each of which highlights some aspect of the main function that we perceive the organization to be, or ought to be, performing, and are now trying to mould these into a mission statement, our Root Definition.

There will be some conflict between providing a full description in our Root Definition and our overall aim to be concise. We should also ensure that the level of detail is consistent throughout the definition. However, we also need to get something down on paper fairly quickly so that we can discuss our thoughts with the problem owners.

In choosing which Relevant Systems to incorporate into our Root Definitions, we need to make a conscious decision as to the direction in which we think we are heading. If we select Relevant Systems which have come from our primary tasks, we are likely to get a fairly conservative Root Definition that effectively describes the mission of the organization. This is appropriate if we believe that we are dealing with a problem perceived to be one of organizational design or information system provision and where the mission itself is not contentious. A Root Definition derived from issues of concern is a more radical proposition as it may challenge fundamental attitudes or major policy decisions. An insightful relevant system is more critical, if not essential, for dealing with a problem situation like that (Checkland and Wilson, 1980).

As mentioned above, we should develop more than one Root Definition through the remaining stages of the SSM process. This is a wise precaution since it would be embarrassing to have our one and only set of desirable and feasible changes rejected by the client, although we should not in any case allow ourselves to get so detached from the perceptions and likely responses of the people involved that our suggested changes will meet this fate. Right now, we should be sharing our thoughts on Relevant Systems with the problem owners; we also could have involved as many problem owners as possible when trying to Brainstorm our Relevant Systems. Trying out alternatives does not require much extra work: the bulk of our effort has already been made. It may be appropriate in certain circumstances to take a primary task and an issue-based Root Definition through to a conclusion. Woodsons is possibly such a situation; they are in such a mess that it is debatable as to which direction we should take. Should they concentrate on improving their internal communications, or would the company benefit from a strategic policy rethink?

Woodsons is a manufacturing company. There are often problems in a manufacturing setting in getting agreement on what should constitute the Root Definition (Rhodes, 1985, p. 93). Everybody usually agrees what transformation is taking place, but this may be constrained by the desire to 'satisfy' the market effectively, or by the need to use production resources efficiently. Is it possible to balance the needs of these two constraints? Those holding prime positions within an organization, such as managing director, production manager, sales and marketing director, chief accountant, will have an opinion on how this should be. Unless agreement is achieved at the outset, attempts to produce conceptual models and arrive at feasible and desirable changes could turn out to be to no avail.

At Woodsons, no official policy has ever been made concerning this. There did not seem to be a need until recently. In practical terms the company has been led by the sales team and market forces, but there has not been a problem until now. We shall assume that there is tacit approval (with certain reservations) for this state of affairs to continue.

The Root Definition I have chosen to work with is shown in Frame 11.7. In devising this I have assumed that, if Woodsons' mission were not a matter of controversy, then building a model based on a primary task-based Root Definition would be helpful; although I have included an explicit reference to obtaining materials from external sources and distributing loudspeakers, as these are two of the areas that are problematic in the real world currently.

Frame 11.7 *Woodsons Ltd: Root Definition*

A (privately owned) limited liability commercial system which designs and builds high quality hi-fi loudspeaker enclosures (and whose production capacity is led by market forces), from materials (in particular, speaker chassis units) obtained from external sources, and who sell and distribute these enclosures primarily to independent hi-fi retailers.

The problem situation at Woodsons appears to be due mainly to a lack of communication. Since the crisis in the early 1980s, they had been doing well, until recently. They had staved off Far Eastern competition in their sector of the hi-fi market, and even produced a steady growth in sales! A further consideration in my choice of a relatively conservative rather than an insightful Root Definition was for it to lead to a model whose logic will be most universally understood, in order to demonstrate as simply as possible the steps involved in SSM. Compared to many of Checkland's Root Definitions, mine is quite verbose and explicitly details many aspects of the transformation process. This has also been done deliberately to facilitate the explanation of the model building process.

In a real situation, amongst other ideas, I would have pursued a Root Definition that would focus attention on the R&D activity taking place at Woodsons, and which could be derived from the Relevant Systems:

- A system for building and testing loudspeakers.
- A system for improving the design of loudspeaker systems.
- A system designed to enhance the quality/esoteric image of UK hi-fi, particularly its excellence in loudspeaker design.

This idea is used as an illustrative example in Chapter 7.

Another possibility could have been a Root Definition leading to a model highlighting changes needed to enable the realization of the aim implied within the Relevant System:

- A system for providing an effective investment for the owner.

Next, we should verify its 'completeness' by checking it against the list of the essential elements of a Root Definition, listed on pages 117–119 (see Frame 11.8).

Frame 11.8 *Woodsons Ltd: checking the Root Definition*

Possible contenders for:

Customers:	The independent hi-fi retailers*
Actors:	The company's employees
Transformation:	The design, manufacture and marketing of loudspeaker enclosures to meet market demand
World view:	Commercial enterprise
Owners:	The owner of the company
Environment:	The speaker chassis suppliers, competitors, hi-fi retailers, end users

* By Checkland's definition (see pages 11 and 78) we could include under 'customers' employees, owner, perhaps even close neighbours of the end users of the loudspeakers – but I feel the significant ones are sufficiently mentioned under other headings.

Building the Conceptual Model

The next stage in SSM is to construct a Conceptual Model of the systems described with the Root Definitions.

The first stage in our model building is to look at our Root Definition and list all the (transitive) verbs, describing things we 'do', or human activities. We try if we can to put them down in some sort of logically coherent order. Scanning the Root Definition for the 'Woodsons' case study we come across the following verbs pertaining to the system:

- design
- build
- obtained
- sell
- distribute.

These describe the main activities necessary for our system to perform as desired. Next, we examine this list (and the Root Definition) for any other activities implied by them, but not explicitly mentioned in the Root Definition. For example, the activity 'obtain materials' implies 'maintaining relationships with potential suppliers'. Another implied business activity would seem to be 'appreciate the nature of of independent hi-fi retailers', if we hope to sell loudspeakers to them. We should be aiming for somewhere between five and ten main activities altogether.

During our model building we must guard against allowing activities (even subsystems of activities) known to take place in the real-world problem situation to creep into our Conceptual Model. Only activities which can be logically deduced as taking place from what has been described in the Root Definition should be included. Remember, we are building an *abstract* 'alternative' view of the present situation, in the form of an 'ideal' system, to compare against the reality. We should also be concentrating on what is going on, what activities are taking place – for example, 'distribute loudspeakers' – while totally ignoring how this could be accomplished, as this is irrelevant at this point.

Any difficulties encountered constructing our Conceptual Model may indicate that some detail in our Root Definition is missing or inappropriate. Going back and forth between the two, making refinements to them, should be considered as a normal part of the process of model building. However, we must resist the temptation to simplify the Root Definition solely to alleviate these difficulties.

Once we have a list of the minimum necessary activities to accomplish the mission set out by the Root Definition, we need to decide which activities in this list are logically dependent on other activities, and select an appropriate control mechanism, so that we can complete our diagram or Conceptual Model.

The former can be done by using Woodburn's (1985) mnemonic DIME: Dependency ⇐ Information, Material and/or Energy (see page 120). Woodburn also suggests that, since we have asked about these significant amounts of information, materials and energy and have named them (for example, production schedules, speaker chassis), they can be included in the Conceptual Model. This has the potential for making the Conceptual Model more informative and also easier to comprehend. However it has been argued by Checkland (1989) that this can result in a model too complicated to be useful when making our comparison with the real world via our Rich Picture. Our initial 'top-level' or overview model should depict only major dependencies. Parts of this model will be elaborated in separate diagrams, and flow versions could be prepared from these if required.

The Conceptual Model for Woodsons, along with the definitions of the efficiency, efficacy and effectiveness performance criteria, is shown in Figure 11.4. The definitions of efficiency and efficacy are fairly 'standard' for a commercial system. The 'seven-blob' control mechanism reflects that the system is privately owned by an entity that is outside the system.

Having identified the main activities taking place within our system, we now need to decide whether any of these activities should be broken down into a number of smaller activities. For example, the activity 'build loudspeakers' almost certainly comprises a number of activities such as 'draw up a production schedule', 'manufacture quality loudspeaker cabinets', 'assemble loudspeaker systems', etc., some of which may be of particular interest to us as they may be involved with the problems we have detected, such as the 'communications' one.

Any activity in this model we feel would benefit from being explored more deeply, for example 'build loudspeakers', 'sell loudspeakers ... ', etc. can be expanded in a subsystem model. We do this by first agreeing what its Root Definition should be (see Frame 11.9) and then building the subsystem Conceptual Model in the same way as our 'top level' model. Figure 11.5 shows a Conceptual Model for the 'build loudspeakers' subsystem.

Frame 11.9 *Woodsons Ltd: Root Definition of the subsystem 'build loudspeakers'* (refers to Figure 11.5)

A wholly owned subsystem of a commercial manufacturing system [Woodsons] that manufactures quality loudspeaker cabinets and assembles complete loud-speaker systems from materials and designs supplied by other subsystems: 'obtain materials', 'design enclosures' [purchasing, R&D] to satisfy orders obtained by another subsystem 'sell loudspeakers . . .' [sales].

Figure 11.4

Conceptual model for Woodsons

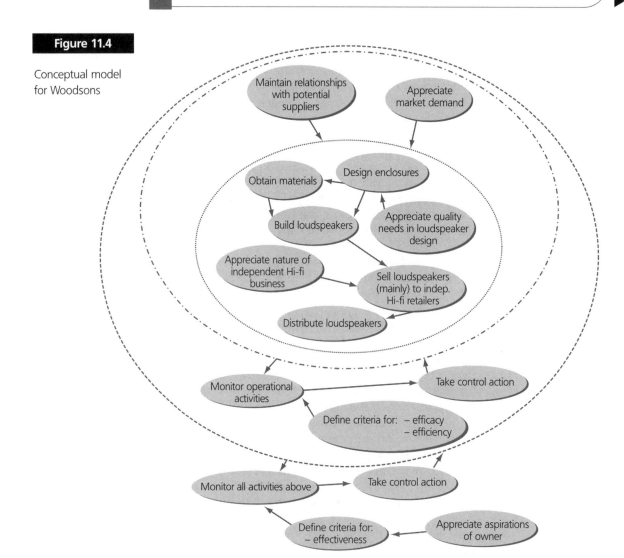

Efficacy: business demonstrably in operation.
Efficiency: returns from the business/cost of resources used in running it.
Effectiveness: owner's aspirations being met while maintaining the reputation of British-designed loudspeaker enclosures.

Figure 11.5   Woodsons Ltd – Conceptual Model for the 'build loudspeakers' subsystem

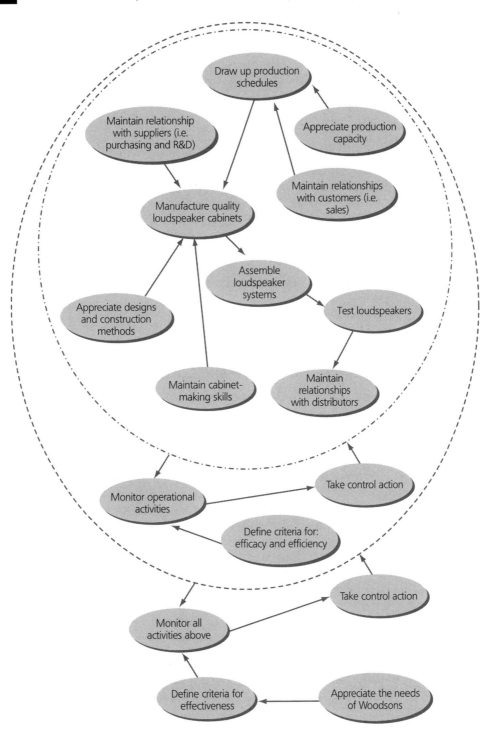

Customers:	Sales
Actors:	Production staff
Transformation:	Build cabinets; assemble loudspeaker systems
World view:	It is commercially viable to manufacture loudspeaker systems internally
Owner:	Woodsons Ltd
Environment:	'Purchasing', 'R&D', 'sales', 'distribution'

A 'standard' way of describing the activity 'feeding' 'determine effectiveness' in this situation could be along the lines 'appreciate corporate strategy/objectives'.

We build further subsystems models until we feel that we have explored all the potentially useful areas of our system and have sufficient detail to compare with our Rich Picture. We might, for example, feel that to fully appreciate the problems at Woodsons, our abstract systems model should contain detail of the activities 'sell loudspeakers . . .', and probably 'design enclosures' and 'distribute loudspeakers', at least. Do not forget that we may have decided earlier to continue with several (top-level) Root Definitions. The conceptual models constructed from these may also require expansion of some of their activities into subsystems.

All our models should be checked for completeness against the **Formal Systems Model**, see Frame A2.4.

Comparison of Rich Picture and Conceptual Model

Once we have 'checked out' our models, we should not spend too much time adding finishing touches to them before actually using them. We can always refine them later if necessary after initiating the comparisons. We now compare the real-world problem situation as depicted by our Rich Picture with each set of Conceptual Models. These comparisons, we hope, will inspire ideas for systemically desirable (consistent with our system model) and culturally feasible changes, which will improve the problem situation. Culturally feasible changes are those possible given the history of the situation and its present characteristics (e.g. prevailing cultural norms and power structures), coupled with individually shared experiences and prejudices. Determining what is culturally feasible should be done with the people involved in the problem situation – ultimately it will be they who decide. It may be difficult to meet both systems and cultural criteria, but if something is not culturally acceptable the chances of it ever being implemented are remote.

Checkland (1981) has found that different kinds of study require different methods of comparison and suggests four ways in which we can perform this comparison.

1. Where the Conceptual Model and reality are very different, we should not try to convince the problem owners that according to our model they have been doing things wrongly in the past. A wiser course of action is to

produce a checklist of questions that you can ask of the real-world problem situation. For example, for each activity in the model:

(a) Does this happen in the real world?

(b) If not, why not?

(c) If so, who does it and why?

- Have the people doing this been considered to be successful?
- If not, why not?
- Why is the activity done this way?
  - Has the activity been considered to be successful?
  - If not, why not?
- Which activities (in the real world) are dependent on it
- Why is this?
  - Is this the same as in the model?
  - If not, why not?
- Which activities (in the real world) provide feedback to it?
- Positive or negative?
  - Is this the same as in the model?
  - If not, why not?
- Does it provide information for control/decision making use?
  - If not, should it?
- What links (if any) does it have with the (real-world) environment?
  - Is this the same as in the model?
  - If not, why not?

2. We could take an incident in the problem situation and 'replay' it through our model, comparing what has happened historically with what might have happened if our conceptual model were to be implemented in the real world.

3. If we suspect that major strategic changes may be required, typically where we have begun to question the utility of an activity, it is probably best to use the comparisons to provide questions of a very general nature, such as asking what is different between the model and reality and why this is so.

4. In well-structured problem situations, we could construct an activity model of the actual problem by redrawing our Rich Picture to show just the activities actually taking place and how they are interlinked. Doing this carefully, ensuring that activities that are common to both the real world and the Conceptual Model are drawn in similar positions on the two diagrams, allows us to physically overlay the real-world situation with our Conceptual Model, vividly showing the differences between the two.

Comparisons of 'what is' with 'what perhaps should be' are fine as long as there is a something already existing to compare with! When you are designing a new system (such as in the 'John Smith Institute' example in Chapter 7), we can only compare it with 'some defined expectation', a theoretical ideal. Such an analysis is likely only to show up basic omissions in the design.

With Woodsons I have opted for the third route, as there appear to be major changes necessary within that organization. In Frame 11.10 I have listed some of the differences that were evident when comparing the set of conceptual models arising from the Root Definition in Frame 11.7 (that is Figures 11.4, 11.5, and the subsystem model for 'sell loudspeakers . . .') with the Rich Picture in Figure 11.3.

Frame 11.10 *Woodsons Ltd: comparisons between Rich Picture and Conceptual Models*

In the Rich Picture there was:

- No apparent market research
- No effective planning of R&D
- Misguided R&D
- Poor communications and reporting channels
- Insufficient dissemination of customer information
- No feedback from production to sales
- No apparent policy re. production capacity determining sales or vice versa
- Production section under severe 'pressure'
- Complaints about incomplete orders, late deliveries, etc.
- Erratic supplies: LSI supplying Woodsons as a 'favour'
- Computers which are under-utilized.

Although we have been working with the problem owners throughout, their reactions now to our comparisons may reveal inadequacies in our initial analysis or in the formulation of our Root Definition. We may have to do some backtracking to the earlier stages of the process to fill in these deficiencies.

Systemically desirable and culturally feasible changes

The purpose of these comparisons is primarily to initiate a debate with the people concerned with the problem situation, and therefore some form of agenda needs to be prepared. The comments and suggestions comprising this agenda should be couched in terms of 'what' rather than 'how'. This has the benefit that, if acceptable, it leaves the problem owners to determine the best methods in their particular circumstances rather than forcing a specific solution on them. For example, 'We feel that the sales team should receive regular updates of the production schedule including advice on work in progress' indicates what we feel may be missing from Woodsons' present operations. However, 'We suggest that a ZY42000 computer system should be installed to facilitate production scheduling and that a terminal giving access to this machine should be placed in the sales office' is just one, and possibly not the most appropriate, way of describing how the former change may be implemented.

We now need to reflect on the differences that have been noted between the Rich Picture and the Conceptual Model for Woodsons, and try to generate a set of suggested changes that can be incorporated into the agenda for our debate. Some of my ideas are in Frame 11.11.

Frame 11.11 *Woodsons Ltd: systemically desirable and culturally feasible? changes*

- Conduct some market research, perhaps initiate an independent analysis of Woodsons' market.
- Adopt an agreed R&D policy, for example, a small team engaged in relatively esoteric research while the rest are developing existing products.
- Improve internal communications, especially between production and sales; for example, distribution of regular production schedules, advice on work in progress, sales figures, market research data, information about R&D projects.
- Consider ways of encouraging teamwork across divisions.
- Consider the expansion of the production department's workforce.
- Institute a proper purchasing/stock control system with particular emphasis initially on second-sourcing loudspeaker chassis units.
- Investigate whether better use can be made of the computing facilities, e.g. production scheduling, customer database etc.

Implementation of the changes

The changes we may have suggested are of a number of different types, such as:

- changes in structure, organizational groupings, departments, reporting structures, lines of command/functional responsibility, communications, physical layout;
- changes in procedures, changing the way that some activities are done (such as changing the processes by which informing and reporting takes place within the structures of the organization);
- changes in policy, repositioning the company, modifying goals and strategies.

These types of change are relatively simple to specify and not too difficult to carry out, especially if the persons desiring the change have the necessary authority or influence. However, although these changes may be easy to bring about, they may still have unexpected consequences. The use of Rich Pictures in the early stages of the process should have minimized the possibility of overlooking any important interactions or interconnections that might cause such problems. A further precaution the problem owners could take would be to carry out something similar to Kepner-Tregoe's **Potential Problem Analysis** (see Chapter 9) before actually embarking on implementation.

Although given the authority and resources it may be easy nominally to effect some changes, commitment is necessary to carry them through effectively. We have seen (Chapters 3 and 9, see also Chapter 13) that people are often antipathetic to change and need to be 'sold' its benefits. If all the problem owners have had the opportunity to play a part in resolving the problem situation, then changes such as those above should be achievable. SSM does tend, however, to assume that these participants are rational beings and responsive to fair and reasoned arguments backed by irrefutable and impartial evidence!

There is another type of change we may feel is necessary!

- changes in attitude both at an individual level and universally throughout an organization, as in attempting to change people's expectations concerning the behaviour associated with certain roles.

Realizing changes of this type is a difficult task to accomplish. The extent of this difficulty will depend on the type or content of the organizational culture in which the change is to take place and its strength, and whether the attitudes at the centre of interest are those of individuals or are widely shared by many within the organization. Checkland (1981) advises that if a deliberate attempt is made to change attitudes, continuous monitoring of the effects are essential, because of the unpredictability of such an operation.

Many people believe that it is anything from foolish to downright impossible, even rather sinister, to try deliberately to change people's attitudes. They say that such things happen only as the result of personal and collective experience. However, that is not to say that people's attitudes, expectations and influence are not suitable material for our debate with the problem owners. If there is to be any change in attitudes as a result of an SSM (or any other kind) of intervention, it will probably come about as a by-product of the participants having been involved in the experience of sharing their perceptions of the problem situation.

Postscript

Suppose we give our report to Woodsons and they say that our suggestions are impractical, or decide simply to do nothing. What should we do? The answer is nothing. We have to accept this state of affairs. The first of these possibilities should not occur if we have considered enough possibilities along the route and have checked periodically to make sure we were remaining within the bounds of cultural feasibility. If they decide to do nothing, even though we have put in a lot of work!, we must simply accept their point of view, as sometimes doing nothing may seem to the problem owners to be the best policy.

Timing

The initial stages, the determination of the politics of the situation and the gathering of hard and soft data required for the production of the Rich Picture take the bulk of the time involved in the process, perhaps weeks or months. Devising the

Root Definitions and the construction of the Conceptual Models may only take hours or days in a project lasting several months. This is why it is recommended to construct and try out several models; apart from being desirable, it is also practically feasible. The amount of time required by the later stages, starting with the comparison of the models with the problem situation (via the Rich Picture) and culminating with the debate over what constitutes systemically desirable and culturally feasible changes, is a little less easy to predict, depending as it does on the complexity and sensitivity of the circumstances 'discovered' during the intervention. It will typically take days or weeks considerably longer if we include in this estimate the time taken to implement and monitor the changes agreed.

SSM and information systems development

This book is about (general) problem-solving processes and techniques, not about information systems development (ISD); but since information and communication technology (ICT) and the information systems (IS) that are built from them are so critical/fundamental to organizations these days, and the 'changes' delivered by the SSM we have just been discussing are likely to impact on the existing IS within that organization, it seems reasonable to spend a little time here describing how SSM can be linked with the (many) ISD methodologies that are around.

In the last 20 years there have been many different ways[1] proposed for 'grafting' SSM (as a 'front end') on to ISD methodologies, or embedding ISD methods within *SSM*[2]. Research into and discussion about which is the best way continues; however, John Mingers (1995) summarizes some of the problems as follows:

- Is it worthwhile to link SSM with structured ISD methodologies in a fairly mechanistic way? Can we find a way to do this without compromising either?

- Most of the 'richness' of SSM, particularly information gathered concerning different viewpoints and possible activities, must be lost if we have to fix on a single agreed Conceptual Model which most approaches do. Does this not go against the philosophy/rationale of SSM anyway?

- Do we graft on or embed? Who is best equipped to do this, SSM practitioners or IS analysts? When should managers/users cease to be involved in the process? Which ISD methodology should we link with? Exactly how and where do we link the methodologies?

Mingers (1995) does offer his answers to some of these questions. He maintains that the philosophical incompatibility does not seem a very significant problem! Embedding is better than grafting on (because it encourages user involvement from the beginning and makes the (ISD) process more focused on learning). He feels that a fairly systematic link would be desirable and that there is no reason, and in fact it is very desirable, not to restrict the link to just one conceptual model – why shouldn't we have our own individual personalized IS?

On the basis of the above, I present a way (mostly due to Wilson, 1990) for achieving some sort of 'link'. We will quickly 'skate over' whether we should attempt to produce just one consensus primary task (or issue-based!) Conceptual

Model, or 'carry forward' several Conceptual Models that we can map on to the real world. We have at least one model, which may have been 'expanded' to a number of levels (subsystems). First we need to identify the information categories associated with each activity (on the lowest level of each model; for example, 'draw up production schedules'). That is, what information is required by the people performing the activity in order for them to do it successfully (and where does this comes from), what information do they generate, modify or simply pass on to others whilst performing the activity, and what metric (if any) is used to measure that performance. This can be recorded in tables or diagrams such as the table shown in Figure 11.6.

To determine exactly which specific data items constitute these information categories we would need to talk to the people who (in the real world) would be carrying out these activities. For this we need to 'connect' (managerial) role definitions with the activities for which they have decision-making responsibility ('work practice mapping'). A data model can be created for each information category.

The relationship between these information categories and activities can then be shown in the top half of a chart called a 'Maltese Cross', as shown in Figure 11.7. There will undoubtedly be an existing (manual or computerized) IS, with its information processing procedures (IPP). These IPPs and their data inputs and outputs are recorded in the bottom half of the Maltese Cross. A comparison of the top and bottom halves of the Maltese Cross will now reveal the additional information requirements needed by the proposed changes to the problem situation our conceptual model(s) have described.

Figure 11.6 Woodsons Ltd – example of (part of) an information categories table

Information	Draw up production Schedules	Activity Manufacture quality loudspeaker cabinets	... ...	Test loudspeakers
Inputs	Product ID, order quantity & delivery date	Location of raw materials		Product ID & serial number
	Work in progress	Design specifications		Test specifications
	Production resources available			
Outputs	Weekly production schedule	Number of cabinets produced (by product ID)		Product ID & serial number
	Materials requirement	Order number assignment		Test results
Measures of performance	Completeness and timeliness of schedule	Number of cabinets produced (by product ID) against plan		Accuracy and completeness of test results
				Timeliness
				Cost of testing

Figure 11.7 Woodsons Ltd – example of part of a Maltese Cross

Information categories:

Activities → / IPP →	Draw up production schedules	Manufacture quality loudspeaker cabinets	Test loudspeakers	Information category	IPP 1	IPP 2	IPP 3	IPP 4	IPP 5
				… … …					
				Work in progress					
				Production resources available					
		×		Weekly production schedule				×	
				… … …					
				Location of raw materials					×
				Design specifications	×				
		×		Number of cabinets produced					
				… … …					
			×	Product ID & serial number		×			
				Test specifications					
			×	Test results		×			
				… … …					

Information processing procedures:

Activities → / IPP →	Draw up production schedules	Manufacture quality loudspeaker cabinets	Test loudspeakers	Information category	IPP 1	IPP 2	IPP 3	IPP 4	IPP 5
				… … …					
				Test results					
			×	Test specifications		×			
			×	Product ID & serial number		×			
				… … …					
				Number of cabinets produced					
		×		Design specifications					
		×		Location of raw materials					
				… … …					
				Weekly production schedule					
	×			Production resources available					
	×			Work in progress		×			
				… … …					

Information categories:

This sounds like a very simple process, but of course life is not like this; there will be IPPs that provide most, but not all, the data items in an information category, perhaps another IPP might provide the rest, so some detailed 'reconciliation' is probably going to be needed.

Other attempts to link SSM with ISD methodologies try to convert conceptual models into what are called **data flow diagrams**, which essentially show how data and/or information flows into and out of a 'system' and to and from the (business) processes within it. (They also show which processes create/update, or just require access to, any data/information stored.)

Summary

This chapter has illustrated how the various SSM models and techniques encountered in earlier chapters come together to form the 'full' Soft Systems Methodology. It has also given a brief indication of how SSM can be 'interfaced' with hard information systems development methodologies.

Endnotes

1. An outline and brief comparative evaluation of these ways is given by John Mingers in Stowell (1995).
2. Because of their underlying rationales, it is not considered appropriate to embed SSM (or bits of it) into a 'hard' ISD methodology, though this has been done, e.g. SSADM4+.

Really complicated problems – the issues of tackling large complex problems

This chapter elaborates the issue of multiple problem ownership, which complicates the problem-solving process, in two contexts: first with just a few problem owners (stakeholders), and second with a lot of them. In so doing, a comparison of the soft systems and Synectics approaches discussed earlier will be attempted with a view to offering a synthesis of the two processes that could be applicable in some of these situations

Introduction

As argued in Chapter 1 the processes and techniques offered in this book are intended for solving problems/making decisions that are by no means straight-forward anyway, but here we will look at an issue that further complicates the problem-solving process.

It has been assumed in most earlier chapters that the problem being solved 'belongs' to one and only one person, even when there has been talk of using a group of people to assist in the problem solving. This is seldom the case in real life, so we need a way to reach a solution that is mutually acceptable to several problem owners, each with a stake in the problem. As we shall see shortly, the basic **Synectics** CPS process (see Chapter 10) can be modified to accommodate a few problem owners.

It is usually desirable to have all stakeholders (problem owners) involved in the problem-solving process. This presents more than a logistical problem when we have a problem situation that affects many people. Although Synectics have a technique called **Decision Point Planning** to cope with this (see page 304), an amalgamation of the **SSM** and Synectics processes might be a better way of dealing with such situations.[1]

Multiple problem ownership – Synectics

The Synectics approach (only a part of which we have so far seen) makes an even more significant contribution to problem solving when applied to multiple problem owner situations. It helps us sort out who actually 'owns' which bits of the problem situation and provides us with the means for separating what they call 'consequential problems' (where the actions resulting from implementing my preferred solution may directly impinge on what other people do and cause difficulties for them) from irrelevant 'second opinions' such as: 'Well, I wouldn't have solved the problem that way!' (Since we are all different from each other, this is highly likely!)

We are now going to look briefly at an example which illustrates how the Synectics process can be modified to cope with more than one problem owner (the Synectics **Consensus Meeting**). (The following is only one of several ways Synectics deals with the complexities of real-world organiza- tional problems.) Whilst doing so, we will also see another type of excur- sion, the **example excursion**, which is based on the **direct analogy** (see Chapter 7).

A consensus solution is only achievable if all problem owners have the will to solve the problem. Most people come to the session with preconceived ideas and solutions. Under 'normal' circumstances they turn up not to prob- lem solve, but to persuade others to accept, to defend or to fight for these ideas/solutions. We need to create the climate wherein they are prepared to put their preconceived ideas/solutions aside (temporarily) (see below) and use their creativity to get a solution that they all feel good about – a win–win sit- uation. That is creating a frame of mind where everyone concerned is going to continue to work together until we get this solution. This is the hardest part, the rest is relatively easy!

Where two or more people are concerned with the same problem situation, what we can do is to go through the stages discussed earlier in an attempt to solve the problem as far as one person is concerned (during which time the other problem owner(s) act(s) solely as a group resource). When we have done this, the solution for the first client becomes the starting point (problem) for the second client and we repeat as much of the process as is necessary to make this a solution for them as well. This is not as circuitous a procedure as it sounds.

Abstract examples have limited utility as a practice exercise for the Synectics process, more so here than in Chapter 10, owing to the lack of real and involved problem owners to select and evaluate ideas, and to offer direction at the appropriate moments. It would be better to practise the Synectics process on one of your own problems. However, since there is a need for this second illustrative example, I have tried to choose a problem situation that most readers will be acquainted with and probably have opin- ions about. The scenario I have chosen is 'the degradation of holiday resorts as they become more popular' and concerns the mythical seaside resort of Northcliffe Sands.

We have been asked by David Eastman, the chairman of the Northcliffe town council, to facilitate (process lead) a small group of interested parties who wish to tackle the problem as stated in Frame 12.1. The group consists of representa- tives from both the Hoteliers' and the Retailers' Associations, the chief county planning officer, a spokesman for the local fishermen, a couple of residents and a distant relative of Eastman's who is in Northcliffe on his annual holiday with his family.

> **Frame 12.1** *Northcliffe Sands: task headline*
>
> How to increase revenue from tourism without 'spoiling' the location?

In Frame 12.2 you will find a brief description of Northcliffe Sands and David Eastman's account of the problem situation as he sees it.

> **Frame 12.2** *Northcliffe Sands: the problem situation*
>
> Northcliffe Sands is a small seaside town of approximately 10,000 people. The only road into the town competes with the River Froam for the limited area of flat land in the Froam valley. Unbelievably, Northcliffe Sands, with its wooded estuary, picturesque harbour and its golden sands, has only just been discovered by tourists.
>
> Over the last ten years the number of summer visitors has increased, from just the occupants of a couple of guest houses and a trickle of passing touring caravans, to a steady stream of many thousands of visitors during the peak months; so much so that they at times outnumber the indigenous population.
>
> David Eastman describes his problem as follows:
>
> There is considerable concern amongst the local residents that the town's amenities and things like the roads and sewers are rapidly becoming unable to cope with this number of people, and that their environment is suffering accordingly. There are always traffic jams in the narrow streets, cars and motor-caravans are parked everywhere, and fishing boats unloading and some vans delivering to the shops contribute to the chaos! And then there are the dinghy sailors driving through town with trailers: one reason for this sudden increase in visitors is that Northcliffe Sands seems to be ideal for sailing.
>
> Those in business have got used to the increased profits the tourists bring, and some of them are greedy for more. Other locals believe that this desire for more and greater profits is destroying their community. It's our job to run things the way people want us to, but everything we do is wrong! To give you one example, we had a scheme to make some of the lanes near to the harbour into a pedestrian precinct. Our aim was to try to keep traffic out of the middle of town and restrict access to the harbour: for everybody's benefit we thought. We were accused of pandering to the tourists and the retailers' lobby at the expense of curtailing the movements of the locals by one pressure group, and attempting to reduce or disrupt trade by keeping passing motorists away from the town centre and restricting where their delivery vans could load and unload by another.
>
> At first all the local tradespeople and hoteliers welcomed the extra business that the increase in tourism brought to the area; now even some of them are beginning to realize that this may come to a premature end if the attractiveness of the location is destroyed. They are also worried about the interest recently being shown in the area by large national retailers and hotel chains.

▶

This problem has come up at many recent town council meetings, and also at a number of special public meetings organized by the various pressure groups, but very little agreement has been achieved as to how best to proceed. The town council has devised a number of plans to improve roads, car parks and amenities, but they have invariably been thwarted by local opposition. Also, large expenditure needs sanction from the County. There is also a growing number of influential 'semi-retired middle-class newcomers'. Their viewpoint is not one of only resisting further expansion in tourism, they want to return to a situation that existed before many of them ever came to the area!

I wish we could get just the tourists' money but not them. We could then carry on living in the way to which we have grown accustomed, and we could return things to the way they used to be.

We will assume that the planning meeting (see Chapter 10) with David Eastman has already taken place and that we have started to open the problem up with some **Goal Wishing** on the background information to the problem (Frame 12.2). Anyone wishing to see further illustrations of **Backward/Forward Planning** can find an indication of what might have been said in Appendix 5. I have included in Frame 12.3 some of the **springboards** that I thought might have been generated by Goal Wishing.

Frame 12.3 *Northcliffe Sands: some possible springboards*

- I wish we could get just their money.
- I wish we could attract only rich tourists.
- How to justify increasing all our tariffs?
- How to create and maintain a relative exclusivity?
- I wish the Froam valley was an 'assault course', only the best tourists can get through it.
- I wish we had a toll bridge on the Froam Valley Road.
- How to make tourists pay for the new infrastructure?
- How to limit the number of guest houses?
- How to attract only tourists that are conservation minded?
- I wish we could attract only those tourists who respected our environment.
- I wish it would always rain on the undesirable tourists.
- How to make a lot of people seem to be less?
- How to lengthen our holiday season?
- I wish we could push all traffic (jams) off the harbour wall.
- I wish we could persuade retailers to take deliveries only on certain days at certain times.

- I wish we could institute a 'sailboat' tax.
- I wish we had more than one slipway.
- I wish we could stop arguing.
- How to promote the idea that the quality of life is more important than profits?
- How to 'educate' the retailers/hoteliers?
- How to show that the suggested improvement schemes are for the benefit of everybody, not just the tourists?
- I wish we could show the benefits of a pedestrian precinct.
- How to persuade the big retailers not to come to Northcliffe?
- I wish we could please everybody.
- I wish I could demonstrate the unfairness of the 'no expansion' policy of the 'newcomers' to the long-standing local residents.
- I wish we could enforce our local bye-laws.

An example excursion

We are trying to solve the problem first for the chairman of the town council, David Eastman. He has now been asked to select a few of the springboards that have just been generated. Look at Frame 12.4 to see which springboard our problem owner has chosen to work with and the comments he made about its appeal.

Frame 12.4 *Northcliffe Sands: the chosen springboard*

The springboard we are going to work with is . . .

How to make a lot of people seem to be less?

David Eastman says: That sums up our problem in a nutshell. I have absolutely no idea how we might actually resolve the problem in this way, but if you could somehow accomplish this we would get the best of everything. A lot (more) of people means increased revenue to pay for the improvements we need to make, and if we can make them seem to be less in the effect they have on the community of Northcliffe we remove the biggest immediate threat temporarily, and this will give us the chance to get together and perhaps agree on how to sort out the best way to 'repair' the damage to our environment that we perceive has taken place.

As facilitator, we are aware that a number of sensible ideas have already been suggested and rejected, and although we have produced some quite speculative springboards, we have also noticed differing and even contradictory opinions being shown by some of these. We have concluded that our best policy might be to take the group on an excursion, not just to get more speculative ideas, but also for the 'bringing together' effect that excursions often have.

An **example excursion** would be introduced in a similar way to the **imaging excursion** on page 247, as a means for getting right away from the problem, a means of generating some apparently irrelevant material that we may be able to 'connect' with the problem situation in order to find some innovative solutions. We now cover up everything to do with the problem so far, and ask the group for examples of 'things that seem a lot less than they are' from the world of biology. As usual we write up all these ideas, and encourage group members to explain their sources if not volunteered. Some examples can be found in Frame 12.5.

Frame 12.5 *Northcliffe Sands: example excursion from the world of biology*

Locusts – all you see is one black cloud.

Raspberries – they tend to hide under the plant's curling leaves.

Trees in a wood – there are probably a lot more than you think when you look at say a wooded hilltop from a distance.

Oil-seed rape – there must be millions of plants in a field but all you see is this vivid mass of bright yellow; it's pretty too.

Stick insects – we have a dozen of them in a jar at home, big ones and little ones, but they are very difficult to see amongst the privet twigs unless they move.

I'm sorry, its not an example, but I've got this image of a holidaymaker-eating Triffid in my mind that I need to get rid of.

Sky-larks – you can hear them but seldom see them because they fly so high.

Honey bees – a friend of mine has a handful of hives, but you very rarely see the bees in his garden. I don't know why this is, perhaps they are scattered far and wide or are in the hives most of the time making honey.

Bats – I know they only come out at night, but they are so small and so quick that you tend not to see them either, until they nearly bump into you.

The choice of appropriate 'worlds' depends largely on the leader's experience of which particular worlds have worked well in the past. Biology is often a good resource for direct analogies (see Chapter 7).

It often happens that, when encouraged to think of 'strange' things or images, a compelling idea comes to our mind when we do not particularly want it. My 'Triffid' in Frame 12.5 was such an image and was stopping me from making other connections. I became almost obsessive about trying to fit in this solution where I did not really want one, until I was able to exorcise it in this way. Since this is known to block further ideas, it is perfectly in order for a group member to 'dump' ideas like this. Far from doing any harm to the flow of 'examples', voicing an idea like this is likely to encourage imagination.

Having generated a number of 'examples', we return to the springboard we were working with by uncovering it, and ask the group to try to make connections between the excursion material and the problem. This stage is called by some the **force fit**. Some ideas that our Northcliffe group might have come up with are given in Frame 12.6. Note again the use of **headlines** and background.

Frame 12.6 *Northcliffe Sands: force-fit ideas*

Create more shopping arcades

I was thinking of the leaves of raspberries curling around the fruit and hiding it, and that reminded me of the entrance to the 'mall' – you can hide tourists in shopping arcades.

Provide better access to North Beach

I liked the idea of lots of things looking less from a distance, you know, the trees in the wood; oil-seed rape plants are the same really, but their yellow made me think of a beach. Very few people use North Beach, even though it's a lovely wide long beach, because you can only reach it around the headland. It's also some distance from the town centre!

Camouflage the tourists

Thinking about the stick insects and how well they are hidden by their camouflage I thought, let's make it a bye-law for everyone to wear sand-coloured T-shirts, shorts and swimming costumes on the beach.

Suggest to the boatyards that they should consider running flotilla cruising holidays

A friend of mine has a really nice 30-foot cruising catamaran called *Sky Lark*. I'm always very envious when I see him sailing out of the harbour to wherever. That made me think that, if we could persuade our day sailors to take up cruiser sailing, we could sell them a week's supply of food and drink and then pack them off to sea. This way we *could* have their money and not them!

Lock the holidaymakers in their rooms

I was thinking of the bees being shut up in their hives busily making honey.

Let's open a casino

This is building on the last idea, the association honey–money led me to thinking about shutting people up in a room where they (or rather we) could make some money.

▶

> *Get the Northcliffe Bus Co. to run more organized bus tours*
>
> I was thinking about bees as well, but about them being 'invisible' because they are so dispersed. Let's spread our tourists all around the area with organized bus tours.
>
> *Build a multi-screen cinema*
>
> That one about bats and not seeing them in the dark appealed to me, and something someone said earlier about shutting people up in a room and taking their money, then I thought, so why not a dark room?

We now ask the problem owner to select from these ideas, and then proceed into the **itemized response** phase of the process to develop and evaluate those ideas which he selects. We shall skip this stage and move straight to a possible solution for our first problem owner, to see how things continue from there. Before we do, you might like to consider what positive features and concerns you would have come up with in David Eastman's position of trying to develop the idea 'Build a multi-screen cinema', assuming that Northcliffe already has a small but financially secure cinema. Appendix 5 contains an illustration of my thoughts on the way such an itemized response might proceed. In actual fact, I am going to let David Eastman settle on a different solution, since the one above is likely to be too specific an idea to fully resolve his problem, though it could form part of a 'total package'. In Frame 12.7 I have described briefly how the final stage of the 'closing down' part of this problem might have occurred for our first problem owner.

> **Frame 12.7** *Northcliffe Sands: 'closing down' for one problem owner*
>
> ---
>
> After selecting several of the force-fit ideas and developing them using itemized response, David Eastman announces the following:
>
> I can see something definite forming in several of those ideas, what I might call 'dispersion'. At the moment, everyone tries to get in and out of the town centre at least a couple of times a day. If we can encourage them to do this less often, by making this less necessary or more attractive not to do so, I believe we can meet my initial objectives, which was to relieve the immediate pressure.
>
> I can see lots of ways we can do this; some are very long term, such as encouraging the sailing fraternity to make a move towards the idea of flotilla cruising, but there are also a number of things we can do now. For instance, Fred Johnson has wanted to build a proper campsite behind the 'Dog and Duck' for years, but we keep refusing to let him expand because of our fears of increasing the number of campers. If we let him do that, and then enforce the prohibition of camping/caravanning, etc. from the vicinity of the town, we could even run a regular minibus service up to Fred's pub.

Another thing we could do is provide parking and picknicking areas up in the woods, perhaps even set up some woodland walks, etc. Proper access and a car park at North Beach should also discourage the current tendency for beach-goers to dump their cars on or around the harbour, so as to gain access to the beach by walking around the cliff path, etc. A slipway on the estuary we could do almost right away; I know where we could build it at very little cost – we'll still charge for using the harbour slipway though!

I am content for the moment; I have got some things I can pursue. My only outstanding concern is, as always, I need everybody's agreement to go ahead with them. I know that we are now going to try to resolve the problem for the rest of you, and I feel that this may develop later as we do that, along with perhaps some more ideas.

Returning to the problem of a problem shared

To get a workable solution for Northcliffe we need to get everybody's agreement and commitment to some form of plan. We know that the town council has considered restricting access to vehicles, more car parks, improved road systems, etc. and now our first problem owner has several more new ideas. He says he is content for the moment. He knows that if the worst happens and no consensus is achieved his turn will come around again, and so we are able to take his 'dispersion' possible solution and offer it to our next problem owner as an idea.

This next problem owner is Mrs Fleanor Smyth-Wilson, representing the views of the 'semi-retired middle-class newcomer' faction. As facilitator, we ask her to check her understanding of the 'dispersion' idea by paraphrasing it, and to do an itemized response on it – ask her for some features about it that she likes, and then ask for her main concern. Let us suppose her reactions are as indicated in Frame 12.8.

Frame 12.8 *Northcliffe Sands: itemized response from second problem owner*

I can see that getting tourists out of the town centre and on the beach will certainly ease congestion in the centre and make things more civilized.

I have always said that we could do with a local minibus service to help the elderly get around; perhaps we can combine the two ideas.

I also think that this idea may incur little or no loss in income for the retailers and hoteliers, that's always their complaint against my ideas.

My major concern would be that it could 'back-fire'. By providing ways of 'dispersing' the tourists we might eventually end up attracting even more of them!

We would now ask the group to generate ideas for ensuring that the 'dispersion' policy works, and then ask our second problem owner (Eleanor Smyth-Wilson) to select, paraphrase and perform an itemized response on her favourite idea(s). We would continue spiralling through this process until she is content with our solution so far. After our second problem owner has a possible solution, we offer this to the third problem owner as a starting idea, and so on (see Frame 12.9).

Frame 12.9 *Northcliffe Sands: the third problem owner*

Let us suppose that we have satisfied Mrs Eleanor Smyth-Wilson that any additional amenities, such as campsites, car parks, beach access roads, slipways, etc., can be provided at the same time as strict restrictions on similar features are enforced elsewhere, i.e. it is possible to 'relocate' or disperse tourist activity in this way. We have even managed to incorporate her minibus hobby-horse and her enthusiasm for conservation issues into the grand plan as well. She is (at present) well pleased, and so this possible solution for her is offered to our next problem owner.

Our third problem owner might be Peter Frith, the manager of Northcliffe's biggest food shop, and thereby representing all the other retailers in the town. After remarking that he can see a number of merits in our second problem owner's 'solution', including the fact that, with the reduction in traffic congestion which the revised 'dispersion' policy should ensure, his delivery loading/unloading difficulties would disappear, he might state his major concern as follows:

I am worried about the possibility that, with the tourists scattered all around the nearby countryside and coming into town less often, my trade could suffer if 'fringe' retailers set up in business where the tourists actually are.

I don't care whether my customers come in to my shop once a week or every day, as long as they purchase the same amount of stuff overall. In fact once a week could make my staffing problem easier to handle by reducing the number of 'rush hour' periods I have to try to plan for. I never seem to have the right number of people on duty to cope with the number of customers I get at a given time! But if someone like Fred opens his own campsite shop in competition to the town, it could have a serious effect on us!

Our next step would be to ask the group for ways of overcoming our third problem owner's concern. I believe that we have pursued this story long enough now to show how the problem is 'handed over' from one problem owner to another, so I will stop at this point. However, for the sake of completeness, Appendix 5 contains a couple of ideas we might offer Peter Frith.

When we have been right through the problem owners in this way, we should return to the first (David Eastman) to see whether he is still happy with the possible solution. Although he is unlikely to be totally opposed to his initial 'solution' now that it has been modified by the other problem owners, additional concerns may have arisen which he wants the group to address. If need be we must go right around the circuit of problem owners again. It is very unlikely, however, that this process could develop into a never-ending circle. Each problem owner knows that s/he will have an opportunity to offer his or her ideas and concerns and his or her own chance to develop a solution. This tends to 'relieve the pressure' and encourage the participants to reorientate themselves from attacking other peoples' ideas which they see as threatening to their pet solutions, to where they actively and readily support other people's ideas and wholeheartedly help to find a mutually acceptable way of modifying them to everyone's benefit. Finally, when we seem to have arrived at a consensus solution we should ask whether any group member still has any outstanding concerns, and deal with these appropriately.

Another approach to consensus

The Consensus Meeting approach described above is the variant that is best used when we are dealing with a 'functional' work group; that is, when there is a 'boss' who is ultimately responsible for the success of the solution, who wants/needs the approval of the others in his/her department/team, and they need to feel able to 'go along' with that solution and have no consequential problems arising from it, in order for it to be a success. It was appropriately used in the above case because the problem was 'predominantly' Eastman's and he certainly would have been called to account by many factions if the solution had 'failed'. And because the nature of the council's role – serving the best interests of the local people – means that the people do need to 'go along' with final solution for it to be successful.

An alternative approach is offered by Synectics when we are dealing with a multidisciplinary work group; for example, a new product development group consisting of a diverse bunch of people from departments such as marketing, R&D, production, finance, etc. Although obviously commonly connected, say, with the (problem of the) new product launch, their views on the problem situation will be somewhat disparate,

- How can we finalize the content of the ad campaign when we don't know what the final features of the product will be?
- How to find another way of providing the 'xyz' functionality of the product.
- How to fit in the initial production run during our busiest time if the product development is delayed any more.
- I wish we knew whether we need to make a provision for some additional marketing spend in the next financial year.

and there may be little or no 'overlap' in their springboards.

In this situation, we would start with a springboard generation stage, from a task headline such as 'How to ensure a successful product launch for the . . .' from the project leader, nominally as our problem owner, just as we did above. And then ask each of the problem owners to select which, say five, springboards are the ones that they would like to work on. The result of this could be depicted in matrix form as in Figure 12.1.

It should then be obvious if there is any overlap and, if so, how much, between the various views of the problem situation. If there is overlap, then we would work on those springboards first, as above. If there is little or no overlap, we would work with each problem owner separately on the springboard s/he selects as being the most representative of the problem as s/he sees it, going through the whole (basic) Synectics process x times and, we hope, resulting in x solutions (one for each problem owner).

To determine if we have any consequential problems we then ask each problem owner to say everything s/he likes and/or is concerned about regarding the other (than their own) solutions. This is called a 'group itemized response'. We might then 'go' for the solution(s) with the least number of concerns against it, probably not the best plan; or work on the concerns one at a time as 'new' problems (the person who expressed the concern being the problem owner), until we have overcome them all and have no remaining consequential problems.

If David Eastman (or indeed any of the other problem owners) had come to our original problem-solving meeting with, what was for them, a solution, we could have started the Northcliffe Sands problem-solving session with a group itemized response and carried on from there. The Synectics process is very robust and flexible!

Comparison of the SSM and Synectics approaches

Before we go on to consider how we handle a problem with lots of problem owners, we need to compare the Synectics CPS process with SSM. These two methods have many similarities, particularly at the ideological level. For example, they provide more 'front end' stages with no pre-judgements (unlike some other methodologies), attempting to ensure we are solving the right problem. There are also some differences. The aim of this section is to summarize and extend the comparisons we started to make earlier, concentrating particularly on the differences. This should enable you to decide whether these are significant enough to preclude the use of one or the other technique under certain circumstances but, perhaps more important, this section shows how a synthesis of the two methodologies can be usefully achieved.

The most apparent difference is right at the very beginning. With the SSM, a lot of data is gathered initially in an attempt to take into consideration the whole picture. From this we try to develop insightful perspectives on the problem situation. Synectics, on the other hand, values the 'ignorance' of many of the

Figure 12.1			Springboard choice		
Problem owner	1st	2nd	3rd	4th	5th
Alan	7	8	27	15	23
John	8	23	11	4	21
Raj	23	3	8	19	11
Sade	19	8	24	11	23
. . . . . .					

Consensus matrix

Note: this shows an unusually large amount of agreement, so first we should work on the springboards 8, 23 and possibly 11.

problem-solving resources (group members) for its potential in providing us with fresh views of the problem situation, maintaining that there is no need for the majority of the group to understand the problem in order to assist with its resolution. The subsequent 'scatter gun' approach of Goal Wishing then amplifies the brief description of the problem given by the problem owner into many other views of the problem situation, both possible and wildly speculative.

Whether we prefer a fairly 'systematic' means of getting many perspectives on the problem situation (with SSM) or the more 'random' approach of Synectics, we should be aware of:

1. the greater difficulty of later getting away from the problem having once gathered large quantities of data, and
2. that Goal Wishing is more likely to send us down the route towards innovative solutions.

I have said before (pages 34 and 230), when we have a problem situation of such complexity that the number of problem owners is well into double figures, the employment of the Synectics process may require a restructuring of the problem situation and the involvement of several groups of problem solvers, which could possibly incur some administrative difficulties. And, since it could be argued anyway that collecting a lot of data in these circumstances is often necessary, SSM may seem to be a more appropriate way to proceed. This latter point should not be taken as a criterion for choosing between methodologies, because Synectics is not opposed to gathering and using data, it simply does not place the same importance on this initially. Not unrelated to this is the time factor. A Synectics session may take only a few hours, while an SSM intervention may take weeks or months. The data collection aspect of SSM is obviously a time-consuming activity, but the time required is also a function of the complexity of the problem situation. If we tackled situations as complex as SSM often does using only Synectics, we would need to have many problem-solving sessions, interspersed with planning meetings and plenary discussions, all of which would take considerably more than a few hours.

Both approaches require the use of skilled practitioners, but in rather different ways. The Synectics approach requires a trained and highly skilled facilitator (process leader). Someone conducting an SSM investigation, however (although possibly needing some process-leading skills during discussions with the problem owners), needs to have knowledge and experience of systems theory, because in an SSM study it is the consultants who effectively 'do the problem solving' in so much as it is they who 'carry out' the process. This really is the fundamental difference between the two methodologies, although both emphasize close liaison with the problem owners, and it is they who ultimately determine what constitutes a solution. With the Synectics approach the consultant/facilitator only guides the process; it is the problem owner who does the problem solving. SSM's involvement in the problem content has another implication; Checkland speaks of our obligation to 'donate the technique' when the intervention is completed; this is admirable, but not quite so easy as it is with Synectics.

Returning to the actual stages in the process, both systems attempt to ensure that whoever commissions the problem solving is checked out as to whether they have the motivation to reach a conclusion. With Synectics the client is by definition (and so necessarily) a problem owner; this need not be so with an SSM study; and, anyway, it will probably be impractical with SSM to ascertain the motivation of all the problem owners.

Both approaches embark, after the 'initial analysis', on amassing ways of viewing the problem situation (**Relevant Systems** *v.* **Goal Wishing**). It is likely to be more difficult for a lone SSM problem solver to produce as many different perspectives as a group performing Goal Wishing. This is why it is recommended (see page 270) that the Relevant Systems are obtained at least partially from a **Brainstorming** (or Synectics' Goal Wishing) session with the problem owners.

A further difference is encountered in the idea generation phase. When there is a need to get right away from the problem, bring in new material and start to put together some thoughts which will, we hope, lead to the resolution of the problem, SSM calls upon abstract systems thinking. Synectics, on the other hand, uses excursions. (Though I see the conceptual model-building process as a sort of excursion!). The former is a very logical development of a systems model from a beginning idea (Relevant System/**Root Definition**); the latter is a somewhat irrational process. Excursions are likely to be more effective at getting this distance, because many unskilled SSM practitioners will experience difficulty in leaving the problem behind after they reach a Root Definition. With the absurdities of some types of excursion it is virtually impossible not to forget the problem!

If the problem situation is such that eventually (once the problem has been 'identified' and suitable changes have been suggested) a 'hard' systems analysis and design process (for example, SSADM, Structured Systems Analysis and Design Method) will need to be initiated (e.g. in a highly technological environment), the building of the conceptual model in SSM will have been an extremely useful starting point.

The finale of SSM is the discussion with the problem owners of the changes suggested by the comparison of the conceptual model(s) with the real-world situation. Even if the SSM facilitator has kept in close touch with the problem owners throughout the intervention, this meeting has the potential for a conflict of views over these systemically desirable and culturally feasible changes. Such a meeting is likely to achieve more consensus if some Synectics' principles are incorporated.

Participation in a Synectics problem-solving session nearly always improves communications between group members and builds team spirit. If this does happen, then this will assist the implementation of the possible solution later. The SSM process, because of its *modus operandi,* is not likely to have the same effect; except perhaps in a minor way because the problem owners have been party to an indirect exchange of viewpoints.

Synectics is committed to openness because of its positive secondary effects on team building. A frank interchange of differing views is not so likely to happen with SSM. Although in an SSM intervention we need to collect the soft attitudes, opinions, prejudices, likes and dislikes, etc. of the people involved, they are not necessarily (in fact rarely) passed on by the facilitator to other interested parties. Synectics seems to be prepared to lose the occasional battle that might result from this openness, perhaps knowing that eventually even confirmed autocrats have to acknowledge that other people have a right to express an idea or a contrary viewpoint without risking crucifixion. The SSM approach is a little more cautious. This does not imply that the SSM practitioner can be less skilled in open-mindedness, inspiring trust and confidence in others and the other human relations attributes required by a Synectics facilitator/process leader. These qualities are still needed for gathering information from problem owners. It is just that the SSM process usually tries to avoid the potential conflicts that complete frankness between problem owners might give rise to.

There is a potential difficulty with Synectics of getting all the appropriate people involved. The bosses, whose presence may be essential, may be reluctant to give up their time for a problem-solving session. If they can be encouraged to participate, then the process leader is going to have to work harder generating the desired atmosphere for creativity where, temporarily, everyone is equal, everyone's contributions have the same merit and openness prevails. Technically, it is easier to collect the '**soft**' information in a personal interview, as one might in an SSM investigation; it would certainly be less time-consuming for those questioned. But we still need approval from an authority figure to guarantee that an SSM intervention can be carried out effectively. Finally, because the problem owners actually take part in the problem-solving process with Synectics, there is less danger that at the end of the day the problem-solving facilitator will be completely 'off-track' in respect of the solutions obtained by the process.

A complicated problem

I have tried to show that Synectics and the SSM are probably two of the best problem-solving processes currently available for dealing with the complex and interwoven people problems we come across every day. Having shown their similarities and contrasted the differences in their approaches, it is appropriate now to demonstrate how this might affect our choice of methodology by posing what I hope is the most complicated scenario so far, and then considering which of the processes mentioned in this book might be used in this situation, and how. It is *not* my intention that you should attempt to try actually to resolve this problem situation now; just simply read through the story in Frame 12.10 and start thinking about how you might tackle it.

Frame 12.10 *Business Equipment International Inc.: the problem situation*

Our story is set in the marketing section of Business Equipment International Inc. (BEI) who are part of a multinational organization manufacturing and selling office equipment. Their product range is quite diverse and includes equipment such as computers, photocopiers, fax machines, etc. They also develop the software required by some of the machines they sell. All product development takes place through the coordinated operations of the marketing departments of the ten national companies. Except, of course, for some fairly esoteric research work going on at BEI's separate and very prestigious Advanced Designs Laboratory (ADL) on the west coast of North America. Most of the

▶

innovative ideas that come out of ADL eventually end up filtering into the company's product range, via periodic research reports sent out to the marketing divisions throughout the world.

Within the marketing section there are a number of fairly autonomous departments, each one mainly handling its own particular function. These departments are new products (NPD), existing products enhancement (EPE), customer services (CS) and software and logistics (SLG). SLG is responsible for the development of the software required by the computer products sold by the company. Its chief product is an 'integrated office' suite of programs that incorporate a fairly full management information system. It is also very much into computerized project management. It is possibly for these reasons that SLG is also responsible for coordinating the development projects of the other three departments.

The morale of SLG is generally good, comprising a small, friendly and cohesive group of people; however, initial investigations suggest that the six line managers within the group have considerably different perceptions of their own roles within SLG, and those of their fellow managers. So despite the group's apparently satisfactory 'team spirit', their overall effectiveness could, in the opinion of the group (departmental) manager, be improved.

SLG's operations are further complicated by the apparent lack of cooperation between the other departments within the marketing section and themselves. From SLG's viewpoint, its role within the section should be to monitor the progress of the other departments' projects so as to ensure the overall efficiency of the section, and to provide access to, and coordinate the usage of, the additional resources required from time to time by the other departments.

For example, by monitoring a project being conducted by, say, EPE, the purpose of which is to determine the most cost-effective upgrade that can be offered to customers owning computer equipment more than two years old, SLG would be aware that what EPE desperately needs at this time is some input from a programmer with experience of the latest developments in systems software. If they also knew (as they should) that Kwame in NPD has this expertise, and is kicking his heels (on his latest project) whilst waiting for some test results to come from the States, they could put the two parties in touch.

Currently hanging over the head of the whole operation is the threat of rationalization. There is a perceived need to increase its productivity whilst decreasing costs, thus improving profitability. This may be the reason why the other three departments view any enquiry from SLG with a certain amount of suspicion, and respond to such requests usually somewhat belatedly and always with incomplete information. Out of sheer necessity, however, the other three departments are continuing to maintain (and are often improving) links amongst themselves. The SLG manager has been heard to defend his group's lack of brilliant performance with comments such as 'They're just not talking to us any more!', 'They keep leaving us out of important discussions and decisions'. Obviously, this attitude is not helping SLG perform its coordinating role!

We (in the role of a new, keen, junior and thus highly expendable manager) have been asked by Stefano Pantoni, the SLG manager, to suggest how the department (or indeed, the section) should best deal with this mess. He wants our advice on suitable problem-solving methods that might help him to resolve the unsatisfactory situation that he perceives himself and his department to be in.

Michael Pantoni's initial thoughts are that SLG should tighten up its own internal operations before any attempt is made to resolve the wider issues.

What should we suggest to Stefano Pantoni? One place to start could be to invite Pantoni, his six line managers and some six or so other people from within the department to a Brainstorming session on 'How to improve the internal operations of SLG'. I was once involved in a Synectics-style problem-solving session for a charitable organization concerned about the low profile and confusing image they were portraying to the general public. They were seeking ways of improving this situation in the hope of gaining more funds and resources for their work. This situation has certain similarities with the situation at BEI. In the early stages of the session with this charity, it became apparent that there were some very different perceptions of what the organization's mission actually was, and that this might have been why they had so far been unable to decide on the best way to proceed in changing their image.

SLG's six line managers have different perceptions of their own and each other's expected contributions to the overall objectives of the department. This may be why, despite relatively ideal working conditions, SLG is perceived (by its manager and others outside the department) as not being as productive as perhaps it should be.

The use of the early stages of the Synectics process (for example, Goal Wishing) are invariably effective with regard to 'opening up' the problem. This is particularly so when you have a problem situation with several owners, as it provides a 'safe' environment for the airing of the differing perceptions, attitudes, opinions and beliefs of the problem owners. With the charity, by the time we had filled two walls with some 100 springboards (some obtained using an excursion), the group members knew better what each other's opinions were, had realized that there was a greater degree of agreement amongst these than they thought, and were getting close to coming to an agreement on a common mission.

Since a friendly and unantagonistic attitude supposedly exists amongst both SLG generally and its senior management, an ideal place to start might well be a Synectics-style problem-solving session with the line managers and their boss, Stefano Pantoni; the purpose of which would be to reach a consensus on the roles of the six line managers in the context of the department's overall mission. We would work first with Stefano Pantoni as the client or problem owner, because he has ultimate responsibility for the department's activities. Then we would try to resolve the problem as seen by each of the individual line managers in turn (as with the Northcliffe Sands problem we discussed earlier in this chapter).

Even if we were less ambitious and were satisfied at this stage with just a sharing of views, Synectics is likely to be more effective than 'straight' Brainstorming. On the other hand, if it seems reasonable to be more 'ambitious' and question the department's stated objectives as well, we would still have a highly suitable vehicle for this in Synectics. We might have been able to use SSM to equal effect on these same issues within SLG; however, since we apparently have the makings of 'team spirit' already, it would be a shame not to capitalize on this and get the active participation of the seven managers together simultaneously in the resolution of the problem situation.

The wider issues of the marketing division and SLG's place within it is a far more complicated situation, which involves considerably more interested parties (problem owners) and possible 'outside' forces from the rest of the company.

It is conceivable that, once SLG has been seen to sort out its internal 'problems', our wider concerns may start to dissipate as Pantoni seems to hope. However, there seems to be a fundamental communications problem fermenting in the middle of all this, which I suspect will worsen in the time it takes SLG to demonstrate its 'new efficiency'. Furthermore, if the root cause of this is due to a fear of rationalization and the perception that SLG's data gathering may be a part of this, seeing a 'new, dynamic and together' SLG arising from the midst of things is just as likely to put the fear of God into the other three departments even more! Perhaps the marketing section's director (through Pantoni) should be advised to commission a soft systems study of the whole section's operations, preferably to be undertaken by an independent consultant. The distrust that appears to exist between the departments from our initial investigations seems to indicate that it would be difficult for someone within the division to gather the subjective 'political' information that we need. This should not, however, preclude the possibility of conducting another multiple problem owner Synectics-style session with the four departmental managers, the marketing section's director and one other person from the lower echelons of each department, to thrash out the communications problem. This could be done in addition to the SSM study, as a means of gathering perceptions of the situation, and people's **best current** thinking on possible solutions. Or it could be our first (and cost-effective) attempt to resolve the wider concerns before someone has to decide whether to invest a considerable amount of time and money on a full SSM study.

If at the end of our problem solving we have a number of possible solutions, systemically desirable and culturally feasible changes, which we need to choose between, then it would be reasonable to employ Kepner and Tregoe's **Decision Analysis** to help us with this selection.

Finally, when we have our chosen solution it would be wise to use something akin to **Potential Problem Analysis** to check out our ideas, before we start to expend effort, time and money on implementation of our chosen solution.

Steps towards a synthesis

From my suggestions on tackling the BEI problem, it should be possible to see how we might augment an SSM intervention with some elements of Synectics. First, we might use Goal Wishing with groups of problem owners as a means of gathering much of the soft data that we require; for instance, their perceptions of the problem situation, what their individual concerns are, some **beginning ideas** and perhaps also their best current thinking on possible solutions. The idea behind best current thinking is that it is generally accepted as not being perfect, and it is being offered as a basis for discussion. It will not be dissected and examined in minute detail and we will not be called upon to defend it.

Second, the generation of Relevant Systems (and even the distillation of these into Root Definitions) may be achieved by Goal Wishing with groups of problem owners as well. We might actually find that some of the springboards from the data collection sessions imply Relevant Systems that we should consider. Do not forget that a relevant system is just a (systemic) way of looking at the problem situation (a suggestion about what is, could or should be the main purpose of all this human activity?) which we hope may turn out to be relevant later on (in the sense that the comparison of the conceptual models, built from them, with the real-world situation will suggest useful changes). For example, person X may see SLG as a 'software development system', person Y as a 'project management system', or person Z as an 'intelligence gathering system' for the US parent company. Many of the **springboards** obtained during Goal Wishing will express ways of looking at the problem situation. Remember that I have likened **Cognitive Mapping** (see Chapter 6) to an 'extended and more systematic' form of **Backward/Forward Planning** and Goal Wishing and so that too finds a place here.

Finally, after SSM's comparison stage, when we get down to discussing with the problem owners which of the changes suggested by our systems thinking are not only systemically desirable but also culturally feasible, we might choose to run this debate in the form of a Synectics Consensus (problem-solving) Meeting. We might start things going by asking each of the problem owners to give an itemized response to the suggested changes. This should give us an indication of the amount of agreement that exists over which of these would provide an acceptable resolution of the problem situation, and also highlight each problem owner's outstanding concerns. Then we would try to resolve each problem owner's concerns in turn and, we hope, end up with a proposed course of action that is acceptable to everyone concerned.

Turning things around, how could aspects of SSM enhance the Synectics process? This is more difficult since the *modus operandi* of SSM (in the sense that the person conducting the SSM investigation becomes involved with the problem content) is antipathetic to the Synectics approach. However, I can see how Conceptual Model building from certain, appropriate ('this could/should be our mission' type) springboards followed by comparison with reality (which parallels Synectics' force fit procedure) could be modified and employed in a group setting so producing an alternative type of excursion.

Also, whilst Synectics already use some drawing exercises as 'ice-breakers' and excursions, it might be fun (and productive) to invite all the problem owners to produce a cartoon (a sort of mini **Rich Picture**) of their view of the problem situation. These could then be displayed (possibly anonymously) and used as raw material for springboards and ideas; for example, we might ask people to choose a cartoon they like (other than the one they have drawn) and offer springboards describing what they think the cartoon 'depicts' and how it relates to the problem situation. This could be a means of gathering individual perceptions of the problem situation when people are anxious about providing this information verbally. Or could be used to 'exchange' perceptions between groups working on different parts of the problem situation.

Coping with lots of problem owners

You will remember that the usual Synectics group size is approximately six to eight people and that the Synectics Consensus Meeting method for dealing with multiple problem ownership (we saw earlier), attempts to resolve the problem for all the problem owners 'cyclically', dealing with only one problem owner at a time. This, as we said before, might cause us some administrative/logistical difficulties with a large number of problem owners.

SSM's ability to cope in these circumstances would seem to recommend it as the the ideal problem-solving process, either used 'straight' as in Chapter 11 or 'enhanced' as above – thus incorporating the more important attributes of the Synectics approach, such as the group interactions. However, Synectics does have a technique that can help us specifically to tackle problem situations complicated by having many problem owners, as well as assisting in planning the implementation of change. It helps deal with the 'problem' of many problem owners by providing a reasonable way of breaking down a complex situation into parts. **Decision Point Planning** (DPP) evolves from Synectics' definition of a problem as 'the gap between the present situation and a more desirable one'. This more desirable situation is often only vaguely perceived. Let us suppose that earlier discussion with the problem owners has revealed a fair degree of consensus as to where they want to end up, but they are uncertain as to how to get there.

In group sessions (which can be larger than usual) we map out the things that the problem owners feel ought to be done, their implications in the sense of what needs to be done before or after them and all the decisions that they need to make *en route* in order to navigate successfully the gap from where they know they are now to where they think they want to be. The resulting diagram that charts this proposed odyssey, which often runs to several sheets of paper, looks vaguely similar to a flowchart except that only two symbols are used. A rectangular symbol is used to contain the actions that need to be carried out, whilst an annotated diamond shape (as is usual) denotes the decisions to be taken. The arrows denote the logical dependency of one activity on another (Figure 12.2).

Once all problem owners are content that all essential actions and decisions have been suitably recorded (the diagram may go through several versions before this is so), we then fill in the names of the people who have **action responsibility** (see page 320) for the various parts of the project and any decisions to be taken, along with those others who are directly involved to the extent that what may happen could impinge on their action responsibility. By this means, as we can identify each problem owner with (only) certain specific part(s) of the situation, and a fairly complicated problem can be safely broken down (restructured) without fear of missing important interconnections and interactions. We should then be able to break off into smaller problem-solving groups in order to tackle any outstanding concerns that we still have with our part(s) of the project. When we have resolved all these issues the DPP can serve as the basis of an implementation plan.

Concluding comments

DPP extends the utility of Synectics into many complex problem situations, even those with many problem owners, though it could still be argued that it falls short of the holistic approach to which SSM aspires. My main concern with SSM, however, is the small amount of involvement the problem owners may have with the actual problem solving. Without involvement we cannot expect any commitment to the changes we obtain, which I feel is the more serious issue. Although we may be obliged by the client to operate in this way (as an external problem-solving consultant, as opposed to a facilitator), it is not a desirable state of affairs. This is why, if a synthesis of these two methods is to be achieved, it would have to come by injecting Synectics techniques into the basic SSM structure, the aim being to incorporate more problem-owner participation within SSM. SSM applied skilfully can get very close to tackling the 'whole' of a complex problem situation, whereas Synectics can encourage more open communications and help build team spirit, and thus can often offer a (positive) **cultural change** along with a solution.

In time the distinction between the two systems may become even less clearcut. Checkland and Scholes (1990) has already attempted to show that SSM is not just a strategy for special highlighted major studies into complex situations, but is equally usable as a way in which a manager can go about his or her normal day-to-day managerial work. Likewise, Synectics is not just a creative problem-solving process, but a continuously developing body of knowledge, skills and techniques concerned with innovation, problem solving, communications and teamwork. It is also the name of the international group of companies responsible for the ongoing enhancement of the original Synectics concepts. DPP, is a part of their efforts to apply Synectics principles to project management, and is but one example of this.

Figure 12.2

Part of a Decision
Point Plan

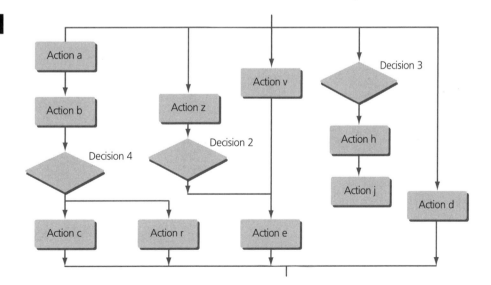

Summary

This chapter has shown how the issue of multiple problem ownership which complicates the problem-solving process, can be dealt with. Also, by comparing the SSM and Synectics approaches, it has indicated how a synthesis of the two processes can be achieved to good effect.

Endnote

1. This chapter assumes that the reader has read and is familiar with the contents of Chapters 10 and 11.

13 Group problem solving

This chapter explores some of the issues concerned with problem solving in groups, such as leadership, motivation, communication, team-building, etc. and their relationship with creativity.

Introduction

It is claimed that many of the processes and techniques designed to encourage creative thinking work best in a group setting. Two of the reasons for this are that the comments and ideas made by other people fire our imaginations, and in the right circumstances we have a tendency to build on other people's ideas. I believe this to be especially true with **Synectics**. However, the conclusions of research conducted into group productivity are mixed; for example, Arnold Meadow and Sidney Parnes in the 1950s seemed to verify that a **Brainstorming** group was more productive than an equal number of individuals working alone, but not using Brainstorming principles (see also Chapter 3). Others have indicated that a Brainstorming group is not as productive as the same number of individuals working alone, but who *are* also using Brainstorming principles (as might happen in a non-interactive **Brainwriting** group.

Subsequent research on enhancing group productivity has tended to concentrate on factors such as group cohesiveness. According to David Buchanan and Andrzej Huczynski (1985, p.203), the level of cohesiveness of a group can be estimated from such things as 'whether members arrive on time, the degree of trust and support between them and the amount of satisfaction they gain from their group membership'. Irving Janis (1982) suggested that in some cohesive groups, an overriding desire for consensus and unanimity could lead to poor decision making due to the suppression of internal dissent and the consequent failure adequately to evaluate alternatives. Generally, however, it is felt that group cohesiveness is an important positive factor determining productivity. As far as creative thinking is concerned, trust and support (see Chapter 3) are vital elements of an environment that enhances creativity.

Jay Hall (1971) concluded that what made a group more effective than individuals was when group members actively searched for areas of disagreement early on in their discussions, and then resolved the subsequent conflicts into a consensus decision. Ineffective groups tended to 'opt out' of such conflicts and reached a common view by 'averaging' their diverse opinions. This led him to devise a set of rules for reaching a consensus, listed in Frame 13.1.

> ### Frame 13.1 *Rules for attaining consensus*
>
> In attaining consensus, the following guidelines should be observed:
>
> - Avoid arguing for your own individual judgements. Approach the task on the basis of logic, and consider carefully the comments of others.
> - This is not a competition; if a stalemate is reached over something, search for a mutually acceptable alternative.
> - Do not alter your opinions just so as to avoid conflict and reach agreement. Support only those suggestions which are basically similar or complementary to your own, and change your mind only when something has been objectively and logically argued. Always be suspicious of a quick agreement.
> - Avoid conflict-reducing techniques such as a majority vote, averaging or the 'trading' of points of agreement when reaching your consensus.
> - View differences of opinions as a help rather than a hindrance in decision making. They are natural and should be expected. A wide range of information and opinions can lead to better solutions.

A well-formed group can come up with more and 'better' ideas for solutions and can make better decisions than individual members of the group working on their own. Furthermore, with a problem situation with several owners, if we have all the problem owners within the group and we manage to reach a consensus solution, there should be no acceptance problem (see also page 187).

Let us now look at how best the dynamics of the situation should be arranged so as to encourage the group members to think more creatively. This involves discussion of two main issues: first, leadership, and second, being a good team member. Together, the interpersonal skills required of these roles can ensure that an appropriate climate for creativity is both established and maintained.

Leadership

First thoughts

Most people believe that groups must have leaders, though some observers feel that 'creative' groups do not seem to have one permanent and easily recognizable leader. They seldom do have a 'traditional' chairperson/manager, but in virtually all cases such a group needs, and has, a leader of some kind. It is not always self-evident who this leader is because a different leadership style is involved and because with an 'experienced' creative group the person assuming the role of leader may vary as the group's objectives and/or a group member's needs change.

Connected with this is the trend for many years now to distinguish 'supervision', and possibly also 'management', from 'leadership' – 'management controls, arranges, does things right; leadership unleashes energy, sets the vision so we do the right thing' (Bennis and Nanus, 1985, p.21.) (see also Frame 13.2). The diagrammatical representation of the functions of management in Figure 13.1, showing the 'usual' five functions, plus a sixth one, 'communicating', illustrates this split. Although undoubtedly an oversimplification, Figure 13.1 does make the distinctions that, first, supervision and leadership have little or nothing in common and that, second, as a consequence of this, our traditional view of managing can no longer be seen as being the same thing as leadership (see Frame 13.2).

Frame 13.2 *Supervision v. leadership*

Graham (1988, pp.74–8) notes that supervision is usually associated with a leader–subordinate relationship implicit in which is a certain 'coerced compliance' brought about by 'the fear of punishments, the promise of rewards, or the desire to fulfil contractual obligations', and which is maintained by the use of positional power (reward, coercion and legitimacy). In connection with leadership, we speak of a leader–follower relationship where followers are psychologically linked to the organization because of identification (involvement based on pride of affiliation) and/or internalization (involvement based on a congruence between individual and organizational values), along with which comes the idea that 'followers freely choose to be influenced by those who lead them', and which relies on the use of personal power (expert and referent).

Note: See also Frame 9.8 for more discussion of power

Figure 13.1

Leadership, supervision and management

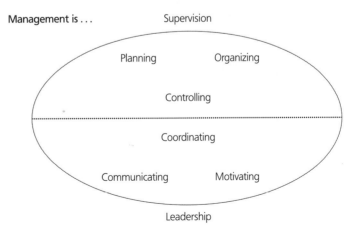

So what do we mean by a leader?

People find themselves in a leadership role for a variety of reasons and possibly could obtain that position solely by virtue of personal charisma, tradition (for example, by birth or seniority), situation (being in the right place at the right time) or appointment. To be accepted as a 'true' leader requires other things; the once popular (now a bit dated but still advocated by some) 'contingency' approaches to leadership are a good place to start to explore this.

Action-centred leadership

If our group needs a leader, it is essential that s/he is a **functional leader** (see Frame 13.3), who holds the position because s/he adjusts his/her behaviour (what s/he does) to meet both the task-related and the personal and interpersonal needs of the group. Primarily, this leadership style needs to be fundamentally democratic rather than authoritarian. We want the members of the group to contribute all they can to the group's task and an authoritarian and/or task-orientated approach is not conducive to this, especially if what we want are beginning or half-formed ideas! However, effectiveness with a democratic and/or people-orientated style of leadership requires rather more than this (that is, just doing the right things) from the leader's behaviour.

Frame 13.3 *Action-centred leadership*

The concept of functional leadership was pioneered by John Adair (1979). His model of leadership maintains that leadership effectiveness comes from what the leader does to meet the needs of the task, the group and the individuals within it. It encourages a flexible style of leadership which may be predominantly concerned with the task, the group or an individual, depending on the priorities and the circumstances.

Examples of the functions the leader needs to fulfil are:

- Task – defining tasks and setting/achieving objectives, planning the tasks, allocating work responsibilities and resources, setting, monitoring and controlling the quality of/and checking performance, reviewing progress/time-keeping.
- Group – establishing behavioural norms by example, maintaining morale and building team spirit, encouraging and providing a sense of purpose, setting standards and maintaining discipline, ensuring good communications, acting as spokesperson for the group.
- Individual – attending to personal problems/resolving conflicts, providing motivation, recognizing and using individual abilities and contributions, providing positive feedback, training and developing skills.

However, Robert Bales (Bales and Slater, 1956) suggests that it is untenable to have a leadership style concerned both with the needs of the task and those of the people within the group. This poses a problem, since often we have situations where a (project) task that has to be 'managed', and people need to be 'led'. He goes on to say that groups perform best when the roles of task 'manager' and human relations 'leader' are occupied by different people. Bales identified the task specialists by asking group members questions such as 'Who contributed the best ideas for solving the problem?' and 'Who did the most to guide the discussion and keep it moving effectively?' The human relations specialists were likewise identified with the question 'Who do you like?' A third group role emerged from this analysis: that of the 'scapegoat'!

Joe Kelly (1969, p.217) describes the interplay between these two leadership roles as follows:

> It is possible to think of the task specialist as working at the task which structures the behaviour and attitudes of the group members, and which frequently makes people anxious and disturbs the equilibrium of the group. The anxiety generated by this kind of initiative may well be siphoned off and directed towards the scapegoat. The human relations specialist, who is usually a very warm and receptive personality, now comes to the fore and takes care of the casualties, bandages up the victim, and sponges down the task specialist, without diverting the group too much from its primary purpose of achieving the task.

F.E. Fiedler (1978) concluded that the suitability of a task as opposed to a people-orientated approach is connected with the relative favourableness of the task or problem situation. The task-orientated leaders seemed to him to be more effective in the extreme situations (very favourable and very unfavourable conditions), whereas the people-orientated leaders were more effective at other times. The favourableness of the conditions depended on whether the task was highly structured or unstructured, whether the leader's positional power was high or low (see Frame 9.8), and whether the followers felt that their relationships with the leader were good or poor. These three variables are difficult to measure, and so the leader has to rely heavily on intuition when selecting a leadership style on this basis alone. Also, this view of leadership ignored the needs of the followers and that sometimes a leader's technical competence is more important than his or her personality. All the same, it does demonstrate the importance of the context.

So where do we go from here?

Process leadership

Generally, most **CPS** groups benefit from having what we call a **process leader** who is neither the problem owner nor the task specialist. Process leaders take little or no part in the problem content, but monitor group dynamics so that they can guide the problem solving through the most appropriate processes and techniques after first having established and then whilst maintaining a suitably conducive group climate. They do not normally offer any ideas, develop any solutions or perform any evaluation during the problem-solving session.

The precise nature of their input to the content of the problem depends on the process/technique being employed. In 'traditional' **Brainstorming** (see Appendix

3), for instance, the leader, though generally contributing no ideas during the actual session, does offer direction for the group's ideas, and may do some 'sifting' of them afterwards. To this extent s/he is not a true process leader. The leader of a **Synectics**-style group (see Chapter 10) should not take any part in the problem content whatsoever, because the group always contains a problem owner (or client) who performs these functions when invited to do so by the leader.

This division between content and process seems to correspond with that of task and people at first sight. The problem owner is the task specialist, whilst the process leader looks after the well-being of the group; but there is a major difference. The process leader of a Synectics-style group does take care of the psychological needs of the individual and of the group. S/he is encouraging and supportive whilst ensuring that the climatic 'rules' are adhered to but, at the same time, s/he guides the group through the problem-solving process. This separates the task specialist from the process leading and eliminates many potential conflicts without taking the ultimate task control away from the problem owner.

This experience with CPS groups suggests that the traditional style of running meetings is not ideal for problem solving, as the 'traditional' manager or meeting chairperson tends to choose the direction of discussion, make instant judgements on relevance and usefulness, stick rigidly to the agenda and allocate assignments and tasks. While these are all important activities when used appropriately, George Prince (1970, pp.3–4) believes that traditional-style meetings are invariably less productive than they could be because:

- It is not always clear to group members precisely what is required of them – does the chairperson want to give information, gather ideas, seek reactions or genuinely solve problems?
- When meetings are used to solve problems or help make decisions 'creativity is a vital component because it develops alternatives, enriches possibilities and imagines consequences'. The chairperson can discourage the conditions necessary for creativity.
- The chairperson is invariably the person with the most senior 'rank' and 'it is accepted practice for him to use this power and for other members to play to it'.
- Our tendency to criticize ideas prematurely (see Chapters 3 and 10) results in many useful ideas being abandoned.

It is generally considered to be poor leadership not to make it clear as to what you, the leader, are doing and what your expectations of the group members are. The other failings are all ultimately functions of the task specialist, being the leader of the process. Prince believes (1970, pp.5–8) that people at meetings exhibit a behaviour that is a combination of sensitivity and aggressiveness, which ostensibly seem to be in conflict, but which are precisely the qualities we need for inspired problem solving. 'Aggressiveness presses us to adventure beyond the rules, to speculate outrageously . . . sensitivity alerts us to both opportunities and shortcomings.'

The chairman must ensure that these are used constructively. However, traditional meetings are very often perceived as competitions. If, as inevitably happens, we experience some disparagement (see also, the *effect of* **discounts**, pages 61–2), we then devote our attention and skills to repairing and refurbishing our self-image, preferably at the expense of our rivals (see also Figure 3.2). Having an impartial process leader helps us get away from these old attitudes. Prince concludes that a good leader is one who:

- defends each group member's image, because s/he 'knows that each member cherishes his own individuality above any problem to be solved';
- directs all aggression against the problem; and
- demonstrates that a meeting can be a winning situation for everyone concerned.

The ability to do these things is certainly something we would expect from a process leader; referring back to what a functional leader does (in Frame 13.3), a process leader performs many of these functions as well. In fact, a process leader should be fulfilling all the 'group' and 'individual' maintenance functions, and most of the 'task' functions as well. The exceptions here will be some overall planning of the problem-solving activity which will usually be done by both the process leader and problem owner together; and 'defining tasks (problems) and setting objectives', this activity can be left solely to the problem owner.

Leadership revisited

In more recent thinking on leadership, Diane-Marie Hosking and Ian Morley (1988, pp.90–1) suggest that 'the only sure means of identifying leaders is through the analysis of leadership processes'. They maintain that by studying the leadership process, the leader–follower relationship, certain 'acts' emerge as contributing to a 'social order' that protects and promotes the values and interests of the groups to which we belong. Leaders are those who 'consistently make effective contributions to [this] social order, and are both expected and perceived to do so by fellow participants'. These leadership acts are performed with a degree of skill, and Hosking and Morley say the skills of leadership are similar to those of negotiating. Klaus Bartolke, however, commenting on their ideas in the same text (1988, pp.153–5), questions whether the concept of equating leadership skills with those of negotiating is universally applicable and, although calling it a 'useful theoretical construction', suggests that in some situations the skills of **joint problem solving** may be more appropriate.

Hunt *et al.* (1988, p.1) comment, on the diversity and controversial nature of recent leadership research, that we still appear to be some way away from achieving consensus on what constitutes effective leadership, or on precisely what 'leadership' is. The views of Hosking and Morley have been briefly introduced above, but alongside this we find that certain aspects of the earlier trait and style theories seem to be re-emerging and acquiring a new upsurge of interest. For example, the concept of charismatic leadership has been reappraised from the perspective that it is not 'solely a function of the leader's personality' but is more to do with the perceptions of followers which may or may not be situationally contingent. Charismatic leadership is often defined these days as something like a new or different view of things portrayed by the leader, which is perceived by his/her followers as being 'cognitively, emotionally, behaviorally and consequentially "real" for them' (Boal and Bryson, 1988, p.12).

Transformational leadership

Closely related to charismatic leadership is the concept of **transformational leadership** (Frame 13.4). Where the latter differs is that it actively encourages followers to think for themselves and to develop their own visions to further the group's objectives. Bruce Avolio and Bernard Bass say that, apart from charisma, 'transformational leaders also need the ability to recognize the needs, aspirations, and values of their followers and the skill to conceive and articulate strategies and goals that will predispose the followers to exert their best efforts' (1988, pp.36–8). Transformational leaders must also be able to 'read' situational factors, such as the prevailing organizational culture, in order to determine what is possible and when the time is right to attempt changes in the outlook of individuals and/or organizations. These leaders do not just 'react to environmental circumstances – they create them'. Is this another way of describing a process leader?

Frame 13.4 *Transformational leadership*

Bruce Avolio and Bernard Bass advocate (1988, pp.30–5) a model of leadership developed by Bernard Bass (1985) which incorporates both previous thoughts on transformational leadership (James MacGregor Burns, 1978) and some earlier ideas concerning transactional leadership. This model attempted to explain how, through 'heightened motivation', followers are encouraged to 'perform beyond expectations'. Although the main emphasis is on the 'transformational' aspects of leadership, they maintain that, in order to be an effective transformational leader, we must have the skills of a transactional leader as well.

Bernard Bass claims to have identified five (now six) factors within what Avolio and Bass see as effective leadership. Two are those of transactional leadership (a form of leadership essentially rooted in path–goal theory):

- **Contingent reward**: the leader is seen as frequently telling (or consulting with) followers about what to do to achieve a desired reward for their efforts.

- **Management-by-exception**: the leader avoids giving directions if the old ways are working . . . (and) . . . intervenes (to correct followers' mistakes) only if standards are not met.

The different interpretation now being placed on these factors is that it is by encouraging them 'to work for transcendental goals instead of immediate self-interests and for achievement and self-actualization instead of safety and security' that followers are motivated to perform beyond expectations.

The rest of Bass's factors are transformational leadership factors:

- **Charisma**: the leader instils pride, faith and respect, has a gift for seeing what is really important and has a sense of mission (or vision)

▶

which is effectively articulated – now called **idealized influence**. This is described as the leader being envisioning, confident and setting high standards for emulation.

- **Inspirational motivation**: the leader provides followers with challenges and meaning for engaging in shared goals and undertakings.
- **Individualized consideration**: the leader provides coaching, mentoring and growth opportunities; for example by delegating projects to stimulate and create learning experiences; pays personal attention to followers' needs – especially those who seem neglected – and treats each follower with respect and as an individual.
- **Intellectual stimulation**: the leader provides ideas that result in a rethinking of old ways, and enables followers to (question assumptions) look at problems from many angles and resolve problems (more creatively) that were at a standstill.

Commenting on the ideas of Avolio and Bass, Jill Graham is optimistic about transformational leadership, because not only does it encourage follower autonomy, but also has the means to sustain it. 'Individualized consideration and intellectual stimulation are the pump primers used by transformational leaders to make followers more self-confident, self-reliant, and critical people, all of which reduces the likelihood that followers will fall into habituated subordination' (1988, pp.73–9). In fact, she sees intellectual stimulation as 'facilitating radical thinking, even to the extent of inviting followers to challenge the positions of the leader'.

Appealing though this description of transformational leadership may be in that it appears to support the Synectics concept of **autonomous teamwork** (see later). Graham warns us that, when measuring the impact of transformational leadership on the basis of effective follower performance, there is a distinct risk of attributing inappropriate characteristics to the leader (including many popular myths). And this is assuming that the charisma that a leader is perceived to have is partly the cause of effective follower performance. Enhanced follower performance could well be due to something that possibly has nothing to do with the leadership; for example, being intrinsically motivated by the task itself.

There have been other criticisms of transformational leadership, including the rather obvious comment that charisma can be used for good or ill (to con and manipulate people). Bass and Steidlmeier (1998, p.2) have responded with the equally obvious statement that if the other aspects of transformational leadership are perfomed effectively and in an appropriate manner then that cannot be.

> The ethics of leadership rests upon three pillars: (1) the moral character of the leader, (2) the ethical values embedded in the leader's vision, articulation and program which followers either embrace or reject, and (3) the morality of the processes of social ethical choice and action that leaders and followers engage in and collectively pursue.

In other words, if the 'right' moral and ethical values are in place, the leadership is truly transformational. Consensus or not, a simple search on the Internet quickly reveals the popularity of transformational leadership.

Some more thoughts on leadership

A growing trend on thoughts on leadership is its connection with **emotional intelligence** (EQ). Daniel Goleman (1997) defines this as:

- knowing what you are feeling and being able to handle those feelings without having them swamp you,
- being able to motivate yourself to get jobs done, be creative and perform at your peak, and
- sensing what others are feeling, and handling relationships effectively.

While all are relevant, the last point would seem to be particularly pertinent to leading a CPS group (see also Chapter 14).

Summarized below is some general advice on leading a creative team, provided by Nolan (1989, pp.266–7): 'the more the environment a team works in requires innovation, and the greater the extent of external change, the more team members need a style of leadership that is open, honest and constructive'.

- Be yourself. Your personal integrity is your most valuable asset.
- Know yourself; exploit your strengths and get help where you need it.
- Define your role as leader. People need to know where they stand; to know that, they need to know where you stand.
- Provide a model of behaviour that you want practised in the team.
- Always disclose what you are thinking and planning to do.
- Give constructive feedback.
- Give honours judiciously.
- Be consistent.

Finally, two quotes that summarize leadership rather nicely:

> A leader can only be a leader if followers are willing to follow.
>
> (Buchanan and Huczynski, 1985, p.389)

> Leadership is the lifting of a man's [or woman's] vision to higher sights, the raising of a man's [or woman's] performance to a higher standard, the building of a man's [or woman's] personality beyond its normal limitations.
>
> (Drucker, 1955, p.195)

Facilitation of CPS groups

After all this discussion about leadership, what we can say here is that whatever is an appropriate form of leadership in other situations, what we have referred to as a 'process leader' is well suited to problem-solving groups.

Whilst I prefer the term 'process leader' (it is descriptive and unambiguous), others use the term 'facilitator' in relation to leading CPS groups (and unfortunately for other, different roles! For example, teachers as facilitators of learning). Paraphrasing Van Gundy (1992, pp.38–40), a facilitator needs to be confident; possess self-knowledge (of his/her strengths and weaknesses regarding facilitation); be patient; have good verbal and nonverbal communication skills; be capable of keeping track of thought processes; be sensitive, open-minded, tolerant of ambiguity and able to take prudent risks; be playful and possess basic creative-thinking skills.

Drawn and adapted mostly from Sedgwick (1996) and Quinlivan-Hall and Renner (1994), listed below are some of the tasks of a facilitator or process leader:

- deals with the meeting's administrative and planning matters,
- selects a process appropriate for the meeting's purpose,
- ensures a clear, common understanding of the meeting's purpose,
- guides the meeting process,
- models the desired behaviours by personal example (listening, non-defensiveness, withholding judgement, etc.),
- balances participation by eliciting and controlling (e.g. by body language) the flow of contributions,
- maintains the 'group memory' (flipcharts) without editing/'censorship', showing respect and acceptance of all ideas expressed,
- keeps the group members on track,
- observes/senses the state of the process and describes process obstacles,
- advises and coaches/trains the group on problem-solving techniques,
- focuses the group's energy on the common task,
- intervenes and discourages/protects group members from personal 'attacks',
- employs conflict resolution techniques when required,
- recognizes individual and group efforts,
- paraphrases and/or requests group to reflect on the meeting's progress,
- promotes consensus wherever,
- refrains from getting involved with and/or giving personal opinions on the meeting content.

Motivation and teamwork

It can be seen from our discussions of leadership above that an important aspect of leading is encouraging our followers to be motivated. Furthermore, we have also seen (Chapter 3) that to be creative and effective problem solvers we need to be (sufficiently) motivated. Frame 13.5 summarizes some theories of motivation.

Frame 13.5 *Motivation*

Abraham H. Maslow (1943) suggested that there were five groups of needs that drove us onwards:

- Physiological needs – food, sex, sleep, sheer activity, etc.

▶

- Safety needs – a safe, orderly, threat-free, predictable, organized environment.
- Love needs – love, affection and belonging (feeling part of a group).
- Esteem needs – self-respect and self-esteem (strength, achievement, adequacy, confidence, independence, freedom) and the esteem of others (reputation or prestige: recognition, attention, importance or appreciation).
- Need for self-actualization – self-fulfilment.

Somewhere within these groups lies a desire to know and to understand, and be creative.

Clayton Alderfer has more recently proposed that these needs can be classified into just three groups, spread along a horizontal continuum:

- Existence needs – material desires (physiological needs, security, money, etc.).
- Relatedness needs – people relationships (social and esteem needs)
- Growth needs – self-actualization (creative desires).

Charles Handy (1985, pp.34–42) offers the following as our best current thinking on motivation. His model (based on Expectancy Theory) assumes that we are self-activating beings and can to some degree control our own destiny and our own responses to the pressures that others bring to bear on us, that we can select our goals and choose the paths we take in an attempt to attain them. Each of us has a set of needs (such as those suggested by Maslow (Lawler, 1969) and Aldefer) and a set of desired results, and so we perform a calculation to determine how much 'E' (which stands for effort, energy, excitement, enthusiasm, emotion, expenditure of time, expenditure of money, expenditure of passion, etc.) to invest in a particular course of action. This decision, although often unconscious or instinctive, can at other times be conscious and deliberate.

The way we do this calculation is different for each of us and is based on three elements:

- the strength (salience) of the need,
- the likelihood that the amount of 'E' we intend to expend will lead to a particular result,
- the effectiveness (instrumentality) of this result in regard to reducing the need.

(See also Georgopoulos *et al.* (1957), Vroom (1964) and Lawler (1969).

These are all related to our self-concept, the roles we occupy, the extent to which the terms of our psychological contract are met and, of course, our perception of all these things. If any of these elements are zero, then we do nothing!

There are attractive features in all these theories and, despite their inadequacies, they do give us a few 'handles' with which to understand other people's behaviour. But the bottom line is we can not as yet reliably determine someone's motivation from observing their behaviour (and so be able to influence that behaviour by providing the appropriate motivational 'inputs'), and to be honest I hope we never will! So where does that leave us? It would seem that from the research done trying to validate transformational leadership that (an appropriate degree, depending on the person, of) autonomy is a motivating factor. The action research conducted by Synectics seems to confirm this (see below).

Selfish cooperation

As individuals we each possess different needs, abilities, aspirations and goals, but because we *are* individuals, we often have to cooperate with others in order to fulfil these things. Organizations are after all 'groups of people united by a common goal' (Morgan, 1989) though, as Gareth Morgan remarks (1989, p.30), such a phrase masks 'almost all the interesting features of organizations in practice . . . they are rarely so rational and so united as the definition suggests'. For some years now the notion of working together so as to create a 'winning situation for everyone', both between groups of people (or organizations) with different and perhaps conflicting goals and within groups (from the whole organization down to a small group of individuals) has been popular.

Though it has been shown to work 'between organizations' at Synectics and Apple Computer (Sculley, 1988), in some instances this philosophy, interpreted as 'building markets for all rather than competing for market share', is not appropriate, for instance, when several television companies are competing for a single franchise – the market cannot be easily expanded because of the limited number of frequencies available within the internationally agreed television broadcast bands. But most of the time, organizations can work together in this way for the benefit of all. And it can certainly work in small groups.

CPS and teamwork are inextricably linked. The climate of openness, trust and general emotional support required for creative thinking, once established and maintained for a while, has a tendency to spill over into the relationships between group members outside of the problem-solving sessions. Almost inevitably, the overall team spirit of a group that works regularly together in this way will improve. Synectics recognized this phenomenon in their experiences with managers as facilitators/trainers in CPS and innovation. This led to the development of the concept of **autonomous teamwork** (also referred to as **innovative teamwork** by Synectics Inc. and **selfish cooperation** in Nolan, 1981), which evolved via this idea of 'winning situations for everyone'.

Autonomous teamwork

Vincent Nolan (1989, pp.238–9) describes autonomous teamwork as follows:

> People work with maximum commitment and energy when they are doing what they have chosen to do, and are doing it in the way they believe is best for them. If they have no emotional ownership of the task, if they are doing it only because they have been told to, or because it is merely a means of earning a living, they cannot bring their full energy and enthusiasm to it. . . . As well as valuing their personal autonomy, people

also like to work with others; they like to be helpful, to be supported and to identify with a whole (preferably successful) that is larger than themselves. It is natural, therefore, for people to work in a team, especially if it operates in a way that values and encourages individual autonomy.

This also suggests that, to secure the highest level of motivation and commitment from a group of people, we should do our best to preserve their individual autonomy over the way they make their contributions to the group's general aims. Some system has to be in place for this to work. One that provides frequent opportunities for us to exchange openly with each other our needs, wishes and frustrations and to discuss, contribute to and make a special effort to reach consensus over the team's objectives, strategies and values, as well as the means to resolve (but not compromise on) the 'conflict of interests' which will inevitably arise. It also requires a certain amount of positive effort on the part of the individuals concerned, and relies on them taking responsibility for their own actions.

When we 'join' a group we enter into an implicit psychological contract. We agree to help with the group's objectives in anticipation that membership of that group will satisfy our needs for security, friendship, belonging, support, empowerment, a sense of achievement, etc. As long as we perceive this contract as being 'honoured' we are motivated to contribute to the group's activities and prepared to undertake these responsibilities. Synectics are quite specific that we should feel responsible, for those things we actually do to further the team aims, and refer to this as our **action responsibility**. This, along with **open-minded communication** and CPS skills (see Chapter 10), form the basis of autonomous teamwork.

Within this area of action responsibility, Nolan states,

> team members are left to carry out their own job in their own way, without advice, help, ideas, criticism or opinions from their own colleagues, unless they ask for such, except when what they are doing or proposing to do impacts on another team member's area of responsibility. (1989, p.243)

The team is there to offer help only when it is asked for, thus respecting the individual's autonomy, and will assume that the individual is able to ask for this help when it is needed. It is an essential part of this kind of teamwork that requiring help is viewed as a willingness to learn, and not as an inadequacy, which is more usual in our culture. Unsolicited offers of help are not unheard of in such a team, however there is an obligation on the giver to ensure that the offer is not seen as a criticism.

The team must also provide the day-to-day emotional support and encouragement we need to achieve our own objectives and those of the team and to enhance our self-confidence and self-esteem. The keystone of all of this is mutual trust, or the assumption that everyone is working to their best in order to achieve both their own and the team's objectives. While an atmosphere of mutual trust takes a long time to build it can very easily be destroyed. The advice Nolan offers is always to 'assume constructive intent on the part of colleagues, particularly when things go wrong' (1989, p.250). Finally, at least one member of the team should be skilled in CPS, so that when conflicts of interest do occur, as they will do, the team is able to generate alternative ways of meeting the same given objective. This should enable us to find an alternative which will satisfy all those concerned and hence resolve the conflict.

So it would appear that, along with autonomy, a sense of belonging, feeling valued, being offered 'challenges', having a sense of personal achievement and being in the appropriately supportive climate that needs to go along with these things, are all factors that can enhance our motivation.

Group membership

Leadership and group development

Bruce Tuckman's four stages, that we are believed to go through as we come together to form a group (Tuckman and Jensen, 1997) are described in most management texts, so a brief description should suffice here. Initially, we will be tentatively trying to determine the group's purpose, its composition, who should lead it, and our place within it (*forming*). This is followed by a conflict stage where these matters are thrashed out (*storming*). If we survive this process, we can then settle down to establishing the way we intend to fulfil the group's function and what behaviours and degrees of openness, trust, etc. are appropriate for achieving this end (*norming*). Only then can our group start *performing* productively.

John Sedgwick (1996) offers a new way of looking at 'forming, storming, norming and performing': rather than letting other things just happen whilst we are trying to get on with the task in hand, we accept that not only does the task need to be 'organized' and done, we need to develop trust within the group. If at each stage we deliberately try to build the trust element, the task side will come together and be effective far quicker.

Beginning with the 'starting' (forming) stage we, as facilitator/leader, first try and create an open and supportive climate, determining 'how we will talk to each other'; then we are able to discuss the purpose and goals of our group ('what are we here for') with less wariness, competitive behaviour and anxiety. At the 'developing' (storming) stage, we need to decide how we are going to deal with the differences (resolve conflicts) that are certain to occur. Perhaps then we can determine/decide roles and responsibilities, without any confrontations, animosity, vendettas, etc. A sharing of our preferred Belbin roles (see Frame 13.8) at this time would identify some potential conflicts that need to be addressed.

Next, in the 'consolidating' (norming) stage, we should concentrate on valuing our differences and bonding (or 'how we can combine our strengths'); this should ease agreeing the procedures and methods we are going to adopt to get the task done. By now, we should be effectively getting on with the task (performing), but we do not stop there. Sedgwick's fourth stage, 'extending', involves reaching out and connecting with others so that we can build partnerships with those whose goals we share.

As far as problem-solving groups are concerned, the establishment of the composition, purpose and norms of the group is usually in the domain of the process leader. Our only concern then is how to get to the performing stage as soon as possible. If we assume that our leader can 'skilfully' perform the necessary 'leadership acts', can quickly gain the group's trust and commitment and can communicate and demonstrate the appropriate behaviours required of the group, then the warm-up exercises recommended elsewhere in this book will serve to reinforce these desired group norms.

What goes on during a group activity?

Effective communication is an integral part of successful problem solving. Without it, we are unable adequately to ascertain other people's cognitions, beliefs, attitudes, opinions, expectations and values concerning the problem situation, or subsequently relay back to the owners of the problem our ideas and possible solutions. In a group problem-solving situation, not only do we have the above interchanges of information taking place, but this is being done face to face amidst all of the usual interpersonal interactions occurring within the group. We may also be asking people to do or say some 'strange' things to encourage creativity, which makes it paramount that every participant must understand what is expected of them, and what the 'ground rules' are. So let us now look briefly at the communication process within a group.

Robert Bales in the late 1940s/1950s identified 12 types of communication between members of a problem-solving group. These are summarized in Frame 13.6. Groups B and C are associated with the task being performed by the group, whereas A and D relate to the human relations within the group. Together these acts determine the type and quality of the process employed by the group to reach its objectives. These different acts of communication were observed from overt behaviour and checked by questioning group members afterwards.

Frame 13.6 *Communication within groups*

Classification of acts of communication (Bales and Slater, 1956, p.267)

A. Positive reactions
- Shows solidarity, raises others' status, jokes, gives help, reward
- Shows tension release, shows satisfaction, laughs
- Agrees, shows passive acceptance, understands, concurs, complies

B. Problem-solving attempts
- Gives suggestion, direction, implying autonomy for other
- Gives opinion, evaluation, analysis, expresses feeling, wish
- Gives orientation, information, repeats, clarifies, confirms

C. Questions
- Asks for orientation, information, repetition, confirmation
- Asks for opinion, evaluation, analysis, expression of feeling

▶

	• Asks for suggestion, direction, possible ways of action
D. Negative reactions	• Disagrees, shows passive rejection, formality, withholds help
	• Shows tension increase, asks for help, withdraws 'out of field'
	• Shows antagonism, deflates others' status, defends or asserts self

Given that it is commonly felt that these acts of communication constitute an exhaustive list of behaviours, which do we wish to encourage for creative thinking and problem solving, and which should we try to eliminate? At first sight it would appear that those in group D are of little or no value and are thus best discouraged. However, Bales himself identified group C as being generally negative with respect to accomplishing the task, and others have since tended to agree with him.

Synectics similarly believe that there are four main interactions that take place when people work in groups, which affect the group's productivity. These can be described as:

- offering ideas, suggestions and information to the group;
- supporting someone else's contribution;
- evaluating or rejecting someone else's contribution;
- asking questions.

While these activities are a very natural and necessary part of working in a group, Synectics warn that all four of these interactions are just as likely to have a detrimental effect on a group's productivity. For example, questions can be used as a put down: 'You're not really suggesting that we do that are you?' Other examples of the negative effects of these interactions are:

- Ideas can be used as the ammunition in one-upmanship games.
- Someone may present an idea so forcefully that it inadvertently overshadows or excludes equally worthy contributions from less forceful group members.
- Praising the merits of an idea ingenuously, or just more than it is worth, is a fairly effective way of killing an idea.
- Too much support too soon may also encourage a group to settle on a solution before it has been adequately thought through.
- Being prematurely critical of an idea may at best cause a basically good idea to be rejected, and at worst may inhibit further positive participation from the contributor.

We should also remember that the effect of these interactions can be contrary to their intentions, no matter how positive those intentions may have been.

Synectics place particular emphasis on the use of questions. We often need to ask questions to clarify our understanding of what someone else has said, and to gather information. But questions asked at the wrong time, for instance, when it is not desirable or really necessary to understand what has just been said (see *listening for ideas* on page 240), inevitably slow down the flow of ideas. Synectics also believe that often what is actually happening when people ask questions is that they are checking out the 'goodness' of their idea prior to voicing it – the old **self-censor** again (see Chapter 3). What they are really saying is 'Who, what, when, why or how is . . ., because if such and such is the case, perhaps we could . . . (idea)'. Being on the receiving end of questions often makes us defensive. One very simple thing each of us can do, which in the long term can considerably improve our communications, is to (honestly) give the reason for wanting to know the answer to a question, as we ask it.

As we have been looking at aspects of leadership and the typical interpersonal interactions that take place within a group, we have been dealing with some of the behaviours required of the members of a creative work group. Chapter 3 contains other indications of our expectations of their contributions and now would seem to be a good time to summarize all of these qualities.

Group membership skills

Harold Leavitt (1978, p. 198) remarks that

> almost all of us are quite expert on many matters of group process, but, curiously, we seldom use what we know to improve the operation of groups. We are expert in the sense that we can go home after a meeting and describe the group's psychology and social structure in considerable detail over dinner, and we know which particular behaviours were dysfunctional to the group.

My experience concurs with this opinion and I believe that our first responsibility as members of any group is to be open about our feelings, and to attempt to deal with any perceived 'injustices'. This may exacerbate any interpersonal conflict present in the group but, as Leavitt goes on to say (p.211), 'the preferred course would seem to be to promote rather than limit communication, that is, to accept and deal with information about personal feelings and personal needs as well as with information about pertinent facts'. The variety of perceptions, opinions and personalities amongst group members is one of its most valuable resources.

In a CPS group, everyone is expected to give freely of their ideas, both obviously useful or interesting ideas and wildly speculative ones. Thus, we have an obligation to suppress as best we can any conceptual blocks that we possess, and also our natural tendency to criticize others immediately they make a suggestion. Quinlivan-Hall and Renner (1994, p.11) describe the tasks of CPS group members as:

- take an active role – participate
- commit to the group and the process (if a participant cannot commit the time and energy to being a full-time member, the group may either accept a part-time role or ask the person to leave)

- remain open to new information and ideas
- display patience with others and the process
- listen – listening shows respect for others
- avoid participating in 'shark attacks'
- share the responsibility for managing the process
- confront those interfering with the group's progress
- help facilitator and recorder to stay in their roles
- do homework and follow through on commitments.

The personal and interpersonal skills required by a group or team member (when they are not leading) are nicely summed up by Colin Hastings *et al.* (1986, pp.97–8), who speak of the need for team members to be 'active followers' and say the following about these people. Particularly note the references concerning asking for help; this, as we have seen, is a fundamental aspect of autonomous teamwork. If we are given this autonomy, and have taken responsibility for our own actions, we will be left alone to get on with it without interference from others. This means that if we need help we are expected to ask for it.

> They know when to be in on the action and when to pull out. They know when to give help and when to ask for help. At times, they will provide push and direction but equally they are able to allow themselves to be pulled by others. Their willingness to follow does not come from the passive obedience to the leader or others, but from their active loyalty, respect and personal commitment to all the members of the team. They are willing to be led by any of the team members provided that they can be persuaded that it is in the best interests of the team as a whole. But above all they assume responsibility. They take it upon themselves for instance to ensure that they understand how their role affects other people's roles. They are driven by a desire not to let other people down, and when, as can always happen, this looks likely they take active steps to help their colleagues avoid or minimize the consequent problems.
>
> When they don't understand they ask. Members of 'superteams' have no fear of looking foolish if they don't know because they recognise that they will need to learn from and value each other if the team is to benefit from its diversity of talent.

Selecting groups/teams

Many people have tried to 'convert' Bales's classification of communication 'types' into a list of group roles, patterns of behaviour that a person may adopt when participating in group working. His original four roles (task specialist, human relations specialist, scapegoat and the rest of the group) have been expanded to as many as 15. Some researchers have 'divided' their roles between task/problem related and people/process related subgroups, others have not. This dilemma indicates the existence of 'grey' roles that defy this type of subclassification, for instance, the 'gatekeeper' role – someone that knows a lot of things or knows where/from whom to find them out. This is a useful person, with access to a wealth of information and contacts, but is this role assisting the problem directly, or the process of problem solving?

We also mentioned earlier Tuckman's 'storming' (for roles) stage in group development. The reason for this seems to stem from the generally agreed belief that, whatever these roles are, we need a 'balance' of them for a successful team, and that we each have our own preferences for occupying certain roles! So we will explore these ideas a little further.

There is a method for ensuring the balance of teams based on the use of Kolb's **Learning Style Inventory** (1976), which highlights the connection between how we learn and our problem-solving skills (see also **MindSpring** theory, Chapter 3). This inventory furnishes four scores which indicate the extent to which we prefer to use *active experimentation, reflective observation, concrete experience* and *abstract conceptualization* as methods of learning. Kolb suggested that teams should have all-round performance, with at least one team member who is predominant in a particular quadrant for all four quadrants shown in Figure 13.2. This figure also shows how certain group roles and the **left/right brain** concepts (see Appendix 7) have been associated with this grid in the past.

Listed in Frame 13.7 are the group roles identified by Belbin (1981) as being needed for a 'fully effective group', with other roles I came across at the Manchester Business School (CMBS) in the early 1980s, and the six management styles of **Action Profiling**, another technique used for selecting and ensuring the balance of a group.

Figure 13.2

Learning style

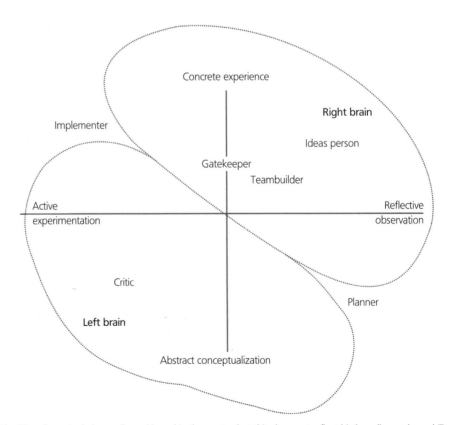

The 'Coordinator' role is usually positioned in the centre, but this does not reflect his/her all-round capability.

Frame 13.7 *Group roles*

R.M. Belbin	Source unknown (MBS)	Action Profiling
Chairman	Coordinator	
Teamworker	Teambuilder	
Shaper		Determined
Resource-investigator	Gatekeeper	
Plant	Ideas-person	Exploratory
Monitor-evaluator	Critic	⎧ Investigative ⎨ ⎩ Evaluative
Company worker	⎧ Implementer ⎨ ⎩ Planner	Anticipatory
Completer-finisher		Timing

I have equated the descriptions of the two sets of roles with each other and with these management styles, by comparing Belbin's description of his eight roles (see Frame 13.8), Carol-Lynne Moore's (1982) summary of the six styles 'measured' by Action Profiling (see Frame 13.9) and my recollection of the MBS roles. There appears be some consensus between these three views of group/team roles, though there were two instances where this 'match' proved a little troublesome. First, the Company worker, the 'practical organizer' whose forte is 'schedules, charts and plans', is certainly an Implementer, but sounds like a Planner as well, two diametrically opposed types on the Learning Style grid. Whilst it is by no means impossible to find someone with that propensity, I suspect it would require two people to fulfil that role. Second, I had a little trouble assigning the Anticipatory and Timing styles of Action Profiling, since both the Company worker and the Completer-Finisher, the person who 'checks the details' and 'chases' us about keeping to schedule, seem to have aspects of both these styles.

Frame 13.8 *R.M. Belbin's team roles*

It is possible to identify eight distinct management styles:

Chairman

Coordinates the team's efforts.
  Calm, self-confident, disciplined, focused and balanced. Talks and listens well, is open and without prejudice. Not especially intelligent or creative.

Teamworker

Looks after the personal relationships in the team.

▶

Socially aware, mild-mannered and sensitive. Is supportive by being a good listener, encouraging, harmonizing and understanding. Uncompetitive, but can be indecisive.

Shaper

Spurs the team into action.

Highly strung, outgoing and dominant. Has drive/passion, and is not slow to challenge ineffectiveness, complacency or self-deception. Can be provocative, irritable and impatient.

Resource-investigator

Keeps in touch with other teams.

Extrovert, enthusiastic, curious and easy to get along with. Responds to a challenge. Brings new contacts, ideas and developments to the group. Can lose interest after the initial enthusiasm.

Plant (Innovator)

Provides creative thinking in the team.

Introverted but intellectually dominant, being the most imaginative and most intelligent member of the team. Unorthodox and a maverick. Can be 'up in the clouds', careless of details and may resent criticism.

Monitor-evaluator

Provides critical thinking in the team.

Also intelligent, but analytical rather than creative. Sees all the options and is able to dissect ideas/see flaws in arguments. Is dependable, has good judgement. May not have the inspiration, personality/ability to motivate others.

Company worker

Gets the work done (Implementer)

Practical organizer, who turns ideas into manageable tasks. A good administrator, methodical, predictable, hardworking, trustworthy and efficient. Is conservative in outlook and can lack flexibility.

Completer-finisher

Keeping the team on its toes.

Painstakingly orderly and conscientious. Checks work details, schedules, etc., identifies errors and omissions, and 'chases' others with his/her sense of urgency. Worries (sometimes unnecessarily) about things. His/her relentless follow through is not always popular.

To which, Alan Chapman (www.businessballs.com) has added.

Specialist?

Provides rare knowledge and skills.

◄
> Single minded, self-starting and dedicated, but contributes only in a narrow area and can dwell on technicalities.
>
> *Belbin (1981) and Handy (1985 pp.166–7)*

Very seldom do we have the luxury of choosing our team and so it is perhaps a little unrealistic to put forward these roles solely as a tool for group selection. However, they can be used as a sort of checklist to determine how 'balanced' our group is and could possibly offer assistance in selecting additional or replacement members for the team. A word of warning for anyone intending to check the 'balance' of a group; we need to guard against such an exercise throwing up a *halo effect* (see page 52) around the perceived shortcomings of the present group membership.

Frame 13.9 *Action Profiles*

Our Action Profile describes the style with which we approach problems (apply 'attention' to the problem situation), make decisions (establish our 'intention' to choose between the alternatives generated by the problem solving) and go about the implementation of the chosen course of action (exhibit our 'commitment' to that decision). These three aspects of problem solving and decision making contribute six basic management styles (investigative, determined, timing, and exploratory, evaluative, anticipatory), depending on whether we are a more 'assertive' ('focusing, pushing and pacing their actions to make things happen') or 'perspective' ('by relating their decisions to each other or to the whole they design their decisions to achieve the desired results') person. No one style is 'right', we are a mixture of various proportions of all six. The aim is once again to ensure that the team is strong in all areas. Knowing a person's Action Profile tells us how that person likes to work, and takes away much of the frustration caused by them 'unexpectedly' not doing things in quite the way that we would have done!

Action Profiles also show our propensity to share our problem-solving and decision-making processes with others, or to work on our own, as well as ratings on several other more general decision-making skills, such as adaptability. It does not attempt to measure our aptitude at problem solving and decision making. Synectics Ltd have used Action Profiling not only to attempt to ensure an overall balance in their team, but also to highlight and forewarn team members where potential clashes might occur between individuals because of their differing styles of working, so that these individuals can compensate for this in advance when dealing with each other, and, since the consultants often work in pairs, to match them up in a complementary way.

Carol-Lynne Moore (1982, pp.16–17)

If we assume that our group has a process leader with coordinating and team-building skills, a determined task specialist/problem owner (shaper), and preferably a gatekeeper already, five additional personality traits can be identified that would be useful to us. We would like to have someone who is imaginative and prepared to speculate openly and explore ideas (ideas person); someone who tends to be analytic and logical (investigative) and has a natural tendency to evaluate possibilities (critic, 'analyst' is a slightly less pejorative term); a practically minded person who quickly sees how something can be done or organized and can/will carry this through (implementer); somebody whom I would describe as a person who pays minute attention to details and has a good sense of timing (finisher); and finally someone who is a good planner, is perceptive to the necessary stages of development and who can anticipate the consequences of these (planner). It should always be remembered that real people will possess several of these qualities and will do so in varying proportions. The advice therefore is to select (if you have the opportunity) a group of people who together provide a complete set of the qualities mentioned above.

Conflict resolution

We started this chapter with some rules on attaining consensus, so it seemed appropriate considering our recent discussions of group members' differences by finishing with some advice on conflict resolution. Based on ideas from Sedgwick (1996) and de Bono (1985) the suggestion is:

Instead of what usually happens:

- see potential for conflict and put up defences (the point of no return!?),
- get righteous (no hope after this!),
- start 'sabre rattling',
- escalate conflict by continuous minor skirmishes, or by a full-scale pre-emptive strike;

try to:

- see the potential for conflict (call a 'time out'),
- explore (the differing) perceptions of the situation,
- sort perceptions into areas of agreement, areas of disagreement and irrelevants,
- problem solve remaining issues to reach mutually acceptable solutions.

It is obviously easier for a third party or facilitator to 'see' the potential for conflict between two people, than it is for those two people to do so on their own, but it is not impossible!

The Synectics CPS process, in the form of their **Consensus Meeting** (see Chapter 12), and especially their **itemized response** (see page 170) and **open-minded communications** (see page 233) techniques are very helpful in resolving the 'remaining issues' (Nolan, 1990).

Summary

The key points to be derived from this chapter are: first, that for CPS and many other groups as well, what we require is a different type of leader from the conventional stereotypes, a process leader who can create the atmosphere of openness and trust required for creativity. Second, though our process leader is an important factor in ensuring a successful outcome from our group's endeavours, he or she cannot do this alone. Along with our process leader must come a willing band of highly motivated and committed, active followers, prepared to share the responsibility for any success and provide emotional support in times of difficulty. Last, high degrees of autonomy and emotional involvement in the group's activities (elicited from feeling that their individuality is valued) would appear to be factors in ensuring the high level of motivation required.

14 Creativity, EQ, SQ, NLP, metaphors, etc.

> The objective of this chapter is to briefly explore a few recent ideas/theories that seem to be connected with creativity, such as emotional and spiritual Intelligence, the significance of metaphors in our everyday lives, neurolinguistic programming, different styles of creativity, etc.

Introduction

In the last couple of decades a number of concepts and theories have emerged/evolved that seem to have more than just a 'passing' connection with creativity. We will now briefly delve into these things, starting with the concept of multiple intelligences.

Multiple intelligences

IQ tests are very good at measuring whatever it is they are measuring, but most people now agree that this is not 'a single, general capacity for conceptualization and problem solving'. For a start, they do not seem to measure our creative thinking abilities too well. J.P. Guilford (1950) said that, although there was probably a 'modest relationship' between IQ and creativity, 'we must look well beyond the boundaries of IQ if we are to fathom the domain of creativity'. In a similar vein, J.W. Getzels and P.W. Jackson (1962) say

> we are not saying there is no relationship between IQ and creative thinking. Obviously, the feeble minded by IQ standards are not going to be creative. But at the high average level and above, the two are sufficiently independent to warrant differentiation.

Michael Kirton (1994b, p.xvii), whose ideas we came across in Chapter 3 (page 46) and which we will explore further later, suggests that although our creative style has little to do with IQ we may have a 'level' of creativity that *is* related to our IQ. So are there different types of intelligence? The answer would seem to be yes – Howard Gardner (1993a) describes seven varieties of intelligence: linguistic, musical, logical-mathematical, spatial, bodily-kinesthetic and two personal intelligences, but where is creative thinking? According to Gardner (1993a, p.xxi), 'creativity should not be thought of as inhering principally in the brain, the mind or the personality of a single individual', but thought of as emerging from the interactions of the individual, what they are doing and what the surrounding 'field' thinks of that. We saw in Chapter 3 that one of the reasons we may feel that our creativity has been attenuated or inhibited is because others may not see that what we are doing is creative (even though it might be) and that creative-thinking skills can be (re)developed, so I cannot accept Gardner's comment in its entirety.

However, of particular interest to us here are the two 'personal' intelligences, described by Gardner (1993b, p.9; 1989) as:

- '*Interpersonal intelligence* is the ability to understand other people; what motivates them, how they work, how to work cooperatively with them.' (Gardner with Krechevsky, 1993, p.9). It includes the capacity 'to discern and respond appropriately to the moods, temperaments, motivations and desires of other people, (Gardner and Hatch, 1989).'

- '*Intrapersonal intelligence* is a capacity to form an accurate veridical [truthful, realistic] model of oneself and to be able to use that model to operate effectively in life' (Gardner and Krechevsky, 1993, p.9). The key to self-knowledge, it includes 'access to one's own feelings and the ability to discriminate among them and draw upon them to guide behaviour' (Gardner and Hatch, 1989).

Goleman (1996, p.38) reports that later Gardner 'split' interpersonal skills into leadership, the ability to nurture relationships and keep friends, the ability to resolve conflicts and the skills of social analysis. Gardner also has said (1993a) that 'some form of Spiritual Intelligence may exist'.

Keep these last three paragraphs in mind as we move on.

Emotional Intelligence

A definition of **Emotional Intelligence** (EQ) was given in Chapter 13, page 316, but here are some others.

Victor Dulewicz and Malcolm Higgs (1998), reviewing the work of other researchers[1] into EQ over the last 15 years summarized its components as follows:

- Self-awareness (knowing one's emotions, recognizing a feeling when it happens)
- Emotional management (handling feelings so that they are appropriate)
- Self-motivation (and delaying gratification)
- Empathy (recognizing emotions in others)
- (Handling) relationships (managing emotions in others, having social competences)
- Communication (including being open-minded, speaking one's mind and listening)

- Personal style (including being able to manage stress and take responsibility, and being self-controlled).

The first five of these were identified by Salovey and Mayer (1990) and some of their descriptions are given above.

Victor Dulewicz and Malcolm Higgs (1999, pp.7–11) then went on to identify seven elements (or competencies), which contribute to EQ, and have developed a measure of EQ based on these:

- *Self-awareness* – the awareness of our own feelings and the ability to recognize and manage these feelings in a way which we feel that we can control, which includes a degree of self-belief that we can do this.

- *Interpersonal sensitivity* – the awareness of the needs and perceptions of others in arriving at decisions and proposing solutions to problems and challenges taking account of these – the ability to build from this awareness and achieve 'buy-in' to decisions and action ideas – the willingness to keep our thoughts on solutions open and actively listen to, and reflect on, the reactions and inputs from others.

- *Emotional resilience* – the ability to perform consistently in a range of situations under pressure and to adapt our behaviour appropriately – a facility to balance the needs of the situation and task with the needs and concerns of the individuals involved – the ability to retain a focus on a course of action or need for results in the face of personal challenge or criticism.

- *Motivation* – the drive and energy to achieve clear results and make an impact and both balance short- and long-term goals with an ability to pursue demanding goals in the face of rejection or questioning.

- *Influence* – the ability to persuade others to change a viewpoint based on the understanding of their position and the recognition of the need to listen to this perspective and provide a rationale for change.

- *Decisiveness* – the ability to arrive at clear decisions and drive their implementation when presented with incomplete or ambiguous information using both rational and 'emotional' or insightful perceptions of key issues and implications.

- *Conscientiousness and integrity* – the ability to display a clear commitment to a course of action in the face of a challenge and to match 'words with deeds' in encouraging others to support the chosen direction – the personal commitment to pursuing an ethical solution to a difficult (business) issue or problem.

Clearly EQ subsumes Gardner's personal intelligences.

David Ryback (1998, p.64), building on the concept of EQ, offers us some principles for a *new team ethic* as the way forward for successful organizations:

- Building trusting relationships and effective communication through risk-taking openness, effective listening skills and learning to respect differences of opinion while building on a consensus that proves worthwhile.

- Creative innovation through group discussions that foster openness and playful opposition.

- Fostering a sense of self-appreciation and team pride through group discussion focused on patterns of successful decision making and appropriate actions based on emotional insights.

- Learning to distinguish between decisions based on fact and those based on emotion, as well as the most effective balance between the two for each particular individual.

- Reducing stress through the encouragement of healthy fitness habits and relaxation techniques.

… which he says has the following benefits: a (self-managed) team with less conflict, a greater sense of mutual support, more cooperation and enhanced communication skills, a better understanding of their roles in achieving goals and a stronger sense of being appreciated. This is not dissimilar to the concept of Autonomous Teamwork we came across in Chapter 13 (see page 319) that developed out of the Synectics CPS process!

Spiritual Intelligence

Moving on from here, Danah Zohar and Ian Marshall (2000, p.5) describe EQ as having a sense of, and being able to judge, the situation you are in and knowing how to respond/behave appropriately *within* it – the boundaries of the situation; whereas **Spiritual Intelligence** (SQ) allows us to ask 'why we have these rules or this situation [in fact whether we want to be here in the first place] or whether either could [or be made to] be different or better'; that is, working *with* (the boundaries of) the situation.

SQ, Zohar and Marshall say,

> allows human beings to be creative, to change the rules and to alter the situation … [and] gives us, our ability to discriminate, our moral sense, an ability to temper rigid rules with understanding and compassion and … to see when compassion and understanding have their limits. … We use SQ to wrestle with questions of good and evil and to envision unrealized possibilities – to dream, to aspire, to raise ourselves out of the mud.

They maintain (2000, p.12) that IQ is the product of serially connected, neural tracts and are typically 'point-to-point' like those in the optic nerve, and in the brain stem and spinal cord, 'which allow the brain to follow rules, to think logically and rationally, step by step'. EQ is the product of (parallel) associative neural networks, also found in various parts of the brain and body, but especially in the cortical regions. These neural networks have a learning ability and are responsible for our associative thinking; 'our emotion driven, pattern recognizing, habit building intelligence'. Then, citing the works of neuroscientists such as Wolf Singer and Rodolfo Llinas in the 1990s, they claim that it is the recently discovered, all encompassing, unifying, synchronous 40 (+/−5) Hz 'waves' of neural oscillations all over the brain – which provide us with what they call 'unitive thinking', the 'essential feature of consciousness' – that are the neurological basis of SQ.

Zohar and Marshall (2000, pp.15–16, 33) say that the indications of a person with a highly developed SQ include:

- the capacity to be flexible (actively and spontaneously adaptive)*
- a high degree of self-awareness
- a capacity to face and use suffering
- a capacity to face and transcend pain
- the quality of being inspired by vision and values
- a reluctance to do unnecessary harm
- a tendency to see the connections between diverse things*
- a marked tendency to ask 'Why?' and 'What if?' questions and to seek 'fundamental' answers*
- a facility for working against convention.*

(Note that quite a few of these traits marked* we have already linked with creativity.)

Such a person 'is also likely to be a **servant leader**[2] – someone who is responsible for bringing higher vision and values to others and showing them how to use it, in other words, a person who inspires others' and who 'has a sense of deep values and who consciously serves these values in his [or her] leadership style'.

Zohar and Marshall's (2000, pp.135, 161) so-called 'Lotus of Self' maps six personality types (based primarily on the work of J.L. Holland,[3] with 'reinforcement' from the works of Jung[4] and R.B. Cattell[5]), and offers us 'six paths towards greater Spiritual Intelligence' based on these, which are:

- Path of Duty
- Path of Nurturing
- Path of Knowledge
- Path of Personal Transformation
- Path of Brotherhood
- Path of Servant Leadership.

Since you may have more than one of these traits already well developed, there may be more than one (development) path you can/should 'travel', culminating in fully developing/travelling all six!

Zohar and Marshall also offer us (2000, p.263) seven practical steps to a better SQ:

- Become aware of where I am now.
- Feel strongly that I want to change.
- Reflect on what my own centre is and on what are my deepest motivations.
- Discover and dissolve obstacles.
- Explore many possibilities to go forward.
- Commit myself to a path.
- Remain aware that there are many paths.

Story so far

If everything above is true, then it would appear that to be creative we must have a high EQ and SQ, so perhaps we should try to develop these things at the same time as developing our creative-thinking skills if we want to be truly creative. However, I think that there may be a different 'spin' we can put on this. Given (as we have said earlier) that participation in group CPS experiential training courses, such as those run by Synectics, and the partaking in group CPS sessions on real problems involving others, encourages open-minded communication, awareness of these others' perceptions, feelings and behaviour and hence team-building, as well as your creative-thinking skills, these things may encourage/lead to the development of our EQ and SQ!

NLP

The essence of **Neurolinguistic Programming** (NLP) can be summarized as follows:

> NLP is a practical set of models, skills and techniques for thinking and acting effectively in the world . . . a way of studying how people excel in any field and teaching these patterns to others (O'Connor and Seymour, (1995, pp.xiii, 1)

NLP 'builds' considerably on the concept of **mental set** that we came across in Chapter 3 (see page 52) and 'positive thinking'. Joseph O'Connor and John Seymour (1995, p.4) explain that the world is so vast and rich that we have to simplify what we 'see' to give it meaning. We do this by attending only to those aspects of the world that interest us, and ignoring others. However, these *filters* that we put on our perceptions determine what sort of world we live in. They say, 'If you go through the world looking for excellence, you will find excellence. If you go through the world looking for problems, you will find problems'. The latter part should not be taken too literally; it does not contradict what we have said elsewhere about the desirability of proactively looking for problems, it simply suggests that if we are always looking for the negative side of things, that's all we will ever see.

> Very narrow beliefs, interests and perceptions will make the world impoverished, predictable and dull. The same world can be rich and exciting. The difference lies not in the world, but in the filters through which we perceive it. (O'Connor and Seymour, 1995, p.4)

We have many natural, useful and necessary filters, so what are they? First, we have already seen in the quote above that our beliefs act as a filter, and so does language (we will pursue this below when discussing **metaphors**). Second, there are some basic NLP filters (referred to as **behavioural frames**), which are essentially to do with the way we think about how we act – there often being two ways of doing this. We have already seen that we can look at new situations as problems and deal with them as some unnecessary evil that we have to cope with, or, we could think of them as 'outcomes' (learning experiences, opportunities, challenges, etc.).

Other examples of filters are: the propensity of some to ask 'why' rather than 'how' questions (instead of worrying about why something happened try to understand how it happened). Instead of 'dwelling' on failure, see it as feedback from a situation you can learn from. See things as possibilities (what you can do, what choices are there) rather than necessities (the constraints of the situation) (compare with **tunnel vision**, page 53). And adopt an attitude of curiosity and fascination rather than one of making assumptions – children learn quickly because they are, at least initially, curious and (because they know they don't know) and are not worried about looking stupid (see also, Chapter 3) (O'Connor and Seymour, 1995, pp.5–6). When we are thinking, that is, communicating with ourselves, or communicating with others, we should take care where we place our attention and try to enlarge our filters so that we notice things that we had not previously.

What else can/should we do? O'Connor and Seymour (1995, pp.8–9) tell us that NLP is all about *outcome, acuity* and *flexibility*. We need to know what we want from a situation; that is, have a clear idea of our desired 'outcome'. We need to make sure we 'see' what we are getting (sensory 'acuity'). And keep changing what we do until we get what we want ('flexibility').

If you do not know where you are going, it makes it difficult to get there.

If what you are doing is not working, do something else, anything else.

Our desired outcomes should be stated in a precise and positive way, be primarily in our control, and be of an appropriate size given the resources we have (**Synectics' Backward/Forward Planning**, see page 107 may be helpful in getting the 'size' of your outcome right). It can also be helpful to **visualize** both it and the ways we are going to know that we have achieved it.

O'Connor and Seymour (1995, pp.77–82) describe Robert Dilts's Unified Field of NLP as a simple, elegant model for thinking about personal change, learning and communications. It provides us with a number of interdependent levels at which we can learn and change ourselves. It enables us to understand and (if appropriate) rebalance these things

Central to everything is our *spiritual* level, the deepest one – this guides and shapes our lives and underpins our existence (Why am I here? What is my purpose?). Then comes *identity* – our basic sense of self, our core values and mission in life. From out of these (should) come our *beliefs* – the basis of our daily actions; then our *capability* – the behaviours, general skills and strategies we use; our *behaviour* – the actions we carry out no matter what our capabilities; and the *environment* – the surroundings and other people we react to.

Problems arise from a lack of balance, for example our actions (behaviour) may not be commensurate with our capabilities (perhaps because we do not believe in what we are doing any more), or we may just be placing too much/little emphasis on certain levels, for example putting into your actions (behaviour) more than you need (or wanted) to do because of your work ethic (your beliefs). Neither of these situations is desirable, both can cause stress and everything associated with it. And one thing we should be wary about is that 'behaviour is often [wrongly] taken as evidence of identity or capability' (O'Connor and Seymour, 1995, p.80). Frequent consideration of what we are doing in relation to these levels can pinpoint where we need to change.

As hinted at above, apart from self-development, NLP has things to say about communicating with others and facilitating CPS groups. Achieving our desired outcomes often involves working cooperatively with others. In both these situations, creating a rapport, and feelings of trust, with and amongst a group of people is paramount.

Rapport can be created by the language that we use; for example, saying 'Yes and . . .', rather than 'Yes but . . .' helps gain rapport. But when you are trying to communicate with others and/or trying to create rapport, you should not just be attending to verbal communications. In any interaction, Mehrabian and Ferris (1967) say, words contribute the least, at 8 per cent, to our understanding; body language (55 per cent) and voice tonality (38 per cent) contribute far more. Or, as Richard Bandler and John Grinder (1990, p.17) put it, 'you will always get answers to your questions insofar as you have the sensory apparatus to notice the responses. And rarely will the verbal or conscious part of the response be relevant'. And remember, 'the meaning of your communication is the response you get' (Bandler and Grinder, 1990, p.61).

The main ways of creating rapport are, not surprisingly, connected with non-verbal communication. These are (deliberately) matching your body language, the tonality (speed, volume and rhythm) of your speech, your eye contact and/or even your breathing patterns to those of another. 'Mirroring' someone else's body language is natural, you will find that you cannot help doing it with people you get on with really well, but this *can* be done deliberately. We are talking about trying to 'match their body language sensitively and with respect, [this is] not mimicry, which is [the] noticeable, exaggerated and indiscriminate copying of another person's movements, and is usually considered offensive' (O'Connor and Seymour, 1995, p.20). In NLP terms this is called **pacing**. Once we have achieved that then it may be possible to **lead** someone to do different things by subtly changing our behaviour if we so wish.

Acting as a facilitator, once rapport and trust have been achieved, you can use body language to control the group. For example, given a seated group and a standing facilitator, one way of 'breaking up' a potential conflict over the merit of someone's idea is to step between them, turn your back on the vociferous critic and address the idea giver. Having captured his/her idea you can turn to the other person and try to capture the idea 'behind' his/her criticism.

There is far more to NLP than this, in particular regarding its use in psychotherapy, but I hope you will already be seeing the connections with creativity and EQ: the positive outlook it encourages in us cannot help but make us more open-minded (and hence creative), and the suggestions/tools regarding communications and creating rapport should improve our awareness of and relationships with others, thus developing our facilitation skills and our EQ.

Metaphors

We have seen earlier (Chapter 7) that the use of metaphors can be invaluable when generating ideas, but recent research suggests that rather than being something we call upon when problem solving, metaphors pervade all of our everyday lives. As George Lakoff and Mark Johnson (1980, p.3) put it, 'our concepts structure what we perceive, how we get around in the world, and how we relate to other people . . . [and] our conceptual system is largely metaphorical'.

We defined and gave examples of metaphors earlier (pages 141 and 147), but here are some more. 'The essence of metaphor is understanding and experiencing one kind of thing in terms of another. (Lakoff and Johnson, 1980, p.5). 'Metaphors work by representing one experience (usually more abstract, vague or intangible) in terms of another experience (usually more concrete, explicit or commonplace)' (Lawley and Tompkins, 2000, p.19).

James Lawley and Penny Tompkins (2000, p.10) tell us that metaphors can be verbal (overt, embedded), nonverbal (body language, sounds – sighs, grunts, etc.), material (physical things) and imaginative (images, feelings, sensory perceptions). An example of an overt verbal metaphor is 'he has got *muscles of steel*', and an example of an non-overt verbal metaphor is 'I'm feeling *up* today'. Metaphors are pervasive in the English language.

Metaphors enable people to understand, reason about and explain abstract concepts, [and] help people organize complex sets of thoughts, feelings, behaviours and events into a coherent whole (Lawley and Tompkins, 2000, p.19).

Lawley and Tompkins (2000, pp.6–7) maintain that metaphors are made up of symbols and explain this with the example, 'I feel like my back is being pinned against a wall' (the metaphor) which contains the symbols 'I', 'my back', 'a wall' and implies another, 'whatever or whoever is doing the pinning'. The idiosyncratic way each of us uses metaphors and symbols can reveal our personal history, our spiritual nature, our sense of destiny and the 'unknown and hidden' aspects of our lives.

Their interest in metaphors is mainly from the psychotherapeutic point of view, where **symbolic modelling**, a process which uses **clean language**[6] (developed by David Grove) is used. This facilitates a person's discovery of 'how their metaphors express his/her way of being in the world – including how that way of being evolves', . . . '[this self-modelling] lays the foundation for a beneficial change in the configuration of their metaphor landscape [the sum total of their symbolic perceptions], which in turn results in new patterns of thoughts, feelings and behaviours' (2000 pp.17, 82). However, they say (2000, p.23) that 'symbolic modelling can also be applied to the more general endeavour of modelling human cognition and learning'. Recognizing and understanding someone's use of metaphors can create empathetic rapport and facilitate communication. Appreciating our own use of metaphors can lead to self-development – by examining the metaphors we live by we can construct our (symbolic) model which corresponds to the way we perceive ourselves, others and the larger scheme of things. A connection here with NLP should be obvious.

Assuming that our conceptual systems are mostly metaphoric, the implications are even more significant than what we have said above.

> Our understanding of what the mind is matters deeply. Our most basic philosophical beliefs are tied inextricably to our view of reason. . . . Reason includes not only our capacity for logical inference, but also our ability to conduct inquiry, to solve problems, to evaluate, to criticize, to deliberate about how we should act, and to reach an understanding of ourselves, other people and the world. (Lakoff and Johnson, 1999, pp.3–4)

The changes to traditional philosophical thought that this new view of things requires are significant, and are given below.

Changes to our understanding of reason:

- Reason is not disembodied, but arises from the nature of our brains, bodies and bodily experiences.
- Reason is evolutionary (and) builds on and makes use of forms of perceptual and motor inference present in 'lower' animals.
- Reason is not 'universal' in the transcendent sense.
- Reason is not completely conscious, but mostly unconscious.
- Reason is not purely literal, but largely metaphorical and imaginative.
- Reason is not dispassionate, but emotionally engaged.

(Lakoff and Johnson, 1999, p.4)

If metaphors are a fundamental part of the natural order of things, then perhaps we should be more aware of the role they play (especially when relating/communicating with others) and should practise/develop our ability to think up and use metaphors.

MindFree – bringing it all together?

George Prince with Kathleen Logan-Prince (2002) has built on his original MindSpring theory (see Chapter 3) to provide us with a way of dealing with life and the people we meet *en route* which they call MindFree®. Their **emotional field theory** says that our

> behaviour is governed by our *'internal field'* – the collection of information in our minds and bodies – and its perception of the information coming to us from the world. This information comes to us through all our senses in the form of words, vocals (tones, hesitations, etc.) and non-verbals, thoughts, feelings, signs and signals such as facial expressions and gestures. It is transmitted by sound waves, electromagnetic waves and gravity. (2002, p.xxix).

It is our interactions with the *fields* generated by other people and things that create our relationships with them. During our encounters with others we are surrounded by various and changing interpersonal fields. To develop ourselves and our relationships with others we need to be able to manage these fields.

We have learnt earlier (Chapter 3) about the destructive force of **discounts**; we need to learn how to deal effectively with the anxiety they can cause. But managing these fields is more than that, as Prince with Logan-Prince (2002, p.122) say,

> emotional Intelligence is the capacity to be aware of fields and respond to them to invite cooperation and friendliness – to bring out synergy. It requires us to manage our impulses and anxieties to avoid destructive and defensive actions. Emotional intelligence is the ability to manage our transmissions without demeaning or diminishing the other while maintaining our integrity. Emotional intelligence is knowing how to create relationship fields that advance interpersonal security, reduce defensive perversity and invite collaboration and synergy. In addition it is knowing how to handle destructive inputs.

It is not just their use of the term 'Emotional Intelligence' that links this to our earlier discussions of EQ: I see these abilities as essential in someone with a high EQ.

As we develop, Prince with Logan-Prince say (2002, pp.21–2), we are 'governed' by two instinctually rooted life forces: one which drives us towards being an emotional separate, autonomous person who can think and act for ourselves, and another that drives us towards togetherness, a person who is connected with others, can get along with them, and belongs.

As we learn about ourselves and the people and things around us in order to become the former, this 'differentiated' independent person, we naturally make 'mistakes'. Unfortunately, the way these mistakes are often dealt with by others makes us think we are losing the togetherness/belonging thing and that makes us anxious and defensive. We 'look out for' these potentially anxiety-making moments and refrain from saying, thinking and/or doing things that might be seen as mistakes. An inordinate desire to please these others can also lead to us adopting a strategy of what Prince with Logan-Prince (2002, p.25) call **impression management** where, instead of presenting ourselves as the 'flawed and often uncertain, with a full share of weaknesses, together with some strengths and competences' person we are, we try and present an 'ideal' version of ourselves. But impression management creates an inner field that brings out the least in us.

If we carry on making mistakes, as we will do if we continue to learn, we seem to adopt a tendency to self-punish which, Prince with Logan-Prince say (2002, p.58), we deludedly feel has possible benefits, such as pre-empting us from punishment by others, protecting us from feeling meaningless, and focusing our attentions on our shortcomings. Sadly, it has many (they list 16) possible damaging effects, such as a lowering of our self-esteem and confidence, a slowing down of our learning and understanding, the creation of blocks to creative thinking, the undermining of our initiative, a lack of whole-heartedness and commitment and a reduction in our joy of being. We should adopt an attitude of self-affirmation, not self-punishment.

The three elements of our inner field that support effective relationships and collaboration with others are *empathy*, *self-awareness* and *integrity*. Empathy 'requires unconditional, wholehearted listening, that is listening without the defensive barrier of my assumptions and prejudices' (Prince with Logan-Prince, 2002, pp.13–14), trying to listen more metaphorically than literally. For this we need to be confident enough in our own beliefs and principles so that we will not feel threatened and become defensive when faced with those of others. We also need to have enough trust in our integrity (which 'governs' our willingness to cope with 'threatening' situations rather than avoid them) and self-awareness (awareness of our thoughts, wishes and feelings – our true self) that we are willing to risk the danger of having to give up and change our position.

We should strive for what Prince with Logan-Prince (2002, p.18) call **practical intimacy**™ with others, 'a state of mind and emotion in which I have the courage to be unrehearsed and undefended'. Self-disclosure like this is encouraged by empathy from others, but someone has to start first!

What else should we try and do? Prince and Logan-Prince (2002, pp.109–20) go on to offer the Synectics behaviours and techniques (described elsewhere in this book), as 'thinking tools' for changing our internal fields to make them more open to our almost limitless imagination, and things such as **wishing, imaging, approx-**

imate thinking, excursions and **open-minded evaluation** (**itemized response**). They list 16 'pluses' for using **excursions**, such as exercising and strengthening our capacity for making unlikely connections, building respect for our own resources and our ability to call on them, being more relaxed and tolerant of the thinking of others, being able to entertain proposals with obvious (to us) flaws and being better listeners. So developing our CPS skills is a good idea also.

There is far more to MindFree than this, but I hope that this brief account is sufficient to show the significant connections between the practice of the processes/techniques and behaviours of CPS (especially Synectics), EQ and developing as a person capable of dealing with what life has to 'throw' at us and relating well to others.

'Measuring' creativity

Introduction

Puccio and Murdock (1999) conducted a survey of measures designed to assess creativity and constructs related to creativity and produced a list of more than 200 measures – not all of these measures they say are of equal value!

There is also some debate as to whether it is more worthwhile to measure the absolute level of our creative-thinking skills, however we define these, or explore different 'styles' of creative thinking. The work of J.P. Guilford (see Frame 3.2) and E. Paul Torrance (1974) are possibly the most well known of the former type of measure, though the Myers-Briggs personality test is often cited in creativity 'circles', usually as a means of validating other tests.

Torrance's Tests of Creative Thinking, although not universally accepted as creative level measures, have been widely used for evaluating creativity programmes. And though Torrance made no claim to sample the entire universe of creative abilities, he did claim that the tasks his tests involved do sample a rather wide range of abilities associated with creative behaviour. However, there seems also to be some dispute concerning what should be measured in these 'level' tests. Overall, Torrance's fluency, flexibility and originality subtests apparently do correlate with Kirton's 'level' measures, but there could be a significant difference between extreme adaptor and innovator groups when it comes to fluency (Isaksen and Puccio, 1988).

Anyway, whilst not wishing to decry the work of Guilford and Torrance, because it *is* nice to understand what constitutes creative thinking, if there are different styles of creative thinking (and there is considerable evidence that there is), I feel that it is more helpful for our individual personal development and the development of any groups/teams to which we belong, to appreciate the different (cognitive) styles we prefer to employ when problem solving. Rather than spending time seeking a measure of our level of creativity, I feel we should strive just to be as creative as we can.

Miller, Cougar and Higgins (1996) claim that Michael Kirton's **Adaption-Innovation Inventory** (KAI) and Miller's own **Innovation Styles Profile** are the two most widely used instruments for determining creativity styles. However, I feel that Gerard Puccio's **FourSight** measure is also rather useful.

Innovation Styles Profile

The four cognitive styles distinguished in Miller's ISP are:

- *Modifying* – using facts and finding ways to take new actions that build and improve on what already exists. Persons using this style are more comfortable with facts and making decisions, seeking solutions by applying methods that have worked in the past, that enable them to maximize available resources and be responsive to immediate needs.

- *Exploring* – using insights and finding ways to perceive new connections and metaphors that yield even newer insights. Persons using this style tend to question assumptions and gather a large amount of information in the expectation that it will help them approach the problem from new angles.

- *Experimenting* – using facts and finding ways to perceive new variables and elements to combine and test. Persons using this style seek solutions by applying pre-established processes and experimental trial and error, enabling them to take risk in stages whilst focusing on good research design.

- *Visioning* – using insights and finding ways to take new actions to reach an ideal. Persons using this style trust their instincts and intuition, and tend to be more interested in long-term direction and goals even though the path of their attainment is unclear.

(Miller et al., 1996, p.227)

An interesting result from Miller's *et al.* (1996, p.229) research is that 'IS [information systems] professionals had significantly different scores on the ISP . . . [indicating that] managers of IS personnel cannot automatically assume that general research about behaviours of subordinates applies also to IS'.

Kirton adaption-innovation inventory

As we said earlier (page 46). Michael Kirton (1994b, pp.xiv–xxvi) believes that as individuals we adopt a particular (cognitive) style when it comes to creativity and problem solving that places us somewhere along his adaption-innovation continuum.

For him the domain of 'creativity and problem solving' does not include variables such as knowledge, scope, opportunity and motive – these things, according to Kirton, just provide the stimulus to do something or the material for idea generation (1994b, p.xvii). He does now include (in addition to level and style), (cognitive) process (e.g. Guilford's **cognition** [what you know], **memory, evaluation, convergent thinking** and **divergent thinking**) and technique (knowing when a particular technique is needed, and being practised in its use) (1994a, pp.xix–xxii).

The difference in thinking style between those placed on the adaptor side of his continuum, as opposed to the innovator side, he says, 'is the amount of structure each of us prefers to have, and how much of that structure needs to be consensually agreed' when undertaking a piece of problem solving. Depending on the circumstances, generally adaptors need more of both (Kirton, 1994c, p.xiv) – 'adaptors have a preference for doing things better . . . while innovators trade off immediate efficiency in their preference for doing things differently' (1994, p.9).

Having said this Kirton also insists that 'without structure there can be no analysis of the past and no learning; no projection to the future, no prediction and no theory; no classification of events, no abstraction of principle, no order in the universe; no language and no thought' (Kirton, 1994c, p.3). The characteristics of adaptors and innovators can be found in Table 14.1.

Kirton (1994c, p.14) explains that 'the [KAI] inventory consists of 32 items, each of which are scored by the subject on a scale of 1 to 5, giving a theoretical range of total scores from 32 to 160 with a theoretical mean of 96'; however, the general population ranges from 45 to 146, with a mean value 95. Apparently, and I can confirm this from experience, 'large differences in scores between individuals (and groups) leads to increased difficulties in collaboration, even communications' (Kirton, 1994d, p.52). We can try and work around these problems by introducing 'bridgers' (people with an intermediate score who can communicate with those with the more extreme scores), or by the potential collaborators adopting a 'coping' style (one that is not natural to, or preferred, by them, but one they can just about deal with which is nearer in score to their fellows). But a gap between how a person prefers to solve problems and how he is expected to do so in practice 'could if the gap were large and lasted over a long time, cause strain and stress' (Kirton, 1994b, p.xxiii). So 'bridgers' and coping behaviour do not necessarily help.

KAI scores have been found (Kirton, 1994c, p.54) to differ between persons of different occupations, age, sex and level of education but only by small amounts: 'the most steady and persistent of these small variations is that females tend, on average, to be more adaptive than males'.

When discussing correlations between personality differences and creative style later, Kirton (1994c, p.28) further tells us that

> the habitual adaptor ... is more left-brain dominated, is, wrongly, inclined to perceive himself as much less creative, is more dogmatic, intolerant of ambiguity, and inflexible. ... is more introverted, humble, conscientious, controlled, subdued and emotionally tender; more anxious but no more neurotic than [habitual] innovators. Furthermore, adaptors are lower in self-esteem, have a lower capacity for status and less marked self-confidence. They prefer to take fewer risks, avoid over sensation, and have a greater need for clarity.

The habitual innovator has the opposite characteristics.

It is perhaps not surprising that there is a relationship between whether we are adaptors or innovators and our preferred learning styles: innovators go for the active (holistic, 'here and now', hands-on) approach, whereas adaptors prefer a reflective (detailed, sequential, linear) mode of learning.

Isaksen and Puccio (1988, p.669) have reported that:

> although the broad separation between level and style can be supported [by their research], it may not (and should not) be as pure as Kirton suggests. In fact, to improve teaching, training and other interventions aimed at problem solving, decision making and creativity, it may be necessary to understand better the relation between creative level and style.

However, if people's KAI scores are known, shared and the different styles appreciated, as far as team-building/productivity is concerned a diversity of KAI

Table 14.1   Characteristics of adaptors and innovators

The adaptor	The innovator
Characterized by precision, reliability, efficiency, methodicalness, prudence, discipline, conformity.	Seen as undisciplined, thinking tangentially, approaching tasks from unsuspected angles.
Concerned with resolving residual problems thrown up by the current paradigm.	Could be said to search for problems and alternative avenues of solution, cutting across current paradigms.
Seeks solutions to problems in tried and understood ways.	Queries problems' concomitant assumptions: manipulates problems.
Reduces problems by improvement and greater efficiency, with maximum of continuity and stability.	Is catalyst to settled groups, irreverent of their consensual views; seen as abrasive, creating dissonance.
Seen as sound, conforming, safe, dependable.	Seen as unsound, impractical; often shocks his opposite.
Liable to make goals of means.	In pursuit of goals treats accepted means with little regard.
Seems impervious to boredom, seems able to maintain high accuracy in long spells of detailed work.	Capable of detailed routine (system-maintenance) work for only short bursts.
Is an authority within given structures.	Tends to take control in unstructured situations.
Challenges rules rarely, cautiously, when assured of strong support.	Often challenges rules, has little respect for past custom.
Tends to high self-doubt. Reacts to criticism by closer outward conformity. Vulnerable to social pressure and authority; compliant.	Appears to have low self-doubt when generating ideas, not needing consensus to maintain certitude in face of opposition.
Is essential to the functioning of the institution all the time, but occasionally needs to be 'dug out' of his system.	In the institution is ideal in unscheduled crises, or better still in helping to avoid them, if he can be controlled.
When collaborating with innovators:	**When collaborating with adaptors:**
Supplies stability, order and continuity to the partnership.	Supplies the task orientations, the break with the past and accepted theory.
Is sensitive to people, maintains group cohesion and co-operation.	Appears insensitive to people, often threatens group cohesion and co-operation.
Provides a safe base for the Innovator's riskier operations.	Provides the dynamics to bring about periodic radical change, without which institutions tend to ossify.
May be seen pejoratively by innovators who feel that the more extreme adaptors are far more likely to reject them and their ideas than collaborate with them.	Seen by adaptors as being abrasive and insensitive (despite the innovator's denials), often because of the attacks innovators [explicitly/implicitly] make on their theories and assumptions.
Tend to be seen by innovators as stuffy and unenterprising, wedded to systems, rules and norms which, however useful, are too restricting for their liking.	

Reproduced with permission from Table 1, pp.10–11, in Michael Kirton (ed.) (1994c) *Adaptors and Innovators: Styles of Creativity and Problem Solving*, 2nd edition. London: Routledge.

scores is good and should be welcomed (not just tolerated), but needs 'insightful careful handling by *everyone*' (Kirton, 1994b, p.xxvi).

FourSight

Gerard Puccio (2002a, p.3) maintains that 'innovation calls for breakthrough thinking – a blend of insight, imagination, analysis and action'. FourSight™ is a psychometric tool for encouraging innovation in the workplace (or anywhere else for that matter) developed by Puccio (www.foursightonline.com). Based on over 13 years of research and field tests, this validated creativity style assessment offers individuals, groups and organizations a simple, striking profile of exactly where they excel and where there may be room for improvement with regard to four distinct phases of the innovation process; that is, where we need to *clarify* (Data/Problem Finding), *ideate* (Idea Finding), *develop* (Solution Finding) and *implement* (Acceptance Finding). It developed from Puccio's realization that certain individuals felt more 'comfortable' and tended to perform better at some stages of the **Osborn-Parnes CPS** process than they did at other stages (Puccio, 2002b).

The profile gives you four scores, and any individual may find that they are particularly good at one or more (perhaps all) of them. The accompanying feedback booklet provides different names and short descriptions of the personalities of the four basic styles, along with how they are likely to annoy other types and how we should treat them to alleviate this conflict. It also provides names (and descriptions) of the combinations of these four basic styles; for example, a 'high clarifier' and 'high developer' Pullio calls an 'analyst'; a 'high developer' and 'high implementer', a 'finisher'; and a 'high clarifier, developer and implementer', a 'realist', etc.

In brief: clarifiers are focused, orderly, serious, methodical and deliberate; ideators are playful, social, flexible, independent, imaginative, adaptable and adventurous; developers are reflective, pragmatic, planful, cautious and structured; implementers are persistent, determined, action-oriented, decisive and assertive (Puccio, 2002a, pp.8–11).

As with **Action Profiling** (see Chapter 13), a FourSight profile of team members' scores 'may help individuals become more tolerant and appreciative of different styles of problem solving' by helping 'team members realize why they behave and interact the way they do when solving problems together. As a result, this information improves communication and creates a better working atmosphere' (Puccio, 2002b, p.2). Put another way, FourSight applied in this way should improve individual and group performance, through more effective collaboration leveraging our individual differences, whilst reducing stress and conflict (www.foursightonline.com).

When trying to build teams, Puccio (2002a, p.19) recommends that first you should go for ability not preferences for a particular style. After that, if we are looking to develop a team that is going to endure (work together for some time) and face complex challenges, we should go for a diversity of style preferences. However, if we need a team for a 'specific, straightforward and short-term assignment' – for example, generating new product ideas, carrying out a specific task – we might favour a team composed mostly of the relevant style, that is, ideator and implementer respectively.

Efforts have been made to validate FourSight against several other well-known measures, including Kirton's KAI and the Myers-Briggs personality test, with good results.

Concluding comments

If a reader wishes to explore his/her creative-thinking styles further, then contact details for the originators of some of these tests can be found in Chapter 16.

Summary

This chapter has identified a few recent ideas/theories that seem to be connected with creativity, namely emotional and spiritual Intelligence, metaphors, neuro-linguistic programming, etc., and explored the 'measurement' of creative-thinking styles.

Endnotes

1. Goleman (1996, 1997); Gardner with Krechevsky (1993); Gardner and Hatch (1989); Salovey and Mayer (1990); Steiner (1997); Cooper and Sawaf (1997); and Lee (1996).
2. A term coined by Robert Greenleaf (1977).
3. J.L. Holland (1958, 1977) suggested the existence of six vocational personality types: conventional, social, investigative, artistic, realistic and enterprising.
4. Jung's personality trait dimensions were introversion $v.$ extraversion, thinking $v.$ feeling, sensation $v.$ intuition, and, although the subject of criticism, they became the basis of the Myers-Briggs Personality Test. Several combinations are incorporated here.
5. R.B. Cattell (1957) offered us a number of motivational factors. Dismissing physical drives/instincts, negative versions of others and learnt behaviours, the following six are 'kept' for use here: gregariousness, intimacy (parental), curiosity, creativity (sex), construction, self-assertion.
6. A set of questions for asking about someone's metaphors and symbols, which solicit responses from that person (which are uncontaminated by the facilitator's vocabulary, ideas, presuppositions and solutions), in a way that values them and enables that person to become familiar with the hidden workings of his/her perceptual patterns (Lawley and Tompkins, 2000, p.81).

15 Computer-aided problem solving

The objective of this chapter is to describe a few computer software packages that we can use to assist with our problem solving, and to consider the general role of ICT in creativity and problem solving.

Creativity, problem solving and computers

Over recent decades a variety of computer software applications have been produced that claim to assist with the problem-solving process. These have ranged from simple text outliners and drawing programs, through ones that actually did assist our creative thinking (by prompting us with appropriate stimulus material), to those that claimed to facilitate the whole problem-solving process. Proctor (1999) found it useful to categorize these as what we might call 'inspirational', that is, those that provide stimuli for **Ideation** and help us (re)structure our thoughts and ideas, and simple ideas processors. However, now the more sophisticated inspirational packages normally contain idea-processing functions as well.

Adjuncts to these were applications usually referred to as 'groupware', which enable work group collaboration (both when geographically or temporally separated and when located in the same physical space – computer-enhanced meetings; see Frame 15.1), some of which also incorporated a degree of idea stimulation/structuring and processing. Many of the *current* batch of inspirational packages (see below) now also have their own inbuilt/add-on modules that enable some degree of idea sharing and/or collaboration.

> **Frame 15.1** *Computer-aided meetings*
>
> *Computer-enhanced meetings*
>
> In the area of group problem solving, computers are being used to 'enhance' the proceedings of local meetings, where everyone concerned is gathered physically in the same room. The portrayal of opinions and

▶

ideas, previously written on whiteboards and flipcharts, is accomplished via overhead projectors and TV monitors connected to a network of computers; participants key in their ideas rather than voice them. These give us the facility of instant call-back of any material, as well as enhancing it; for example, by rearranging its order and subsequently publishing it. GroupSystems™ (for Windows) is probably the best-known of these packages. Advantages often claimed from these systems is the lack of the confrontation/conflict which normally occurs when opinions and ideas are voiced, and increased productivity.

The implications for creative problem-solving groups of the use of this technology depend on whether the problem-solving group's leader is simply someone operating the computer network or whether s/he is also process leading the meeting. If it is considered desirable and efficient for the leader to do both jobs, then they need training in *both* the skills of process leading (see Chapter 13) and those of using the information technology. As a process leader normally has a lot to do already, being relieved of writing up group responses may permit him/her to run the session better.

Remote 'conferencing'

A potentially more serious problem is that it is getting more common for geographically separated people to communicate with each other via computers, fax machines, telephone conferencing, etc. for the purpose of 'group' problem solving. This means losing even more of the all-important face-to-face human interactions that contribute to creativity, not to mention the relative anonymity that these media offer which can be abused.

There are also other 'everyday' applications, such as spreadsheets and e-mail packages, that can assist problem solving and/or collaboration.

Since other authors (Van Gundy, 1992; Proctor, 1999) have already attempted to review the abilities of many of these programs, and because with passing time software products like these come and go or can change quite rapidly, it seems pointless to describe their functionality and peculiarities in great detail again here. However, a few examples (of the inspirational and ideas-processing type – which is what I feel should be our main interest here) that have been around for some time will be briefly described to give a 'feel' of what is currently available. They are all geared to assisting one particular problem-solving process/technique, which should be obvious from the write ups below.

IdeaFisher – creative Brainstorming

IdeaFisher claims (www.ideafisher.com) to be 'the world's first and only *Metaphoric Associational Thesaurus*', and cites the following example to explain the difference between a traditional thesaurus and IdeaFisher's ability to produce metaphorical associations. Comprising (as they usually do) only of lists of synonyms (and the odd antonym), a normal thesaurus would produce for the word 'red' (meaning colour) 10–20 words such as crimson, garnet, rose and rust (*Chambers Twentieth Century Thesaurus* (1986) gives 52!). Although IdeaFisher also contains the most popular synonyms like these, it also produces (and this is its primary purpose) metaphoric associations for 'red', such as cardinal*, apple, blood*, fire [flaming*], blush*, angry, Red Cross, red-eye flight, etc. (Chambers had those marked with an * and others such as carroty, foxy, healthy, shame-faced, wine!). Anyway, IdeaFisher reckons to have nearly 700 metaphoric associations listed for 'red' alone. Also, it has continuous 'loops' throughout all of its 65,000 word database. For example, red ~ fire ~ forest fire ~ forest ~ tree ~ spotted owl ~ bird ~ fly ~ red-eye flight, etc.

IdeaFisher has millions of these virtually unlimited associational combinations. Its database of words, phrases and concepts are categorized and cross-referenced in many ways, including 432 'topical' categories such as:

ability/skill/talent	. . . wheels/tyres/gears
accidents/disasters/survival/rescue	width/thick/thin/broad/narrow
accurate/precise/correct	winter sports/skiing/ice-skating
aggressive/fierce/wild/uncivilized	
agriculture/farming/ranching	yellow/orange
airflow/wind/blow/fan . . .	young adults/middle age

In addition, IdeaFisher contains tens of thousands of idea-prompting questions covering 15 specific task-orientated areas such as general problem solving, advertising/promotion, new product/service development, strategic planning, conflict resolution, etc. Some of these banks of questions come as 'standard' with the software, others are available as add-on modules. You can also add your own personal associations to IdeaFisher.

Using any word or concept (or pairs of them) as a trigger, IdeaFisher produces a rich association of ideas to suit any problem context, 'the kind of connections that lead to creative solutions'.

Decision Explorer (neé COPE) – (Cognitive) Mapping

According to Banxia (www.banxia.com), the flexibility of **Decision Explorer**® allows it to support many mapping techniques for use both by a single user and in group work (as a Group Decision Support System – GDSS). These include **mind mapping** and **Cognitive Mapping** (see Chapter 6). The supplied user guides give instructions on a specific mapping technique (Cognitive Mapping), however, they say it is not necessary to use this particular technique to achieve results – the most important factor is that your chosen mapping technique is applied consistently.

Banxia correctly point out that mapping (on its own) will not always give you instant answers, but claim that as the model of the issue is built, the key factors soon become apparent and then you can start to identify and explore potential solutions. Decision Explorer maps are not intended to be static pages, but dynamic views of a much larger model, on which we can keep working and adding to over time.

They say that there is no limit to your map's page size, and the quoted 8000-concept capacity of the software does seem big enough for most things!

Banxia also claim that:

Decision Explorer is a proven tool for managing 'soft' issues – the subjective, qualitative information that surrounds/pervades complex or uncertain situations. It allows you to capture in detail people's thoughts and ideas, to explore them, and then gain a new (empathetic) understanding of and insight into their situation.

Decision Explorer contains many facilities that help you analyze the maps you have created, for example, it can show 'clusters' of closely linked concepts, find concepts which have many links, and detect loops of influence (vicious and virtuous circles).

Decision Explorer® has been developed by academics at the universities of Bath and Strathclyde and now by Banxia Software, in conjunction with major organisations. This innovative tool now has hundreds of major international users. (www.banxia.com)

A useful introduction to Cognitive Mapping can be found at http://www.banxia.com/depaper.html. And an excellent fully featured (but obviously limited in scope: 30 concepts) demonstration version of Decision Explorer, complete with an instruction guide, Cognitive Mapping tutorial, online tutorials etc. can (at the time of writing) be downloaded free from: http://www.banxia.com/dexplore/demo.html.

ThoughtPath (neé Mindlink) – Synectics

ThoughtPath™ is based on the **Synectics** CPS process, and contains several modules including a set of *triggers* (idea-generation techniques), a (full) CPS process, the ThoughtPath Warehouse™ (to manage all your ideas and concepts) and a creative workout Gym. There is also an idea generation 'option', which uses the triggers in a 'cut-down' version of the problem-solving process that lets you generate ideas quickly without having to follow the entire CPS process. This is ideal for problems where ideas for solutions will not require any, or very little, development.

These modules 'have been integrated to strategically guide the user through their most complex problems and opportunities, always pushing toward solutions that are fresh, exciting and workable' (www.thoughtpath.com).

Triggers can be accessed throughout the ThoughtPath problem-solving process and are intended to be like the 'breaks' we often need to take when working on a tough problem. For example, making some coffee, going for a walk or talking to a friend often (by taking our minds away from the problem) result in us being able to see the problem in a new light when we return to it.

They are mental **excursions** (see Chapter 7) incorporating imagery, writing, word analogies, role playing, etc. that are 'fun to do and are guaranteed to get those creative juices flowing'. ThoughtPath claims to ensure 'the freshness and spontaneity of its triggers by maintaining over 40 categories of triggers and thousands of objects that can be accessed through various triggers'.

ThoughtPath's problem-solving process is divided into two distinct phases: *idea development* and *solution development*. Since it is based on the Synectics process this is a little confusing, because the first involves **Goal Wishing** and idea generation, and the second, **Itemized Response** (Idea Development!) and action planning.

ThoughtPath describes the process as follows:

- Phase 1 – *problem definition* (where we organize our thoughts and perspectives on the problem and define it as clearly as we can), *wishing* (where we make some wishes, explore a wide range of possibilities and desired outcomes), *idea generation* (where we review the list of wishes, especially those that represent totally new lines of thinking on our problem and ThoughtPath helps us explore the most intriguing of these wishes).

- Phase 2 – *solution statement* (where we identify the concerns we have with our **most promising ideas** and overcome them, and develop an action plan for moving ahead with our solution) and *solution formats* (where ThoughtPath provides us with the tools for creating clear, attractive reports for our ideas/solutions). The pre-designed formats are built to provoke your memory for any relevant details (www.thoughtpath.com).

The ThoughtPath Warehouse offers a variety of different functions that are intended to allow you to make the most of your problem-solving efforts across many problems. Obviously, it allows you to store and later 'access' thoughts that you have had/ideas developed on any of your problems addressed within ThoughtPath. You can also catalogue your thinking within a specific problem. You can attach key words to any of your thoughts allowing later querying, even to the extent of using these thoughts as triggers in other problem-solving sessions.

The ThoughtPath Warehouse claims to have powerful import, export and merge functions which allow you to share problems/knowledge over a network or multiple, separate machines.

The Gym contains a series of self-paced exercises designed to improve your creative-thinking skills, and which automatically change each time you use them to avoid repetition.

TechOptimizer – TRIZ (Invention Machine)

Invention Machine provide several software packages in the area of 'intellectual asset management', one of which is *TechOptimizer*™.

According to Invention Machine, TechOptimizer 4.0

> empowers breakthrough and iterative innovation, enhances problem solving by using the proven product-development methodologies: TRIZ and Value Engineering and provides access to the world's largest, commercially available knowledge base of scientific effects. (www.invention-machine.com)

This knowledge base, it is claimed, facilitates knowledge sharing across industries by using abstracted representations of technical systems and concepts, and 'stimulates out-of-the-box thinking by pooling knowledge from different disciplines'. With the addition of more than 900 new scientific effects, examples and animations, the scientific effects library in the latest version of TechOptimizer now consists of more than 8400 physical processes and their practical industry applications.

TechOptimizer has a 'partner' package **CoBrain 2.6** which, using advanced semantic processing, not only captures and organizes intellectual assets such as the ideas/solutions obtained from TechOptimizerI, along with WWW data/ information, but facilitates its sharing enterprise-wide.

CoBrain, they say (www.invention-machine.com)

provides enterprises with a number of distinct benefits. It prevents effort duplication, supports organization-wide sharing of best practices, empowers day-to-day problem solving, enables senior executives to optimize R&D strategy and resource allocation and integrates external and internal information into unified corporate knowledge.

Innovation WorkBench – TRIZ (Ideation International)

Ideation International offer a suite of software packages, based on the **TRIZ** process, and claim that they provide 'a total innovation system that provides engineers with expert I-TRIZ assistance in solving challenging technological problems. Proven to help users develop implementable solutions that at times represent true technological breakthroughs' (www.ideationtriz.com).

The *Innovation WorkBench*® 2.9 (IWB®) includes a number of modules:

- *Innovation Situation Questionnaire*® *(ISQ)*. This is a tool that facilitates the preliminary problem analysis, by helping the user 'to structure and document information about a problem situation into a format useful for problem solving' and view the problem from multiple perspectives at the same time, reducing what Altshuller (1999) called **psychological inertia**.
- *Problem Formulator*™. This analytical tool that gives the user 'the ability to model systems or problem situations in terms of cause-and-effect relationships', and 'attack' it more effectively by restructuring it into a subset of simpler (typical) engineering **contradictions**.
- *System of Operators*. This is the I-TRIZ knowledge, based on Altshuller's original analysis of many thousands of patents worldwide (but currently including over two million), and which now includes 440 **operators** – innovation 'secrets'. Boris Zlotin and Alla Zusman (1999) describe why and how this updated set of operators – which include TRIZ's **40 Principles** (see Chapter 7) and **Standard Solutions** – have been 'abstracted from the successful results of previous inventors spanning a broad cross-section of technological areas'.
- *Innovative Illustration Library*. A 'library' of more than 1200 examples of the practical applications of these operators.
- *Innovation Guide*. A compendium of articles describing physical, chemical and geometric effects, along with more than 1000 engineering applications of this knowledge, integrally linked to the System of Operators.
- *Evaluation module*. This module 'provides access to proven methods to help users benchmark design concepts, anticipate and prevent problems with solution implementation, and foresee the potential evolution of a solution and/or system'.

IWB also comes with extensive 'e-learning' tutorials on the use of both IWB and TRIZ.

At the time of writing, demonstration copies of Ideation's software is available for downloading from their website (www.ideationtriz.com). The same website also contains several useful articles on how they have been updating TRIZ in recent years, along with examples of the application of this 'new' I-TRIZ.

eThink

The management consulting and training company Kepner-Tregoe Inc. have also produced a software package, **eThink**®, that guides the user through the use of the five Kepner-Tregoe techniques: **Situation Appraisal**, **Problem Analysis**, **Decision Analysis**, **Potential Problem Analysis** and **Potential Opportunity Analysis**, 'organizing and capturing the data and the thinking behind' the problem resolution, decision, etc. that s/he has used them to help with.

Whatever this completed process is, they say, the output from the software 'becomes a record that can be referenced when faced with similar issues in the future. It also can be quickly exported to a report or a Microsoft PowerPoint presentation' (www.kepner-tregoe.com), or otherwise shared with/disseminated to others in the group or organization.

The data is collected and structured in (and can also be retrieved from) *KT* **Memory Bank**®, while eThink's **Groupware Capability**™ deals with the data/information sharing, permitting both local and remote collaboration – a group effort can remain open and ideas and comments contributed to it until such time as the 'owner' or originator of the issue decides.

eThink's **Action Tracker**® component then enables us, as individuals, groups and managers, to coordinate and monitor actions that we have decided to take. It collects and organizes items while we are working through an issue, either on our own or with others, capturing all the concerns, necessary actions, deadlines, responsibilities, etc.

eThink also has another facility, which allows you to integrate their rational techniques into your own procedures and 'systems' that define your present work routines, so forming **Process Application Kits**® (PAKS). They now supply 'standard' PAKs for some critical areas of business, such as 'troubleshooting a customer complaint', 'protecting a new product launch' and 'selecting a vendor'.

Groupware

When writing the first edition of this book, I was concerned about the use of groupware (for a definition, see Frame 15.2) to 'facilitate' problem solving in groups. Having seen face-to-face problem-solving groups work very effectively with a trained **CPS** (especially Synectics) facilitator/process leader, I personally felt that it is a bit of a waste not to utilize those things that makes each of us different by 'managing' (with a trained facilitator/process leader) the potential conflict which this may cause, by going for a method (computer-enhanced meetings) which deliberately attempts to avoid this conflict, or inhibits it (other groupware) when the group participants are geographically and temporally separate. If circumstances dictate the use of information and communication technology and groupware then we should do our best to emulate the face-to-face experience.

I wrote:

It would be useful to devise a protocol in keeping with the spirit of CPS, that we could adopt for [computer-aided] group problem solving at a distance even though it would be difficult to ensure adherence to this. Perhaps 'proper' video conferencing [not using web-cams, until we all have broadband access to the Internet], video telephones, and one day, live holographic images will be the answer to this problem. By seeing our fellow group problem-solving participants, we can pick up their body language and regain some of the sense of being in the same room.

What has happened since then?

Frame 15.2 *Groupware*

In recent decades we have seen the evolution of groupware '*any* technology which improves group productivity' (my emphasis) (Briggs and Nunamaker, 1994, p.61) but, as can be seen from this definition, this could mean anything from a fax machine, through a video conferencing system, to quite sophisticated computer software operating over a wide area network specifically designed to enable group problem solving and decision making

There are essentially two types of groupware: those that are designed to facilitate communications (for example, Microsoft Outlook, Lotus QuickPlace/Sametime/Domino) and those intended to facilitate group problem solving and decision making (for example, Group Systems). There is obviously an overlap here because the former, say in the form of an e-mail/computer conferencing system, *can* help a group work collaboratively on a problem even though they do not have problem-solving techniques and meeting structures programmed into them (Group Systems incorporates Brainstorming, actually **Brainwriting**, as an idea-generating technique).

Research into the benefits of groupware has attempted to measure many aspects of group 'productivity' including: efficiency, effectiveness, participant satisfaction, level of information exchange, degree of consensus achieved, amount of conflict and participation equality. Unfortunately, the different types of groupware employed somewhat confused things.

Elspeth McFadzean (1996b, p.6) concluded that the results of this early research into the effectiveness of groupware were mixed and inconclusive, though they do seem to 'have added value to group meetings by increasing the depth of analysis and increasing the amount of participation each group member undertakes'.

She goes on to say that if we apply Briggs and Nunamaker's (1996) Team theory of group productivity – which relates productivity to goal congruence, team processes (our attention 'conflict' between communication, deliberation and information access) and distractions – to the assessment of the benefits of group decision-support systems that employ parallel and anonymous communication, we find that they do permit participants 'to "talk" and "listen" all at once', and 'to communicate contentious issues without fear of retribution'. Group Systems' Brainwriting, categorizing and voting functions also help with deliberation (McFadzean 1996b, p.11).

So some of these GDSS do produce some benefits, and it has been shown that information technology solutions like these do tend to work better if the group members have previously met face-to-face. But at the time McFadzean was making the comments above, what programs like GroupSystems still needed was the incorporation of more creative techniques than straight Brainwriting – as well as a built-in 'facilitator' as mentioned above. InSync, see below, has both these things!

InSync – Synectics Technology

A computer CPS package/collaborative solution that is worth looking out for is **InSync®** from Synectics Technology. This package, which has already been used successfully for several years by Synectics' clients is, at the time of writing, going through a major enhancement process. By the time you read this, it should be available to both organizations (whether clients of Synectics or not) and in a 'lite' form for the general public.

Building on the features offered by software packages such as GroupSystems, InSync provides a rules-based meeting structure, based on the Synectics CPS process, that enables electronic collaboration and problem solving, whether the group members are together in the same physical location, or separated by place or time. Not only does it provide a meeting structure based on probably the best CPS process for producing innovative solutions (for example, products, strategies and ways of working) to a broad range of business problems and opportunities; it provides an electronic facilitator 'in the box'.

The workflow guided processes lead participants through the task-analysis, **springboard**/idea-generation and Idea-Development stages of the Synectics process (see Chapter 10), and culminate in some action planning. Along the way the system will 'evaluate' the participant's responses and suggest the next appropriate step through auto-prompting, introducing **excursions** etc. It will also sense when future responses are due and will remind users of upcoming events.

The facilitation feature accommodates both novices and experienced Synectics practitioners (providing the former with appropriate coaching on techniques and the overall CPS process) and can be easily configured by each user group to meet their preferences for aggressive, moderate or more passive facilitation interventions.

InSync accepts input to the meeting from PDAs, PCs, telephone and fax. Other features that InSync provides are e-mail, a calendar, 'to do' lists, contact management, data mining, participation management and personalization (of, for example, facilitation, excursions).

The software's inbuilt 'performance monitoring' of individuals and teams enables the innovation process to be customized and (hence) optimized, and the teams to be developed. Excursions (see also Chapter 7) can be customized by participant, client or industry, and problem-solving session templates are available for tactical or strategic collaboration and innovation.

InSync will be available in several languages (including English, French and Spanish), be platform independent and will integrate with virtually any external application. Some of the enhancements being made at present are the ability to capture speech and transcribe it to text, the translation of meeting content into other languages, and the inclusion of visualization tools. It will also be adaptable to cultural and industry specific differences and provide access to web crawlers and hence access to any additional information available on the worldwide web.

Synectics claim that problem-solving group participants are 75 per cent more productive when using InSync, because

> They find they can input their ideas as they occur to them, without waiting for their 'turn to speak' and without getting in each other's way. Participants are not afraid to speak their minds since all inputs are anonymous and with this security, they feel safe to make connections with one another's ideas and take the mental risks that lead to breakthrough. Similarly, selection of ideas is also anonymous leading to a richer selection, free from fear of 'going with the flow'. (www.synecticsworld.com)

Can computers problem solve or be creative?

Herbert Simon has suggested (1960a, pp.1–8) that we can position decisions along a continuum running from 'highly programmed' at one end to 'highly nonprogrammed' at the other. He contended (1960b) that we had (using Operational Research and computers) the 'technical capacity' to automate many of the decisions that fall at the programmed end of this spectrum. He also predicted that it would not be long (a couple of decades) before 'heuristic programming' would permit us to automate nonprogrammed decisions by computer as well.

Forty years on, it is true that, if a set of rules can be written down that take us systematically through, say, an appropriate machine fault diagnosis routine (similar to those found in car maintenance manuals), an analysis of our entitlement to tax allowances and our tax liabilities, or a procedure which determines what would be the best form of insurance investment for us or whether we are a good credit risk, etc., then an expert system (see Frame 15.3) could be constructed that apparently possesses this expertise and which could advise us accordingly. In other words, computerization of a programmed decision is a practical reality, and is becoming quite a common occurrence.

Frame 15.3 *Expert systems*

An expert system is a computer program that attempts to encapsulate some knowledge possessed by a human expert. This expertise need not be of a highly academic nature, but simply rare knowledge possessed by only a limited number of people within an organization, or fairly mundane information that we need to access frequently but do not hold permanently in our memory; for example, train timetables.

An expert system consists of a knowledge base – a collection of facts (such as, there is a train leaving Bristol at 07.15 every weekday which stops at Reading and Slough, and arrives at London Paddington at whenever) and rules (for example, if you are travelling from Salisbury to Slough you need to change trains at Basingstoke and Reading); a means by which it can question the user and thus gain the further information (such as desired destination and arrival time, departure point, etc.) it needs in order to perform some query ('What is the last train I can catch from Salisbury that will get to Slough by 09.30?) and reach a conclusion; and a procedure for working through the rules in order to deduce the most appropriate advice (on available trains) to offer the user.

Even if a set of rules such as these were difficult or impossible to obtain, as long as we have an appropriate set of examples of the expertise that we are interested in 'capturing' on a computer (with respect to machine faults, we would need to have a number of breakdowns, a record of the sort of things which we checked, the symptoms noticed, along with the fault that was eventually deemed to be the cause of the problem), an expert system could still be devised using a process known as **Rule Induction** or with artificial neural networks. Some people consider that this process typifies machine learning, but should/would a computer running such an expert system be considered as having problem-solving skills? I can foresee that computers may perform some rudimentary problem solving for us once, of course, some human has written the expert system. But I have no fears of computers replicating human ability to solve people problems, at least not until someone develops a foolproof way of predicting human behaviour by mathematical means!

What about computer creativity? They can certainly produce '3-D' representations of buildings, cars, etc. that will permit us to look at the object from all directions, including from the 'inside'. They can generate very realistic animated graphics and reproduce the sound of any instrument in an orchestra (and a few that aren't). Impressive though these things are, it is ultimately the human operator's creativity that we are marvelling at; all the computer has done is to make it easier for that person to realize his or her ideas. The nearest a computer gets to producing what can even vaguely be referred to as creativity is the generation of fractal landscapes, which are apparently constructed from randomly generated squares 'distorted' by perspective. Though visually stunning, these are not very far in essence from the concept of a computer writing a bestseller by extracting an appropriate number of words at random from a dictionary.

Summary

This chapter has described a few computer software packages that we can use to assist with our problem solving, and has discussed the general role of information and communications technology in creativity and problem solving.

16 Other sources of information on problem solving

> The objective of this chapter is to provide for the reader with some other sources of information that may be of interest.

Websites

Organizations 'promoting' creative problem solving:

Creative Education Foundation

The Creative Education Foundation set up by Alex Osborn many decades ago has run an annual CPS conference/training event, the Creative Problem Solving Institute (CPSI), in June for many years.
www.cef-cpsi.org

Creative Problem Solving Group

The Creative Problem Solving Group, Inc. is headed by Scott Isaksen. This is where you will find some of the people responsible for the ongoing development and promotion of the Osborn-Parnes CPS process. A number of useful articles can be downloaded from this site.
www.cpsb.com

Centre for Creative Learning

This is where you will find the other half of the Isaksen-Treffinger 'partnership', Donald Treffinger; also a brief summary of the latest version of the Osborn-Parnes CPS process and the facility to purchase the latest books on this subject.
www.creativelearning.com

Synectics

Synectics Inc. is an international training and consultancy firm, originating from Boston MA.
www.synecticsworld.com

Synectics Education Initiative

Born out of a group of Synectics enthusiasts working in the UK (as teachers, lecturers and educational psychologists, etc.), SEI is fundamentally a training and consulting organization, specializing in supplying services to public sector organizations, principally education. The training processes are designed to enable the development of a culture of experiment and innovation within the client organizations.

SEI is an educational charity promoting: 'the teaching and application of creativity throughout the formal education system. The processes include creative problem solving and also the development of open-minded communication and win–win teamwork'.

SEI's definition of creativity includes the development of appropriate attitudes and behaviours. Therefore, it is concerned with 'helping people to be more open minded, more constructive, more cooperative, better team workers, more flexible and more responsive to changing situations. The by-product of this is a great improvement in learning skills'.

www.synecticsworld.com/whatis/SEI.htm

European Association for Creativity and Innovation

The EACI's mission is to 'contribute to a better understanding, practice and acceptance of creativity and innovation in Europe'. They claim to do this by organizing conferences, building a network of people interested in creativity and innovation, stimulating research and distributing research publications.

www.eaci.net

Creativity networks and events

Many other countries have their own 'creativity network' type organization, for example, Canada and Australia. If you do not mind 'ploughing' through typically 17,000 hits (when you insert 'creative problem solving' and 'network' into your search engine), it is worth doing a periodic search for these and anything else to do with creativity. You might find sites such as

www.creativityday.org

www.creativity-unlimited.org (the author's website, and where occasional updates/additions to this book can be found) and

www.creativityland.net.

Organizations 'promoting' TRIZ

Technical Innovation Center

Technical Innovation Center, Inc. is a training and consultancy organization and claims to be the leading publisher of books on TRIZ in English, including Genrich Altshuller's three books. Their website www.triz.org contains some useful articles that can be downloaded for free, including Lev Shulyak's Preface to Altshuller' book *40 Principles*. TIC is also the founder and sponsor of The Altshuller Institute for TRIZ Studies (www.aitriz.org).

TRIZ Journal

www.triz-journal.com

Kepner-Tregoe

Founded in 1958, the Kepner-Tregoe management consulting and training company, 'dedicated to the belief that effective action follows clear thinking', is still going strong and is contactable on www.kepner-tregoe.com.

They now claim to specialize in skill development, operational improvement, and strategy formulation and implementation. Their rational thinking techniques are now supported by computer software called eThink™, see www.kepner-tregoe/ethink/ethink.html.

Soft systems

Searching for 'Soft Systems Methodology' on the Internet, like 'creativity', brings in far too many sites to evaluate easily, though the following one may be of interest:

Systems Study Group

Amongst other things, the Systems Study Group are researching into computer software to facilitate the SSM process.
www.deakin.edu.au/infosys/research/ssg

Useful books and articles

Soft systems

Peter Checkland's latest offering is:

> Peter Checkland and Jim Scholes (1999) *Soft Systems Methodology in Action: Includes a 30 Year Retrospective*, Chichester: John Wiley and Sons. 0-471-98605-4.

To find out more about 'merging' SSM with an information systems development methodology try:

> Brian Wilson (1990) *Systems: Concepts, Methodologies and Applications, Second Edition*, Chichester: John Wiley and Sons. 0-471-92716-3.

And if you are interested in other soft systems processes/techniques (along with some 'hard' ones):

> Robert L. Flood and Michael C. Jackson (1991), *Creative Problem Solving: Total Systems Intervention*, Chichester: John Wiley and Sons. ISBN 0-471-93052-0.

Contrary to what the title suggests, this book is not about the creative problem-solving processes described herein, but a useful text describing several hard and soft systems approaches (including SSM) and suggesting how a 'synthesis' of these approaches might be adopted.

TRIZ

If you are interested in finding out more about TRIZ than I have been able to say here, this is a good book to read next. It contains many examples of the application of TRIZ.

Genrich Altshuller (1999) *The Innovation Algorithm: TRIZ, Systematic Innovation and Technical Creativity*, Worcester, MA: Technical Innovation Center Inc.

At the time of writing, several interesting articles on the recent developments of TRIZ are available free from www.ideationtriz.com and www.creax.com.

Creative problem solving

Still probably the best book on Synectics is:

Vincent Nolan (1989) *The Innovator's Handbook: The Skills of Innovative Management — Problem Solving, Communication and Teamwork*, London: Sphere Books. 0-7474-0452-6.

Although the 'colloquial' presentation may not appeal to some, the content of the following book is good and gives an up-to-date account of George Prince's current thinking.

George Prince with Kathleen Logan-Prince (2002) *Your Life is a Series of Meetings . . . Get Good at Life*, 1stBooks Library. 1-4033-1093-9.

Scott Isaksen and Donald Treffinger's (1985) book *Creative Problem Solving: The Basic Course*, Buffalo, NY: Bearly Ltd, if you can get hold of it, is a good practical guide to the Osborn-Parnes CPS process. This book, though, describes Version 3 of their CPS process; we are now on Version 6.1 (see Appendix 7) which is described in detail in the first of the books below.

Isaksen, S.G., Dorval, K.B. and Treffinger, D.J. (2000) *Creative Approaches to Problem Solving: A Framework for Change, Second Edition*, Dubuque, IA: Kendall/Hunt Publishing Co.

Treffinger, D.J., Isaksen, S.G. and Dorval, K.B. (2000) *Creative Problem Solving: An Introduction, Third Edition*, Waco, TX: Prufrock Press.

Other interesting things

EQ

There are many books on EQ, several by Daniel Goleman, who popularized the subject. Possibly a good place to start is his book:

Daniel Goleman (1996) *Emotional Intelligence: Why It Can Matter More Than IQ*, London: Bloomsbury Publishing. 0-7475-2830-6.

SQ

Apart from presenting the authors' evidence for the existence and nature of SQ, this book offers a short questionnaire to give us 'some idea' of our personality types regarding SQ, our Lotus of Self.

Danah Zohar and Ian Marshall (2000) *Spiritual Intelligence: The Ultimate Intelligence*, London: Bloomsbury Publishing. 0-7475-3644-9.

NLP

For a very readable introduction to neurolinguistic programming try:

Joseph O'Connor and John Seymour (1995) *Introducing NLP: Psychological Skills for Understanding and Influencing People*, London: Thorsons (HarperCollins). 1-85538-344-6. (First published in 1990.)

Metaphors

A good place to start appreciate the significance of metaphors in our everyday lives is . . .

George Lakoff and Mark Johnson (1980) *Metaphors We Live By*, Chicago, IL: University of Chicago. 0-226-46801-1.

. . . and, if you fancy exploring the deeper philosophical implications of this try the heavier (in all senses of the word):

George Lakoff and Mark Johnson (1999) *Philosophy in the Flesh: The Embodied Mind and its Challenge to Western Thought*, New York: Basic Books (Perseus Books). 0-465-05674-1.

Creativity and EQ measures

FourSight

The FourSight creativity-style self-score inventory and feedback booklet can be purchased from www.foursightonline.com. The FourSight Technical Manual, providing information about the origins and development of Foursight, can (at the time of writing) be downloaded free from the same site.

EQ map

Robert Cooper and Ayman Sawaf's EQ map, a 20-page EQ inventory, can be found in:

Robert Cooper and Ayman Sawaf (2000) *Executive EQ: Emotional Intelligence in Business*, London: Texere Publishing. 1-58799-099-7. (First published in 1997.)

REQuES

David Ryback's EQ executive survey, REQuES, a 60-item inventory, can be found in an appendix of:

David Ryback (1998) *Putting Emotional Intelligence to Work: Successful Leadership is More Than IQ*, Boston MA: Butterworth-Heinemann. 0-7506-9956-6.

Summary

This chapter has provided some other sources of information about the things discussed in this book, which may be of interest to the reader.

Kepner-Tregoe

This appendix provides some background information on Kepner and Tregoe's thinking processes.

Introduction

In the late 1950s and early 1960s, Charles Kepner and Benjamin Tregoe studied examples of both good and bad management, looking for ways of thinking that could be used to differentiate between them. They concluded that the best managers, or those considered by other managers to be 'the most effective and successful', used 'variations of four distinct routines or patterns of thinking, in handling problems and decisions' (1981, p. vii). In the first edition of their book (1965), the Kepner-Tregoe approach to problem solving and decision making (KT), their philosophy of **rational management**, was a set of guidelines on good thinking practices for managers, a 'leader's guide' for the team manager rather than advice for those working in a team. Whether you are managing others or not, many of these ideas offer useful guidance for self-management as well.

In *The New Rational Manager* (1981) they concede that teamwork is important in organizational effectiveness. Their view is that teamwork will improve if everyone has been trained in KT, because KT serves as a 'common language' providing a rational description of the cause of a problem or the outcome of a decision. There are no misunderstandings, no possibilities for bad communications, no 'moving goal posts'. There is, however, more to building an effective team than this; good communication is a necessary but not a sufficient condition. They also support the view that people are resistant to change and need to be 'sold' its advantages. They maintain that the introduction of KT, and the development of teamwork, is best encouraged and implemented in a 'top-down' fashion.

An overview of KT's rational thinking

The four patterns of thinking identified by Kepner and Tregoe are exemplified by the following questions managers ask every day (Kepner and Tregoe, 1981, p.20).

- What's going on?

- Why did this happen?
- Which course of action should we take?
- What lies ahead?

These four patterns[1] are called **Situation Appraisal, Problem Analysis, Decision Analysis** and **Potential Problem Analysis**, and are summarized in Frame A1.1.

Frame A1.1 *Four patterns of thinking (Kepner and Tregoe)*

Situation Appraisal

- Assessing and clarifying situations;
- Sorting things out;
- Breaking down complex situations into manageable components;
- Achieving and maintaining control of events.

Problem Analysis

'Cause and effect' thinking:

- Accurately identifying, describing, analysing and resolving a situation in which 'something has gone wrong without explanation'.

Decision Analysis

Making choices between courses of action:

- Determination of the reasons for and purpose of making the decision;
- Consideration of the available options;
- Assessment of the relative risks of each option.

Potential Problem Analysis

Anticipating the future:

- What might be and what could happen;
- What problems might occur;
- What decisions will have to be made.

Charles Kepner and Benjamin Tregoe (1981, pp.21–6)

The KT approach: conclusions

Kepner and Tregoe intended their approach to be a complete system of rational thinking that would help managers become more effective problem solvers and decision makers. Whatever the disputes over whether or not this is the case, to gain any benefit from the process, it must be applied systematically. Because of the 'rigidity' associated with the idea of a systematic and logical method for doing anything, the implementation of a KT approach could be criticized as inflexible. It need not be. More significant, the approach's systematic nature could make it vulnerable to external pressures, such as constraints on time, lack of information, availability of support staff, distractions, disruptions and crises, not to mention the effects of intra-organizational politics. If we are planning to use the KT approach (or any part of it) we need to be aware of these things.

To an extent, the process should be 'self-correcting' in regard to some of these pressures. Situation Appraisal involves a trouble-shooting element and, indirectly, time management considerations aimed at providing extra time for operating the approach or dealing with the inevitable disruptions. Potential Problem Analysis is also intended to help us minimize the number of unexpected events and crises that might happen.

The claimed benefits of the approach are that we will feel 'secure in knowing that all necessary questions are being asked, all critical information considered, and all bases covered', and that from this condition of security we will be free 'to work imaginatively and creatively in pursuit of the resolution, choice, or plan that is not only safe and correct, but perhaps unusual or outstanding as well' (Kepner and Tregoe, 1981). Whether or not these claims are valid, the external pressures mentioned above have the potential for wrecking any such sense of security.

For this reason Kepner and Tregoe seem to prefer the adoption of their approach on a 'top-down', 'organization-wide' basis rather than by individuals within the organization. However, we need to remind ourselves here of the view that, while solutions to problems are rational, the process of finding them is not. In any quest to develop our problem-solving, communications and teamworking skills, we have to look some way beyond the KT approach. It is not a total problem-solving/decision-making package, and as a method for managing others, I have severe reservations about it. However, there is still much to commend in the KT approach if it is viewed as a 'bundle' of practical common-sense advice intended to improve our self-management skills and the way we organize our own individual tasks.

The management consulting and training company, Kepner-Tregoe Inc., 'dedicated to the belief that effective action follows clear thinking' still exists, and seems to continue to do well.

Endnote

1. Kepner-Tregoe now has a fifth technique, **Potential Opportunity Analysis**, which claims to provides a systematic way to identify and seize opportunities.

A system by any other name

Since creative thought is the most important thing that makes people different from monkeys, it should be treated as a commodity more precious than gold and preserved with great care.

(Hall, 1962)

This appendix essentially supports the explanation of the systemic approach to problem solving examined in Chapter 11 and pages 78–80, 83–6, 116–25. The first objective of this appendix is to introduce some basic systems ideas, the understanding of which are assumed in Chapter 12. Second, through a critical evaluation of 'traditional' (or 'hard') systems thinking as a problem-solving tool, we hope to show how **soft systems** thinking preserves the best aspects of systems thinking in general, whilst remedying the deficiencies of the 'hard' systems approach. And, third, we will attempt to clarify the systems terminology used in tackling the other two objectives. An immediate example of this terminology is that the word 'systemic' does not mean the same thing as 'systematic' (usually defined as closely following a set of rational and logical steps or procedures), but simply 'using "systems" ideas'. Before the exposition of systems ideas in detail, a brief description of how and why the Systems Movement came into existence will provide a frame of reference for these ideas.

The origins of the Systems Movement

For many centuries, scientists have tried to establish a set of laws that would explain (and ultimately allow us to predict) some of the mysteries of life and the universe. This is a rather large endeavour, and there has been a tendency arbitrarily to break these investigations down into several fields of research, namely, physics, chemistry, biology and, more recently, psychology and the social sciences. But, looking back over the development of the sciences, the nature of these subdivisions does seem to possess some form or coherence. The various sciences did not just happen simultaneously, but developed sequentially.

This sequential emergence of the sciences seems to parallel the degree of complexity of the things being studied. These fields of study, our arbitrarily contrived scientific disciplines, now appear to fall into a hierarchy based on this complexity, and also on the way in which one science presupposes the laws of another. For example, chemistry tells us how elements react (which physics does not) but relies on physics to explain their atomic structure; biology tells us how living things procreate but depends on chemistry to describe the workings of DNA. Attempting to classify the sciences like this reminds us of their fundamental interrelatedness. This is necessary in that, as our knowledge increases and, with it, the complexity of the things we wish to study, the tendency is to break down our fields of research into even more specialized areas of investigation, such as astrophysics, nuclear physics, organic chemistry and marine biology. This tendency could, however, lead us to miss some significant connections and interrelationships. Our ignorance or neglect of the complex interrelationships between the components of our world, for example, means it may no longer be possible to control some of the (eco)systems that we have tampered with. But this is not our only problem.

Coincidental with this expansion of the sciences and our consideration of things of greater complexity has been the realization that the main method of scientific research, that of the application of systematic and objective analytical thought, becomes less effective and appropriate. Using the three Rs, **reductionism**, **repeatability**, **refutation**, that is, analysing a complex situation in order to find ways of breaking it into small enough bits (reductionism) for us to design experiments (that can be validated by virtue of their repeatability) to test (refute) hypotheses that we have formed concerning certain specific aspects of this situation, does not seem to work as well in studying human behaviour as in investigating, say, the way heated inanimate objects cool down in various environments. The failure of operational research techniques, and management science generally, to deal with problems of managing an organization is an illustration of this.

The more complex a situation becomes, the less easy it is to find ways of isolating suitable little bits of it on which we can design and conduct appropriate experiments. And even if we could do this, the potential dangers we encountered earlier (in Chapter 1), when discussing the consequences of restructuring a problem situation (that is, the possibility of missing the crucial issue because it falls between two fragments of the problem situation), would be equally applicable to our planned set of experiments. Specialization further compounds this problem.

The increasing complexity of the entities now studied, the spreading awareness that they may also be intricately related and form part of much wider systems and the fear of the results of increased specialization, have prompted some scientists to consider the feasibility of a holistic approach; that is, taking the problem situation as a whole and adopting a systems approach. In view of this it is perhaps not surprising that among the pioneers of the Systems Movement was a biologist, Ludwig von Bertalanffy. It was the realization by people like him that the entities they studied seemed to be collections of interrelated parts, that each entity had attributes or properties different from those of its constituent parts, that it had some sort of purpose – a reason for its existence – and was itself part of another collection, that led to the creation of the concept of a 'system'. As Peter Checkland puts it (1987a, p.2), when it comes to trying to understand the world we live in, systems ideas are 'potentially useful since our intuitive knowledge of the world suggests that it is densely interconnected'. And so the Systems Movement has evolved (see also Frame A2.1). A fuller and more rigorous account can be found in Checkland (1981).

Frame A2.1 *The study of systems*

One of the aims within the Systems Movement has been to devise a (General) Systems Theory, an abstract meta-science, which would be 'above' all the other sciences in the hierarchy mentioned earlier and would thus (it was hoped) contain a set of laws that would explain and generally 'sweep up' all the awkward phenomena found in the other sciences. To some extent this has been quite successful, but there is still a long way to go to the realization of this aim, if indeed it is attainable! But the use of systems concepts (that is, systems thinking) does appear to be a viable (and many people would now say more appropriate) alternative to analytical thinking when we are delving into areas where the latter experiences some difficulties. It certainly helps us understand and deal with many situations on which analytical thinking falls down. Peter Checkland (1981) believes that eventually systems thinking, along with analytical thinking, will be thought of as 'the twin components of scientific thinking'.

Systems thinking

A system is a totally abstract mental construct that we have invented in order to understand the real world that much better. It does this by providing us with a means of modelling our perception of things in the real world. The system itself does not actually exist in the real world (see also Frame A2.2), although there is some confusion because we now tend to use the word 'system' to describe everyday things which we do and which are often tangible entities that can be sensed. For example, 'the minister announced today that there will be further cuts in the educational system'; 'the company's newly installed computer system "crashed" again today'; or even 'Voyager 1 has now left the solar system and is heading off into outer space'. These things may have some of the properties of a system, and could no doubt be usefully *thought* of as systems, but they are not systems in the sense that we speak of them here.

Frame A2.2 *Systems and systems thinking*

A system is:

> *a group, of people, things and or ideas connected by some common reason or purpose, that is clearly differentiated from its surroundings, and which has attributes or properties that are different from those its mem-*

▶

bers have individually, and the belonging to which alters those members in some way . . . as perceived or conceived by an individual human being.

Systems thinking is:

the process of trying to use this (systemic) image (with the properties that we have attributed to it), to help us understand the real world.

We may think of the following as systems:

- a sunflower
- the solar system
- an Apple Macintosh microcomputer
- physics
- humanism
- Total Quality Management
- the National Health Service
- The United Nations.

Checkland argues (1987a, pp.7–8) that the reason why we now use the word 'system' too casually and perhaps incorrectly in our everyday language is due (at least in part) to the success the original concept achieved as a model of perceived reality. Although there may appear to be no real harm in using the same word to describe both the thing that exists in the real world and the mental concept that we use to help our understanding of it (so long as we always remain aware of this difference), this confusion has already made systems thinking more difficult to understand, inhibited its development and slowed its attainment of more universal acceptance as a useful learning and problem-solving process. This is particularly so in regard to human affairs for, as Checkland has said (1987a), the confusion caused by the dual usage of the word 'system' is important because it constrains and limits systems thinking, without this being noticed. The constraints are not too damaging in relation to the use of systems thinking to conceptualize objects in the natural world – such as frogs and foxgloves – nor in relation to the design of man-made objects such as cars and cow sheds. But the confusion is very damaging in relation to attempts to use systems ideas in trying to understand the phenomena of the social world, since it restricts the application of a systems approach there to a crude form of functionalism.

This differentiation may seem pedantic, but it is necessary if we are to understand and apply the useful findings of the Systems Movement effectively. If we persist in thinking that the thing 'out there' is a system, we may inadvertently and probably incorrectly attribute to it the properties of a system. For instance, the organization whose problem we are trying to help resolve may well be 'a collection of people, things and ideas'. But are they necessarily 'connected by some *common* reason or purpose'? It is doubtful that they are if they have a major problem, and even if they are, can we be sure that this organization has all the necessary control processes and feedback that it needs in order to survive the changes taking place in the environment around it?

A secondary consequence of this is that we may fall into the trap, as some systems analysts have, of assuming that the thing we are studying does have some sort of integrity. It is often referred to inadvisably and perhaps wrongly as the 'original system', when it is at best an *implementation* of a system, and could in fact be the implementation of an idea that has no systemic coherence at all. Having made this mistake we are likely to analyse only *how* it is doing something, then, noticing anomalies with this, we 'patch them up' in an attempt to improve its performance. During this, however, we may have failed to consider whether this activity should actually be done in the first place or to question the very purpose of the thing's existence.

Although a 'system' was always intended to be an abstract concept, there has been a certain ambiguity in the writings of systems thinkers. If blame for the spread of this confusion is to be apportioned anywhere, however, then some of it must lie with those people who reapplied systems ideas during the 1950s and 1960s from science into the area of human affairs.

'Hard' systems thinking

Having said that the perceived need to view things holistically came with the realization by some scientists of the complexity that pervaded everything, including ourselves, I should add that it was not long before other people applied systems ideas to the planning, appraisal and execution of complex human endeavours, typically those which evolved out of a desire to translate the discoveries being made in scientific and technological research into realized applications that would benefit mankind by fulfilling *some defined need.* These people, however, tended to think that systems *could* exist 'out there' in the real world, and that the (system) models which they built were representations of something that did or would exist in it. All that was then necessary, they believed, was to take a systematic approach to the 'engineering' (contriving and modifying) of these systems. From the 1950s onwards there were many attempts to provide this systematic way of conceiving, designing, evaluating and implementing these projects. This began what is now called **hard** systems methodology – or at least one strand of it – which in essence reduces problem solving to defining the system, defining the system's objectives and engineering the system to meet those objectives (Checkland, 1985).

There would appear to be three main 'strands' in the development of hard systems thinking: Systems Engineering (SE), (RAND) Systems Analysis (SA) and Operational Research (OR), although these have evolved into a number of variants. A statement of the nature and purpose of OR has already been given in Chapter 1. Checkland describes SE and SA as:

> Systems engineering comprises the set of activities which together lead to the creation of a complex man-made entity and/or the procedures and information flows associated with its operation. Systems analysis is the systematic appraisal of the costs and other implications of meeting a defined requirement in various ways. (1981, p.138)

OR is different from the other two primarily because it was intended to help with *tactical* decisions concerning *existing* 'systems', as opposed to SE and SA, whose origins are in research projects and planning respectively and are thus concerned with *strategic* issues and *not yet existing* systems. Although having slightly differing aims, there is much similarity between them, particularly with regard to their underlying assumptions, as Checkland (1981, Chapter 5; 1983) has argued. Consequently, Frame A2.3 uses only the steps involved in SE to serve as an illustration of the hard systems approach.

Frame A2.3 *Systems Engineering*

The seven stages in the process of SE identified by A.D. Hall (1962) are typical of hard systems methodology:

- Problem definition – essentially a definition of a need.
- Choice of objectives – a definition of physical needs and of the value system within which they must be met.
- Systems synthesis – creation of possible alternative systems.
- Systems analysis – analysis of the hypothetical systems in the light of their objectives.
- System selection – selection of most promising alternative.
- System development – development up to the prototype stage.
- Current engineering – system realization beyond prototype stage and including monitoring, modifying and feeding back information to design.

All these methodologies assume that the problem situation can be expressed as a need, and our objective is to find the best way to satisfy this need. Here is Checkland (1981, p.139) talking about SE and SA:

> The words differ somewhat but the thought is always the same, that at the start of the study it is essential to know, and to state, what end we want to achieve, where we want to go. Given that definition, the systems thinking then enables us to select a means of achieving the desired end which is efficient, if possible economically efficient.

Although he later (1978, 1981) revised his views on problem 'solving', Ackoff (one of the pioneers of OR), writing in 1957, similarly summarized the essence of hard systems thinking by saying that 'All problems ultimately reduce to the evaluation of the efficiency of alternative means for a designated set of objectives'. In other words, hard systems thinking assumes that **goal seeking** is what we are about.

Another key feature of the hard systems approach was the belief that not only was it quite reasonable to strive for optimal solutions, but that such things could actually be attained. This was until Herbert Simon pointed out (see Chapter 1) that this was seldom possible in practice, and that we should be content with a solution that **satisfices** – one that is the best we can presently manage under the circumstances.

Because of some initial successes in areas where a specific need had been identified, people tried to apply hard systems thinking to less well-defined situations such as **people** problems, where it met with considerably less success, partly due to the imposition by the methodology of the limited form of functionalism mentioned above. (Ironically, the attempts to introduce this form of systems thinking into the social sciences came at a time when the limitations of functionalism were encouraging a search for better alternatives.) **Soft** systems thinking was intended to salvage the best aspects of the hard systems approach whilst providing a more adequate means of tackling open-ended **wicked** real-world problems. So what exactly was wrong with the hard systems approach?

The problem with 'hard' systems thinking

Probably the most important shortcoming of hard systems thinking is summarized by Checkland thus:

> SSM was developed because the methodology of systems engineering, based on defining goals or objectives, simply did not work when applied to messy, ill-structured, real-world problems. The inability to define objectives, or to decide whose were the most important, was usually part of the problem. (1985, p.763)

Checkland (1983, p.667) and others believe that with most real-world problems, especially those in which several people have a stake, defining the objective will always be a problem because everyone involved will see the problem situation from different perspectives and are thus likely to have different objectives. It will seldom be obvious whose objectives we should be addressing. Hard systems thinkers do not see this as a problem. For the RAND analyst or the systems engineer there is no question as to whose value system we should use when selecting our problem definition. It would be the real-world decision taker who has the decision problem, or the originator of the specification for the SE team, respectively. That the hard systems approach does not consider that 'the likely victims of the system in question, those who decree its creation, its designers or, indeed, any other group with any interest in the outcome of the study' may have a valid view of the problem situation is, to Checkland, a major weakness.

Fundamental differences between hard and soft systems thinkingi

The difficulties in defining objectives in real-world problem situations involving people led some systems thinkers to doubt whether 'goal seeking' was an appropriate description of them. Sir Geoffrey Vickers (1965, p.33) is known for first questioning whether human systems should be thought of like this:

> To explain all human activity in terms of 'goal-seeking', though good enough for the behaviour of hungry rats in mazes, raises insoluble pseudo-conflicts between means and ends ... and leaves the most important aspect of our activities, the ongoing maintenance of our ongoing activities and their ongoing satisfactions, hanging in the air as a psychological anomaly called 'action done for its own sake'.

The problem with means and ends occurs if we think of ends as being goals, for then no end can ever be more than a means. We almost invariably strive for particular goals because we perceive that through their attainment we can establish or maintain some ongoing process, for example, the continuing satisfaction of certain needs. A better description of what **human (activity) systems** are about, Vickers believed, was **relationship maintaining**. The idea that we continuously seek to attain one goal after another is fallacious and based on the assumption that we desire objects rather than relationships. 'No one "wants an apple" . . . [we] may want to eat it, sell it, paint it, admire it, conceivably even merely to possess it – a common type of continuing relation', in other words, what we want to do is 'to establish or change some relation with it'. Any goals that we do seek are to do with 'changes in our relations or in our opportunities for relating; but the bulk of our activity consists in 'relating' itself' (Vickers, 1965, p.33).

Another contribution Vickers made to the development of soft systems thinking was to stress the importance of realizing and accepting that people perceive problem situations in different ways, and that their individual system of values and beliefs affects this perception.

> Appreciation manifests itself in the exercise through time of mutually related judgements of reality and value. These appreciative judgements reflect the view currently held by those who make them of their interests and responsibilities, views large implicit and unconscious which none the less condition what events and relations they will regard as relevant or possibly relevant to them, and whether they will regard these as welcome or unwelcome, important or unimportant, demanding or not demanding action or concern by them. Such judgements disclose what can best be described as a set of readinesses to distinguish some aspects of the situation rather than others and to classify and value these in this way rather than in that. I will describe these readinesses as an appreciative system. (1965, p.67)

This concept of an appreciative system, would seem to be an elaboration of what has been called **mental set** in Chapter 3.

It was from these beginnings that Checkland developed his **Soft Systems Methodology** (SSM), which can be seen as 'a formal practical expression' of the idea of appreciative systems. SSM is a problem-solving strategy designed (amongst other things) to incorporate various people's perspectives of the problem situation and their differing objectives, thus overcoming the second weakness of the hard systems approach. Because of the importance that the soft systems approach places on this, they are never so presumptuous as to assume that their systems are models of the real world. As Checkland (1985, p.764) says, 'the models of **human activity systems** in SSM do not pretend to be models of the world, only models which embody a particular stated way of viewing the world'. These are models such that by comparing a number of them with the real-world situation, we hope to gain a better understanding of what is going on 'out there' and how things perhaps should be if we are to improve the situation from those perspectives.

Hard systems thinking assumes that we know where we are going, and hence what sort of changes are required in order to improve the situation, so all we have to do is affect these changes in the most efficient way. Soft systems thinking, on the other hand, accepts that we do not always know what changes are needed, but believes that by considering the situation from these various viewpoints we will discover the changes we need to make. We have found a way by which learning can effectively replace optimizing or satisficing our implied aim when we left Chapter 1. This learning process is in theory (and probably in practice) a cyclic and never-ending one. There will be no 'final solution' with soft systems thinking, but that is not necessarily a bad thing.

A reprieve for hard systems thinking?

Having criticized the hard systems approach it seems appropriate to conclude this section on a positive note. As stated earlier (Chapter 1) it is not that OR, or the hard systems approach generally, is no longer of use and should be replaced, but that it is only suitable for a certain subset of problems. Where there is nothing problematic about the purpose of the organization, division or section we are investigating, and there is agreement over what needs to be done to resolve the problem situation, hard systems thinking can help us, as it did with projects intended to satisfy specific human needs in the early days of SE.

Checkland (1985, pp.765–6) says that soft systems thinking should be seen as the general case of that which hard systems thinking is 'the occasional special case'. He goes on to say that at a 'basic operational level there is very often a complete consensus on what needs to be done and what constitutes efficiency in doing it'. In these situations, when we have a well-defined problem and our objectives are clear – for example, a mail order company which is unable to satisfy its orders within a reasonable amount of time because of an inadequate stock control 'system' – the use of the powerful techniques of OR, SSADM (Structured Systems Analysis and Design Methodology) etc., are appropriate and can assist us in resolving our problem. But equally there will be many other situations, such as deciding what products are to be offered in our mail order catalogue, which will be different matters altogether, with many differing views of them and requiring an entirely different treatment.

In an attempt to 'balance' the score, this final quote comes from Geoff Cutts, an exponent of one aspect of current hard systems thinking,: 'It is essential to only consider the use of SSADM in an environment which is predominantly well-structured' (1987, p.14).

More systemic thoughts

If we look again at the definition of a system at the beginning of this chapter, you will notice that it finishes with 'as perceived or conceived by an individual human being'. Many definitions fail to emphasize this point. Whether or not there is any need to make the distinction between perception and conception is debatable, because in everyday usage we tend to use the words 'perceive' (become or be aware of through the senses, get knowledge of by the mind, understand, discern) and 'conceive' (form in the mind, imagine or think about, understand) almost interchangeably. This is particularly so with regard to 'understanding' things, which essentially is what systems are all about. Perception is so intimately linked to intentionality (the way the mental processes of consciousness are directed at whatever we are thinking about) that the whole process can be viewed as one of conception. Some might even say that perception is no more than the mechanism of conception. But to use just one word (and it is usually 'perceive' that occurs in those definitions of a system that do stress this point) might seem to preclude the other. What happens when we do some 'systems thinking' depends to a certain extent on whether we are trying to make sense of something we have seen, heard, etc., or are dreaming up (designing) something new.

When we look at the public sector provision for educating the young in our country, with a view to trying to improve it, we may think of it as a system. That is, there is educational provision 'out there' somewhere, we have this concept of a system in our minds and we use this concept to help us order, structure and generally make sense of our perceptions of this provision. When we are designing something which is 'new', say the setting up of a desk-top publishing facility for a small manufacturing company, we may also wish to view this as a system. It is likely that for this, we will be using a different system (but again a mental construct) to help us organize our recollections of the company's needs and our previous experience of similar installations. Thus systems thinking can involve both perceiving and conceiving something as a system. We have not as yet said exactly what is involved in systems thinking however.

John Beishon and Geoff Peters (1981, p.14) describe systems thinking as

> looking at situations, topics, problems, etc., as a complex of interacting parts which can be divided into specific systems and within these, subsystems, and if necessary into sub-subsystems, and so on. Identification of these various systems is followed by an examination of the relationships among them, including the flows of influences (or information), materials and energy and the routes these take among and within the systems involved.

Before taking it any further than this (in Chapter 11), we need to consider whether there are different types of system, and to look in more detail at the properties of a system.

Classification of systems

The universe may be thought of as being made up of systems within systems. Various attempts have been made to classify these systems. One such effort, by K.E. Boulding in 1956, did this on the basis of complexity. Starting with static structures, such as crystals, it went through various types of 'mechanical' and organismal systems and finally culminated with Man, socio-cultural systems and transcendental systems. Another, by N. Jordan in 1968, attempted to classify systems according to three 'dimensions', **Structural** (static) *v.* **Functional** (dynamic), whether or not they are **Purposive**, and their **Connectivity**. The latter term means when some elements (or the connections between them) are changed, removed or destroyed and the remaining elements may also be affected or not. Essentially this is a distinction between organismal and mechanical systems. But as yet there is no agreed way of partitioning the universe like this.

Checkland (1981), however, has suggested the following minimal classification of systems types as being sufficient for our purposes here.

- natural systems, e.g. a molecule, the universe;
- designed physical systems, e.g. a hammer, the lunar module;
- designed abstract systems, e.g. mathematics;
- human activity systems, e.g. British Airways, Greenpeace;
- transcendental systems, e.g. God.

If we assume that the patterns and laws of the universe are not capricious, then the distinguishing feature of natural systems is that they cannot be other than they are. Designed systems, on the other hand, because they have been devised and possibly fabricated by human beings, could be. A human being is part of a natural system, but he or she may create and use designed systems, possibly from elements of another natural system, and indeed may do this whilst belonging to a human activity system. A human activity system can be thought of as a system in which a collection of human beings interact with each other and perform certain activities in an organized and purposeful way, as perceived by some human's point of view.

It is not necessary for members of a human activity system to know that they belong to it. Because the systems have to be perceived by an individual (who perceives things in different ways to others) a human activity system can obviously be other than it is.

We need to be careful how we classify so-called 'social' systems which, put in simple terms, are those groups of people to which we knowingly belong, the membership of which carries with it certain responsibilities and obligations, and from which we have certain expectations. Examples of these social systems are an ethnic group, our family, the Boy Scouts, a trade union or a commercial enterprise. Since it is possible to identify for any of these groups a set of human activities which are characteristic to that particular group, they might be thought of as human activity systems. But the interpersonal relationships and emotional attachments which could be thought of as characteristic of natural groupings, our gregarious tendencies, although mostly prevalent in tribal and family groupings, can and do occur in many of the other social systems as well, so should they be thought of as natural systems?

Checkland (1981, pp.120–1) says that a distinction which he attributes to the sociologist Tonnies more than adequately solves this dilemma. Under this classification scheme, a social system is thought to be a natural system if we naturally belong to it and do so with our whole selves. If, as well as this, we choose to be a member of some other social system (for a while) in order to achieve some specific goal, but assign only a part of ourselves to membership of that social system, then it is best thought of as a human activity system. For instance I am, as a whole person, naturally part of the community I live in (a natural system); however, I donate some of my time and mental effort to the organization I work for (a human activity system) and I do this for a reason. (And it's not the money!)

The significance of this distinction is that as individuals we can and usually do belong to more than one social system. Some of these will be natural systems and others will be human activity systems. We will thus have allegiances to more than one social system, and the nature and strength of these allegiances will be different also. We are often bound to natural social systems by very strong emotional ties, whereas with human activity systems the attraction may be only one of

extrinsic rewards, which are possibly available elsewhere. Even if our membership of a human activity system is because of some intrinsic motivation, we have
chosen it for some reason and the basis of this decision could change; for example, our needs and objectives may alter, or we may perceive that the organization
is no longer fulfilling our psychological contract (see Chapter 13). If forced to
choose, would not many people place the welfare of their family ahead of that of
the organization they work for or even their country? This potential conflict of
goals, loyalties and responsibilities should never be forgotten, in fact it should be
deliberately considered (with a view to ensuring some degree of compatibility
amongst them) in any systems thinking that we do. We are, after all, using this
(systemic) approach so as not to overlook interconnectednesses like this: we are
attempting to get as complete a picture of things as possible. Our aim here is to
use systems concepts to help us deal with 'people' problems, situations which are
characterized by human beings trying to take purposeful action, so our main
concern would seem to be with human activity systems. These systems may
include both natural and designed subsystems, and may also themselves be
included within other natural or designed systems, and perhaps even transcendental systems!

The significance and fragility of human activity systems are illustrated by the
following quotes:

> Social structures (organizations) are essentially contrived systems. They are made of
> men and are imperfect systems. They can come apart at the seams overnight, but they
> can also outlast the biological organisms which originally created them. The cement
> that holds them together is essentially psychological rather than biological. Social
> systems are anchored in the attitudes, perceptions, beliefs, motivations, habits, and
> expectations of human beings. (Katz and Kahn, 1966)

> Nearly all systems which include human beings are unstable and their instability is
> nearly always the unwilled result of man's actions, monstrously multiplied in power by
> technology but not correspondingly informed by increased understanding … The
> extent to which we can redesign any part of it without disastrous impact on any other
> parts is very limited and we do not know and probably cannot fully know its limitations.
> (Vickers, 1981, p.19)

The characteristics of a system

As we have seen, a system is a purposeful collection of interrelated elements, the
whole of which can be distinguished from those things which are not part of the
system, that is, its **environment**, by its properties and the interconnectedness of
its components. Therefore, there must be a **boundary** between the system and
the environment in which it exists.

In the first instance, we can define **closed systems** as those which are totally
self-contained and do not interact in any way with the environment that they are
in. A particular feature of closed systems is that they tend towards a state of dis-
order, chaos and total breakdown (or more technically, entropy).

Entropy is a term taken from the study of thermodynamics, and in the study
of systems is used to mean the tendency of a system to move towards a chaotic

or random state, where it is unable to fulfil its function properly (there no longer exists a potential for energy transformation or work to take place). One example of entropy is the phenomenon that if you shut a human being up so that he or she can have little or no interaction with their environment – anything from 'solitary confinement' to the extent of suspending a person in salt water of the right density to simulate weightlessness, and which is warmed to body heat, all done in a lightproof, soundproof container – that human being will eventually go stark raving mad! Usually entropy is associated with mechanistic systems; for example, an automatic drilling machine which senses the arrival of a new part on a nearby conveyor belt, grabs hold of it, orientates it and then promptly drills x number of holes in it. If left to its own devices, however, with no interaction (maintenance) from outside, it will cease to perform its drilling operations accurately and eventually break down completely, as wear develops on its drill bits and elsewhere.

The ubiquitous digital watch could be thought of as an example of a **dynamic** closed system. Assuming that it comes supplied with a new battery, it will continue to display the correct time (within an accuracy of a few seconds per month) for a couple of years or more without any interaction with its surroundings (providing the watch is not going to be subjected to a harmful environment which it was never designed to withstand). Slowly the energy being provided by the battery will diminish and, upon reaching a certain minimum threshold, the timekeeping accuracy will deteriorate or, as is more usual, the display will disappear rendering the system of no further use without a battery transplant. It is interesting to note though that this type of closed system has an internal regulatory or **control mechanism**. The quartz crystal controls the electronic oscillations and hence the timekeeping, in the same way as the escapement mechanism controlled the release of the clockwork 'power source' and the movement of the cogs in an old-style analogue watch. Our drilling machine would have a control mechanism, probably a program stored in a microprocessor. There are other things which can be thought of as **static** closed systems, such as a suspension bridge, which do not have such a control mechanism. All of these systems have a reason for their existence though. The digital watch, the drilling machine and the suspension bridge can be thought of as designed physical systems; they were designed by human beings for a purpose.

This discussion has introduced certain features of a system, such as the boundary with its environment, entropy, its purposefulness and its possible possession of a control mechanism. To identify automatic drilling machines, watches and suspension bridges as merely closed systems, however, is an oversimplification. The distinction between open and closed systems is neither as precise nor as useful as this introduction may suggest.

An **open system**, while having all the characteristics mentioned above, is a system that does interact with its environment. There will be continual exchanges of material, information and/or energy taking place between an open system and its environment. We cannot really accept that replacing the battery in a digital watch is an example of energy being exchanged between the environment and the system because the current thinking is that, in order to be an open system, a system must take an active part in these exchanges. A solar-powered digital watch would stand a better chance of being considered as an open system. It is true that the solar-powered watch does not go out hunting for energy sources, but it does have an internal subsystem, the solar panel and its associated circuitry, which (actively) 'absorbs' light energy and converts it into electrical energy whenever it has the opportunity to do so.

What we can say about both the drilling machine and our solar-powered digital watch is that, although they take something in from their environment (undrilled parts, solar energy) and give something back to it as well (drilled parts, information about the time), neither of them has any way of detecting the effect that these outputs are having on their environment. Open systems do. If we took our solar-powered digital watch and added to it some electronics that could pick up radio waves containing time signals such that it could then automatically adjust its timekeeping from these signals, we might be getting even nearer to an open system.

Should a domestic gas-fired central heating installation be thought of as an open or closed system? It takes in energy in the form of gas from the environment. It converts this into hot water, which it transports (via pipes) to radiators that in turn export heat energy back to the environment. The installation also has sensors which monitor the temperature of the environment and its own water temperature and communicates this information (provides some *feedback*) to the control mechanism which determines the behaviour of the installation; that is, it provides information that allows the control mechanism to *decide* whether to switch the water heating mechanism on or off. It seems to remain in a fairly stable state, maintaining its environment at a constant temperature. But if a central heating boiler is left to its own devices (i.e. we do not intervene in its normal operations by having it regularly maintained), it too will eventually break down. Does this condemn it to being a closed system?

Open systems are thought of as having a dynamic but reasonably stable relationship with their environment; the interchange of material, information and energy is such that the system *itself* manages to allay the onslaught of entropy. If our domestic central heating required no maintenance, or was somehow self-maintaining, it would definitely be an open system. Human activity systems are open systems. There does appear to be, however, a desire amongst systems thinkers to subdivide open systems like these into two further categories.

Some open systems simply respond to stimuli via some sort of feedback loop. These are the ones that react to environmental conditions in a seemingly perpetual self-correcting fashion, just barely (if the feedback mechanism is effective) postponing the inexorable decline into entropy's chaotic state. There are also thought to be other open systems which 'make the first move'; that is, their interactions with the environment are not just responses to stimuli. These systems are proactive rather than reactive. Their exchange of materials, information and energy with the environment is such that not only do they hold back the devastating effect of increased entropy, but they can also improve their position by overcoming the effects of entropy (that is, they gain negative entropy). This suggests that they are potentially able to achieve a degree of 'immortality', or continuity anyway. The form of these systems is more persistent than their constituent elements, which would need to have been replaced many times over in order to achieve the systems' relative longevity. These open systems also have the potential to fall apart at any time very quickly. It is a very delicate balance for, as Sir Geoffrey Vickers warns us (1983, p.13) 'no open system lasts for ever. Its stability can never be taken for granted', as it 'fluctuates' during its regulatory process, and it can easily go beyond a point of no return 'and dissolve or change into something else'.

The main problem with the discussion so far is that things which are often thought of as closed systems are almost invariably components or subsystems of larger open systems, and so it is unrealistic to think of them as totally isolated entities. If the pricing and design of our battery-operated digital watch is such that we would replace the battery rather than throw it away and buy a new watch, then it can be thought of as part of a (time-knowing) system that does interact with its environment, a system that also contains a human being who buys and fits a new battery when one is required. Even if we could not replace the battery, it could still be thought of as a part of an (open) profit-making system by someone. It could be said, therefore, that closed systems are nothing more than a philosophical abstraction.

The early, and unsuccessful, attempts at modelling organizations with closed systems highlight the danger of placing too much emphasis on the existence of closed systems, as it encourages the reductionist thinking we are trying to get away from. It is, however, open systems that are of special interest to us here, because we now believe that social systems, and organizations in particular, are best regarded as open systems. There are undoubtedly many that apparently behave like the first category of open system mentioned above, but surely to be described as successful, organizations should be such that they are perceived as the second category of open system.

Conclusions

Studying the behaviour of things we regard as systems is not without difficulty. First we have to overcome the cultural norm summed up by the old adage that tends to govern our thinking: 'If it's working fine, leave it alone!' This advice would be all right if we could guarantee that systems always drift slowly and gracefully into a state of entropy. This is seldom the case.

Another problem is that it is difficult to predict all the possible behaviours of a system until we have seen it fail. Unfortunately, we often have to wait for a system to fail before all its possible behaviours are revealed. When that happens there are many vested interests which ensure that full records of what happened are difficult to trace. In addition, system malfunctioning often occurs suddenly and catastrophically; one cannot expect people to start making detailed observations in the middle of a crisis.

We have now introduced all the features that an open system, such as one of the human activity systems that we are about to encounter, should have. The so-called **Formal System Model** described in Frame A2.4 can be thought of as a summary of these features. In Chapter 7 we construct models of various systems and use the Formal Systems Model as a checklist to ensure that our model contains all the elements that it, and the system it represents, should have.

Frame A2.4 *Formal System Model*

The Formal System has (Checkland, 1981, pp. 173–4):

- an ongoing purpose/mission . . .

which might be unattainable in a soft systems situation,

- a measure of performance . . .

which permits regulatory action,

- contains a decision-taking process,
- components which are themselves systems,
- components which interact . . .

or show a degree of connectivity (which may be physical, flows of energy, materials, information, or influence) such that effects/actions can be transmitted through the system with which it interacts,

- exists in a wider system (environment),
- a boundary . . .

an area within which decision taking has real power to cause action,

- resources . . .

physical, human and/or abstract which are at the disposal of the decision-taking process,

- some guarantee of continuity or long-term stability.

The complete 'original' Brainstorming CPS process

This appendix illustrates the 'complete' Brainstorming process as originally described by Alex Osborn.

What is Brainstorming?

Brainstorming was conceived originally as a 'complete' problem-solving process, intended to provide the means for dealing with several of the stages we tend to go through when tackling a problem. When compared with the stages in the problem-solving 'model' presented in Chapter 2, the Brainstorming process involves redefining the problem, generating ideas and finding possible solutions, developing feasible solutions and evaluating solutions.

Brainstorming was intended to be a group problem-solving process, relying on the interactions between the ideas and imaginations of group members for its success and productivity.

An outline of the whole process is given in Frame A3.1. This process has now been superseded by what is known as the **Osborn-Parnes** CPS process.

Frame A3.1 *Outline of the Brainstorming process*

Pre-meeting with the problem owner to define the problem, determine its suitability, and to discuss what constitutes an acceptable solution.

- Warm-up session – which may include problem redefinition in its later stages.
- Brainstorming session ('proper') – incorporating additional techniques: wildest idea, checklists and Attribute Listing as appropriate.
- The processing (and evaluation) of ideas:
    - Subsequent acquisition of ideas.
    - Selection of most promising ideas.
    - Development of selected ideas.

– Verification
– Presentation of the 'best' ideas.

When to use the full Brainstorming process

It used to be thought that virtually all problems could benefit from a Brainstorming approach, though some might need breaking down into parts to ensure that problem was not too general. Brainstorming is not now considered suitable for complex problems, and even in the 1950s Osborn advised that 'the guiding principle is that a problem should be simple rather than complex. Failure to narrow the problem to a single target can seriously mar the success of any brainstorm session' (1957, p.238).

The problem 'How can we improve the profitability of our household products division?' is far too diverse a problem situation for Brainstorming to tackle in one go (if at all). If we were to attack this problem from a number of specific 'viewpoints' – such as: How can we reduce production costs of our leading household product? What other markets are there for our plastic containers? What additional products could we 'easily' add to our existing range? How can we improve the marketing of our kitchenware? – we would stand a greater chance of success. Although addressing any one of these problem definitions is feasible with Brainstorming, tackling all of them may not be. There will be a limit to the number of Brainstorming sessions that time permits, even if we ignore any additional difficulties likely to be caused by the perceived interconnectedness of some of these specific problem definitions.

Brainstorming is not normally used with complex problems these days owing to a change in opinion over the desirability of restructuring such problems. Not only is it difficult to separate a complex problem situation into a number of discrete and independent parts, but this process may result in the actual problem area being 'missed' completely. Other methods seek to avoid the dangers of restructuring a problem, for example, the **Soft Systems Methodology** described in Chapter 11. Osborn paraphrases his own advice with 'orientation of aim is often half the battle'. This particular observation is realized by the inclusion of an entire stage, **Goal Wishing** (see Chapter 6), in the early part of the Synectics process. Brainstorming is best used only on quite specific problem areas (see Frame A3.2); these other problem-solving strategies are better on more complex problems.

Frame A3.2　*Typical applications of Brainstorming*

- Finding a name for a new product/service.
- Finding alternative uses/new markets for existing products.
- What improvements can we make to this product/service/process?
- Where can we find more time/space/resources so that we can . . . ?
- Potential problem analysis.
- Obtaining a cross-section of views on a specific topic.

Tudor Rickards (1974) has listed a number of specific problem areas for which Brainstorming may be unsuitable. Among these are problems requiring a high level of technical expertise, problems involving the manipulation and motivation of people, and those problems where written material needs to be created and/or considered.

One feature that may indicate a problem is suitable for Brainstorming is if the merit of the ideas or possible solutions once acquired is fairly self-evident, and/or they do not require much further development before they become feasible; for example, finding a name for a new product.

Preparing for a Brainstorming session

If, as suggested (in Chapter 3), the Brainstorming group contains some 'novices', then these 'new' guests need to be given some idea of what to expect. Preferably, they should at least have taken part in a training session, and are thus not totally inexperienced; but if they have never participated in any form of Brainstorming before they should be sent a description of the Brainstorming process which includes an explanation of its purpose and its rules.

All participants should be sent a 'background' memo, informing them of the time and place of the meeting, and giving them an indication of the problem to be brainstormed, along with some 'typical' ideas.

Finally the group leader needs to note down his/her own ideas in order to gain some impression as to the 'directions' s/he considers it worth guiding the group along on the day. A **checklist** may be useful for this.

The tasks of the secretary and leader during the meeting

A member of the group should take on the role of secretary and should normally be positioned near the leader. The secretary should write up all the ideas offered and may paraphrase them, though if possible this should be avoided. No form of censorship or bias should be invoked. Osborn advises that the ideas should be numbered as they are written up, because knowing how many ideas have been produced acts as an encouragement. He also states that reading from lists prepared earlier should not be allowed.

The Brainstorming session begins with the leader explaining the problem that the group is to work on and reminding the group of the 'ground rules'. The leader should then use a warm-up exercise, to set up a 'climate' which ensures that no 'external' criticism comes from the other group members when we start putting forward ideas. The leader should also encourage the participants not to allow their own built-in **self-censor** (see Chapter 3) to stop them from putting ideas forward, especially since often our critical faculties are so ingrained that we are not always aware of the self-censor's operation. Techniques such as **Synectics'** excursions (see Chapter 7) help to overcome this.

During the course of the Brainstorming session 'proper', the leader has a number of other tasks to accomplish, such as enforcing the rules and counteracting the tendency of the group to break up into several smaller meetings. Since combinations of ideas are what is most wanted, the leader should also give 'builds' priority when ideas are flowing fast. Originally participants were asked to raise their hands when they had an idea to contribute, and Osborn recommended snapping one's fingers to indicate a 'build', although this may not be appropriate in all cultures!

Last, the leader should remind the group that if ideas are coming too fast for the leader and secretary to 'manage', then the group members should note down their ideas on paper until they get a chance to suggest them.

An application of Brainstorming: naming a product

One of the most frequent applications of Brainstorming is naming a new product or service. To illustrate the Brainstorming process we will now work through such a problem. A brief outline of the story surrounding our product is given in Frame A3.3.

Frame A3.3 *Drug Stores Ltd: the problem situation*

Drug Stores Ltd is a nationwide chain store, with 130 branches throughout the country. They sell a wide range of proprietary brands of cosmetics and toiletries, 'over the counter' pills and medicines, and a limited number of 'health' foods and drinks, plus a number of miscellaneous items. Drug Stores are about to launch their own brand of cosmetics and are trying to think up a suitable name for this new range of products. They are hoping that these products will appeal primarily to the younger woman and provide them with a strong foothold in this market.

Pre-meeting with the problem owner

The pre-meeting normally involves just the leader and client. One reason for this is to make the leader aware of the constraints on the range of acceptable solutions in any real-world situation, owing to financial, social, political and legal considerations, or just client preferences, so that the leader can guide the group's efforts. However, because it is difficult for someone to be conscious of these constraints and still remain uncritical, it is probably best if the Brainstorming group itself remains unaware of them.

Warm-up exercise and Brainstorming session

On the day of the Brainstorming session, the first thing we need to do after the introductions is to 'get into the mood' of the occasion with a warm-up exercise (see Chapter 3).

The next stage in the process is the Brainstorming session 'proper'. The list shown in Frame A3.4 was obtained by a group of students during a training session, and took approximately 15 minutes to achieve (a few ideas have had to be censored before publication!). Some of these suggestions are probably not going to go much further in the process ('S & M' and 'Bondage' for example), but as catalysts for our imaginations they have already served their purpose. However, there are many quite reasonable suggestions in this list, which I am sure you will agree are at least as marketable as existing product names (such as 'No. 17', 'Rimmel', 'Maybelline' and 'Max Factor').

> **Frame A3.4** *Drug Stores Ltd: a name for a new range of cosmetics*
>
> | | | |
> |---|---|---|
> | New Faces | Fantasy | Lady of the Night |
> | Complexions | Wishing Well | Bondage |
> | Bright Eyes | Images | S & M |
> | Camouflage | Reflections | Stallion |
> | Deception | War Paint | Pagan |
> | Metamorphosis | Creations | Neanderthal |
> | Naturelle | Ecstasy | Innuendo |
> | Illusions | Bitch | Aura |
> | Images | Street Corner Look | Peaches & Cream |
> | Collage | Red Light | English Roses |
> | Dreams | | |

The processing (and evaluation) of ideas

After the Brainstorming session is completed, the ideas generated have to be evaluated. Osborn said that, despite some disagreement about this, most people believe that evaluation should be done by a panel of people different from those who took part in the original session, thus preventing any 'my baby' problems coming into the evaluation. However, the original group will experience frustration if no feedback is available concerning the fate of their ideas. Osborn suggests that the **most promising ideas** should now be selected (usually by the original group leader) and passed to an evaluating panel for further consideration; but he does not indicate how rigorous this screening procedure should be. There is a danger here: this selection of the 'good' ideas from the 'bad' can be a retrogressive step. Nolan (1989, p.60) believes that there is a distinct possibility that 'new' ideas may not be considered to be 'good' ideas because they have no track record (see Chapter 8). Allowing the original idea-generating group to make the selection and to take part in the evaluation may ensure the retention of more of the 'new' speculative or unusual ideas, but the real solution is probably to have a more sophisticated and 'idea-friendly' evaluation process such as that incorporated into the Synectics approach (see **itemized response** in Chapter 8).

Osborn breaks down the processing of the ideas into several stages:

(1) Subsequent acquisition of ideas   On the basis that the participants frequently come up with more ideas after the Brainstorming session, when they have had a chance to 'sleep on it', participants should be canvassed for additional ideas after the event. One way to do this is to send to each participant a list of the ideas produced in the session along with a request for any further thoughts that group members may have had on reflection. If this can be accomplished by personal contact a greater number of returns will probably be achieved.

(2) Selection of most promising ideas   Usually the group leader 'screens' the ideas, removing those not likely to benefit from further consideration, leaving

those that seem 'most promising'. Osborn would probably define 'most promising' more tightly than I do and because of this I need to incorporate an additional selection process after Osborn's stage (3). I would not eliminate all the speculative ideas as there is some merit in retaining these at least until the next stage. However, in most Brainstorming sessions suggestions are made which serve process purposes (relaxing the group, sparking off the imagination of others, etc.) but which would seem questionable if repeated outside the Brainstorming session. These ideas, and perhaps also the more impractical ones, would be eliminated; for example, we would abandon those names produced which are too similar to an existing product or have an 'unfortunate' translation in another language.

(3) Development of the selected ideas   The best ideas, it is claimed, 'are usually combinations of other ideas' and participants have already been encouraged to build on the ideas of others. However, Osborn suggests that further building by the evaluation panel with the screened list of ideas can have particularly beneficial effects.

(4) Verification   The merit of the ideas selected above should now be ascertained by the most appropriate means; the potential success of our new product, its name or the chosen marketing campaign can be 'checked out' by market research.

(5) Presentation of the 'best' ideas   Osborn suggests (1957, p.254) that good advice to start with when considering the presentation of the results of a Brainstorming session is: 'The way to sell an idea to another is to state your case moderately and accurately' (Benjamin Franklin) and, 'The time to discuss an idea with others is after you have thought it through' (Dr William J. Reilly).

We must now go through these stages with the ideas we have for a name for Drug Stores' new product range. Let us assume we have supplemented our list of names by a few more thought of after the Brainstorming session (1). How can we now reduce this to our short-list which will ultimately be subjected to the verification process? I prefer to let the original group play a major part in this. We first need to make an initial selection (2) to eliminate the 'non-starters'. We want to retain most of the more novel or unusual ideas at this stage. After removing these 'non-starters' we would hold another meeting (3) whose primary task is to see if any further ideas can be found by a combination and/or development of the ideas we have so far. We now need to perform the additional selection process mentioned earlier, before going on to Osborn's verification stage (4). For this type of problem I tend to use **Reverse Brainstorming** (see Chapter 8) to evaluate the list of ideas as this coarse method of selection is often all that is required. However, although Reverse Brainstorming may 'suggest' suitable assessment criteria for our ideas, before starting any final selection we should be fairly clear as to what these ought to be. We should not rely on the Reverse Brainstorming process to provide them. Frame A3.5 suggests some possible criteria for our problem and indicates which of our ideas may now have been eliminated from further consideration.

> **Frame A3.5** *Drug Stores Ltd: what makes a product name successful?*
>
> Possible selection criteria (desirable qualities) might be:
>
> - whether it is memorable
> - uniqueness
> - ease of incorporation into a jingle/slogan
> - mass appeal
> - descriptiveness
> - projecting the right image, degree of quality, etc.
>
> On this basis we might reject names from our list if:
>
> - the name is too long to incorporate into a 'snappy' slogan;
> - it does not have mass appeal or will not (we think) appeal to the type of customer we wish to attract;
> - the name has 'unfortunate', strange or inappropriate connotations.
>
> This would rule out names such as 'New Faces', 'War Paint' and 'Bitch'. Not having any one of the desirable qualities listed above may have been thought of as a 'fault' in our Reverse Brainstorming session.

If we have more ideas left after this than our current need requires, we can change the gradation of our filter from coarse to fine by involving more of the criteria in Frame A3.5 but, even now, we should think very carefully before totally rejecting an idea. For example, 'Bright Eyes' might well be a usable name for eye make-up (if the rabbit connotation is not a problem), although not particularly suitable for an entire range of cosmetics. There is a case for retaining many of our ideas for a future occasion.

Our short-list might be:

- Illusions
- Images
- Naturelle
- Reflections
- Red light.

If we need a more sophisticated evaluation of the short-list to reduce these ideas down to one or two, then we can adopt the **Grid Method**, or a full **Decision Analysis** (see Chapter 8).

Introduction to logical thinking

This appendix explains some principles of logical thinking.

Virtually all of the explicit training we receive in problem-solving skills through our educational system is in '**logical thinking**'. What precisely is this? Does it include 'common sense'? And how can we apply this to real-world problems? The term 'common sense' can mean anything from something which is intuitively sensible to something which is rationally sensible, or logical.

By doing something logically we normally mean that we are methodically working through a rational series of steps in the hope of systematically converging (by a sort of process of elimination) on our desired objective; for example, the solution to a problem. If there is any choice along this route, decisions we have to make regarding which of several possible directions to go in next, the appropriate choice can normally be inferred from what has gone before, and the facts we have established *en route*. Logical thinking, whilst systematic, rational and mainly 'convergent' in nature, is often referred to as 'analytical thinking'. Analytical thinking, the main tool of scientific research and mathematics, is usually thought to involve finding ways of separating a given phenomenon (the object of our interest) into its component parts, so that by studying these we can make guesses (hypotheses) about their nature which we can then test out and modify as necessary. The hope is that all this will ultimately help us to discover and establish some underlying principles that explain the nature and/or behaviour of the phenomenon we are studying.

The split between **creative thinking** and logical thinking is often paralleled with that between **divergent** and **convergent thinking**. This is not quite a perfect match, as creativity is thought to include some convergent/logical (evaluative) processes. But analytical thinking is predominantly convergent and so the bulk of this appendix concerns strategies of this type. However, while we draw somewhat artificial boundaries between creative and analytical thinking, this should not be allowed to divert our attention from the fact that most of the time we need *both* for effective problem solving.

In their introduction to logical thinking skills, Peter Grogono and Sharon Nelson (1982) differentiate between 'strategies' and 'tactics'. Tactics are specialized methods which are very likely to work with a certain limited set of problems, whereas strategies are more universally applicable, but can in no way be guaranteed to solve any one particular problem. Strategies are more of 'a method worth trying' when you do not know which specific tactic you 'should' be using. We will consider only logical techniques that would be referred to in this classification system as 'strategies'.

In the way of general advice, Grogono and Nelson say we should state the problem clearly and understand it. We need to identify what we know with regard to the data that we have, and the restrictions or limitations that are imposed on the situation, some of which may not be explicitly evident. This understanding also includes having a clear idea of what constitutes a solution; we should not attempt to solve a problem by logical means until we are sure that we know exactly what it is that constitutes a solution. If we do not know what the problem is exactly, or have no precise concept of what form a desired or acceptable solution might take, we should first be using the methods described in other sections of this book in order to help us establish what these might be, or at least in what directions we might best look to find them out, not rushing off trying to find a solution.

Logical strategies

Grogono and Nelson (1982) offer a number of different logical strategies which are described below.

Abstraction

Expressing the problem in abstract terms assists us establish what we do know about the problem. It is also useful for cutting away superfluous information (but we must make sure that it *is* superfluous, rather than just 'difficult to fit in' with the rest of the information that we have. To implement this strategy we need to select an appropriate method of notation, the building blocks of our abstract model. For instance, should we express the problem algebraically, diagrammatically or verbally? This choice is important because, as we have already seen in Chapter 3, one of our conceptual blocks is 'an incorrect choice of language problem-solving strategies'.

Let us suppose that, from an annual summary report derived from company personnel records, we know that, of the 17 qualified engineers working for us, 6 have experience of the petrochemical industry, 10 have been involved with civil engineering contracts and 3 of them have worked in neither of these fields. And now we want to know how many have worked in both. We could express this problem in an algebraic form:

$$p + c + b + n = 17, p + b = 6, c + b = 10, n = 3$$

but it is also possible to express it in tabular form (see Figure A4.1), or in a more visual form similar to the drawing in Figure A4.2. The answer is that 2 of our engineers must have previous experience working in both fields (see Appendix 5).

You may have been able to visualize the problem without a diagram or a table; you may have used mental arithmetic or perhaps trial and error. You probably did not have to call all 17 engineers into your office, or go back to the personnel files (that is, solve the problem without abstraction) to find out who had worked in both fields. When faced with a situation like this most of us will use some method of abstraction – one that we are happy to work with and one that suits the problem situation. The art is knowing which one; when in doubt, try several!

As I have already said, when using abstraction we are generally forced to sort out the relevant information from the superfluous variety, but often we are obliged to go further than we might wish and work with a simplified abstract model. We should always be aware that with most complex, real-world problems, our abstract model is very rarely an exact representation of reality.

Progress by inference

This is what most people think of as logical thinking. The problem statement will contain or imply certain facts, and possibly indicate the rules we may apply to these facts. From these we can infer the truth or validity of other facts and rules that will, we hope, come closer to determining the unknown thing which is our problem. In the engineers problem above, from knowing that 3 engineers out of the 17 had no previous experience in either of the fields, I was able to infer that 14 engineers must have experience in at least one. A byproduct of this process is that it can identify any missing data which we should attempt to find.

There are actually two types of inference. Deductive inference (**deduction**) is trying to infer from what is known to be true or valid about things (objects, people, situations or events) generally, that it is also true or valid for a specific example of them. Inductive inference (**induction**) is attempting to infer from what is known to be true or valid about a specific example (or from a 'pattern' perceived in a number of particular examples) something that is also true or valid for these things generally. The former is the more reliable process and tends to be the most used; the latter is often in practice little better than an inspired guess.

		Petrochemical		
Experience		Y	N	Totals
Civil	Y			10
	Y		3	
Totals		6		17

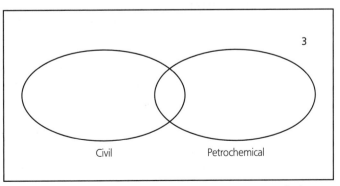

Engineers

Break the problem into subproblems or stages

We may be able to resolve a relatively complex problem by dividing it into parts and solving each part in turn, paying due attention as we do so to the dangers inherent in restructuring problems. This can be done both in a vertical fashion (assuming that the problem situation was originally structured so as to permit this) and also in a lateral direction by considering the problem as a succession of subgoals to be achieved. For example, if our problem is to produce reliable forecasts of the demand for one of our products or services, an appropriate subgoal might be to find some economic indicators that show a good correlation with the unit sales of that product or service.

Working backwards

If our goal or objective is clear, but we cannot see how to get to it from where we are, we may find it easier to work logically backwards from the solution until we get to our present situation. At each backwards step we would ask ourselves something like: 'What has to be or needs to be done just before this, in order to make it possible?'

Look for 'stock' solution methods

Grogono and Nelson (1982) stress the importance of our past experience in problem solving. Each 'new' problem need not be treated in isolation: we are likely to have recollections of previously solved problems that have a direct relevance to the new one. Our first line of attack should always be to establish whether or not there are any standard solution methods available for this category of problem; for example, using **Linear Programming** to determine the optimal production mix of a manufacturing plant.

Consider similar problems

If no stock solution is applicable, we could look at whether a modified version of a method we had previously used successfully on a similar problem might work in the new situation.

Investigate special/more general cases of the problem

In simple terms mathematical induction is a process by which you first attempt to prove that a special case of something is true, and that if the something is true for one case it must be true for another. Real life is never quite as easy as this, but we can often get hints and clues about how to go about tackling a more general problem by considering how we have solved a special case of it. The converse of this can also be helpful. If we believe that the current problem can be thought of as a special case of a wider family of problems, for which a particular solution method has been found to be generally useful, we might consider trying this method. For example, **Network Analysis** has been found to be a useful tool in many planning and scheduling situations; it might be a useful technique to use next time we need to plan something.

Transforming the problem

In its simplest form transforming the problem is a sort of abstraction. We do not like the form the problem is in so we change or transform it into another form, a new frame of reference we find easier to work with. Expressing geometric problems in terms of algebra appeals to some people! Taken to its 'illogical' conclusion this idea spans a range of possibilities from a change of notation to a **Synectics excursion**.

Checking for validity

Finally, and commensurate with the philosophy of the logical approach, after carrying out one or more of these strategies and having arrived at a solution, we should then check both our solution and our argument for validity.

Part of this method is in direct contradiction to methods described elsewhere in this book. Sorry! The art of effective problem solving is knowing at what point in our problem solving we should be thinking logically, and when we need to cast this aside temporarily and do some creative thinking.

Danger! Logical thinking

Logical thinking invariably starts from a set of 'facts' and 'rules', some assumptions or premises we make about the problem situation. It should be obvious that if we start our logical thinking from a false premise, making incorrect or inappropriate assumptions, we will end up logically and systematically deducing an incorrect or inappropriate solution. This should place considerable responsibility on the problem solver to ensure that any logical thinking starts from the right place. Often, in practice, such considerations are not made or at least not made carefully enough. The cavalier attitude some people adopt towards the formation of assumptions seems to indicate a belief that the logical process will compensate for any 'minor deficiencies' in this respect. It will not.

Worse than this sloppy use of logical thinking is its deliberate abuse. Because we believe in its potency and effectiveness, a semblance of logical thinking can be used to justify, legitimize or give credibility to what might be perceived as an inappropriate decision or solution. This is not just the use of an apparently rational argument to cover up unsatisfactory decisions and solutions, although this does happen and we need to be watchful for it. It is also the deliberate intent to disguise (managerial) prejudice by surrounding it with a screen of false rationality, covering a favoured idea or course of action, which may have no rational or generally approved justification, with a camouflage of pseudo-logical netting. If we believe *intuitively* that something is the right thing to do, then we should declare it as such; most people will respect us for our openness. It is usually only those who are aware that their view is highly prejudiced, or have ulterior motives, who find it necessary to justify their case with false logic.

It has been argued by Buchanan and Huczynski (1985) that technology can be used as a political tool by management and this provides a good illustration of the abuse of logic. Management wishing to tighten up or change work practices might argue: 'We have to do things differently now so as to meet the requirements of the new computer system we have installed. This will improve the way we allocate and utilize our resources and ultimately our profits and your rewards in our new profit sharing pay scheme'. The faults in this 'logic' are relatively easy to see: the unquestioned assumption that a new computer system and considerable reorganization *will* improve profits. Those intent on abusing logic in this way often do so much more skilfully than this.

When to be logical

Given the 'health warning' above, perhaps I should now suggest when we should consider the use of a predominantly logical or analytical approach to our problem solving, remembering that this means doing some logical or analytical thinking, not just using a systematic approach. Systematic usually means 'closely following a set of logical steps'. By this definition all the problem-solving strategies in this book can be called 'systematic', because they all contain steps or stages, and the originators of these strategies would maintain that the steps are organized the way they are because of some underlying rationale. There is nothing wrong or inherently limiting in being systematic, so long as we remain flexible as well. If our problem solving is not systematic, then it is difficult for us to learn from our past experience of problems how to improve our problem-solving skills. Some strategies require mostly logical, analytical thinking; others involve mostly creative or systemic thinking.

In most problem situations there will be times when we will want to 'open' things up – gathering information, getting different perspectives on the situation (redefining the problem), generating ideas, developing possible solutions – and shortly after each of these we may wish to perform some sort of selection or evaluation. And, of course, eventually we seek **closure**; we want to converge on to some possible solutions. It is during these 'convergent' phases that logical thinking is likely to be appropriate. However, if the problem situation is well defined and we have a clear idea as to what will constitute an acceptable solution, then a predominantly logical approach is likely to be the order of the day. For example, if everyone concerned is in agreement that we need to find ways of altering our present distribution system in order to reduce transport costs, then employing Operational Research techniques in a logical and systematic manner may well be the best line of attack. If our problem is essentially diagnostic in character, such as a machine fault, then a predominantly logical approach in the form of Kepner and Tregoe's **Problem Analysis** is likely to be most appropriate (see Chapter 6).

Concluding comments

Despite the fact that we are dealing with tame, logical problems here, Grogono and Nelson also emphasize the need for 'insight', the sudden realization that using certain symbols or a particular notation, considering a 'special case' or transforming a problem in some way is the key to the solution of the problem in hand. We are talking about the same connection-making process as we use with creativity, but this time the raw material comes from theoretical knowledge, rather than apparently irrelevant perceptions and memories.

The classic text by Polya (1957) on logical problem solving delves into these concepts in greater depth and would be useful to any reader with an interest in this or mathematics.

Additional materials for examples

This appendix contains some further illustrations of the application of the techniques discussed in the main text.

Decision alternatives: MUST and WANTS

Two further examples of the classification of criteria into MUSTS and WANTS, for decisions relating to a couple of civil engineering projects, are listed below (see also Chapter 8).

New marina development

MUSTS

- Capacity for 500 15-m berths
- Deep non-tidal moorings
- Freehold site
- Outline planning permission

WANTS

- Proximity of other marinas
- Low cost of land purchase
- Low development costs
- Space for residential accommodation
- Good transport facilities nearby (motorway, airport, railway)
- Local acceptance
- Sheltered moorings (against tidal extremes/storms)
- Local amenities (cinemas, restaurants)

Site for new hotel

MUST

- Outline planning permission for at least 200-bedroom hotel
- Projected net present value of investment more than x%
- Development area

WANTS

- Good long-term investment
- Expansion possibilities
- Good position
- Local amenities (cinemas, restaurants, etc.)
- Proximity of similar establishments
- Condition of local tourism industry
- Future demand
- Availability and quality of local staff
- Weather profile

Note: it could be important to know whether the situation is within a developing area. Gaining some form of government development grant may be more important than long-term investment.

Northcliffe Sands

(Chapter 12)

Backward/Forward Planning

Task headline

How to increase revenue from tourism without 'spoiling' the location?

Backwards

1. 'If we had now managed to solve this problem, what other higher-level problems would it solve? What would it allow you to do?'
2. 'Increased funds would mean that we could get on with some long overdue and much needed improvements to the town's amenities etc., and be able to do it in a more flexible way.'
   (i) I wish we could speed up the implementation of the long overdue and much needed improvements.
   (ii) I wish we had more flexibility in the way we can handle the town's development.
3. 'If you were able to get on with the "implementation of. . . the improvements", what could you do then?'

4. 'By improving some of the town's facilities, we would be able to lessen some of the fears that the local residents have about their environment being "destroyed", and at the same time, the "breathing space" that this would bring us, would allow us time to think things through – we wouldn't always be in a near-crisis situation.'

   (iii)   How to reassure the local population about the possible future development of the area?

   (iv)   How to find time to think in the middle of a crisis?

Forwards

5. 'If we had now "increased our revenue from tourism without 'spoiling' the locations" what benefits would we get from this?'

6. 'It would stabilize our local economy, and enable us to do some long-term planning and development. It would improve the general environment and increase the standard of living of the indigenous population.'

   (v)   How to bring more stability (less seasonality) to our local economy?

   (vi)   How to improve the quality of life of the indigenous population?

7. 'What is stopping you doing all this?'

8. 'We can't seem to reach any agreement on what actions to take.'

   (vii)   I wish we could stop arguing and make a few decisions.

Itemized response

Itemized response on 'I wish we had a multiscreen cinema'.

Positive features

- It would keep a fair number of tourists 'hidden' away from sight and concentrated in one place for several hours a day. This would be really useful on rainy days.
- We would be generating more revenue (for somebody!).
- It should improve this facility for the indigenous population at the same time, even more so if it has an alternative off-season use.

Concerns

The major concern might be . . .

   The cost of converting our single-screen cinema into a multiple one and the additional running costs.

An idea to overcome the concern

Offer the owners help with the cost of conversion, in exchange for multiple use of the facility; for example, the local arts centre theatre group presentations, conferences, etc.

   or . . .

   The general decline in cinema attendance.

An idea to overcome the concern

Since we have a large, transient and changing 'captive' audience coupled with the fact that they are on holiday (people tend to do things on holiday that they do not do otherwise, or do things more often than they normally do) we are more likely to be able to buck this national trend. We should also be able to adopt the policy of going for volume ticket sales at low prices if necessary.

Ideas to satisfy Peter Frith's concern

Since planning permission will be required by potential fringe retailers, Peter Frith will be forewarned of possible competition. He and the other retailers could either:

- offer to supply a fringe retailer with any goods that s/he wishes to sell at competitive 'trade' prices; or
- offer to run the fringe retail operation as an extension of their own businesses, paying rent and/or a small commission to the landowner, or whoever manages the campsite, hill-walking/nature centre, etc.

Little can be done about the sale of home-produced products except to secure from the council an assurance that all health, hygiene and trading laws are observed.

The engineers problem: abstraction

(Appendix 4)

Figure A5.1 contains all the information that we have been told about the situation. By taking the subtotals that we have away from the grand total, we can easily find the 'missing' subtotals 11 and 7. By bringing the 3 into play we can similarly deduce what numbers should be in the other 'gaps' in the table and hence the required information.

Figure A5.1 attempts to represent the (overlapping sets of) previous work experience of the engineers as two circles. Whilst not so immediately helpful in this instance (with the same basic problem but with different information

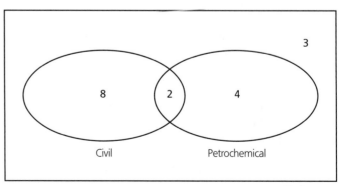

'knowns' and 'unknowns' the diagram can be more explicit than the table), we can (relatively) easily determine that there must be 2 engineers who have petrochemical and civil engineering experience. If there are 3 with neither experience there must be 14 within the two overlapping circles. But 6 engineers with petrochemical experience have to be placed in the right-hand circle, and 10 in the left, civil experience circle. $10 + 6 = 16$, therefore $(16 - 14) = 2$ engineers have to be in both circles.

The algebraic proof is as follows:

Let p be the number of engineers with only petrochemical experience
     c be the number of engineers with only civil experience
     b be the number of engineers with both types of experience
     n be the number of engineers with neither experience

then $p + c + b + n = 17$ (1)
      $p + b = 6$ (2)
      $c + b = 10$ (3)
      $n = 3$ (4)

one possible solution method is . . .

from (1) – (4) we get $p + c + b = 14$ (5)
from (2) + (3) we get $p + c + 2b = 16$ (6)
and from (6) – (5) we get $b = 2$

The cognoscenti will realize that all these approaches are mathematical in one form or another – the diagram method being a Venn diagram taken from Set Theory. However, there might have been a totally non-mathematical way of abstracting this problem.

Contradiction matrix – TRIZ

The information provided in this appendix was reprinted from *The Innovation Algorithm*, ISBN 0–9640740–4–4 with permission. All rights reserved.

Published by Technical Innovation Center, Inc., Worcester, MA, USA.

CHARACTERISTICS		Characteristic that is getting worse									
		1	2	3	4	5	6	7	8	9	10
1	Weight of a mobile object	■	–	15, 8 29, 34	–	29, 17 38, 34	–	29, 2 40, 28	–	2, 8 15, 38	8, 10 18, 37
2	Weight of a stationary object	–	■	–	10, 1 29, 35	–	35, 30 13, 2	–	5, 35 14, 2	–	8, 10 19, 35
3	Length of a mobile object	8, 15 29, 34	–	■	–	15, 17 4	–	7, 17 4, 35	–	13, 4 8	17, 10 4
4	Length of a stationary object	–	35, 28 40, 29	–	■	–	17, 7 10, 40	–	35, 8 2, 14	–	28, 10
5	Area of a mobile object	2, 17 29, 4	–	14, 15 18, 4	–	■	–	7, 14 17, 4	–	29, 30 4, 34	19, 30 35, 2
6	Area of a stationary object	–	30, 2 14, 18	–	26, 7 9, 39	–	■	–	–	–	1, 18 35, 36
7	Volume of a mobile object	2, 26 29, 40	–	1, 7 4, 35	–	1, 7 4, 17	–	■	–	29, 4 38, 34	15, 35 36, 37
8	Volume of a stationary object	–	35, 10 19, 14	19, 14	35, 8 2, 14	–	–	–	■	–	2, 18 37
9	Speed	2, 28 13, 38	–	13, 14 8	–	29, 30 34	–	7, 29 34	–	■	13, 28 15, 19
10	Force	8, 1 37, 18	18, 13 1, 28	17, 19 9, 36	28, 10	19, 10 15	1, 18 36, 37	15, 9 12, 37	2, 36 18, 37	13, 28 15, 12	■
11	Tension/pressure	10, 36 37, 40	13, 29 10, 18	35, 10 36	35, 1 14, 16	10, 15 36, 28	10, 15 36, 37	6, 35 10	35, 24	6, 35 36	36, 35 21
12	Shape	8, 10 29, 40	15, 10 26, 3	29, 34 5, 4	13, 14 10, 7	5, 34 4, 10	–	14, 4 15, 22	7, 2 35	35, 15 34, 18	35, 10 37, 40
13	Stability of composition	21, 35 2, 39	26, 39 1, 40	13, 15 1, 28	37	2, 11 13	39	28, 10 19, 39	34, 28 35, 40	33, 15 28, 18	10, 35 21, 16
14	Strength	1, 8 40, 15	40, 26 27, 1	1, 15 8, 35	15, 14 28, 26	3, 34 40, 29	9, 40 28	10, 15 14, 7	9, 14 17, 15	8, 13 26, 14	10, 18 3, 14
15	Time of action of a moving object	19, 5 34, 31	–	2, 19 9	–	3, 17 19	–	10, 2 19, 30	–	3, 35 5	19, 2 16
16	Time of action of a stationary object	–	6, 27 19, 16	–	1, 40 35	–	–	–	35, 34 38	–	–
17	Temperature	36, 22 6, 38	22, 35 32	15, 19 9	15, 19 9	3, 35 39, 18	35, 38	34, 39 40, 18	35, 6 4	2, 28 36, 30	35, 10 3, 21
18	Brightness	19, 1 32	2, 35 32	19, 32 16	–	19, 32 26	–	2, 13 10		10, 13 19	26, 19 6
19	Energy spent by a moving object	12, 18 28, 31	–	12, 28	–	15, 19 25	–	35, 13 18		8, 35	16, 26 21, 2
20	Energy spent by a stationary object	–	19, 9 6, 27	–	–	–	–	–	–	–	36, 37
21	Power	8, 36 38, 31	19, 26 17, 27	1, 10 35, 37	–	19, 38	17, 32 13, 38	35, 6 38	30, 6 25	15, 35 2	26, 2 36, 35
22	Loss of energy	15, 6 19, 28	19, 6 18, 9	7, 2 6, 13	6, 38 7	15, 26 17, 30	17, 7 30, 18	7, 18 23	7	16, 35 38	36, 38
23	Loss of a substance	35, 6 23, 40	35, 6 22, 32	14, 29 10, 39	10, 28 24	35, 2 10, 31	10, 18 39, 31	1, 29 30, 36	3, 39 18, 31	10, 13 28, 38	14, 15 18, 40
24	Loss of an information	10, 24 35	10, 35 5	1, 26	26	30, 26	30, 16	–	2, 22	26, 32	–
25	Loss of time	10, 20 37, 35	10, 20 26, 5	15, 2 29	30, 24 14, 5	26, 4 5, 16	10, 35 17, 4	2, 5 34, 10	35, 16 32, 18	–	10, 37 36, 5
26	Amount of substance	35, 6 18, 31	27, 26 18, 35	29, 14 35, 18	–	15, 14 29	2, 18 40, 4	15, 20 29	–	35, 29 34, 28	35, 14 3
27	Reliability	3, 8 10, 40	3, 10 8, 28	15, 9 14, 4	15, 29 28, 11	17, 10 14, 16	32, 35 40, 4	3, 10 14, 24	2, 35 24	21, 35 11, 28	8, 28 10, 3
28	Accuracy of measurement	32, 35 26, 28	28, 35 25, 26	28, 26 5, 16	32, 28 3, 16	26, 28 32, 3	26, 28 32, 3	32, 13 6	–	28, 13 32, 24	32, 2
29	Accuracy of manufacturing	28, 32 13, 18	28, 35 27, 9	10, 28 29, 37	2, 32 10	28, 33 29, 32	2, 29 18, 36	32, 28 2	25, 10 35	10, 28 32	28, 19 34, 36
30	Harmful factors acting on an object from outside	22, 21 27, 39	2, 22 13, 24	17, 1 39, 4	1, 18	22, 1 33, 28	27, 2 39, 35	22, 23 37, 35	34, 39 19, 27	21, 22 35, 28	13, 35 39, 18
31	Harmful factors developed by an object	19, 22 15, 39	35, 22 1, 39	17, 15 16, 22	–	17, 2 18, 39	22, 1 40	17, 2 40	30, 18 35, 4	35, 28 3, 23	35, 28 1, 40
32	Manufacturability	28, 29 15, 16	1, 27 36, 13	1, 29 13, 17	15, 17 27	13, 1 26, 12	16, 40	13, 29 1, 40	35	35, 13 8, 1	35, 12
33	Convenience of use	25, 2 13, 15	6, 13 1, 25	1, 17 13, 12	–	1, 17 13, 16	18, 16 15, 39	1, 16 35, 15	4, 18 39, 31	18, 13 34	28, 13 35
34	Repairability	2, 27 35, 11	2, 27 35, 11	1, 28 10, 25	3, 18 31	15, 13 32	16, 25	25, 2 35, 11	1	34, 9	1, 11 10
35	Adaptability	1, 6 15, 8	19, 15 29, 16	35, 1 29, 2	1, 35 16	35, 30 29, 7	15, 16	15, 35 29	–	35, 10 14	15, 17 20
36	Complexity of a device	26, 30 34, 36	2, 26 35, 39	1, 19 26, 24	26	14, 1 13, 16	6, 36	34, 26 6	1, 16	34, 10 28	26, 16
37	Complexity of control	27, 26 28, 13	6, 13 28, 1	16, 17 26, 24	26	2, 13 18, 17	2, 39 30, 16	29, 1 4, 16	2, 18 26, 31	3, 4 16, 35	36, 28 40, 19
38	Level of automation	28, 26 18, 35	28, 26 35, 10	14, 13 17, 28	23	17, 14 13	–	35, 13 16	–	28, 10	2, 35
39	Capacity/productivity	35, 26 24, 37	28, 27 15, 3	18, 4 28, 38	30, 7 14, 26	10, 26 34, 31	10, 35 17, 7	2, 6 34, 10	35, 37 10, 2	–	28, 15 10, 36

Characteristics to be improved

11	12	13	14	15	16	17	18	19	20	21	22	23	24	
10, 36 37, 40	10, 14 35, 40	1, 35 19, 39	28, 27 18, 40	5, 34 31, 35	–	6, 29 4, 38	19, 1 32	35, 12 34, 31	–	12, 36 18, 31	6, 2 34, 19	5, 35 3, 31	10, 24 35	1
13, 29 10, 18	13, 10 29, 14	26, 39 1, 40	28, 2 10, 27	–	2, 27 19, 6	28, 19 32, 22	19, 32 35	–	18, 19 28, 1	15, 19 18, 22	18, 19 28, 15	5, 8 13, 30	10, 15 35	2
1, 8 35	1, 8 10, 29	1, 8 15, 34	8, 35 29, 34	19	–	10, 15 19	32	8, 35 24	–	1, 35	7, 2 35, 39	4, 29 23, 10	1, 24	3
1, 14 35	13, 14 15, 7	39, 37 35	15, 14 28, 26	–	1, 40 35	3, 35 38, 18	3, 25	–	–	12, 8	6, 28	10, 28 24, 35	24, 26	4
10, 15 36, 28	5, 34 29, 4	11, 2 13, 39	3, 15 40, 14	6, 3	–	2, 15 16	15, 32 19, 13	19, 32	–	19, 10 32, 18	15, 17 30, 26	10, 35 2, 39	30, 26	5
10, 15 36, 37	–	2, 38	40		2, 10 19, 30	35, 39 38	–	–	–	17, 32	17, 7 30	10, 14 18, 39	30, 16	6
6, 35 36, 37	1, 15 29, 4	28, 10 1, 39	9, 14 15, 7	6, 35 4	–	34, 39 10, 18	2, 13 10	35	–	35, 6 13, 18	7, 15 13, 16	36, 39 34, 10	2, 22	7
24, 35	7, 2 35	34, 28 35, 40	9, 14 17, 15	–	35, 34 38	35, 6 4	–	–	–	30, 6	–	10, 39 35, 34	–	8
6, 18 38, 40	35, 15 18, 34	28, 33 1, 18	8, 3 26, 14	3, 19 35, 5	–	28, 30 36, 2	10, 13 19	8, 15 35, 38	–	19, 35 38, 2	14, 20 19, 35	10, 13 28, 38	13, 26	9
18, 21 11	10, 35 40, 34	35, 10 21	35, 10 14, 27	19, 2	–	35, 10 21	–	19, 17 10	1, 16 36, 37	19, 35 18, 37	14, 15	8, 35 40, 5	–	10
	35, 4 15, 10	35, 33 2, 40	9, 18 3, 40	19, 3 27	–	35, 39 19, 2	–	14, 24 10, 37	–	10, 35 14	2, 36 25	10, 36 3, 37	–	11
34, 15 10, 14		33, 1 18, 4	30, 14 10, 40	14, 26 9, 25	–	22, 14 19, 32	13, 15 32	2, 6 34, 14	–	4, 6 2	14	35, 29 3, 5	–	12
2, 35 40	22, 1 18, 4		17, 9 15	13, 27 10, 35	39, 3 35, 23	35, 1 32	32, 3 27, 15	13, 19	27, 4 29, 18	32, 35 27, 31	14, 2 39, 6	2, 14 30, 40	–	13
10, 3 18, 40	10, 30 35, 40	13, 17 35		27, 3 26	–	30, 10 40	35, 19	19, 35 10	35	10, 26 35, 28	35	35, 28 31, 40	–	14
19, 3 27	14, 26 28, 25	13, 3 35	27, 3 10		–	19, 35 39	2, 19 4, 35	28, 6 35, 18	–	19, 10 35, 38	–	28, 27 3, 18	10	15
–	–	39, 3 35, 23	–	–		19, 18 36, 40	–	–	–	16	–	27, 16 18, 38	10	16
35, 39 19, 2	14, 22 19, 32	1, 35 32	10, 30 22, 40	19, 13 39	19, 18 36, 40		32, 30 21, 16	19, 15 3, 17	–	2, 14 17, 25	21, 17 35, 38	21, 36 29, 31	–	17
–	32, 30	32, 3 27	35, 19	2, 19 6	–	32, 35 19		32, 1 19	32, 35 1, 15	32	13, 16 1, 6	13, 1	1, 6	18
23, 14 25	12, 2 29	19, 13 17, 24	5, 19 9, 35	28, 35 6, 18	–	19, 24 3, 14	2, 15 19		–	6, 19 37, 18	12, 22 15, 24	35, 24 18, 5	–	19
–	–	27, 4 29, 18	35	–	–	–	19, 2 35, 32	–		–	–	28, 27 18, 31	–	20
22, 10 35	29, 14 2, 40	35, 32 15, 31	26, 10 28	19, 35 10, 38	16	2, 14 17, 25	16, 6 19	16, 6 19, 37	–		10, 35 38	28, 27 18, 38	10, 19	21
–	–	14, 2 39, 6	26	–	–	19, 38 7	1, 13 32, 15	–	–	3, 38		35, 27 2, 37	19, 10	22
3, 36 37, 10	29, 35 3, 5	2, 14 30, 40	35, 28 31, 40	28, 27 3, 18	27, 16 18, 38	21, 36 39, 31	1, 6 13	35, 18 24, 5	28, 27 12, 31	28, 27 18, 38	35, 27 2, 31		–	23
–	–	–	10	10	–	–	19	–	–	10, 19	19, 10	–		24
37, 36 4	4, 10 34, 17	35, 3 22, 5	29, 3 28, 18	20, 10 28, 18	28, 20 10, 16	35, 29 21, 18	1, 19 26, 17	35, 38 19, 18	1	35, 20 10, 6	10, 5 18, 32	35, 18 10, 39	24, 26 28, 32	25
10, 36 14, 3	35, 14	15, 2 17, 40	14, 35 34, 10	3, 35 10, 40	3, 35 31	3, 17 39	–	34, 29 16, 18	3, 35 31	35	7, 18 25	6, 3 10, 24	24, 28 35	26
10, 24 35, 19	35, 1 16, 11	–	11, 28	2, 35 3, 25	34, 27 6, 40	3, 35 10	11, 32 13	21, 11 27, 19	36, 23	21, 11 26, 31	10, 11 35	10, 35 29, 39	10, 28	27
6, 28 32	6, 28 32	32, 35 13	28, 6 32	28, 6 32	10, 26 24	6, 19 28, 24	6, 1 32	3, 6 32	–	3, 6 32	26, 32 27	10, 16 31, 28	–	28
3, 35	32, 30 40	30, 18	3, 27	3, 27 40	–	19, 26	3, 32	32, 2	–	32, 2	13, 32 2	35, 31 10, 24	–	29
22, 2 37	22, 1 3, 35	35, 24 30, 18	18, 35 37, 1	22, 15 33, 28	17, 1 40, 33	22, 33 35, 2	1, 19 32, 13	1, 24 6, 27	10, 2 22, 37	19, 22 31, 2	21, 22 35, 2	33, 22 19, 40	22, 10 2	30
2, 33 27, 18	35, 1	35, 40 27, 39	15, 35 22, 2	15, 22 33, 31	21, 39 16, 22	22, 35 2, 24	19, 24 39, 32	2, 35 6	19, 22 18	2, 35 18	21, 35 2, 22	10, 1 34	10, 21 29	31
35, 19 1, 37	1, 28 13, 27	11, 13 1	1, 3 10, 32	27, 1 4	35, 16	27, 26 18	28, 24 27, 1	28, 26 27, 1	1, 4	27, 1 12, 24	19, 35	15, 34 33	32, 24 18, 16	32
2, 32 12	15, 34 29, 28	32, 35 30	32, 40 3, 28	29, 3 8, 25	1, 16 25	26, 27 13	13, 17 1, 24	1, 13 24	–	35, 34 2, 10	2, 19 13	28, 32 2, 24	4, 10 27, 22	33
13	1, 13 2, 4	2, 35	11, 1 2, 9	11, 29 28, 27	1	4, 10	15, 1 13	15, 1 28, 16	–	15, 10 32, 2	15, 1 32, 19	2, 35 34, 27	–	34
35, 16	15, 37 1, 8	35, 30 14	35, 3 32, 6	13, 1 35	2, 16	27, 2 3, 35	6, 22 26, 1	19, 35 29, 13	–	19, 1 29	18, 15 1	15, 10 2, 13	–	35
19, 1 35	29, 13 28, 15	2, 22 17, 19	2, 13 28	10, 4 28, 15	–	2, 17 13	24, 17 13	27, 2 29, 28	–	20, 19 30, 34	10, 35 13, 2	35, 10 28, 29	–	36
35, 36 37, 32	27, 13 1, 39	11, 22 39, 30	27, 3 15, 28	19, 29 39, 25	25, 34 6, 35	3, 27 35, 16	2, 24 26	35, 38	19, 35 16	19, 1 16, 10	35, 3 15, 19	1, 18 10, 24	35, 33 27, 22	37
13, 35	15, 32 1, 13	18, 1	25, 13	6, 9	–	26, 2 19	8, 32 19	2, 32 13	–	28, 2 27	23, 28	35, 10 18, 5	35, 33	38
10, 37 14	14, 10 34, 40	35, 3 22, 39	29, 28 10, 18	35, 10 2, 18	20, 10 16, 38	35, 21 28, 10	26, 17 19, 1	35, 10 38, 19	1	35, 20 10	28, 10 29, 35	28, 10 35, 23	13, 15 23	39

CHARACTERISTICS		Characteristic that is getting worse									
		25	26	27	28	29	30	31	32	33	34
1	Weight of a mobile object	10, 35 20, 28	3, 26 18, 31	3, 11 1, 27	28, 27 35, 26	28, 35 26, 18	22, 21 18, 27	22, 35 31, 39	27, 28 1, 36	35, 3 2, 24	2, 27 28, 11
2	Weight of a stationary object	10, 20 35, 26	19, 6 18, 26	10, 28 8, 3	18, 26 28	10, 1 35, 17	2, 19 22, 37	35, 22 1, 39	28, 1 9	6, 13 1, 32	2, 27 28, 11
3	Length of a mobile object	15, 2 29	29, 35	10, 14 29, 40	28, 32 4	10, 28 29, 37	1, 15 17, 24	17, 15	1, 29 17	15, 29 35, 4	1, 28 10
4	Length of a stationary object	30, 29 14	–	15, 29 28	32, 28 3	2, 32 10	1, 18	–	15, 17 27	2, 25	3
5	Area of a mobile object	26, 4	29, 30 6, 13	29, 9	26, 28 32, 3	2, 32	22, 33 28, 1	17, 2 18, 39	13, 1 26, 24	15, 17 13, 16	15, 13 10, 1
6	Area of a stationary object	10, 35 4, 18	2, 18 40, 4	32, 35 40, 4	26, 28 32, 3	2, 29 18, 36	27, 2 39, 35	22, 1 40	40, 16	16, 4	16
7	Volume of a mobile object	2, 6 34, 10	29, 30 7	14, 1 40, 11	26, 28	25, 28 2, 16	22, 21 27, 35	17, 2 40, 1	29, 1 40	15, 13 30, 12	10
8	Volume of a stationary object	35, 16 32, 18	35, 3	2, 35 16	–	35, 10 25	34, 39 19, 27	30, 18 35, 4	35	–	1
9	Speed	–	10, 19 29, 38	11, 35 27, 28	28, 32 1, 24	10, 28 32, 25	1, 28 35, 23	2, 24 35, 21	35, 13 8, 1	32, 28 13, 12	34, 2 28, 27
10	Force	10, 37 36	14, 29 18, 36	3, 35 13, 21	35, 10 23, 24	28, 29 37, 36	1, 35 40, 18	13, 3 36, 24	15, 37 18, 1	1, 28 3, 25	15, 1 11
11	Tension/pressure	37, 36 4	10, 14 36	10, 13 19, 35	6, 28 25	3, 35	22, 2 37	2, 33 27, 18	1, 35 16	11	2
12	Shape	14, 10 34, 17	36, 22	10, 40 16	78, 32 1	32, 30 40	22, 1 2, 35	35, 1	1, 32 17, 28	32, 15 26	2, 13 1
13	Stability of composition	35, 27	15, 32 35	–	13	18	35, 24 30, 18	35, 40 27, 39	35, 19	32, 35 30	2, 35 10, 16
14	Strength	29, 3 28, 10	29, 10 27	11, 3	3, 27 16	3, 27	18, 35 37, 1	15, 35 22, 2	11, 3 10, 32	32, 40 28, 2	27, 11 3
15	Time of action of a moving object	20, 10 28, 18	3, 35 10, 40	11, 2 13	3	3, 27 16, 40	22, 15 33, 28	21, 39 16, 22	27, 1 4	12, 27	29, 10 27
16	Time of action of a stationary object	28, 20 10, 16	3, 35 31	34, 27 6, 40	10, 26 24	–	17, 1 40, 33	22	35, 10	1	1
17	Temperature	35, 28 21, 18	3, 17 30, 39	19, 35 3, 10	32, 19 24	24	22, 33 35, 2	22, 35 2, 24	26, 27	26, 27	4, 10 16
18	Brightness	19, 1 26, 17	1, 19	–	11, 5 32	3, 32	15, 19	35, 19 32, 39	19, 35 28, 26	28, 26 19	15, 17 13, 16
19	Energy spent by a moving object	35, 38 19, 18	34, 23 16, 18	19, 21 11, 27	3, 1 32	–	1, 35 6, 27	2, 35 6	28, 26 30	19, 35	1, 15 17, 28
20	Energy spent by a stationary object	–	3, 35 31	10, 36 23	–	–	10, 2 22, 37	19, 22 18	1, 4	–	–
21	Power	35, 20 10, 6	4, 34 19	19, 24 26, 31	32, 15 2	32, 2	19, 22 31, 2	2, 35 18	26, 10 34	26, 35 10	35, 2 10, 34
22	Loss of energy	10, 18 32, 7	7, 18 25	11, 10 35	32	–	21, 22 35, 2	21, 35 2, 22	–	35, 32 1	2, 19
23	Loss of a substance	15, 18 35, 10	6, 3 10, 24	10, 29 39, 35	16, 34 31, 28	35, 10 24, 31	33, 22 30, 40	10, 1 34, 29	15, 34 33	32, 28 2, 24	2, 35 34, 27
24	Loss of an information	24, 26 28, 32	24, 28 35	10, 28 23	–	–	22, 10 1	10, 21 22	32	27, 22	
25	Loss of time		35, 38 18, 16	10, 30 4	24, 34 28, 32	24, 26 28, 18	35, 18 34	35, 22 18, 39	35, 28 34, 4	4, 28 10, 34	32, 1 10
26	Amount of substance	35, 38 18, 16		18, 3 28, 40	3, 2 28	33, 30	35, 33 29, 31	3, 35 40, 39	29, 1 35, 27	35, 29 10, 25	2, 32 10, 25
27	Reliability	10, 30 4	21, 28 40, 3		32, 3 11, 23	11, 32 1	27, 35 2, 40	35, 2 40, 26	–	27, 17 40	1, 11
28	Accuracy of measurement	24, 34 28, 32	2, 6 32	5, 11 1, 23		–	28, 24 22, 26	3, 33 39, 10	6, 35 25, 18	1, 13 17, 34	1, 32 13, 11
29	Accuracy of manufacturing	32, 26 28, 18	32, 30	11, 32 1	–		26, 28 10, 36	4, 17 34, 26	–	1, 32 35, 23	25, 10
30	Harmful factors acting on an object from outside	35, 18 34	35, 33 29, 31	27, 24 2, 40	28, 33 23, 26	26, 28 10, 18		–	24, 35 2	2, 25 28, 39	35, 10 2
31	Harmful factors developed by an object	1, 22	3, 24 39, 1	24, 2 40, 39	3, 33 26	4, 17 34, 26	–		–	–	–
32	Manufacturability	35, 28 34, 4	35, 23 1, 24	–	1, 35 12, 18	–	24, 2	–		2, 5 13, 16	35, 1 11, 9
33	Convenience of use	4, 28 10, 34	12, 35	17, 27 8, 40	25, 13 2, 34	1, 32 35, 23	2, 25 28, 39	–	2, 5 12		12, 26 1, 32
34	Repairability	32, 1 10, 25	2, 28 10, 25	11, 10 1, 16	10, 2 13	25, 10	35, 10 2, 16	–	1, 35 11, 10	1, 12 26, 15	
35	Adaptability	35, 28	3, 35 15	35, 13 8, 24	35, 5 1, 10	–	35, 11 32, 31	–	1, 13 31	15, 34 1, 16	1, 16 7, 4
36	Complexity of a device	6, 29 27, 10	13, 3 27, 10	13, 35 1	2, 26 10, 34	26, 24 32	22, 19 29, 40	19, 1	27, 26 1, 13	27, 9 26, 24	1, 13
37	Complexity of control	18, 28 32, 9	3, 27 29, 18	27, 40 28, 8	26, 24 32, 28	–	22, 19 29, 28	2, 21	5, 28 11, 29	2, 5	12, 26
38	Level of automation	24, 28 35, 30	35, 13	11, 27 32	28, 26 10, 34	28, 26 18, 23	2, 33	2	1, 26 13	1, 12 34, 3	1, 35 13
39	Capacity/productivity	–	35, 38	1, 35 10, 38	1, 10 34, 28	18, 10 32, 1	22, 35 13, 24	35, 22 18, 39	35, 28 2, 24	1, 28 7, 19	1, 32 10, 25

35	36	37	38	39	
29, 5 15, 8	26, 30 36, 34	28, 29 26, 32	26, 35 18, 19	35, 3 24, 37	1
19, 15 29	1, 10 26, 39	25, 28 17, 15	2, 26 35	1, 28 15, 35	2
14, 15 1, 16	1, 19 26, 24	35, 1 26, 24	17, 24 26, 16	14, 4 28, 29	3
1, 35	1, 26	26	–	30, 14 7, 26	4
15, 30	14, 1 13	2, 36 26, 18	14, 30 28, 23	10, 26 34, 2	5
15, 16	1, 18 36	2, 35 30, 18	23	10, 15 17, 7	6
15, 29	26, 1	29, 26 4	35, 34 16, 24	10, 6 2, 34	7
–	1, 31	2, 17 26	–	35, 37 10, 2	8
15, 10 26	10, 28 4, 34	3, 34 27, 16	10, 18	–	9
15, 17 18, 20	26, 35 10, 18	36, 37 10, 19	2, 35	3, 28 35, 37	10
35	19, 1 35	2, 36 37	35, 24	10, 14 35, 37	11
1, 15 29	16, 29 1, 28	15, 13 39	15, 1 32	17, 26 34, 10	12
35, 30 34, 2	2, 35 22, 26	35, 22 39, 23	1, 8 35	23, 35 40, 3	13
15, 3 32	2, 13 28	27, 3 15, 40	15	29, 35 10, 14	14
1, 35 13	10, 4 29, 15	19, 29 39, 35	6, 10	35, 17 14, 19	15
2	–	25, 34 6, 35	1	20, 10 16, 38	16
2, 18 27	2, 17 16	3, 27 35, 31	26, 2 19, 16	15, 28 35	17
15, 1 19	6, 32 13	32, 15	2, 26 10	2, 25 16	18
15, 17 13, 16	2, 29 27, 28	35, 38	32, 2	12, 28 35	19
–	–	19, 35 16, 25	–	1, 6	20
19, 17 34	20, 19 30, 34	19, 35 16	28, 2 17	28, 35 34	21
–	7, 23	35, 3 15, 23	2	28, 10 29, 35	22
15, 10 2	35, 10 28, 24	35, 18 10, 13	35, 10 18	28, 35 10, 23	23
–	–	35, 33	35	13, 23 15	24
35, 28	6, 29	18, 28 32, 10	24, 28 35, 30	–	25
15, 3 29	3, 13 27, 10	3, 27 29, 18	8, 35	13, 29 3, 27	26
13, 35 8, 24	13, 35 1	27, 40 28	11, 13 27	1, 35 29, 38	27
13, 35 2	27, 35 10, 34	26, 24 32, 28	28, 2 10, 34	10, 34 28, 32	28
–	26, 2 18	–	26, 28 18, 23	10, 18 32, 39	29
35, 11 22, 31	22, 19 29, 40	22, 19 29, 40	33, 3 34	22, 35 13, 24	30
–	19, 1 31	2, 21 27, 1	2	22, 35 18, 39	31
2, 13 15	27, 26 1	6, 28 11, 1	8, 28 1	35, 1 10, 28	32
15, 34 1, 16	32, 26 12, 17	–	1, 34 12, 3	15, 1 28	33
7, 1 4, 16	35, 1 13, 11	–	34, 35 7, 13	1, 32 10	34
	15, 29 37, 28	1	27, 34 35	35, 28 6, 37	35
29, 15 28, 37		15, 10 37, 28	15, 1 24	12, 17 28	36
1, 15	15, 10 37, 28		34, 21	35, 18	37
27, 4 1, 35	15, 24 10	34, 27 25		5, 12 35, 26	38
1, 35 28, 37	12, 17 28, 24	35, 18 27, 2	5, 12 35, 26		39

PRINCIPLES	
Segmentation	1
Extraction	2
Local quality	3
Asymmetry	4
Consolidation	5
Universality	6
Nesting (Matrioshka)	7
Counterweight	8
Prior Counteraction	9
Prior Action	10
Cushion in Advance	11
Equipotentiality	12
Do it in Reverse	13
Spheroidality	14
Dynamicity	15
Partial or Excessive Action	16
Transition Into a New Dimension	17
Mechanical Vibration	18
Periodic Action	19
Continuity of Useful Action	20
Rushing Through	21
Convert Harm into Benefit	22
Feedback	23
Mediator	24
Self Service	25
Copying	26
Dispose	27
Replacement of Mechanical System	28
Pneumatic of Hydraulic Construction	29
Flexible Films or Thin Membranes	30
Porous Materials	31
Changing the Color	32
Homogeneity	33
Rejecting and Regenerating Parts	34
Transformation Properties	35
Phase Transition	36
Thermal Expansion	37
Accelerated Oxidation	38
Inert Environment	39
Composite Materials	40

Miscellany

This appendix expands on a couple of points raised in the previous text of the book, for clarification purposes.

Left-right and four brains

It has been thought for some decades now that the two halves of the human brain were responsible for different higher cognitive functions; the left hemisphere dealing with verbal ability, logical/analytical thinking, mathematical reasoning and judgement; the right hemisphere being the source of dreaming, feeling, intuition and dealing with visualization, spatial relationships and musical abilities.

In our discussions earlier of **EQ** we encountered a 'vertical' split of the brain into the limbic and cortical parts. N. Herrmann (1990) has used this split to 'extend' Roger Sperry's original left brain/right brain theory into a model of the brain consisting of four parts, each responsible for its own thinking processes:

Left brain

'Upper' (cortical) – logical/analytical problem solving, mathematical reasoning and judgement.

'Lower' (limbic) – monitoring, planning and organizing/controlling things.

Right brain

'Upper' (cortical) – holistic and creative thinking, intuition, visualization.

'Lower' (limbic) – interpersonal, emotional and spiritual feelings and musical abilities.

Version 6.1 of the Osborn-Parnes CPS process

The main source used here for describing the **Osborn-Parnes** CPS process was Isaksen and Treffinger (1985), now thought of as portraying Version 3. The authors themselves criticized this version as too prescriptive – six stages that you had to run through systematically using certain techniques at certain times. We now have Version 6.1 of this process – but do not be alarmed that what you have read in this book is obsolete. The main changes between Versions 3 and 6.1 have been the removal of the prescriptive approach and the addition of a couple of extra stages (actually, they are not stages as such but two activities that continue alongside whatever else you are doing) to help you decide which stage and what techniques would be the best to be using at a given point within a particular **CPS** session (see below). We have deliberately avoided describing the Osborn-Parnes CPS process here as a complete, continuous and prescriptive process, choosing instead to offer various techniques (which have not essentially changed) with guidance as to at which stage in the generic problem-solving process they may best be used.

In Version 6.1, the original six stages have been 'grouped' and renamed (more descriptively), as below:

Understanding the challenge

Uses one or more of . . .

Constructing opportunities	[Mess finding]
Exploring data	[Data finding]
Framing problems	[Problem finding]

Generating Ideas

(If necessary!?)

Generating ideas	[Idea finding]

Preparing for Action

Uses one or more of . . .

Developing solutions	[Solution finding]
Building acceptance	[Acceptance finding]

The two new activities come under . . .

Planning your approach

Appraising tasks

This involves

> determining whether CPS is a promising choice for dealing with a particular task, and taking stock of the commitments, constraints, and conditions you must consider to apply CPS effectively (the people involved, the results you desire, the context in which you are working, and the methods available). (www.creativelearning.com)

Designing process

This requires 'using your knowledge of the task and your needs, to plan the CPS components, stages, or tools that will be best-suited to help you reach your goals' (www.creativelearning.com).

Comments have been made and advice given regarding these activities in various parts of this book, although these names have not been used.

It should also be mentioned that Donald Treffinger (personal communication, 2003) sees these changes made in Version 6.1 as 'a shift in mindset, method, and application' from the earlier Osborn-Parnes CPS process. He believes that they have 'really stepped away' from this now and no longer present their approach as 'simply an extension of their earlier work'.

Summary

This appendix has briefly described a couple of 'brain' theories, and 'updated' the names of the stages of the Osborn-Parnes CPS process.

Bibliography

Ackoff, Russell L. (1957) 'Towards a Behavioural Theory of Communication', in W. Buckey (ed.) *Modern Systems Research for the Behavioural Scientist,* Chicago, IL: Aldine.

Ackoff, Russell L. (1978) *The Art of Problem Solving,* Chichester: John Wiley.

Ackoff, Russell L. (1981) 'The Art and Science of Mess Management', *Interfaces,* 11(1), February (The Institute of Management Sciences).

Ackoff, Russell L. (1983) 'An Interactive View of Rationality', *Journal of the Operational Research Society,* 34(8).

Adair, John (1979) *Action-centred Learning.* Aldershot: Gower.

Adams, James L. (1979) *Conceptual Blockbusting, A Guide to Better Ideas,* 2nd edition, New York: W.W. Norton (first published 1974).

Alcott, Louisa M. (1987) *Little Women,* Ansty, Leicestershire: Charnwood – F.A. Thorpe.

Alexander, John (1979) 'Synectics: Creativity, Problem-solving and Interpersonal Skills', *Bacie Journal,* January.

Allen, M.S. (1962) *Morphological Creativity,* Englewood Cliffs, NJ: Prentice-Hall.

Altshuller, Genrich (1997) *40 Principles: TRIZ Keys to Technical Innovation,* Worcester, MA: Technical Innovation Center, Inc.

Altshuller, Genrich (1999) *The Innovation Algorithm: TRIZ, Systematic Innovation and Technical Creativity,* Worcester, MA: Technical Innovation Center Inc.

Ansoff, H. Igor (1968) *Corporate Strategy: An Analytic Approach to Business Policy for Growth and Expansion,* London: Penguin.

Avolio, Bruce J. and Bass, Bernard M. (1988) 'Transformational Leadership, Charisma, and Beyond', in James Hunt, B. Baliga, H. Dachler and Chester A. Schriesheim (eds) *Emerging Leadership Vistas,* Lexington, MA: Lexington Books, D.C. Heath and Co.

Bales, Robert F. and Slater, Philip E. (1956) 'Role Differentiation in Small Decision-Making Groups', in Talcott Parsons, Robert F. Bales *et al.* (eds) *Family Socialization and Interaction Process,* London: Routledge and Kegan Paul.

Bandler, Richard and Grinder, John (1990) *Frogs into Princes: Neuro Linguistic Programming,* London: Eden Grove Editions.

Bartolke, Klaus (1988) in James Hunt, B. Haliga, H. Dachler and Chester A. Schriesheim (eds) *Emergency Leadership Vistas,* Lexington, MA: Lexington Books, D.C. Heath and Co.

Bass, Bernard M. (1985) *Leadership, Psychology and Organizational Behavior,* New York: Free Press.

Bass, Bernard and Steidlmeier, Paul (1998) 'Ethics, Character and Authentic Transformational Leadership', Center for Leadership Studies, Binghamton University, NY. http://cls.binghamton.edu/BassSteid.html

Beishon, John and Peters, Geoff (eds) (1981) *Systems Behaviour,* 3rd edition, London: Harper and Row (first published 1972).

Belbin, R.M. (1981) *Management Teams,* London: Heinemann.

Bennis, W.G. and Nanus, B. (1985) *Leaders,* New York: Harper and Row.

Boal, Kimberley B. and Bryson, John M. (1988) 'Charismatic Leadership: A Phenomenological and Structural Approach', in James Hunt, B. Baliga, H. Dachler, Chester A. Schriesheim (eds) *Emerging Leadership Vistas,* Lexington, MA: Lexington Books, D.C. Heath and Co.

Boulding, K.E. (1956) 'General Systems Theory: the Skeleton of Science', *Management Science,* 2(3).

Briggs, R.O. and Nunamaker, J.F. (1994) 'Getting a Grip on Groupware', in P. Lloyd, (ed.) *Groupware in the 21st Century,* Westport, CO: Praeger.

Briggs, R.O. and Nunamaker, J.F. (1996) *Team Theory of Group Productivity and its Application to Development and Testing of Group Support Systems,* CMI Working Paper Series WPS-96-1, University of Arizona.

Buchanan, David A. and Huczynski, Andrzej A. (1985) *Organizational Behaviour: An Introductory Text*, London: Prentice-Hall International.

Burns, James MacGregor (1978) *Leadership*, New York: Harper and Row.

Buzan, Tony (1974) *Use Your Head*, London: BBC Publications.

Carnall, Colin (1995) *Managing Change in Organizations*, Hemel Hempstead: Prentice-Hall.

Cattell, R.B. (1957) *Personality and Motivation Structure and Measurement*, New York: World Book Co.

Checkland, Peter B. (1981) *Systems Thinking, Systems Practice*, Chichester: John Wiley.

Checkland, Peter B. (1983) 'OR and the Systems Movement: Mapping and Conflicts', *Journal of Operations Research*, 34(8).

Checkland, Peter B. (1985) 'From Optimizing to Learning: A Development of Systems Thinking for the 1990s', *Journal of the Operational Research Society*, 36(9).

Checkland, Peter B. (1986) 'The Politics of Practice', International Roundtable on 'The Art and Science of Systems Practice', ITASA, November.

Checkland, Peter B. (1987a) *Images of Systems and the Systems Image*, Presidential Address to the International Society for General Systems Research, Budapest, June.

Checkland, Peter B. (1987b) 'Soft Systems Methodology: An Overview', a paper given at a plenary session of the 31st Annual Meeting of the International Society for General Systems Research, Budapest.

Checkland, Peter B. (1989) 'Soft Systems Methodology' in J. Rosenhead (ed.) *Rational Analysis for a Problematic World*, Chichester: John Wiley.

Checkland, Peter B. and Scholes, J. (1990a) *Soft Systems Methodology in Action*, Chichester: John Wiley.

Checkland, Peter B. and Scholes, J. (1990b) 'Techniques in Soft Systems Practice Part 4: Conceptual Model Building Revisited', *Journal of Applied Systems Analysis*, 17.

Checkland, Peter B. and Scholes, J. (1999) *Soft Systems Methodology in Action*, 2nd edition, Chichester: John Wiley.

Checkland, Peter B. and Wilson, B. (1980) 'Primary Task and Issue-based Root Definitions', *Journal of Applied Systems Analysis*, 7.

Churchman, C.W. (1968) *The Systems Approach*, New York: Dell Publishing.

Coldwell, Jon B. (1996) 'Quiet Change – Big Bung or Catastrophic Shift: At What Point Does Continuous Improvement Become Innovation?' *Creativity and Innovation Management*, 5(1), 67–73.

Cooper, R.K. and Sawaf, A. (1997) *Executive EQ: Emotional Intelligence in Leadership and Organizations*, New York: Grosset Plenum.

Couger, J.D. (1995) *Creative Problem Solving and Opportunity Finding*, Danvers, MA: Boyd & Fraser Publishing Co., cited in McFadzean (1996b).

Couger, J.D. and Dengate, G. (1996) 'Measurement of Creativity of IS Products', *Creativity and Innovation Management*, 5(4), December, 262–72.

Crawford, R.P. (1954) *The Techniques of Creative Thinking*, New York: Hawthorn Books.

Cutts, Geoff (1987) *Structured Systems Analysis and Design Methodology*, London: Paradigm.

Cyert, R.M., Simon, H.A. and Trow, D.B. (1956) 'Observation of a Business Decision', *Journal of Business*, 29.

Deal, Terrence E. and Kennedy, Allen A. (1982) *Corporate Cultures: The Rites and Rituals of Corporate Life*, Reading, MA: Addison-Wesley.

de Bono, Edward (1985) *Conflicts: A Better Way to Resolve Them*, London: Harrap.

de Bono, Edward (1990) *Lateral Thinking: A Textbook of Creativity*, London: Penguin (first published by Ward Lock Education in 1970).

Deming, W. Edwards (1986) *Out of the Crisis: Quality, Productivity and Competitive Position*, Cambridge: Cambridge University Press.

Diesing, Paul (1958) 'Socioeconomic Decisions', *Ethics*, 69.

Drucker, Peter F. (1955) *The Practice of Management*, London: Heinemann.

Dulewicz, V and Higgs, M. (1998) *Emotional Intelligence: Managerial Fad or Valid Construct*, Working Paper 9813, Oxford: Henley Management College.

Dulewicz, V. and Higgs, M. (1999) *Can Emotional Intelligence be Measured and Developed*, Working Paper 9901, Oxford: Henley Management College.

Dunphy, D.C. and Stance, D.A. (1988) 'Transformational and Coercive Strategies for Planned Organizational Change', *Organizational Studies*, 9(3).

EACI (1995) 'EACI Dialogue – 1. Definitions', *Periscope*, Spring, Heerlen NL: EACI.

Eden, Colin, Jones, Sue and Sims, David (1983) *Messing About in Problems: An Informal Structured Approach to their Identification and Management*, Oxford: Pergamon Press.

Eldridge J.E.T. and Crombie A.D. (1974) *A Sociology of Organizations*, London: George Allen and Unwin.

Fielder, F.E. (1978) 'Situational Control and a Dynamic Theory of Leadership' in B. King *et al.* (eds) *Managerial Control and Organizational Democracy*, New York: John Wiley. Also in Pugh (1984) pp.372–93.

Firestien, R.L. and Treffinger, D.J. (1983) 'Ownership and Converging: Essential Ingredients of Creative Problem Solving', *Journal of Creative Behavior*, 17(1), 32–8.

Flood, R.L. and Jackson, M.C. (1991) *Creative Problem Solving: Total Systems Intervention*, Chichester: John Wiley & Sons.

Forrester, Jay (1961) *Industrial Dynamics*, Boston, MA: The MIT Press, and Chichester: John Wiley, reported in George H. Rice, 'But How do Managers Make Decisions?', *Management Decision*, 18(4), 197.

Forsth, L-R. and Nordvik, B. (1995) 'Building a Vision – A Practical Guide', *Creativity and Innovation Management*, 4(4) December.

French, J.R.P. and Raven, B.H. (1959) 'The Bases of Social Power', in D. Cartwright (ed.) *Studies in Social Power*, University of Michigan Press.

Gardner, Howard (1993a) *Frames of Mind: The Theory of Multiple Intelligences*, 2nd edition, London: Fontana (first published 1983).

Gardner, Howard (1993b) *Multiple Intelligences: The Theory in Practice*, New York: Basic Books.

Gardner, H. and Hatch, T. (1989) 'Multiple Intelligences Go to School', *Educational Researcher*, 18(8), cited in Goleman (1996), p.39.

Gardner, Howard with Krechevsky, Mara (1993) *Multiple Intelligences: The Theory in Practice*, New York: Basic Books.

Georgopoulos, Basil S., Mahoney, Gerald M. and Jones, Nyle W. (1957) 'A Path-Goal Approach to Productivity', *Journal of Applied Psychology*, 41, 345–53. Also in Vroom (1964), p.239.

Geschka, H., Schaude, G.R. and Schlicksupp, H. (1973) 'Modern Techniques for Solving Problems', *Chemical Engineering*, 91–7, August.

Getzels, J.W. and Jackson, P.W. (1962) *Creativity and Intelligence: Explorations with Gifted Students*, New York: John Wiley.

Goldberg, Phillip (1983) *The Intuitive Edge*, Los Angeles, CA: Jeremy P. Thatcher, Inc.

Goleman, D. (1996) *Emotional Intelligence: Why It Can Matter More than IQ*, London: Bloomsbury Publishing (first published 1995).

Goleman, D. (1997) 'Beyond IQ: Developing the Leadership Competencies of Emotional Leadership', paper presented at the Second International Competence Conference, London, October.

Gordon, William J.J. (1961) *Synectics*, New York: Harper and Row.

Graham, J. (1988) in James Hunt, B. Baliga, H. Dachler and Chester A. Schriesheim (eds) *Emerging Leadership Vistas*, Lexington, MA: Lexington Books, D.C. Heath and Co.

Graves, Desmond (1986) *Corporate Culture – Diagnosis and Change: Auditing and Changing the Culture of Organizations*, London: Frances Pinter.

Greenleaf, Robert (1977) *Servant Leadership: A Journey into the Nature of Legitimate Power and Greatness*, New York: Paulist Press.

Greiner, L.E. (1972) 'Evolution and Revolution as Organizations Grow', *Harvard Business Review*, July/August.

Grogono, Peter and Nelson, Sharon H. (1982) *Problem Solving and Computer Programming*, Reading MA: Addison-Wesley.

Guilford, J.P. (1950) 'Creativity', *American Psychologist*, 5, 444–54, cited in Kirton (1994), p.x.

Guilford, J.P. (1962) 'Creativity: Its Measurement and Development', in S.J. Parnes and H.F. Harding (eds) *A Source Book for Creative Thinking*. New York: Charles Scribner's Sons.

Hall, A.D. (1962) *A Methodology for Systems Engineering*, Princeton, NJ: Van Nostrand.

Hall, Jay (1971) 'Decisions, Decisions, Decisions', *Psychology Today*, November.

Handy, Charles B. (1978) *Gods of Management*, London: Pan Books.

Handy, Charles B. (1985) *Understanding Organizations*, 3rd edition, London: Penguin Books.

Harrison, Roger (1972) 'Understanding Your Organization's Character', *Harvard Business Review*, May/June.

Hastings, Colin, Bixby, Peter and Chaudry-Lawton, Rani (1986) *Superteams: A Blueprint for Organisational Success*, Glasgow: Fontana.

Herrmann, N. (1990) *The Creative Brain*, Lake Lure, NL: Brain Books.

Hofstede, Geert (1980) *Cultures Consequences: International Differences in Work-Related Values*, London: Sage Publications.

Holland, J.L. (1958, 1997) *Making Vocational Choices: A Theory of Vocational Personalities and Work Environments*, 3rd edition, Florida: Psychological Assessment Resources Inc.

Hosking, Dian-Marie and Morley, Ian E. (1988) 'The Skills of Leadership', in James Hunt, B. Baliga, H. Dachler and Chester A. Schriesheim (eds) *Emerging Leadership Vistas,* Lexington, MA: Lexington Books, D.C. Heath and Co.

House, Robert J. (1988) 'Leadership Research: Some Forgotten, Ignored, or Overlooked Findings', in James Hunt, B. Baliga, H. Dachler and Chester A. Schriesheim (eds) *Emerging Leadership Vistas*, Lexington, MA: Lexington Books, D.C. Heath and Co.

Hunt, J., Baliga, B., Dachler, H. and Schriesheim, C. (eds) (1988) *Emerging Leadership Vistas.* Lexington, MA: Lexington Books, D.C. Heath and Co.

Isaksen, Scott G. and Puccio, Gerard J. (1988) 'Adaption-Innovation and the Torrance Tests of Creative Thinking: The Level-Style Issue Revisited', *Psychological Reports*, 63, 659–70.

Isaksen, Scott G. and Treffinger, Donald, J. (1985) *Creative Problem Solving: The Basic Course*, Buffalo, NY: Bearly Ltd.

Isaksen, Scott G., Dorval, Brian and Treffinger, Donald J. (2000) *Creative Approaches to Problem Solving: A Framework for Change*, 2nd edition, Dubuque, IA: Kendall/Hunt Publishing Co.

Janis, Irving L. (1982) *Groupthink*, Boston, MA: Harcourt Brace.

Jensen, J.V. (1978) 'A Heuristic for the Analysis of the Nature and Extent of a Problem', *Journal of Creative Behaviour*, 12, 168–80.

Katz, Daniel and Kahn, Robert L. (1966) *The Social Psychology of Organizations,* New York: John Wiley.

Kelly, Joe (1969) *Organizational Behavior,* Richard D. Irwin Inc. and the Dorsey Press: Illinois.

Kepner, Charles H. and Tregoe, Benjamin, B. (1981) *The New Rational Manager* London:, John Martin Publishing (1st edition published as *The Rational Manager* by McGraw-Hill, 1965).

Kirton, M.J. (1994a) 'A theory explored: preface to first edition', in M.J. Kirton (ed) *Adaptors and Innovators: Styles of Creativity and Problem Solving*, 2nd ed, London: Routledge, pp. x–xiii (first published 1989).

Kirton, M.J. (1994b) 'Five years on, preface to second edition', in M.J. Kirton (ed) *Adaptors and Innovators: Syles of Creativity and Problem Solving* 2nd ed, London: Routledge, pp. xiv–xxvi (first published 1989).

Kirton, M.J. (1994c) 'A theory of cognitive style', in M.J. Kirton (ed) *Adaptors and Innovators; Styles of Creativity and Problem Solving*, 2nd ed, London: Routledge, pp. 1–33 (first published 1989).

Kirton, M.J. (1994d) 'Adaptors and innovators at work', in M.J. Kirton (ed) *Adaptors and Innovators: Styles of Creativity and Problem Solving*, 2nd ed, London: Routledge, pp. 51–71 (first published 1989).

Koberg, D. and Bagnall, J. (1974) *The Universal Traveller. A Soft Systems Guidebook to: Creativity, Problem Solving, and the Process of Design*, Los Altos: William Kaufmann.

Kolb, D.A. (1976) 'Management and the Learning Process', *California Management Review,* XVIII(3).

Lakoff, George and Johnson, Mark (1980) *Metaphors we Live By*, Chicago, IL: University of Chicago.

Lakoff, George and Johnson, Mark (1999) *Philosophy in the Flesh: The Embodied Mind and its Challenge to Western Thought*, New York: Basic Books (Perseus Books).

Lawler, Edward E. (1969) 'Job Design and Employee Motivation', *Personnel Psychology,* 22, 426–35, reprinted in Vroom and Deci (1970, 1989), pp.160–9.

Lawley, James and Tompkins, Penny (2000) *Metaphors in Mind: Transformation through Symbolic Modelling*, London: The Developing Company Press.

Leavitt, Harold J. (1978) *Managerial Psychology,* 4th edition, Chicago IL: University of Chicago Press.

Lee, C. (1996) 'Et tu EQ?' *Training*, 33, 1, 8.

Lesio, P.J. (1984) 'Imaging for Success', unpublished Masters project, State University of Buffalo, NY.

Lindblom, C.E. (1959) 'The Science of "Muddling Through"', *Public Administration Review,* 19(2), and in Pugh (1984) pp.238–55.

Lippitt, Gordon L. (1982) *Organization Renewal: A Holistic Approach to Organizational Development*, 2nd edition, Englewood Cliffs, NJ: Prentice-Hall.

Majaro, Simon (1988) *The Creative Gap: Managing Ideas for Profit*, London: Longmans.

Mann, Darrell L. and Dewulf, Simon (2002) *Evolving the World's Systematic Creativity Methods*, www.creax.com.

March, J.G. (1976) '*The Technology of Foolishness*', in J.C. March and J.P. Olsen (eds) *Ambiguity and Choice in Organizations*, Universitetsforlaget. Also in Pugh (1984), pp.232, 236–7.

Maslow, Abraham H. (1943) 'A Theory of Human Motivation', *Psychological Review,* 30, 370–96. An abridged version can be found in Vroom and Deci (1970, 1989).

Maslow, Abraham H. (1962) 'Emotional Blocks to Creativity', in S.J. Parnes and H.F. Harding (eds) *A Source Book for Creative Thinking*, New York: Charles Scribner's Sons.

McFadzean, Elspeth (1996a) *The Classification of Creative Problem Solving Techniques*, Working Paper HWP 9632, Henley: Henley Management College.

McFadzean, Elspeth (1996b) *The Use of GroupSystems for Windows in a Business School Environment: Some Early Lessons*, Working Paper HWP 9635, Henley: Henley Management College.

McGregor, Douglas M. (1957) 'The Human Side of Enterprise', in 'Adventures in Thought and Action', *Proceedings of the Fifth Anniversary Convocation of the School of Industrial Management*, Boston, MA: MIT Press and also in Vroom and Deci (1970, 1989).

Mehrabian A. and Ferris S.R. (1967) 'Inference of Attitudes from Nonverbal Communication in Two Channels', *The Journal of Counselling Psychology*, 31, 248–52.

Miller, W.C. (1989) *Validation of the Innovation Styles Profile*, Austin, TX : Global Creativity Corp.

Miller, W.C., Couger, J.D. and Higgins, L.F. (1996) 'Innovation Styles of IS Personnel vs. Other Occupations', *Creativity and Innovation Management*, 5(4), December, 226–33.

Mingers, John (1995) 'Using Soft Systems Methodology in the Design of Information Systems', in Stowell (ed.)

Mintzberg, H. (1975) 'The Manager's Job: Folklore and Fact', *Harvard Business Review,* July/August. Also in Pugh (1984), pp. 424–5.

Moore, Carol-Lynne (1982) *Executives in Action,* 2nd edition, Plymouth: Macdonald and Evans (originally published as *Action Profiling,* 1978).

Morgan, Gareth (1989) *Creative Organization Theory: A Resourcebook,* London: Sage Publications.

Moss Kanter, Rosabeth (1983) *The Change Masters: Corporate Entrepreneurs at Work,* London: George Allen and Unwin.

Nolan, Vincent (1981) 'Open to Change: How to Initiate, Cope with and Benefit from Change at Work', *Management Decision,* 2(1).

Nolan, Vincent (1989) *The Innovator's Handbook: The Skills of Innovative Management – Problem Solving, Communication and Teamwork,* London: Sphere Books.

Nolan, Vincent (1990) 'Creativity and the Resolution of Conflict', paper presented to Inno 90 Conference, Lapperante, Finland.

Nolan, Vincent (2000), 'Educating a Nation of Innovators', in V. Nolan, (ed.) *Creative Education: Educating a Nation of Innovators*, Stoke Mandeville, Bucks: Synectics Education Initiative.

O'Connor, J. and Seymour, J. (1995) *Introducing NLP: Psychological Skills for Understanding and Influencing People,* London: Thorsons (first published 1990).

Oldcorn, Roger (1982) *Management. A Fresh Approach,* London: Pan Books.

Osborn, Alex F. (1957) *Applied Imagination,* revised edition, New York: Charles Scribner's Sons, (originally published 1953).

Parnes, Sidney J. (1972) *Creativity: Unblocking Human Potential,* Buffalo, NY: DOK Pub. Inc. (Creative Education Foundation).

Parnes, Sidney J. (1981) *The Magic of the Mind,* Buffalo, NY: CEF/Bearly.

Parnes, S.J. (1991) 'Creative Problem Solving and Visionizing', in S.J. Parnes (ed.) *Source Book for Creative Problem Solving: A Fifty Year Digest of Proven Innovation Processes*, Buffalo, NY: Creative Education Foundation Press.

Parnes, S.J. (ed.) (1992) *Source Book for Creative Problem Solving: A Fifty Year Digest of Proven Innovation Processes*, Buffalo, NY: Creative Education Foundation Press.

Parnes, Sidney J. and Harding, Harold F. (eds) (1962) *A Source Book for Creative Thinking,* New York: Charles Scribner's Sons.

Plant, Roger (1987) *Managing Change and Making It Stick,* London: Fontana/Collins.

Polya, C. (1957) *How to Solve It: A New Aspect of Mathematical Method,* New York: Doubleday Anchor Books (originally published by Princeton University Press, 1945).

Prince, George M. (1968) 'The Operational Mechanism of Synectics', *Journal of Creative Behavior*, 2(1) and in S.J. Parnes (ed.) (1992), pp.168–77.

Prince, George M. (1970) *The Practice of Creativity,* New York: Collier Books (Macmillan Publishing).

Prince, George M. (1975) 'The MindSpring Theory: A New Development from Synectics Research', *Journal of Creative Behavior*, 9(3) in S.J. Parnes (ed.) (1992), pp.177–93.

Prince, George M. (1976) 'MindSpring', *Chemtech,* May.

Prince, George M. (1980) 'Problem Solving Strategies: The Synectics Approach', a management training video produced by McGraw-Hill International Training Systems.

Prince, George M. (1998) *Mind Spring,* London: Changemaker Publications.

Prince, George M. with Logan-Prince, Kathleen (2002) *Your Life is a Series of Meetings . . . Get Good at Life*, 1st Books, Library.

Prince, George M., Weaver, W.T. and Logan-Prince, Kathleen (2000) 'Liberating Creativity and Learning – Part 1: Understanding the Inhibitors of Good Thinking', in V. Nolan, (ed.) *Creative Education: Educating a Nation of Innovators*, Stoke Mandeville, Bucks: Synectics Education Initiative.

Proctor, Tony (1999) *Creative Problem Solving for Managers*. London: Routledge.

Puccio, Gerard J. (2002a) *FourSight Self-score Feedback Booklet*, Evanston, IL: THinc Communications.

Puccio, Gerard J. (2002b) www.foursightonline.com/downloads/ techmanual.pdf. *FourSight Technical Manual*

Puccio, Gerard J. and Murdock, M.C. (1999) *Creativity Assessment: Reading and Resources*, Buffalo, NY: Creative Education Foundation.

Pugh, D.S. (ed.) (1984) *Organization Theory*, 2nd edition, London: Penguin Books (first published 1971).

Quinlivan-Hall, D. and Renner, P. (1994), *In Search of Solutions: Sixty Ways to Guide Your Problem-solving Group*, Vancouver, BC: Training Associates.

Reddin, W.J. (1977) 'Confessions of an Organizational Change Agent: Group and Organisational Studies', *International Journal of Group Facilitators*, 2(1) March.

Rhodes, D.J. (1985) 'Root Definitions and Reality in Manufacturing Systems', *Journal of Applied Systems Analysis*, 12.

Rickards, Tudor (1974) *Problem Solving through Creative Analysis*, London: Gower Press.

Rittel, H.W.J. jr. and Weber M.M. (1974) 'Dilemmas in a General Theory of Planning', *DMG-DRS Journal*, 8(1), 31–39.

Rogers, Carl R. (1954) 'Toward a Theory of Creativity', *Review of General Semantics*, Xl(4). Also in Parnes and Harding (1962), pp.63–72.

Rogers, E.M. (1983) *Diffusion of Innovations*, 3rd edition, New York: Free Press.

Ryback, D. (1998) *Putting Emotional Intelligence to Work: Successful Leadership is More Than IQ*, Boston MA: Butterworth-Heinemann.

Salovey, P. and Mayer, J.D. (1990) 'Emotional Intelligence', *Imagination, Cognition and Personality*, 9, 185–211.

Sathe, V. (1985) *Culture and Related Corporate Realities*, Homewood IL: Richard D. Urwin.

Sculley, John with Byrne, John A. (1988) *Odyssey – Pepsi to Apple*, Glasgow: Fontana/Collins.

Sedgwick, J. (1996) 'Facilitation Skills', Staff development course, Thames Valley University.

Sedgwick, John (2000) 'Managing the Imagination', in V. Nolan (ed.) *Creative Education: Educating a Nation of Innovators*, Stoke Mandeville, Bucks: Synectics Education Initiative.

Shallcross, D.J. and Sisk, D.A. (1989) *Intuition: An Inner Way of Knowing*, Buffalo, NY: Bearly Ltd.

Shulyak, Lev (1997) 'Introduction to TRIZ', in G. Altshuller (ed.) *40 Principles: TRIZ Keys to Technical Innovation*, Worcester, MA: Technical Innovation Center, Inc.

Simon, Herbert A. (1955) 'A Behavioral Model of Rational Choice', *Quarterly Journal of Economics*, 64(1).

Simon, Herbert A. (1957) *Models of Man*, John Wiley and Sons.

Simon, Herbert A. (1960a) 'The Executive as Decision Maker', in *The New Science of Management Decision*, New York: Harper and Row. Also 'Decision Making and Organizational Design' in Pugh (1984), pp.202–8.

Simon, Herbert A. (1960b) 'Organizational Design: Man–Machine Systems for Decision Making' in *The New Science of Management Decision*, New York: Harper and Row. Also 'Decision Making and Organizational Design', in Pugh (1984), p.209.

Simon, Herbert A. (1969) *The Science of the Artificial*, Cambridge, MA: MIT Press.

Smyth, D.S. and Checkland, Peter B. (1976) 'Using a Systems Approach: The Structure of Root Definitions, *Journal of Applied Systems Analysis*, 5(1).

Steele, Fritz (1975) *Consulting for Organizational Change*, Amherst: University of Massachussetts Press, also in Sathe (1985) pp.355–7.

Steinberg, Rhona and Shapiro, Stanley (1982) 'Sex Differences in Personality Traits of Female and Male Masters of Business Administration Students', *Journal of Applied Psychology*, 67(3), pp.306–10. Also cited in Buchanan and Huczynski (1985), pp.386–7.

Steiner, C. (1997) *Achieving Emotional Literacy*, London: Bloomsbury Publishing.

Stevens, M. (1988) *Practical Problem Solving for Managers*, London: Kogan Page/British Institute of Management.

Stowell, Frank A. (ed.) (1995) *Information Systems Provision: The Contribution of Soft Systems Methodology*, Maidenhead: McGraw-Hill.

Taylor, Calvin W. (1962) 'Tentative Description of the Creative Individual', in S.J. Parnes and H.F. Harding (eds) *A Source Book for Creative Thinking*. New York: Charles Scribner's Sons.

Torrance, E. Paul (1974) *Torrance Tests of Creative Thinking: Norms and Technical Manual*, Bensenville, IL: Scholastic Testing Services.

Treffinger, Donald J. (2000) *Creative Problem Solver's Guidebook*, 3rd edition, Waco, TX: Prufrock Press.

Treffinger, Donald J., Isaksen, Scott G. and Dorval, Brian K. (2000) *Creative Problem Solving: An Introduction*, 3rd edition, Waco, TX: Prufrock Press.

Tuckman, Bruce and Jensen, N. (1977) 'Stages of Small Group Development Revisited', *Group and Organizational Studies*, 2, 419–27.

Van Gundy Jr., Arthur B. (1984) *Managing Group Creativity: A Modular Approach to Problem Solving*, New York: American Management Associations.

Van Gundy Jr., Arthur B. (1988) *Techniques of Structured Problem Solving*, 2nd edition, New York: Van Nostrand Reinhold (first published 1981).

Van Gundy Jr., Arthur B. (1992) *Idea Power: Techniques and Resources to Unleash the Creativity in Your Organization*, New York: American Management Associations.

Vaughan, Francis E. (1979) *Awakening Intuition*, New York: Anchor Books.

Vickers, Geoffrey (1961) 'Judgement, The Sixth Elbourne Memorial Lectures', January, *The Manager*, 31–9. Also in Pugh (1984), pp.183–201.

Vickers, Geoffrey (1965) *The Art of Judgement: A Study of Policy Making*, London: Chapman and Hall.

Vickers, Geoffrey (1970) *Freedom in a Rocking Boat*, London: Allen Lane (also published by Penguin, 1972).

Vickers, Geoffrey (1981) 'Sonic Implications of Systems Thinking', in J. Beishan and G. Peters (eds) *Systems Behaviour*, 3rd edition, London: Harper and Row.

Vickers, Geoffrey (1983) *Human Systems are Different*, London: Harper and Row.

Vroom, Victor H. (1964) *Work and Motivation*, Chichester: John Wiley.

Vroom, Victor H. and Deci, Edward L. (eds) (1970, 1989) *Management and Motivation*, London: Penguin Books.

Wall, T., Kemp, N.J., Lackson, P.R. and Clegg, C.W. (1986) 'Outcomes of Autonomous Workgroups: A Long-Term Field Experiment', *Academy of Management Journal*.

Wild, R. (1972) *Management and Production*, London: Penguin Books.

Wilson, Brian (1990) *Systems: Concepts, Methodologies and Applications*, 2nd edition, Chichester: John Wiley (first published 1984).

Woodburn, Ian (1985) 'Some Developments in the Building of Conceptual Models', *Journal of Applied Systems Analysis*, 12.

Zlotin, Boris and Zusman, Alla (1991) *The Problems of ARIZ Enhancement*, Moldova: Kishinev, August and www.ideationtriz.com.

Zlotin, Boris and Zusman, Alla (1992) *An Integrated Operational Knowledge Base (System of Operators) and the Innovation Workbench™ System Software*, Moldova: Kishinev, 22 September and www.ideationtriz.com.

Zlotin, Boris and Zusman, Alla (1999) 'Managing Innovation Knowledge: The Ideation Approach to the Search, Development and Utilisation of Innovation Knowledge', *Izobretenia*, Autumn (also in *Journal for the Altshuller Institute of TRIZ Studies* and on www.ideationtriz.com).

Zlotin, Boris, Zusman, Alla and Kaplan, Len (2000) *Containment Ring Problem: IWB Case Study*, Detroit: Ideation International Inc., and www.ideationtriz.com.

Zohar, Danah and Marshall, Ian (2000) *Spiritual Intelligence: The Ultimate Intelligence*, London: Bloomsbury Publishing.

Zwicky, F. (1969) *Discovery, Invention, Research through the Morphological Approach*, New York: MacMillan.

Subject Index